Fairchild C-82 Packet
and
C-119 Flying Boxcar

Alwyn T Lloyd

An imprint of
Ian Allan Publishing

Fairchild C-82 Packet and C-119 Flying Boxcar
© 2005 Alwyn T Lloyd

ISBN 1 85780 201 2

Published by Midland Publishing
4 Watling Drive, Hinckley, LE10 3EY, England
Tel: 01455 254 490   Fax: 01455 254 495
E-mail: midlandbooks@compuserve.com

Midland Publishing and Aerofax are imprints of Ian Allan Publishing Ltd

Worldwide distribution (except North America):
Midland Counties Publications
4 Watling Drive, Hinckley, LE10 3EY, England
Telephone: 01455 254 450   Fax: 01455 233 737
E-mail: midlandbooks@compuserve.com
www.midlandcountiessuperstore.com

North American trade distribution:
Specialty Press Publishers & Wholesalers Inc
39966 Grand Avenue, North Branch, MN 55056
Tel: 651 277 1400   Fax: 651 277 1203
Toll free telephone: 800 895 4585
www.specialtypress.com

Design and concept
© 2005 Midland Publishing and
Stephen Thompson Associates
Layout by Sue Bushell

Printed in England by Ian Allan Printing Ltd
Riverdene Business Park, Molesey Road,
Hersham, Surrey, KT12 4RG

All rights reserved. No part of this publication may be reproduced, stored in a retrieval system, transmitted in any form or by any means, electronic, mechanical or photo-copied, recorded or otherwise, without the written permission of the publishers.

Contents

Introduction and Acknowledgements 3

Chapters

1 The C-82 Packet 5
2 C-82 Operations 16
3 Procurement, Production and Political Problems 23
4 C-119 Description 31
5 C-119 Flight Testing 45
6 Air Resupply Drop Procedures 50
7 Boxcars in Korea 53
8 The French in Indochina 68
9 European Operations 73
10 Zone of Interior C-119 Operations. . . 79
11 Miscellaneous USAF Packet & Boxcar Operations 85
12 Military Air Transport Service. 90
13 *Drag Net* and Later Projects 94
14 USAF Reserve C-119s. 99
15 Air National Guard Flying Boxcars . 111
16 Gunships 117
17 United States Marine Corps and Navy Boxcars 127
18 Royal Canadian Air Force 134
19 Indian Air Force Boxcars 140
20 Republic of Vietnam Air Force. 142
21 Other Military Packets and Flying Boxcars 144
22 Civilian Packets and Boxcars 150
23 C-82 Packet & C-119 Flying Boxcar Summary Unit Histories & Markings 161

Appendices

1 Production and Mishap Data. 175
2 C-82 & C-119 Block Numbers and Serial Numbers. 178
3 C-82 Packet Units 179
4 United States C-119 Units 180
5 C-82s & C-119s in Foreign Service . 184
6 Civil Registered and Museum C-82s & C-119s in the United States 188

Title page: **C-119C-19-FA, s/n 50-136, was in a line of 443rd TCG aircraft taxying out at Rhein-Main AB, West Germany. The black anti-corrosion paint on the belly ran the full length of the aircraft.** C N Valentine

This page: **This C-119C-13-FA, s/n 49-129, was taking off from Ashiya AB, Japan. The aircraft retained its outboard horizontal stabilizer tip extensions. As indicated by its Blue/White quartered nose markings, the aircraft was assigned to the 36th/817th TCS, 483rd TCW. Compare the differences in the belly anti-corrosion paint with that of the aircraft on the front cover. Also note the black anti-corrosion paint aft of the R-4360 engines.** USAF

Introduction and Acknowledgements

Through history, getting troops and supplies to a combat zone has presented a major problem to military commanders. An effective transport aircraft must possess a capacious compartment for carrying lighter, less dense objects than a bomber. During World War Two, all the major protagonists developed many adequate transports but their designs, semi-monocoque fuselages sealed at both ends and requiring side doors, inevitably impeded their ground cargo handling characteristics. It would take an endloading aircraft to really make airborne operations efficient, and so, unsurprisingly, several nations experimented with the concept.

German design efforts resulted in the Arado Ar 232, which had a pod and boom-type fuselage with a high wing, and the Gotha Go 242, a high-winged, twin-boomed glider that was capable of carrying up to 21 fully equipped troops, plus the Messerschmitt Me 321 Gigant glider with large clamshell doors in the nose to facilitate loading, both of the latter being subsequently converted into powered transports.

Likewise, the Japanese developed a pair of twin boomed end-loading aircraft – one a glider and the other powered. The Kokusai Ku-7 Manazuru (Crane) was a twin-boomed glider with a central fuselage pod that had a hinged door built into it, while the powered Kokusai Ku-105 Ohtori (Phoenix) was developed as a means of hauling badly needed fuel from Sumatra to the Japanese home islands.

The British were also developing endloading aircraft during the early stages of World War Two. The Airspeed Horsa II was the first operational glider to join the RAF's inventory, while the General Aircraft Limited GAL 49 Hamilcar, was the largest and heaviest glider employed by the Allies during the conflict.

In 1944, General Aircraft designed and built the first powered British endloader known as the GAL 58 Hamilcar X. The RAF ordered 100 of these aircraft to serve in the war in the Pacific; however the war concluded and production was limited to only 20 examples.

In the USA, an impending aluminum shortage encouraged aircraft manufacturers to consider the use of alternative materials in new designs.

The Curtiss C-76 Caravan was a wooden twin-engined, tricycle-gear, high-wing transport, with a cockpit mounted on top of the fuselage, whose nose hinged upwards thereby permitting straight-in loading from trucks. While meeting its operational requirements, it never saw operational service.

The Waco CG-4A Haig/Hadrian assault glider was vastly more successful, towed by either a C-46 or a C-47, their upward-hinging noses delivered thousands into battle.

Designed by Willem D Van Zelm, Martin patented the Model 240, a four-engined heavy troop/cargo transport, and the Model 241, a twin-engined cargo transport. Both aircraft were of the twin-boom configuration and incorporated a door at the aft end of the fuselage. Part of the system included a hydraulic ramp that could be lowered to ground level or suspended at truck-bed height to facilitate loading.

These designs, though never built, were more or less contemporary with Fairchild's C-82 and featured similar solutions. Solutions which were to set the pattern for the general layout and operation of many subsequent tactical transports.

During World War Two, the bulk of the US airlift capability was by aircraft which lacked some, or all, of the advantages of these designs. Cargo loading of the Curtiss C-46 Commando and Douglas C-47 Skytrain was difficult at best when making the 90° turn into the fuselage. The conventional landing gear added to the problem when the cargo had to be moved uphill along the sloping floor. The Douglas C-54 Skymaster offered a level floor to assist in loading, but required a forklift to load and unload it.

Fairchild C-82 Packet
In 1941, the US Army requirement for a freight carrier that would afford a large, uninterrupted cargo hold with direct access for ground-level loading resulted in the Fairchild Model 78. This aircraft would carry the USAAF Mission-Design-Series (MDS) designation of C-82, and the name Packet. The twin-boomed, high-wing, podded fuselage aircraft had a fuselage with a cross-section capable of accommodating a variety of standard military vehicles. Power was provided by a pair of 2,100hp Pratt & Whitney R-2800-85 radial engines driving Hamilton Standard three-bladed, constant speed, hydromatic propellers. The crew was to consist of two pilots, navigator, radio operator, and crew chief. Up to 42 paratroops or 34 litter patients could be carried.

Fairchild C-119 Flying Boxcar
During 1947, an XC-82A, s/n 45-57769, was modified to lower the flightdeck and move it forward, delete the ventral fins, and install more powerful 2,650hp R-4360-4 engines. Some additional windows were added to the nose to enhance drop zone visibility. Thus modified, the airframe was redesignated as the C-119A. On 17 December 1947, this aircraft made a first flight that lasted 1 hour and 45 minutes.

In their own way, each of these early heavy-lift aircraft paved the way for endloading military transports. Their high wing designs placed the cargo floor closer to the loading vehicles/equipment and high tails permitted uncluttered access to the cargo area. While underpowered and flown overgrossed, the C-82 and C-119 let Army and Air Force units prove out airdrop and airland techniques, with the C-119 serving ably during combat.

From these aircraft came the Fairchild C-123 Provider, an interim transport aircraft, and the venerable Lockheed C-130 Hercules – which, half a century on, remains the ultimate endloader for tactical operations.

Acknowledgements
No book of this scope could be accomplished without the assistance of a multitude of people and access to numerous data repositories. It is with these facts in mind that this author gratefully acknowledges the support provided by those listed herein.

Capt George Cully, USAF (Ret), and MSgt David W Menard, USAF (Ret) for continual support and guidance.

Lloyd S Jones for his detailed drawings of the C-82, C-119, C-119H, and XC-120

CMSgt Thomas H Brewer, USAF (Ret), Wesley Henry, Jeff Duford, and Vivian White from the USAF Museum for data and photography.

Peter M Bowers, Norman E Filer; Harry S Gann, William T Larkins, MSgt Douglas Remington, USAF (Ret), Victor D Seely, John W R Taylor, Norman E Taylor MSgt USAF (Ret) and Gordon S Williams for access to photography and data.

Robert T 'Tom' Cossaboom, Betty Kennedy, Dr John Leland, and Donald D Little for access to the MATS/MAC/AMC/ARS files at Scott AFB, IL.

Gerald T Cantwell and Dr Kenneth C Kan for data and photos on the Air Force Reserve.

Dr William Elliott and Jane Trimmer for access to data from the archives of the Air Force Systems Command/Air Force Materiel Command.

Lynn O Gamma, Dr Daniel L Haulman, Archie DiFante, James H Kitchens, and Major Lester A Sliter, USAF for access to materials in the Air Force Historical Research Center, Maxwell AFB, AL.

James A 'Al' Moyers, Air Force Communications Agency for data on the Air Force Communications Service.

Walter J Boyne, Dana Bell, and Melissa A N Keiser for access to the National Air & Space Museum files.

Grant M Hales, Air Combat Command Historian, for data on Tactical Air Command use of the aircraft, especially the Eighteenth Air Force, and a sanity check.

Col John Dale, USAF (Ret) for data and photography on Project *Drag Net*.

SSgt Anna Raitt, 62nd MAW Historian, for data and photography on the 62nd TCG C-82s.

Jim Babcock for data on Aero Union fire bombers.

Carl H Bernhardt for details on the Air Resupply and Communications Service.

Captain Claude Girrard for information and photographs regarding TWA's C-82 *Ontos*.

Guy Aceto and Pearlie M Draughn for access to the Air Force Association files.

David C Leisy for data and photographs on flight testing of the C-119.

Wendel Loyd for information and photographs on the MATS Ferrying Squadron.

Mel Duncan for data and photography on the WY-ANG C-119s.

Lt Col Jessie J Craddock, CA-ANG (Ret) for data and photography on the 129th SOS C-119s.

Col Ron Thurlow, USAF (Ret) for data on significant and named C-119s.

Lt Col Donald W Klinko, USAFR, for TAC files at Tinker AFB, OK.

Robert V Aquilina, John Elliott, and Roy Grossneck for data and photography on the USN and USMC.

Dr Carl A Christy, Ray Gagnon, Janet Lacroix, and Lena O'Hara for access to RCAF photography.

J Herb Steward for data and photography on the Steward-Davis *Jet-Pack* conversion on the C-82 and C-119.

MSgt Frederick H Vater, Historian AF Satellite Control Facility, Onizuka AFS, Sunnyvale, CA for the data on the 6593rd TS.

Michael Lombardi and Thomas Lubbesmeyer for data and photography on the North American C-82, now residing in the Boeing Archives.

J R Alvis for data and photography on the 71st SOS, and Col Herman A 'Al' Heuss for data and confirmation on Lt Col Harold E Mitchell, pilot of *Pelican 9* and the IP on the first 71st SOS AC-119G combat mission.

Ted Quackenbush for data and photography on the 483rd TCW.

Frank Lamm for data on the 483rd TCW and data and photography on the PA ANG.

John Andrews; Leatrice R Arakaki; J Ora Baird Jr; H C Casey Burks; Burl Burlingame; Dr Dennis F Casey; John H Cloe; Daniel Crawford; Dr Thomas W Crouch; John Ensign; Harry R Fletcher; SMSgt Stephen M Glidden, USAF; John Gomez III; 1Lt June E Green, USAF; Joylin I Gustin; Dr Robin Higham; J C Hopkins; Frederick D Horky; Cheryl Hortel; Frederick A Johnsen; Lt David Johnson. USAF; Richard Lane; MSgt A Lawrence, USAF; Virgil I Lunning; Pat Reid; Theron Rhienhart; R M Rose; Frederick J Shaw Jr; Robert J Smith; Aaron J Tobiska; Jody Y Ullmann; Lt Col Joe Vollemeck, USAF (Ret); Lt Col Joe Wagovich, USAF (Ret); Robert Woodling; Dr James O Young; 62nd Air Mobility Wing Historian; AC-119 Gunship Association; Aerospace Historian Magazine; Air Combat Command Historian; Air Force Historical Research Agency; Air Force Logistics Command Historian; Air Force Magazine; Air Force Materiel Command Historian; Air Force Reserve Historian; Air Force Satellite Control Facility Historian; Air Mobility Command Historian; Air Rescue Service Historian; Air Resupply and Communications Association; Alaskan Air Command Historian; American Aviation Historical Society; Canadian National Defence Dept of History; Edwards AFB Historian; Glenn L Martin Aviation Museum; Marine Corps Air-Ground Museum; Military Airlift Command Historian; Museum of Flight, Seattle; NASA History Office; National Air and Space Museum; Naval Historical Center; Office of Air Force History; Pacific Air Forces Historian; RCAF Photo Library; Steward-Davis, Inc; Strategic Air Command Historian; Tactical Air Command Historian; Trans World Airlines; United Airlines; USAF Historical Research Center; USAF Museum; USAF Public Affairs (Books & Magazines Branch).

Special thanks is given to: Lt Col David H Anderson, USAFR (Ret); Robert T 'Tom' Cossaboom; Capt George Cully, USAF (Ret); Dr William Elliott; Roger M Fox; Grant M Hales; Col Richard D Iversen, USAF (Ret); Dr Kenneth C Kan; MSgt David W Menard, USAF (Ret); and CMSgt William O Petrie, USAF (Ret) for giving the manuscript a sanity check.

Lt Col David H Anderson had flown KC-97s in SAC, then came to Boeing and joined the Reserve where he flew the C-119. He called them 'Texas Wheelbarrows'. After flying aircraft with significantly better performance he believed he had taken a big step backwards and was not to impressed with the C-119's structure, systems, and marked lack of power that resulted in marginal engine-out capabilities.

Dedication

This volume is dedicated to the men and women who designed, built, operated, and maintained these aircraft. And, especially to the 73rd Troop Carrier Squadron, 932nd Troop Carrier Group, 434th Troop Carrier Wing, Scott AFB, IL who introduced this author to the C-119. It was with this unit he dropped his boyish dream of being a fighter pilot and yearned for multi-engined aircraft. One would count 12 blades, feel a shudder, and see a plume of smoke as each engine roared to life. Most memorable, was the flight aboard *Abe 22* flying from Scott AFB to Charleston AFB, SC when we had one of the ADFs tuned to WBBM in Chicago and listened to Rachmaninoff's 2nd Piano Concerto as we climbed out into the star-studded darkness.

The sole XC-82, s/n 43-13202, as she appeared at Wright Field, OH, on 4 June 1946. The forward crew door was open and an access ladder was hung from the door sill. The tail number was repeated under the left wing and the nose was inscribed *Packet The Flying Boxcar*, replete with a drawing of the latter. P M Bowers

Chapter 1

The C-82 Packet

The Fairchild C-82 Packet is a twin-engined, twin-boomed, high wing, land monoplane of all metal construction, designed for the use as a cargo carrier, troop/paratroop transport, and a cargo drop airplane. The fuselage structure is of semi-monocoque construction. A retractable tricycle landing gear system is installed. The twin booms and empennage were of sufficient height above the ground to permit ease of loading of large objects through the open cargo doors at the aft end of the fuselage.

C-82 Principal Dimensions and Weights

Wingspan	106ft 5in
Fuselage length	60ft 6⅜in
Overall length	77ft 1in
Height	26ft 4in
Wing Area	1,400ft²
Empty weight	31,498 lb
Basic weight	34,098 lb
Design weight	50,000 lb
Combat weight	40,265 lb*
Max TOW	54,000 lb†

* Basic Mission; † Limited by performance

The cargo compartment had a rectangular cross-section that permitted the carrying of a wide variety of equipment, while the tricycle landing gear afforded a level floor to facilitate loading. The floor height was four feet above the ground – truck-bed height. Large clamshell doors swung outboard through an arc of 90° offering complete clearance for loading. Paratroop doors located within the clamshell doors could be opened in flight for troop drops. For heavy cargo drops, the clamshell doors would be removed so that the cargo could be extracted through the large 8ft square opening.

C-82 Cargo Compartment Dimensions

Height	8ft 0in
Width	8ft 0in
Length	38ft 5in
Cargo Floor Area	308ft²

Early Army Interest

In 1934, Fairchild had successfully demonstrated to the Army the XC-31, single-engined, high wing, conventional-geared transport with a large truckbed-height floor and 5ft wide doors.

The Army envisioned a better transport as early as December 1941. However, perceived shortages of strategic materials, particularly metal, drove the idea for an all-wood transport much like the Curtiss C-76 Caravan. At the behest of General of the Army Henry H 'Hap'

While having similar lines – twin boomed, twin-engined, podded fuselage – the performance of the Lockheed P-38M Lightning and Fairchild C-82 Packet was markedly different. Here the P-38 was employed as a photo chase plane for one of the North American C-82N-NTs.
Boeing Archives NAA1050

Arnold, Fairchild proceeded with a transport design by their chief engineer, Armand J Thieboldt. He made the preliminary sketches for the aircraft that became the Fairchild Model 78 in November 1941. On 10 November 1941, the Army decided to identify the aircraft as the C-82 Packet. A year was spent making all of the engineering drawings for this all-wood airplane, then the Army ordered Fairchild to re-do the drawing for an all-metal airplane.

A Desperate Beginning

With the end of World War Two in sight, and for what appear to be political reasons, Fairchild searched for a new face in their management structure who might assure their building of the C-82. Downsizing after the war could have spelled the demise of the aircraft manufacturer. Fairchild obtained none other than the famed race pilot of the 1930s, Bennie Howard who had flown *Mr. Mulligan*, *Ike*, and *Mike*. Bennie

This was the prototype Packet, XC-82-FA, s/n 43-13202, revealing its distinctive lines that would continue throughout the series of aircraft. Museum of Flight

Details of the nose markings on the XC-82 reveal the name *Packet* and a winged railroad boxcar with the words 'THE FLYING BOXCAR' beneath. To the rear were a Douglas A-26 Invader and a Douglas A-20 Havoc. P M Bowers

Howard reported to Hagerstown, Maryland, where he was given a minimal briefing on the new airplane before commencing the taxi tests. The crew were not wearing parachutes and some of the windows had been removed for better ventilation during the hot weather. Several taxi runs at various speeds were made on 10 September 1944; then suddenly the airplane became airborne with a completely unprepared crew on board. They circled the field and landed. When asked how they had managed to get airborne, Howard replied, 'It just felt like flying, so I flew it.' This aircraft was the XC-82, serial number 43-13202.

The XC-82 is known to have been deployed to Saipan in 1944 as part of the test program.

An initial contract called for the production of 100 C-82As, with deliveries beginning in late 1945 – too late to see service in World War Two. A second contract was let for 100 more of these aircraft. In addition to Fairchild in Hagerstown, MD, a second manufacturer was to produce the C-82. A new production line was established at

Below left: **The fuselage, nacelle, and boom stations are shown in this figure.**

Below right: **These side, plan, and section views show the available cargo volume areas within a C-82.** USAF 32840AC

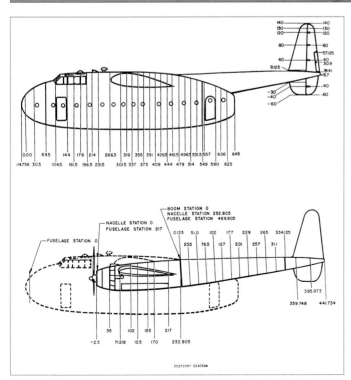

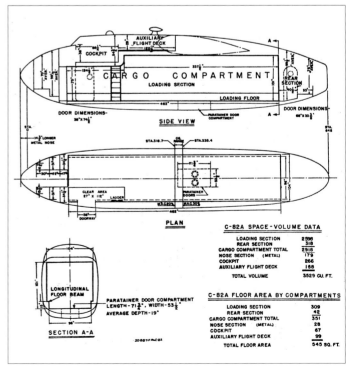

6 Fairchild C-82 & C-119

the North American Aviation plant in Dallas, TX, and a contract for 782 C-82Ns was issued. Only three C-82Ns were completed when the contract for the remaining C-82Ns was terminated on VJ-Day. Fairchild built a total of 220 C-82As between 1945 and September 1948.

The C-82 entered operational service in May 1945, and the production run of 223 airplanes was completed in September 1948. The C-82 was the first Allied endloading aircraft produced in quantity. From 1946, most of the C-82As served in troop carrier units in the Tactical Air Command (TAC). Some of these aircraft were allocated to the Military Air Transport Service (MATS) for use by the Air Rescue Service. Strategic Air Command (SAC) also operated the Packets as base support aircraft for their bomber groups – at its peak having eleven of these aircraft within the command in 1949.

Fairchild C-82 Packet

The C-82 Packet featured clamshell doors in the aft fuselage that permitted ease of loading with its low floor, and allowed parachute delivery of troops or supplies in a matter of seconds. The airplane was capable of carrying a cargo load of 15,000 lb, about double that of the C-47.

Below left: **This figure reveals the C-82 radio antenna locations.**

Below right: **A total of 10 paratainers were carried by the C-82's aerial delivery system located near the aircraft's center of gravity.**

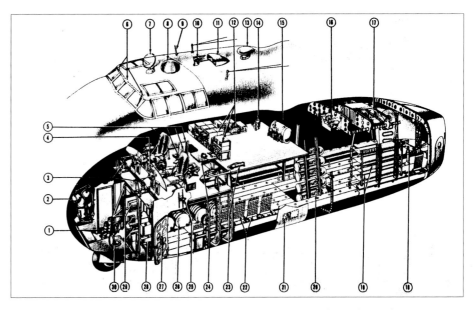

C-82 fuselage components.

1. Nose landing gear
2. Hydraulic system – nose section
3. Flight control columns
4. Instrument panel
5. Crew seats
6. Windshield wipers
7. Manual radio compass antenna – ADF Loop
8. Astrodome
9. VHF command radio set antenna
10. RC-103 blind landing antenna
11. Air scoop – heating & ventilation system
12. Communications equipment
13. Automatic radio compass radio antenna – ADF loop
14. Propeller anti-icing tank
15. Reserve oil tank (Airplanes s/n 44-22959 – 44-22989)
16. Automatic pilot servo motors
17. Type G-1 O_2 cylinders
18. Type A-17 fire extinguisher
19. Litter installation
20. Aerial delivery installation
21. O_2 filler compartment
22. Troop seat installation
23. Type A-17 fire extinguisher
24. Navigator/Radio operator worktable
25. Radio beacon (IFF) antenna
26. Type J-1 O_2 cylinders
27. Type A-2 fire extinguisher
28. Lavatory equipment
29. Automatic pilot equipment
30. Chemical disposal toilet

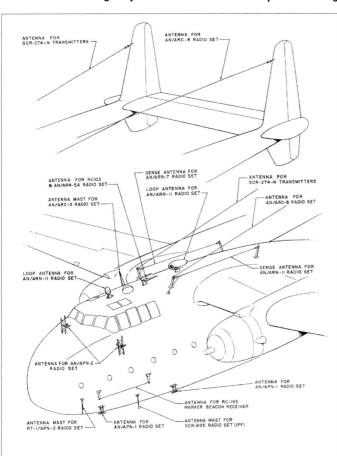

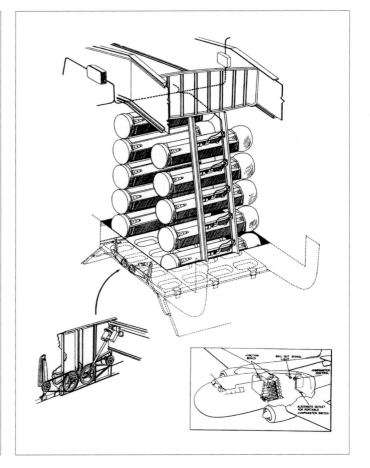

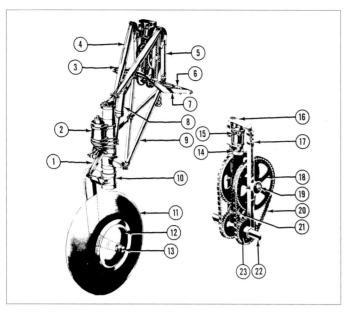
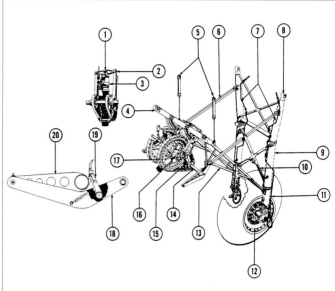

C-82 nose landing gear components.
1. Torque links
2. Shimmy damper
3. Upper truss tie
4. Upper truss
5. Brace tube
6. Retracting arm
7. Locking link
8. Emergency extension shock absorber
9. Lower truss
10. Shock strut
11. Tire
12. Wheel
13. Axle
14. Actuator
15. Cannon plug
16. Actuator tie support
17. Actuator compression beam
18. Large sprocket
19. Adjustment pivot
20. Chain
21. Driver
22. Torque shaft
23. Small sprocket

C-82 main landing gear components.
1. Actuator tie support
2. Retracting mechanism support
3. Actuator
4. Cross tube
5. Emergency extension shock absorbers
6. Connecting link
7. Upper hydraulic lines
8. Upper truss
9. Shock struts
10. Air interconnect line
11. Lower hydraulic lines
12. Wheel and tire
13. Drag strut
14. Torque shaft
15. Small sprocket
16. Adjustment pivot
17. Chain
18. Locking link
19. Down-lock latch
20. Retracting arm

The normal crew of five consisted of: pilot, co-pilot, navigator, radio operator and crew chief/flight mechanic.

Possible C-82 Personnel / Cargo Loads

Airlift	Troops	42
Aeromedical	Litters	32
	Attendants	2
15 x Army paracans	350 lb each	
1 x M2A3 75mm Howitzer	3,500 lb	
1 x M3A1 75mm Howitzer	2,089 lb	
1 x M-4 37mm gun	916 lb	
1 x M-2 40mm anti-aircraft gun & carriage	6,400 lb	
1 x 37mm anti-tank gun & motor carriage	5,500 lb	
1 x M2A1 105mm gun	4,340 lb	
1 x M1918 155mm Howitzer	9,120 lb	

Above left: **This low-angle profile shot of C-82-FA, s/n 44-22962, reveals the various skin panels, belly antennas, cowl flaps, and engine exhaust manifold. Note how the manifold protrudes aft of the cowl flaps, then exits below the wing leading edge.** Via Peter M Bowers

Left: **This low-angle profile shot of C-82A-FA, s/n 45-57804, reveals its CQ-804 buzz number, production number, 174, standard USAF marking, and unit markings on the nose and tail. A black anti-corrosion paint was applied to the belly. Also of interest are the underwing radio altimiter antennas, cabin heater heat exchanger on the exhaust, and additional antennas under the forward fuselage.** USAF 39515

Structure

The semi-monocoque, tension-field structure, aluminum fuselage houses the nose gear, has a raised flightdeck, a capacious aft cabin with a level floor at truck-bed height, a forward access door on the left, and a pair of clamshell aft doors with integral inward opening troop doors. The latter permitted simultaneous paratroop jumps from either side of the aircraft. The clamshell doors could be removed for heavy equipment drops. The floor of the forward main cabin has a bomb bay-like doors installed for dropping paracans. The paratainer box is located between Stations 319 and 391. A section of floor panel covered the paratainer box. Seven longitudinal beams support the cargo deck that is constructed of plywood. Cargo tie-down rings are spaced in 20-inch squares along the center of the cargo deck floor. The fuselage is attached to the wing center section by four large bolts. Spacing for the fuselage frames is 35 inches, except for the main spar frames located directly below the wing box that are spaced at 72 inches. The fuselage is divided into six major sections: main body, sides upper front, upper rear, nose compartment, and rear cargo door compartment.

The wings of the C-82 are semi-monocoque, tension-field structures that are fully cantilevered with an inverted gull design to shorten the main gear struts while retaining the cabin height. The camber of the wings is tapered from root to tip. Each outboard wing panel has a flap and a pair of ailerons attached to the rear spar. Wingtip caps are attached outboard on the wings. The

Top right: **C-82A-FA, s/n 48-585, was the last Fairchild-built Packet. This crisp view reveals the variegated skin patterns. The aircraft had its CQ-585 buzz number on the forward fuselage along with the 220 production number. The upper fuselage details include: an ADF loop antenna, a pair of HF radio antenna masts, an RC-103 localizer antenna, the APU air inlet, and an ADF footfall antenna. The fan-shaped pieces along the wing leading edges were screens for the landing lights. The walkway outlines for the wings, booms, fuselage, and horizontal stabilizer may be seen.** Via N E Taylor

Centre right: **Fairchild demonstrated C-82A-1-FA, s/n 44-22959 (first of the series), in its chromate green finish. Note the wing walk configuration (differing from the Fairchild-built Packets). Large mass balance arms were installed on the elevator and rudders. Note the large loop antenna, followed by the navigator's blister, RC-103 localizer antenna, and ADF football antenna on top of the fuselage. An IFF antenna was installed beneath the left and right forward-most cockpit windows. While classified as an all-metal aircraft, the flight controls were fabric covered. A pair of mass balance weights may be seen on top of the elevator. Compare the shape of the walkway areas on the North American-built C-82 with those on the Fairchild-built Packet on page 10.** Boeing Archives NAA1046

Right: **One of three North American-built C-82Ns was taxiing at the Fort Worth, TX, field. All of the C-82Ns were camouflaged.** North American via F A Johnsen

Above: **A camouflaged C-82N flies over the Texas countryside on a test flight. The black wing walkway stripes are visible.** Via P M Bowers

Left: **C-82A-30-FA, s/n 44-23048 was captured just after lift off. Note the open troop doors for cabin ventilation. The buzz number appeared on the nose and beneath the left wing. An ADF sense antenna may be seen under the forward fuselage. The number 92 aft of the prop warning line indicates that this was the 92nd Packet built.** USAF

Below left: **A Firestone tracked landing gear was installed on EC-82A, s/n 45-57746. The 'E' prefix was to designate the aircraft as exempt, meaning exempt from routine technical orders. Similar tracked gear were installed on a Boeing B-50 and a Convair B-36. Tests showed that, when used on the rough fields the gear was intended to operate from, the tracks became jammed with sod.** W T Larkins

Above: **MPs guarded the tracked-gear EC-82A. Note the flight test camera mounted beneath the aft fuselage.** W J Balogh via MSgt D W Menard

Right: **This patent drawing by Alfred A Gassner depicts the tracked gear components at rotation on take-off.** Fairchild

Below: **EC-82A, s/n 45-57746, was in the flare just prior to touchdown at the Hagerstown Airport. Flight test cameras were mounted beneath the fuselage to capture the operation of the tracked gear.** Fairchild Photo D-1393/ USAF 32536AC via United Technologies Archives

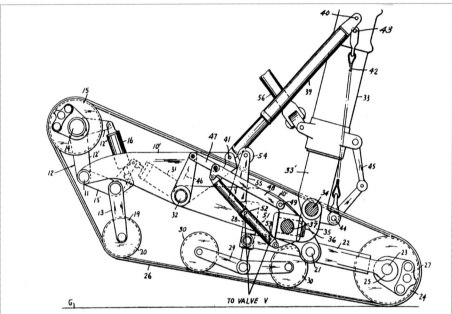

Fairchild C-82 & C-119 11

From top:
C-82A, s/n 44-23004, carried its CQ-004 buzz number on its booms aft of the national insignia. It shared the ramp at Wright Field, OH with B-29 44-68658, a C-47, and a pair of AT-11s. P M Bowers

In transition markings, red bars were added to the national insignia, but the CQ-004 buzz number was applied to the booms. The aircraft was photographed at Wright Field with skis on all three landing gears. Via John Lomez

C-82A, s/n 44-23004, photographed after September 1947 when the USAF became a service co-equal with the Army and Navy, reveals its red-barred national insignia and UNITED STATES AIR FORCE lettering on the fuselage. The aircraft was equipped with skis on the main gear. P M Bowers

C-82A-1-FA, s/n 44-22961, shows how the spray from the main gear wheels partially covered the buzz numbers on the tailboom. The blotches on the forward fuselage must have been the result of touch-painting. A small moveable window may be seen in the trapezoidal window in the forward corner of the cockpit. Boeing Historical Archives NAA1053

wings incorporate a twist and washout to preclude wingtip stalling. A D-duct is incorporated into the wing leading edge for thermal anti-icing. The inverted gull wing raised the fuselage and allowed for shorter landing gear.

For simplicity, the tapered cylindrical booms, vertical fins, rudders, ventral fins, and outboard stabilizer tips are interchangeable left and right. The booms are joined with the horizontal stabilizer with its elevator.

Fourteen circular windows are installed in the main cabin, equally spaced and mounted along the airplane mid-water line. Another such window is installed at the top of each of the troop doors located in each of the cargo doors.

Engines and Propellers

A pair of Pratt & Whitney R-2800-85 engines, equipped with a single-stage, two-speed turbosupercharger powered most of the C-82s. At sea level, the engines delivered 2,100bhp at 2,800rpm for five minutes. The XC-82 was powered by R-2800-34 engines, whereas the first ten production aircraft were equipped with R-2800-22 radials.

While identical tests were conducted using Curtiss Electric reversible propellers and Hamilton Standard hydromatic propellers, production aircraft were equipped with three-bladed Hamilton Standard 33E60 propellers with a 15ft 2in diameter. The propellers are of the constant-speed, full-feathering, hydromatic type.

The air induction system for the engines has a scoop mounted on top of each nacelle. The inlet has three operating positions: direct ram air, filtered air and hot air.

Fuel and Oil Systems

The C-82 operated on 100/130 octane grade fuel. An independent fuel system is incorporated for each engine. Collapsible, bladder-type fuel cells are installed.

Right: **This factory shot shows how a 1¼-ton truck could be loaded into the C-82. The cargo compartment was designed to fit the size of most standard-sized military vehicles of the day.**
Boeing Historical Archives NAA1049

Below: **This C-82N was photographed during rotation at take-off. Note the open sliding window for the co-pilot. In the background are a North American B-25 Mitchell, Curtiss C-46 Commando, and Douglas C-45 Expeditor.**
Boeing Historical Archives NAA1047

Fuel Tanks		C-82	C-82N
Outboard Wing	2 tanks	1,262gal	1,506.0gal
Inboard Wing	2 tanks	1,338gal	1,529.2gal
Total	4 tanks	2,600gal	3,052.2gal

A 55-gallon oil tank is located aft of each engine firewall.

Flight Controls

The primary flight controls of the C-82 consist of an elevator on the trailing edge of the center portion of the horizontal stabilizer, a pair of rudders attached to the rear spars of the vertical fins, and two ailerons attached to the rear spars of each outboard wing panel. The secondary controls consist of inboard and outboard flaps located on either side of each boom, and trim tabs on the elevator, each rudder, and the right inboard aileron. The flaps are NACA two-segment slotted devices. The inboard ailerons droop when the flaps are lowered. The primary flight controls and their respective trim tabs are fabric covered.

A cable-driven system is employed for the primary flight controls and the trim tabs. The flaps are electrically driven.

Landing Gear System

With the exception of the brake system, all other landing gear systems are electrically powered. The nose gear retracts into a well forward of the cockpit, while the main gear retracts into each boom. Each gear strut accommodates a single tire.

Cleveland Pneumatic No 8358 dual oleo struts are installed on the main gear while a single Cleveland Pneumatic No 8357 oleo strut is employed for the nose gear. Each main gear shock strut had an air-interconnection system mounted to the front of the struts to equalize pressure, and improve ground handling characteristics.

The nose gear is non-steerable, and directional control is achieved through differential braking and differential power. The nosewheel is unloaded by applying up elevator, allowing the strut to extend, thereby disengaging the centering cams. With the cams disengaged, the wheel casters in whichever direction it is controlled.

C-82N-NT, s/n 45-25436, was the first of three such aircraft built by North American. The massive nose gear wheel and tire are identical to those on the main gear. The placard centered on the lower portion of the door states 'FIRE EXT. INSIDE', indicative of the fire concerns on these aircraft. Boeing Historical Archives NAA1045

North American engineers were inspecting the engine installation on C-82N-NT, s/n 45-25436. Visible is the fire extinguisher on the inside of the forward entry door. A propeller warning placard appeared next to the door lock lever on the left beneath the fire bottle. An IFF antenna was installed beneath the cockpit window. The web troop seats are visible inside the aircraft. Details of the sheeetmetal ladder are also evident. North American via F A Johnsen

A Houde No A-10818 shimmy damper is installed on the nose gear strut. The nosewheel is free to swivel through an arc 62° either side of neutral.

The main gear wheel brakes are operated by a pair of 1,000psi hydraulic systems with an accumulator mounted in each boom. The systems are cross-connected so that each system powers a set of brakes in each landing gear, thereby assuring partial braking in the event of one hydraulic system failure. Hayes No 2-25B hydraulic expanding tube brakes are installed on Fairchild C-82s 44-22959 through 45-57746 and 45-57765 through 48-587, and all three North American C-82Ns. Aircraft 45-57747 through 45-57764, those equipped with tracked landing gear, are equipped with Goodyear hydraulic spot brakes.

Hayes Industries 56-inch diameter wheels and Type I, 56-inch, 16-ply smooth contour tires are installed on each main gear. A Goodyear 44-inch diameter wheel and Type I, 44-inch, 10-ply, smooth contour tire is installed on the nose gear.

All landing gear doors are operated through direct mechanical linkage to the landing gear retracting mechanisms. While the main gear doors remain open with the gear extended, the nose gear doors close after the gear has completed its extension cycle.

A gear warning system consists of three green and three red lights to indicate whether gear is up or down, and a warning horn that sounds to prevent the pilot from inadvertently landing without the gear down and locked.

Mission Equipment

Canvas seats along each side of the main cabin are provided for up to 41 paratroops. When not in use, the seats are folded up and secured to the sidewall.

A ¼-inch diameter galvanized static line cable is installed on each side of the main cabin. For stowage the cables are coiled and attached at the aft end of the fuselage. For use, the cables are uncoiled and attached to fittings in the forward cabin.

A monorail aerial delivery system installed in the aircraft permitted the delivery of up to 15 Army paracans weighing up to 350 lb each. The aerial delivery rack was installed between Body Stations 319 and 391. This system could be operated either from the cockpit or the jumpmaster's station. When not in use, the paratainer racks were stowed along the top of the fuselage.

A total of 13 posts could be installed in the main cabin to support up to 34 litters when the aircraft was employed for aeromedical evacuation operations.

A three-step entrance ladder is stowed in the forward fuselage by the cargo door. The ladder hangs from the beam at the cargo door and rests against the fuselage skin.

Two 16ft-long metal loading ramps are carried on the aircraft. The ramps hook into the outer edge of the cargo door sill and may be spaced to accommodate various loading conditions. A pair of loading support jacks are provided for installation under the aft fuselage during loading operations.

A set of 26 engine/ordnance tie-down fittings are installed along the centerline beam of the cargo floor. Another 88 cargo tie-down fittings are installed in a 20-inch grid pattern on the cargo compartment floor.

C-82s were also capable of towing gliders. Initially the aircraft were equipped with two lugs installed in the end of the booms, each permitting towing of two 7,000 lb gliders, or a single 18,000 lb glider when the aircraft gross weight did not exceed 42,000 lb. Later production airplanes were equipped with a tow lug mounted on the aft lower portion of the fuselage. The new lug enabled the aircraft to pull a 30,000 lb glider.

Electrical System

The electrical system on the C-82s consists of a single wire, 24-volt DC installation grounded through the airplane structure. The basic system incorporates a storage battery, inverters, two engine-driven generators, two reverse-current relays, and two voltage regulators. In addition, there is an external power circuit and an auxiliary powerplant. The latter could be employed both on the ground and in flight.

The battery, an AN3150, Type G-1, was a 24-volt, 34 ampere-hour shielded storage battery.

A 1,000VA, 400-cycle, 3-phase inverter is installed on the right side of the cargo compartment floor just aft of Station 179.

These limited electrical systems were installed on the C-82:

System	Function
115V, 400-cycle	operating the radio navigation equipment
115V, 400-cycle	operating the automatic pilot
26V, 400-cycle	operating the fuel flow meter
3V, 400-cycle	operating the magnetic compass light

Beginning with airplane s/n 44-22989, the C-82s were equipped with a second inverter that was a 750VA type.

Communications & Electronic Equipment

The C-82s were equipped with a variety of communication and electronic equipment for intercommunication, communication, navigation, and identification.

These radio systems were installed on the C-82s:

Description	Army/Navy Specification
Interphone	AN/AIC-2
Interphone	AN/AIC-3
Glide Path Receiver	AN/ARN-5
VHF Command	AN/ARC-3
VHF Command	SCR-274N
Radio Beacon Receiver	AN/APN-2 (44-22959/45-57737)
Radio Beacon Receiver	AN/APN-12 (45-57738/45-57832)
LORAN	AN/APN-9
Glide Path Receiver	AN/ARN-5A
Automatic Radio Compass	AN/ARN-7
Manual Radio Compass	AN/ARN-11
Liaison	AN/ARC-8
Localizer	RC-103
Marker Beacon	RC-193
IFF	SCR-695B
Radio Set	AN/APS-10 (45-57783/45-57832)

A pair of wick-type static dischargers are mounted on the upper trailing edge portions of each rudder and trailing edge outboard end of each aileron. A single discharger is installed on the trailing edge of each wingtip.

Oxygen System

The C-82s are equipped with a conventional low-pressure demand oxygen system for each of the five crew members. In addition, a separate continuous-flow oxygen system was provided for troops in the main cabin. The latter system supported up to 43 troops. Four Type J-1 cylinders, located beneath the cargo floor, provided oxygen for this system.

Three Type A-6 portable oxygen cylinders, with a 280in^3 capacity, were also provided. For this system, five recharger hose outlets for filling the portable cylinders were located throughout the airplane. These recharger outlets were part of the demand-type system.

The demand-type system was supported by eight shatterproof Type G-1 steel oxygen cylinders mounted in the aft cargo compartment ceiling.

Heating, Ventilating & Anti-Icing Systems

Hot air is provided by four exhaust gas heat exchangers and a secondary heat exchanger. This air is used for heating and anti-icing.

Hot air directed along a D-duct in the wing, horizontal stabilizer, and vertical stabilizer leading edges affords icing protection.

The secondary heat exchanger and air mixer, located in the wing center section, modulates air temperature to provide comfortable air to the cockpit and main cabin. Hot air is also available for windshield and astrodome anti-icing. The two outer forward windshields are of shatter-proof double pane construction that allows hot air to deice these windshields.

EC-82A

During the late 1940s the USAF was investigating a number of operational options; one of which was flying off unprepared fields. As part of this program, a single C-82A, s/n 45-57746, was converted into an EC-82A, equipped with the Firestone-designed tracked landing gear. During this period, the 'E' prefix stood for Exempt, not Electronic. The standard wheels, tires and brakes were replaced by tank-like treads rolled around a set of sprocket wheels and bogies. With the tracked gear, the airplane could operate from both prepared and rough fields. Fairchild design engineer Alfred A Gassner was faced with the initial design. His challenge was to reduce the gear footprint to 25-28psi. In April 1949, a contract was let to retrofit 18 C-82s with this system, however only 12 aircraft were ever modified. Airplanes scheduled for incorporation of the tracked gear were s/n 45-57747/45-57764. Unfortunately it was a bad idea that went south. The tracks easily became jammed with grass and debris. In crosswind landings, the rubber track belts would depart their bogies. Both Fairchild and USAF test pilots were experiencing similar difficulties with the tracked gear, and the program was canceled in December 1949.

The C-82 was also employed for ski tests. Aircraft s/n 44-23004 was equipped with snow skis developed by the Federal Aircraft Works in Minneapolis, MN under contract from the Wright Air Development Center. While retaining its standard landing gear and wheels, a set of wide skis was attached to each wheel around axle height. While development of the skis began in 1945, it was not until April 1948 that tests were conducted at Ladd AFB, AK. The aircraft experienced high nose gear shimmy and the main gear ski actuators lacked sufficient power to raise and transfer the load from the wheels to the skis. The aircraft was returned to Wright AFB for redesign and modification. It was able to resume testing later in 1948 and in early 1949. These tests were conducted at Yellowknife, Northwest Territories, Canada. Nose ski unstick problems continued and on one test the aircraft traversed two miles without getting airborne. On the third attempt, the aircraft was able to get airborne. Though additional work was done to correct the nose ski unstick problem in time for the 1950-1951 tests, the program was abandoned because the take-off distance remained an issue.

C-82A, s/n 44-23004, was assigned to Wright-Patterson AFB, for flight testing. Note the fire bottle and ground power cart. Via P M Bowers

Chapter 2

C-82 Operations

The C-82 Packets roamed far and wide in the pursuits of their business; however their growing pains were most evident during their initial operations. They served within the Zone of Interior (ZI), AK, and in Europe with the USAF, in the services of other air forces, and in civilian roles. In addition to its primary mission as a troop/paratroop/cargo transport, the C-82 served admirably in the humanitarian role.

Project Comet

After World War Two, the United States Army Air Forces served as a subordinate organization within the United States Army. Strategic Air Command (SAC) and Tactical Air Command (TAC) were established on 21 March 1946 utilizing assets and personnel from Continental Air Command (CONAC). Continuing in existence was Air Transport Command (ATC), which had been established in 1942. While ATC was tasked with routine logistical support of both land and air forces within the Army, TAC was assigned the troop carrier mission.

New post-war aircraft requirements were tackled by industry – remnants of the *Arsenal of Democracy* that had been established during World War Two. Many World War Two veterans formed the Air Force Association (AFA) whose mission was to educate America's citizens and Congress on the need for a separate air force. Toward this end there was a series of deliberate exercises to raise America's awareness of airpower. These exercises used the proven Boeing B-29 for long-range flights, placed the fledgling Convair B-36 Peacemaker squarely in the public eye, and demonstrated new fighters and transports. One of these missions was Project *Comet*.

On 2 May 1946, Major General Elwood 'Pete' Quesada, TAC Commander, directed a mass trans-America flight utilizing the new Lockheed P-80 Shooting Star, America's first operational jet fighter. Logistical support would come from the new Fairchild C-82. Project *Comet* called for a formation of 25 P-80s from the 412th Fighter Group (FG) to fly from March Field, CA on a nine-city, thirteen-day excursion to Washington, DC. The mission was threefold:

- To demonstrate to America the need for a strong air force and show them what was being developed for the defense of the nation.
- To assess problems encountered in maintenance and supply during long-range deployments that may be required for a wartime deployment.
- To assist in Army Air Forces recruiting

Shrewd planning on the part of the 412th FG called for a spare flight of four P-80s.

Logistical support was provided by six C-82s from the 36th TCS, 316th TCG, stationed at Pope Field, NC. One Packet could not extend its gear and circled Hamilton Field, near San Francisco, for over an hour. The checklists gave no relief. Radio consultation with Fairchild Tech Reps also proved fruitless and the aircraft

A C-82A from the 20th TCS, 314th TCG, was photographed at Orchard Place AFB, IL (now O'Hare International Airport), on 4 July 1949. The squadron insignia consists of a light blue disc, within a red border, piped white, a yellow caricatured stork carrying a caricatured bug, in the attire of a paratrooper, wearing yellow shoes and gloves and a black helmet, and carrying in the left hand a brown parasol and in the right hand, a Tommy gun. B Kemp via MSgt D W Menard

C-82A, s/n 45-57820, from the 8th TCS, 62nd TCG. The aircraft has Insignia Red Arctic trim applied to the empennage and outboard wing panels. Blue, the squadron color is applied to the nose. The squadron insignia also appears on the nose. The latter is a blue disc, edged black, a caricatured winged work horse yellow, outlined black, branded on hip with a red cross, galloping at full speed, and wearing a revolver in holster fastened to cartridge belt tan about the neck, and a packing box green strapped to his back, all over a silhouette figure, black, descending by parachute to the left toward a large white cloud formation at the bottom.
G S Williams

Right: This ramp is filled with 23 C-82s from the 316th TCG, as denoted by their nose chevrons. The squadron colors are applied to the nose chevrons and some of the vertical tails. Note the variations in arctic markings. Via N E Taylor

Below right: C-82A-FA, s/n 44-23027, is parked at an airshow, where some of the crew members have a bird's eye view of the activities. Red stripes are applied to the nose, engine cowls, and vertical tails, indicating that the aircraft belongs to the 4th TCS, 62nd TCG. This photograph was taken at the 1947 Air Races in Cleveland, OH. The aircraft was assigned to the 62nd TCG at Bergstrom AFB, TX on 1 May 1946, transferred to the 1455th Air Force Base Unit (ATC) at Great Falls AFB, MT, then the 62nd Maintenance & Supply Group, 62nd TCW, McChord AFB, WA on 20 April 1948. The markings appear to have been retained from its assignment to the 1455th ABU, while stationed at Great Falls. W J Balogh via MSgt D W Menard

Bottom: C-82A, s/n 44-23004, was photographed lifting off from Wright-Patterson AFB with Waco CG-15A-WO, s/n 45-5276, in tow. Via MSgt D W Menard

made an ignominious belly landing. Plans called for two C-82s to precede the formation of P-80s and for three Packets to follow.

The first stop was at Tucson, AZ. Capt Ed Burnett, flying a P-80 named *Shifty III*, touched down and its two drop tanks departed the aircraft then bounced down the runway. Fortunately a spare set of tanks was carried aboard one of the C-82s and repairs were effected in short order.

Fort Worth Army Air Field was the next stop. On departure another C-82 experienced gear problems and had to return to Tucson. Its load was divided between two C-47s that were hurriedly dispatched from Long Beach, CA. Then, the C-82 departed with its gear pinned down for the laborious trip back to Hagerstown for an engineering assessment and repairs.

While the leg to Memphis, TN went without a technical hitch, the arrival at Washington National Airport with the advanced maintenance echelon again was subjected to a C-82 landing gear malfunction.

It was airshow time in Washington, and while the fighter pilots discussed their upcoming routine, they were upstaged by a C-82 piloted by Dick Henson, a Fairchild test pilot! He put the lumbering Packet through its paces, including low-level engine-out passes to the delight of the crowd. Members of the 412th FG were extremely displeased with what they considered to be an arrogant display that disregarded safety. The P-80 line chief approached their commander, Col Bruce K Holloway, stating that 'there is going to be a mutiny' if the maintenance personnel were forced to fly on the C-82s for the remainder of Project *Comet*. Col Holloway listened and most of the personnel were able to fly on C-47s for the balance of the trip. In addition, the fighter pilots wrested back their just laurels in a dazzling performance. That evening, Fairchild hosted a cocktail party for the members of Project *Comet* at the Statler Hotel.

The 36th TCS dispatched a replacement pair of C-82s from Pope Field and the remaining flyable Packets were returned to Hagerstown for engineering evaluation of the landing gear. During the departure from Washington on the leg to Tinker Field, OK, a C-82 aborted the take-off due to a fouled spark plug. It caught up with the team on the following day. Another C-82 failed to have the nose gear retract on take-off from Tinker and had to make an air turnback for repairs.

Overall, Project *Comet* succeeded in its mission. The P-80s performed quite well; however the same could not be said for the C-82. Through exercises such as this, an airmindedness was developed within the United States and on 26 July 1947, the National Security Act of 1947 was passed by Congress, paving the way for a separate air force that was co-equal with the Army and Navy. The United States Air Force was activated on 17 September 1947.

From top:
These two 62nd TCG C-82As, s/n 45-57801 and 45-57775, are parked on the muddy wash rack at McChord AFB. 62nd MAW Historian

This view of C-82A, s/n 45-57775, shows the aircraft being hosed down, the precariously perched scrubber, and another airman checking the pump for spraying the water/detergent mixture. 62nd MAW Historian

C-82A, s/n 45-57751, assigned to the 62nd TCG, 7th TCS, participated in a winter exercise. Troop-drawn sleds were used to move the cargo. Note the herringbone tires that improved operations on the snow-covered airfield. Note how the Insignia Red Arctic markings were applied to retain the CQ-755 buzz number. Via G S Williams

C-82A, s/n 45-57735, from the 50th TCS, 314th TCG, was deployed to Goose Bay AB, Labrador. Replete with the Insignia Red Arctic trim, the aircraft sports its red nose denoting the squadron. E Van Houton via MSgt D W Menard

C-82 TROOP CARRIER OPERATIONS

The C-82As operated with seven troop carrier groups and one fighter wing between 1947 and 1953. These units were all part of TAC. (It should be noted that the USAF underwent a change in operating unit designations from groups to wings in the early 1950s.) The 57th Fighter Wing, based at Elmendorf AFB, AK, operated the aircraft for intra-theater airlift with four different troop carrier squadrons that were assigned/attached at various times. Regular theater airlift operations in Europe were flown by the 60th TCG (M) between 1951 and 1953. Six other troop carrier groups/wings were assigned within the Continental United States or Zone of Interior (ZI) and flew airlift, airdrop/airlanding, and humanitarian missions with the aircraft:

Unit	Base
62nd TCG (M)	McChord AFB, WA
64th TCG (M)	Greenville AFB, SC
313th TCG (M)	Bergstrom AFB, TX
314th TCG (M)	Smyrna AFB, TN
316th TCG (M	Greenville AFB, SC
375th TCG (M)	Greenville AFB, SC

The 314th TCG developed assault airlift operational procedures in addition to performing routine training with Army airborne forces.

The 316th TCG had the unique assignment of developing glider operations utilizing the Waco CG-15. In addition, the unit was tasked with freight ferrying within the ZI and overseas.

During the Berlin Airlift, codenamed Operation *Vittles*, the bulk of the airlift was provided by the C-47 and C-54 aircraft belonging to MATS. This relief operation was conducted between 26 June 1948 and 30 September 1949. Towards the end of the airlift operation, parts for a new powerplant in the British Sector had to be flown in. For these massive parts, three different aircraft types were employed – a Boeing C-97 Stratofreighter (from SAC), a Douglas C-74 Globemaster I, and a Fairchild C-82 Packet.

Alaskan Operations

C-82s from the 62nd TCG, Twelfth Air Force, at McChord AFB, WA, were routinely deployed to Alaska for joint operations with the US Army. The aircraft would stage out of Elmendorf AFB and fly to such places as Galena, Nome, and Big Delta AFB. In air transportability exercises, the C-82s would work with units of the US Army's Sixth Army. Mobile control towers would be airlifted for the operations. Ground troops would deploy with sleds. Such deployments were run in winter to test the capabilities of the aircraft, aircrews, and Army forces.

Individual troop carrier squadrons would be deployed to Alaska to provide routine airlift and resupply for the Alaskan Air Command.

Operation *Yukon*

During Operation *Yukon*, the 62nd TCG provided two squadrons and all available aircraft to transport one company of infantry and their field equipment from McChord AFB to Big Delta, Alaska in January 1948. The troops were part of the 2nd Infantry Division.

A long navigation leg was included as part of the mission along the following route: McChord - Seattle - Ellensburg - Spokane - Coeur d'Alene - Mullen Pass - Superior - Missoula - Craig Intersection - Great Falls - Cut Bank - Lethbridge - Calgary - Fanhold - Edmonton - Whitecourt - Grande Prairie - Fort St John - Beatton River - Fort Nelson - Smith River - Watson Lake - Whitehorse - Aishihik - Snag - Northway - Tanacross - Big Delta - Fairbanks - Summit - Talkeetna - Elmendorf. Refueling stops were made at Great Falls, Fort Nelson, and Elmendorf. On the return trip, the reverse route was flown.

Northbound troops enplaned at McChord and deplaned at Elmendorf AFB; whereas southbound troops enplaned at Elmendorf and deplaned at McChord.

Operation *Assembly*

During a six-week period beginning in April 1948, the 62nd TCG deployed to Pope AFB, SC, where it participated in Operation *Assembly*. While on this deployment, the unit trained with the Army's 82nd Airborne Division sta-

From top:

C-82A, 45-57770, also operated with the 50th TCS, 314th TCG on deployment to Goose Bay. A snow remover was operating behind the aircraft. E Van Houton via MSgt D W Menard

Sporting a slight variation in nose trim, this C-82A, s/n 45-57824, was flown by the 316th TCG. In addition, the squadron color appears on the top of the vertical tail. E Van Houton via MSgt D W Menard

The 182nd Packet built was C-82A-FA, s/n 45-57792, seen here with its checkerboard nose. P M Bowers A.3815

C-82A-FA, s/n 45-57743, seen in summertime as denoted by the khaki uniforms. The forward entry door, astrodome, cockpit windows, and clamshell doors are open for cooling. Insignia Red Arctic trim is applied, with buzz number CQ-743 on the lower left wing panel. G S Williams

This 316th TCG ship, s/n 45-575, has yellow trim. A T-6 Texan is taxying up behind the Packet.
W T Larkins via MSgt D W Menard

tioned at nearby Fort Bragg. Not only did the unit's personnel gain valuable experience in logistical planning during the preparation of a Wing Loading and Movement Plan in preparing for the move to Pope, they had their first opportunity to participate in actual tactical situations. While deployed, the 62nd engaged in both tactical flying and living under field conditions involving: *Operations* – Formation Flying, Paradrops, Resupply Missions; *Support* – Field Administration, Maintenance, Subsistence, Movement, Sanitation, Medicine.

During this deployment the unit dropped 6,655 paratroops and 425,346 lb of cargo. The results of Operation *Assembly* garnered the 62nd TCG a letter of commendation from the Chief of Staff of the USAF, Gen Hoyt S Vandenberg.

Pirate Packet

Chance Vought aircraft had developed a new single-engined fighter for the US Navy, known as the XF6U-1 Pirate. The new jet-propelled aircraft was designed to replace the piston-powered Chance Vought F4U Corsair. The Vought aircraft plant was at Stratford, CT. The runways at the field were very short, and the under-powered Pirate would not have been able to take off from there. A solution was at hand with the USAF.

The date, 21 June 1946, commemorated the 13th anniversary of the Chance Vought Company. The Pirate was unveiled and named on this occasion. Several days later, the Pirate was disassembled and covered in a tarpaulin. It was then stuffed into the largest transport capable of carrying it – a C-82 Packet. A second C-82 was employed to carry spares for the XF6U-1. The maiden flight of the Pirate occurred when the C-82 took off from Stratford and headed to Muroc Dry Lake where the Pirate was reassembled for the flight test program.

Fighter Rotation Support

The 82nd Fighter Group (SAC), equipped with North American P-51H Mustangs, had been deployed to Ladd AFB, AK for cold weather training since 14 April 1948. The 62nd TCG dispatched 28 C-82s on 1 July to Ladd AFB for the 82nd's redeployment to Grenier AFB, NH. The complete movement of 505 personnel and 217,066 lb of equipment was accomplished between 2 and 6 July. The 62nd was given only 48 hours notice for the mission. The successful planning and execution of the mission in such a short period were a testament to the high state of operational readiness of the 62nd TCG.

Pass the Ammunition

When an urgent requirement for ammunition arose at Rapid City AFB, SD, the 62nd was tasked to provide the airlift. A force of 31 C-82s was employed in transporting 243,601 lb of 0.50 caliber ammunition in a 36-hour period between 16 and 17 July 1948. This was most likely in support of the 28th Bombardment Group's B-29 deployment to RAF Scampton between July and October 1948.

A similar mission was flown on 16 July when 31 C-82s from the 62nd TCG were dispatched to Wendover AFB, UT; Smoky Hill AFB. KS; and Rapid City AFB, SD to airlift both spare R-3350 engines and ammunition to the 92nd Bombardment Group at Spokane AFB, WA. The 92nd had recently returned from a deployment to Yokota AB, Japan. Visibility was good and the mission was flown in formation.

Operation *Haylift*

In January 1949, a severe blizzard struck the Northwest and reached as far east as Nebraska. Cattle were dying from the severe cold and a lack of food. Ranchers were concerned about the potential loss for their industry. Particularly hard hit were places in eastern and central Nevada. It was estimated that 45,000 cattle and 165,000 sheep were in immediate danger. Highway crews tried their best to gain access to the areas, but their efforts were futile. They would no sooner clear a portion of highway when the winds would heap drifts of snow back over their work. The secretary of the United Stockmen's Association of Nevada, George Swallow, prevailed upon then Governor Vail Pittman, who in turn called Nevada Senator Pat McCarran. The senator conferred with Air Force general officers. As a result, Maj Gen John E Upston, Fourth Air Force Commander, ordered the 62nd TCG at McChord AFB, WA, into action. Previously, this same unit had flown medical supplies and food to the scene of the Texas City explosion disaster and done the same and provided air evacuation to flood victims at Vanport, Oregon.

On 23 January 1949, 17 C-82s departed McChord for McClellan AFB, near Sacramento, CA. The US Navy had given permission for the unit to use the remote field at NAS Fallon in western Nevada. State highway crews worked around the clock clearing the runways in preparation for the arrival of the Packets.

The first plane to arrive from McClellan was piloted by Capt Doyal Saye, liaison officer for the operation. His co-pilot was F/Lt Peter Berry, an RAF exchange pilot. Berry had flown on a similar mission in England when the northern part of that country was snowbound the previous year. Berry was amazed at the distances involved in Operation *Haylift*. He stated, 'Any leg of this flight would have put us way out to sea in England'.

The cattlemen were not pleased with the fact that the Air Force was tasked to help them. All they could see were the snow-covered roads and wanted them cleared for normal traffic. They believed that any airdrop would be too little too late. Apparently they lacked any concept of airpower.

At 0130 hours on 24 January, the first load of hay arrived at Fallon Field. By 0930 the first of 16 C-82s that had overnighted at McClellan arrived. The ships came in at 10-minute intervals. At Ely, 210 air miles away and 1 hour 20 minutes later, the second aircraft landed while the runway was being plowed. Control on the icy runway was touchy at best. The aircraft skidded into a bank of snow at the side of the runway. The crew managed to align the aircraft and get it to the ramp with a dragging brake. They unloaded and got the ship back to McClellan for repairs.

The ranchers complained that their cattle would be lost. National Guard personnel were to redistribute the hay to the ranches. Instead, Col Adriel 'Doc' Williams ordered three of the nine aircraft to take the farmers aboard to direct them for an airdrop. After these drops the cattlemen and the press were quick to give their accolades: 'The air age has come to ranching…only possible way to save the stock…salvation of the livestock industry.'

There were problems. It was cold – 30° below zero at night. The gas trucks at NAS Fallon broke down. Maintenance facilities were lacking. The US Navy dispatched a pair of trucks with 80,000 gallons of gasoline from NAS Alameda to help. Col Williams ordered more aircraft, men, and equipment. Take-offs were difficult – field elevation at NAS Fallon is 4,000ft above sea level; and 6,000ft at Ely. The field elevation translated to a 10% power loss because the manifold pressure drops at the rate of 1 inch per 1,000ft of altitude. Initially they flew at 54,000 lb gross weight, but by the second day this was reduced to 52,000 lb. The runway length at Fallon was 7,000ft; at Ely it was 6,000ft. The

The *Packet Press Room* really had a *Nose for News*. Its name, all in capital letters, was written in two lines, This aircraft was C-82A-FA, s/n 48-573. It housed a mobile newsroom replete with most all of the needs for the newsmen in the field. This aircraft was manufactured as Line Number 208 and carried its CQ-573 buzz number. USAF KKE4875

A second aircraft, C-82A-FA, s/n 48-578 also bore the name *Packet Pressroom*. Its *Nose for News* was written in a single line with initial capital letters. Note that no buzz number was applied to the aircraft. She appeared at numerous airshows. Inside were desks with typewriters and chairs for use by visiting media personnel. The aircraft was also used for the 1948 presidential campaign. W J Balogh via MSgt D W Menard

mountains between Fallon and Ely ranged from 8,000-12,000ft in elevation, with nothing but desolate, rocky, frozen desert wasteland along the route.

Weights of the hay bales varied from 60-150 lb each. Initially the crews used bathroom scales to weigh them prior to loading. When this slowed down the process, they opted to guess the weight and hope to achieve a reasonable center of gravity loading of each aircraft. Even with additional storms, the 62nd TCG managed to deliver 1,000,000 lb of hay.

An additional ten C-82s were provided by the 375th TCG at Greenville, SC. Their job was to shuttle between McClellan, Minden and Ely because of a lack of facilities at Fallon. Hay was also flown to Caliente in southeastern Nevada for stockpiling and redistribution.

Things still looked bleak by 29 January, and a two-man legislative committee prevailed upon the Governor for more assistance. They believed that the haylift would have to continue for four to six weeks. The Governor in turn petitioned President Harry S Truman. The President said that the storm disaster 'makes it imperative that the full resources of the Federal Government be mobilized to furnish such emergency assistance as can be made through Federal agencies.' In essence, he had given Operation *Haylift* a blank check.

By 17 February the storms had ceased and the C-82s had compiled quite a record. They had flown more than 1,600 hours, covering over 270,000 miles, dropping an estimated 4,244,000 lb of hay, saving 300,000 head of cattle.

Governor Vail Pittman was so impressed with the performance of the airlifters, that each participant received an executive certificate, stamped with the State of Nevada Seal and signed by the governor. The certificates read:

CERTIFICATE

In recognition of the courage, skill, and devotion to duty displayed in assisting citizens of the State of Nevada in combating the blizzards and intense cold of the winter of 1948-1949, and in acknowledgment of the vital service rendered to the livestock industry of Nevada in the preservation of great numbers of cattle through the medium of 'Operation Haylift',

I, Vail Pittman, Governor of Nevada, on behalf of the grateful citizens of this State, do declare (Name of Recipient) of the United States Air Force an Honorary Citizen of the State of Nevada, and do bespeak for him the appreciation of the men of good will everywhere.

Domestic Deployment

During a domestic operation, nine C-82 Packets from the 314th TCG airlifted the 1850th Mobile Communications Squadron from Tinker AFB, OK to Eglin AFB, FL so that the communications unit could participate in war games. They transported 990,000 lb of equipment in one lift. This was the first time 8,500 lb radioteletype units had been carried on twin-engined aircraft. The 1850th's jeeps were also carried on the airlift. The loading was completed within three hours, and the aircraft arrived at Eglin with the 1850th's equipment four hours later.

Operation *Vittles* – The Berlin Airlift

Airlifting large pieces of equipment during the Berlin Airlift was a difficult task until five C-82s from the 60th TCG at Wiesbaden AB, West Germany, joined the operation. The C-82s carried jeeps, earth graders, aircraft engines, rock crushers, fuel-servicing units, heavy generators, steam rollers, ambulances, snowplows, steam shovels, cement mixers, communications equipment, aircraft control surfaces, and a variety of other

pieces of equipment. In one instance, a Ground Controlled Approach (GCA) radar unit was broken down into two pieces and carried on a pair of C-82s, then reassembled and placed into operation at Tempelhof Airport in Berlin.

Most of the automobiles airlifted out of Berlin were flown on board the C-82s. These cars were purchased by aircrews in Berlin and flown out on the Packets that had their clamshell doors removed. In one instance, a C-82 lost an engine and the crew had to jettison the car, resulting in a personal loss for the airman.

The 60th Troop Carrier Group in Europe

The 60th TCG, based at Rhein-Main, West Germany, provided much of the intra-theater airlift using C-82s. Three squadrons comprised the 60th TCG – the 10th, 11th, and 12th TCSs. While the 10th and 12th were equipped with 14 C-82s each, the 11th had 13. The Military Air Transport Service provided the pipeline from the ZI to Europe, while the 60th moved the cargo and personnel throughout Europe. During a typical month, the 60th's airplanes would range from Tripoli in North Africa, in support of fighter units deployed there for training, to Oslo, Norway, for demonstrations of American power. The group would support British paratroop training exercises at Abingdon and Aldershot, England or the French at Lourdes, or Strasbourg in France, or Phillipville in North Africa. In addition, they supported the US Seventh Army in Europe. The 60th TCG commander was Lt Col Jay D Bogue, a former crop duster.

During one exercise with the French 41st Airborne Half-Brigade and members of the French Foreign Legion, five C-82s from the 60th TCG airlifted them from Phillipville, Algeria to practice establishing an aerial beachhead and providing perimeter defense. Maj Dixon Arnold commanded the detachment of C-82s, while French General Jean Noiret led the French contingent. During the four-day exercise, the C-82s made 1,800 paratroop drops and poured out tons of equipment from the aircraft without their clamshell doors. Language was the only major barrier to the operation that went off without one casualty.

During Operation *Umbrella*, there was a lack of bombers to act as aggressors for a test of the fighter defenses. To support this operation, the 60th TCG's C-82s acted as incoming bombers.

Two C-82s from the 60th TCS were tasked with the grueling assignment of flying scheduled round-trip resupply missions across the Atlantic as part of Project *Redhead*. The 2nd Bombardment Wing, based at Hunter AFB, GA, deployed its operational component, the 2nd Bombardment Group, to RAF Lakenheath and RAF Upper Heyford for a 90-day period in the summer of 1952. Project *Redhead* was to test the viability of SAC bombers operating from a forward operating location using flyaway kits for spares. There were concerns over replenishing critical parts in order to continue high dispatch reliability. The intrepid C-82 crews flew the priority spares from the Warner Robins Air Materiel Depot at Robins AFB, Georgia. As a result of this logistical support, the Aircraft Out of Commission-Parts (AOCP) rate dropped from 11.28% to 0.65% for the B-50Ds and from 32.5% to 1.73% for the KB-29s – a marked improvement by any standards.

Approximately one-third of the missions of the 60th TCG were flown in support of fighter training in Tripoli. During one month they flew 25 air evacuation missions, and another 25 devoted to French training. They searched for a B-29 down in the Mediterranean, and a C-124 lost over the North Atlantic. A particularly tense operation was the search for a US Navy PB4Y-2 Privateer shot down by the Russians over the Baltic Sea. Flying the Berlin Corridor was no piece of cake because Soviet fighters routinely made harassing runs at the unarmed transports. The exigencies of the Korean War had an impact on the operations of the 60th TCS. Spare parts shortages resulted in back orders of as much as two months. Because of other global commitments of the USAF, the 60th's Packets were two years overdue for a major overhaul, but the maintenance personnel kept them flying.

375th Troop Carrier Wing Activation

The 375th TCW, a Reserve unit, operated C-46 Commandos from the Greater Pittsburgh Airport, PA. The unit was ordered to active service on 15 October 1950, and relocated to Greenville AFB, SC, arriving a day later. The 375th immediately transitioned onto the C-82, which they operated in support of the US Army Infantry School airborne missions at Fort Benning, Georgia. Assigned to the wing was the 375th TCG with its components – 55th, 56th, and 57th TCSs. The wing was inactivated on 14 July 1952, returned to Reserve status, and relocated to Pittsburgh where it reverted to Curtiss C-46s.

64th Troop Carrier Group

The 64th TCG, stationed at Donaldson AFB, SC, achieved a major milestone on 20 August 1952, when they made the largest all C-82 airdrop. The wing sent its aircraft to Pope AFB, NC for a demonstration that was witnessed by cadets from West Point and military attaches from 39 countries. During this mission, 2,160 paratroops were dropped along with heavy equipment including trucks, jeeps, and howitzers. All personnel and all of the heavy equipment landed within the drop zone. The only casualties were six paratroops who reported slight sprains.

The 64th TCG flew two emergency relief missions during October 1952. First, a C-82 was dispatched to Eglin AFB, Florida where it was loaded with a Sikorsky H-5 Dragonfly helicopter and 10 personnel from Eglin for onward movement to Tegucigalpa, Honduras. Later that month one of the group's aircraft went to Wilmington, NC to make an emergency airlift of fire-fighting equipment to Charleston, WV.

When a Reserve C-119 unit, the 443rd TCW, was inactivated at Donaldson AFB, SC on 8 January 1953, the 64th TCG was tasked with moving 270,00 lb of organizational equipment to Altus AFB, OK for use by the newly activated 63rd TCW, Regular Air Force unit assigned to the Eighteenth Air Force (TAC), at that base. The cargo airlift continued into February.

On 25 January 1953, 10 C-82s from the 64th TCG were assigned to airlift equipment belonging to the 366th Fighter Bomber Wing from Alexandria AFB, LA to Griffiss AFB, NY, for Operation *Coldspot*. Aircraft from the 64th TCG and the 465th TCW, a C-119 unit stationed at Mitchel AFB, NY provided courier service throughout the exercise.

During one mission for Operation *Coldspot*, a C-82 from the 64th TCG was airlifting a dump truck to Griffiss AFB. The truck was loaded in such a manner that the crew could not have gotten to the troop doors in the clamshell doors for bailout in the event of an emergency. In addition, the clamshell doors could not be removed in flight thereby precluding an option for jettisoning the truck. While enroute to Griffiss, the No 2 engine failed and the aircraft began losing altitude. Fortunately for all aboard, the pilots were able to make a successful emergency landing.

C-82 DRAWDOWN

As the Douglas C-54 Skymasters and C-124 Globemaster IIs entered into troop carrier units within the ZI, the Fairchild C-82 Packets were phased out of the troop carrier business during late 1949. Sixteen of the 62nd TCG's C-82s were transferred to the 60th TCG at Rhein-Main AB, West Germany during October 1949. Other C-82s went to the 2601st Assault Squadron, Fourteenth Air Force, Smyrna AFB, GA. The remaining C-82s were reassigned to MATS.

C-82s in Troop Carrier Command were withdrawn from the following units as they re-equipped with newer aircraft, as shown:

Date	Unit	Base	New Aircraft
Oct 1948	313th TCG	Bergstrom AFB, TX	C-54
Oct 1949	62nd TCG	McChord AFB, WA	C-54
Aug 1950	314th TCG	Smyrna AFB, GA	C-119
Nov 1950	316th TCG	Smyrna AFB, GA	C-119
Jul 1952	375th TCG	Greenville AFB, SC	C-119
1953	60th TCG	Rhein-Main AB, West Germany	C-119
Jul 1953	64th TCG	Donaldson AFB, SC	C-119

EPILOGUE

Though the Fairchild C-82 Packet was an ungainly and awkward ugly duckling, it served the Post-World War Two active duty forces well. Not only did it afford crews an opportunity to expand on a mission performed during World War Two, but to perfect global all-weather operations. In addition, the airplane performed vital humanitarian missions.

The civilian exploits of the C-82 are covered in Chapter 23.

Chapter 3

Procurement, Production and Political Problems

Any large-scale government procurement program is akin to birthing an elephant when all of the diverse elements involving procurement, production, and politics are taken into account. The USAF/Fairchild C-82 Packet and C-119 Flying Boxcar programs are exceptional examples of the interweavings of these elements and how they can get downright nasty when the right mix of people is involved.

PROCUREMENT & PRODUCTION

There were two major manufacturers involved in producing the C-119, Fairchild Aircraft that had produced the C-82 Packet, and Kaiser, an automobile manufacturer that became an upstart in a volatile aircraft program.

Fairchild Aircraft

Fairchild Aircraft had been in business since the 1930s producing a variety of civilian aircraft, some of which were adapted for military use but procured in relatively small numbers.

When World War Two came about, the US Government preferred to deal with its established aircraft manufacturers such as Boeing, Consolidated, Curtiss, Douglas, Grumman, Lockheed, North American and Piper. Consequently, Fairchild was relegated to building single- and twin-engined trainers at a prodigious rate as their contribution to the war effort. Fairchild's wartime production totals are given in the table below.

Requirements

At the direction of Headquarters AAF, Air Materiel Command (AMC) at Wright-Patterson AFB, OH presented the AAF requirements for a new tactical transport to the AMC Engineering

Fairchild factory personnel complete the forward fuselage of this C-119 on their Hagerstown, MD ramp. For ventilation, the cockpit windows and astrodome are open. Air Force Association

Division to develop a detailed airplane specification. It was up to the Engineering Division to initiate contracts with industry in the form of a request for proposal (RFP). Engineering was responsible for a manufacture of experimental items, for preparation of specifications to secure uniformity and acceptable quality where standardization was possible, and for testing of

Type	Qty	Notes
XAT-13	1	
XAT-14	1	
AT-21	106	Another 39 were built by Bellanca in New Castle, DE; and 30 by McDonnell in St Louis, MO.
PT-19A	3,182	Another 477 were built by Aeronca in Middletown, OH; and 44 by St Louis Aircraft in St Louis, MO.
PT-19B	774	Another 143 were built by Aeronca.
PT-23	2	Another 375 were built by Aeronca, 199 by Howard Aircraft in Chicago, IL; and 93 by Fleet in Canada.
PT-23A	0	150 built by Howard, and another 105 by St Louis Aircraft.
PT-26	670	
PT-26A	0	870 built by Fleet.
PT-26B	0	250 built by Fleet.

prototype models produced by the manufacturers. In the case of the C-82 Packet, there was a sole source contract issued to the Fairchild Aircraft Division at Hagerstown, MD.

AMC's Production Division interfaced with both the Engineering Division and the aircraft manufacturers. As design changes were developed by the Engineering Division, it was up to the Procurement Division to schedule and implement the changes into the manufacturer's production line. The folks in the Production Division were go-getters and looked for the most expeditious means of implementing the changes – it was a challenge to them. A situation that exists to this day began during World War Two when the Production Division accused the Engineering Division of being too slow and too concerned with minor refinements. Conversely, the Engineering Division complained that the Production Division did not consult with them often enough, and many times ignored their advice.

It was the responsibility of the Procurement Division, made up largely of attorneys, to draft the language employed in each of the contracts. Many of them lacked the technical expertise to comprehend the battles between the Engineering and Production Divisions.

The requirement for a tactical transport drove a decision to procure 100 C-82As from Fairchild and open a new plant in Dallas, TX for North American to build 792 C-82Ns. Both companies commenced production in January 1945. When World War Two came to an end in August 1945, the North American contract was canceled, with only three C-82s being built. By June that year, Fairchild had been awarded a contract to build an additional 100 C-82As.

Initial testing of the C-82 appeared so promising that the USAAF awarded Fairchild an initial contract for 100 aircraft before testing had been completed. Tactical flying soon revealed several undesirable characteristics. The main objection was lack of vision afforded the pilots when approaching a drop zone. The nose-high attitude of the airplane obliterated the view of the drop zone. This same condition occurred during a landing, making runway visibility difficult. In addition, the Air Force began demanding that the aircraft have a greater load-lifting capability and an increased cargo volume capacity. The crew visibility problems required a redesigned cockpit; while the load capability necessitated new engines. A wider fuselage was needed to meet the cargo capacity requested by the USAAF. All of these requirements resulted not in a modified C-82A, but an entirely new airplane that would be designated the C-119 Flying Boxcar.

The C-82A was limited to 54,000 lb gross weight at take-off. To raise this limitation while using the R-2800-85 powerplant would result in an airplane taking off at its critical single engine ceiling. It was suggested that the engines be replaced with Pratt & Whitney R-4360 engines driving four-bladed Hamilton Standard reversible propellers; thereby permitting a 64,000 lb maximum gross take-off weight. Use of these engines necessitated a redesign of the wing center section, outer wing panels, forward fuselage, engine mounts, and landing gear. Fairchild Aircraft indicated to the Air Force that these changes might also necessitate lengthening of the tailbooms and only wind tunnel testing would prove this. The longer tailbooms would be necessary for stability and control reasons. Because of the similarity between the C-119A and the C-82A, the decision was made that wind tunnel testing would not be performed by either the USAAF or Fairchild.

Coping with Deficiencies

Because the requirement for a new tactical transport was so urgent, there was no time to adequately test a prototype or a series of service evaluation aircraft prior to entering production. To correct the deficiencies encountered with the C-82, major changes were recommended for the airplane – so many that a new designation, C-119, was issued.

In late October 1946, the Procurement Division informed the Engineering Division that Fairchild believed that the C-119A would be unstable and that a 4ft extension would be required for the booms. Fairchild had further suggested wind tunnel tests of a scaled-down model. The Chief of the Aircraft Laboratory, Engineering Division, stated that wind tunnel testing would not be required to determine the proper configuration for obtaining satisfactory stability and control characteristics for the aircraft. He went on to say that the 4ft boom exten-

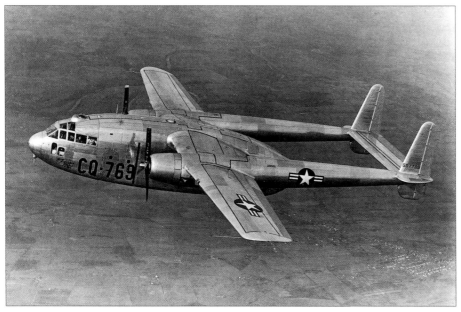

C-82A, s/n 45-57769, was extensively modified to become the sole XC-119A, bearing the same serial number. The name on the nose reads *Fairchild C-119 Packet*, **hence some of the confusion in the name Packet being carried over to the Flying Boxcar. An instrumentation boom was installed beneath the outboard portion of the right wing. Note the extremely long nose gear door.** Air Force Museum A1/C-119A/pho/5

This in-flight view of the XC-119A reveals the upper surface walkway markings. The 'USAF' is missing from the top of the right wing. The picture dates from 1948. Note the large fairing for the astrodome. An instrumentation boom is installed beneath the outboard portion of both wings. The aircraft was eventually to become an instructional airframe at Chanute AFB, OH. USAF

A crane director stood on top of the fuselage to guide the crane operator in moving the boom/empennage assembly into place on the first C-119B-FA, s/n 48-319. Fairchild *Pegasus* Magazine

sion would offset the destabilizing effect of the movement of the center of gravity, and that the modified aircraft with the extended booms should approximate that of the C-82A. However, after the C-119 was committed to production, it was discovered that the stability of the C-119 did not approximate the stability of the C-82A.

On 26 November 1946, Headquarters AAF asked for a complete cost estimate for installing R-4360 engines on the C-82 in lieu of the R-2800 engines. They also asked for a complete redesign of the cockpit and landing gear. Fairchild's proposal for $868,269 to accomplish the modifications was forwarded by AMC to Headquarters AAF on 17 December. These figures did not include the C-82 that was to be furnished by the AAF for the retrofit. Excluding the cost of the aircraft, but adding in the cost of government furnished equipment (GFE), the program was expected to be around $1,300,000. On the following day, Maj Gen Laurence C Craigie, head of the AMC's Engineering Division, stated that the modified aircraft should include all changes necessary to satisfy the requirements of Troop Carrier Command. He went on to say that, while this effort would amount to a major redesign, it would be more expeditious and far cheaper in the long run by several million dollars than entering into a competition for a replacement aircraft.

A 2 October 1946 proposal submitted by Fairchild suggested installation of either R-4360-4 engines with single stage, variable speed superchargers or R-4360-35 engines with single stage, single speed superchargers. Because the R-4360-35 engines were not available, AMC recommended using the R-4360-4 engines. Numerous changes were recommended by the Air Force's Mock-up Inspection Boards thereby causing Fairchild to submit a new specification on 24 February 1947 with the price increasing from $868,269 to $1,214,814 per aircraft. Changes added to the specification resulted in a further increase in the price to $1,255,187. Subsequent negotiations resulted in a price reduction to $1,230,473, permitting Fairchild a 7% profit (submitted on 13 August 1947).

In August 1947, the AAF Aircraft and Weapons Board decided that the cargo compartment should be widened to accommodate a 96-inch wide ground vehicle. Because this decision came in too late, the C-82A converted into a C-119A did not have this change. During 1947, XC-82A, serial number 45-57769, was modified to lower the flightdeck and move it forwards, delete the ventral fins, and install 2,650hp R-4360-4 engines. Additional windows were added to the nose to enhance drop zone visibility. This modified airframe was redesignated as the C-119A. On 17 December 1947, the airplane made its first flight. This lasted 1 hour and 45 minutes.

Early Problems

Shortly into the flight test program of the C-119A, a number of stability and control problems and some structural deficiencies were discovered. Directional control was less on the new airplane than it had been on the C-82A, a condition that was exacerbated during engine-out conditions. Critical asymmetric power conditions resulted, thereby causing the pilot to exert very high rudder pedal forces in order to maintain directional control. It was found that the principal cause of pilot-error accidents with the C-82A was poor single-engine technique used by pilots accentuated by the inherent marginal directional stability characteristics of the aircraft. While Fairchild considered the C-119B to be an improvement over the C-82 in this respect, the Air Force never agreed.

Test pilots flying the C-119A discovered that, when making a tail-low take-off or landing, it was possible to strike the ventral fin on the runway. To preclude such tail strikes, Fairchild removed the ventral fins; thereby further exacerbating the engine-out directional control problem.

About six months prior to the first flight of the C-119A, it was noted that there would be a five-month gap between production of the last C-82A and the first C-119B because a production contract would not be let until after the C-119A had been built and test-flown. Such a production gap would result in an estimated $4,000,000 contract price increase because the manufacturer would have to rehire and train laid-off factory personnel. As a result, Fairchild was authorized to produce an additional 20 C-82As in order to keep the production line open during the C-119A flight test program. On 25 November 1947, Fairchild was awarded a contract for the production and delivery of the first 12 C-119Bs. This contract was let 22 days prior to the first flight of the C-119A.

The C-119B was a further redesign that permitted accommodation of a 96-inch wide ground vehicle in the cargo bay. Power was provided by a pair of Pratt & Whitney R-4360-20 engines, each capable of producing 3,250bhp at 2,700rpm on take-off.

Structural Inadequacies

Structural problems plagued the C-119s. Between January 1950 and July 1951, there were 22 C-119 accidents that were attributed to material failure. This figure equated to 60% of all C-119 accidents during this period. The majority of these failures involved tail surfaces and booms.

Several near-accidents resulted from failure of the vertical fins while in flight. In one instance a C-119 was flying near the coast of France when the crew noticed some unusual noises. The crew chief went aft to investigate. Through the intercom he advised the flightdeck of his findings and he bailed out of a troop door. The flightdeck crew followed his example. The horizontal stabilizer separated from a boom and the airplane crashed just off the shore. Boom failures were believed to be the result of rough field operations, hard landings, turbulence, and prop wash encountered in formation flying. As a result, BuAer requested a 50% increase in boom strength to satisfy the 140-knot critical design load maneuver criteria. While these changes were incorporated on all R4Q-1s, the USAF did not go along with these modifications initially. When Navy flight testing proved the validity of the changes, the USAF initiated a similar program. It should be noted that all of these changes had an impact on the aircraft

On 9 May 1950, C-119C-13-FA, s/n 49-126, carried a completely assembled spare outboard wing panel for a damaged C-119 from Hagerstown, MD, to Camp Campbell, KY. The spare panel, weighing 1,450 lb, was loaded without the wingtip, fuel cells, or aileron. Dimensions for the part were approximately 33ft in length, 8ft at the tip and 13ft at the root. The root end protruded about 10ft 6in from the aft end of the cargo compartment. Three wooden cradles, cables and bolted plates were employed to lash down the bulky piece of cargo. The aircraft was piloted by Lt Col S E Cleveland, the Air Force Plant Representative at Fairchild. Similar transport feats were later accomplished during the Korean War. Fairchild #8-82 via R Woodling

operating empty weight, thereby affecting its payload capability.

In addition to the poor single-engine control characteristics, the C-119 was noted for poor single-engine performance. At 71,800 lb, the C-119B would not climb at any altitude, nor could it turn without losing altitude. It had extremely poor go-around performance. At 60,000 lb, the performance was slightly more satisfactory. While somewhat better, the C-119C also had unsatisfactory single-engine performance at higher gross weights. It was subsequently recommended that the C-119B be limited to a maximum allowable gross weight of 68,700 lb, and the C-119C be limited to 72,300 lb so that the airplane could meet the requirement for a 110ft per minute climb on one engine. These conditions still exceeded the design weight of 64,000 lb.

In addition to the poor control characteristics and performance, the C-119 had extremely poor rudder and aileron effectiveness at low speed, inducing crew fatigue and dangerous formation flying characteristics. Also, Tactical Air Command had established a maximum drop speed that was 10 knots below the safe single-engine speed. (The speed was established to reduce payload scatter over the drop zone.) This operating procedure placed the operational pilot in the position of not being able to fly at a safe speed in order to jettison his cargo if forced to feather an engine during the drop.

Propeller problems plagued the early C-119s. The initial production batch of C-119Bs was not accepted by the USAF until Hamilton Standard could eliminate the oil leakage problem. Approximately five months after initial deliveries of the airplanes, a series of runaway props was experienced due to failures in the pitch change gear teeth. In addition, stress cracks developed in the blades. Blade failure in flight resulted in runaway props or the entire prop departing the airplane. Because of these stress cracks, the blades were stripped of paint so that the cracks could be more readily detected. Hamilton Standard eventually made the necessary design changes in order to eliminate these problems. Improper curing of the cellular plastic rubber core was cited for some of the prop failures.

Between 1 January 1950 and 1 July 1951, C-119s were involved in 38 major and eight minor accidents, resulting in 13 aircraft being destroyed and 25 experiencing major damage with a loss of 36 lives. These material losses totaled $9,558,123. A combination of design errors and unrealistic operating procedures were the causes of many of these losses. Statistical data on the mishaps for both the C-82 and C-119 may be found in Appendix 1.

Procurement and Production

To fill the possible five-month gap between production of the C-82A and the C-119B, Headquarters AAF accepted the second plan for 20 additional C-82As, without any cockpit modifications, for the FY 48 procurement program.

Fairchild submitted a proposal to Headquarters USAF (the USAF replaced the AAF on 17 September 1947) on 16 October 1947 for $22,985,715, which included 37 C-119Bs, spare parts, handbooks and data, and ground support equipment. The first C-119B was to be delivered in December 1948 at an average unit price of $558,745. Because the C-119B had 46.4% commonality with the C-82A and much of the same tooling could be utilized, the unit price was significantly lowered. The contract gave Fairchild a 10% profit.

On 28 March 1948, the Government issued notices terminating its two facilities contracts with Fairchild, effective 31 August 1949, and replaced the three previous contracts with a new facilities contract on 1 September 1949. Maj Gen Orval R Cook, AMC's Director of Procurement and Industrial Planning, approved the contract on 23 September 1949. The new contract covered buildings, machinery, equipment, and repaving the runways at a cost of $7,264,000. Reserve equipment valued at $186,934 was provided. These changes revalued the Government-owned facilities at $3,294,298. The facility expansion and improvement program was done to permit an increase in C-119 production from 10 to 35 aircraft per month.

On 18 August 1948, the Navy's Bureau of Aeronautics (BuAer) submitted a Military Interdepartmental Purchase Request for the procurement of eight C-119Bs, to be designated as R4Q-1s. Deliveries were scheduled for one aircraft per month, beginning in July 1949. BuAer had a requirement that all of the instrument panels be changed to met their specifications. To accommodate this request, production of the R4Q-1s was to be completed with three aircraft in October 1949 and the remaining five the following month. All eight aircraft, with the new instrument panels, were delivered as the 47th to the 54th production articles. These aircraft were built under a supplemental agreement to the FY 48 program. As a result of this BuAer order, the USAF was able to obtain its 99 previous aircraft with a cost reduction of $471,900.

During January 1949, AMC advised Fairchild of its desire to replace the R-4360-20 engines with R-4360-20W engines, effective on the 38th airplane. When this change could not be immediately implemented, it was slipped to the 56th production article and resulted in redesignation of the aircraft as the C-119C. On 5 January 1950, a change order was issued (at a cost of $218,282.01) for installation of R-4360-20W engines on 81 C-119Cs and eight R4Q-1s.

On 31 October 1951, Maj Gen Mark E Bradley, Deputy Director of AMC's Directorate of Procurement and Industrial Planning Division, informed Headquarters USAF that a strike at Wright Aeronautical Corporation had resulted in a slippage of 1,447 R-3350 engines. These engines were destined for follow-on C-119F series aircraft. During the same period, a strike at Douglas Aircraft forced the rescheduling of its C-124 Globemaster II production, resulting in the release of 104 R-4360-20W engines for the C-119 program. In addition, the Navy had 46 R-4360 engines that were in excess to their R4Q-1 program. Therefore, 150 R-4360-20W engines became available for Fairchild. Consequently, the first 75 of the 131 C-119Fs were delivered as C-119Cs. The remainder of the 131 aircraft were delivered as C-119Fs with Wright R-3350 turbocompound engines.

On 21 May 1948, the Air Materiel Command requested Headquarters USAF to approve procurement of an additional 99 C-119Bs. This buy was approved on 3 June. Supplemental Agreement No 1, issued on 19 April 1948, called for the conversion of one of the original C-119B airframes into the XC-120 with a detachable pod. On 18 August 1948, the US Navy's Bureau of Aeronautics (BuAer) submitted a bid for eight C-119Bs, designated R4Q-1s (R for transport, 4 for the fourth model, Q for Fairchild, and -1 for first series of this model), for use by the US Marine Corps.

Design efforts to improve the airplane continued. The YC-119D, a detachable-pod version of the C-119C, and YC-119E, a similar adaptation of the C-119H, were paper projects only.

New War Requirements

On 21 May 1948, the Air Materiel Command requested Headquarters USAF to approve procurement of an additional 99 C-119Bs. This buy was approved on 3 June. Supplemental Agreement No 1, issued on 19 April 1948, called for the conversion of one of the original C-119B airframes into the XC-120 with a detachable pod. On 18 August 1948, the US Navy's Bureau of Aeronautics (BuAer) submitted a bid for eight C-119Bs, designated R4Q-1s (R for transport, 4 for the fourth model, Q for Fairchild, and -1 for first series of this model), for use by the US Marine Corps.

A change in engines to the 3,500hp R-4360-20W, with water injection, resulted in the C-119C. Other changes included the deletion of the outboard horizontal stabilizer tip extensions and the addition of dorsal fins on top of the booms to enhance directional stability. These changes came with airplane serial number 49-119. A contract revision with BuAer resulted in the R4Q-1s being delivered in this configuration. The C-119C first flew in April 1950. The Korean War accelerated the need for these aircraft and as a result, a second source was found – this being the Kaiser Manufacturing Company in Willow Run, MI. A total of 303 C-119Cs was built, the last 41 of this series being made by Kaiser. In addition, Fairchild built a total of 31 R4Q-1s for the Marines.

With the outbreak of hostilities in Korea in July 1950, Headquarters USAF decided that there was a new requirement for 1,800 C-119s for the US and their allies. On 20 July 1950, AMC representatives met with Fairchild Aircraft to discuss an immediate acceleration in C-119 production. Initially, the USAF had planned to give the entire C-119 production run to Fairchild. A new order for 36 additional aircraft, at a total cost of $16,869,809, was given to Fairchild on 8 December 1950.

To meet the projected requirement for 1,800 additional C-119s, AMC personnel met with Fairchild Aircraft to discuss opening a second production line in Omaha. This was in keeping with Pentagon thoughts that key aircraft production should be moved inland as insurance against an enemy attack on manufacturing facilities near the coasts. It was believed that some 15 months would be required to open a new facility in Omaha.

On 12 October 1950, Brig Gen A H Johnson, from AMC's Industrial Planning Division, notified Headquarters USAF that the Fairchild plant at Hagerstown, Maryland could be expanded to produce a maximum of 20 aircraft per month. Gen Johnson also advocated that Government Plant No 8 (at O'Hare International Airport, Chicago) be expanded because Fairchild had been scheduled to partially occupy the facility on 1 December 1950. General Johnson went on to state that: 'It is hereby certified that other suitable capacity for this production is not known to this Command, nor is it believed that same can be obtained elsewhere at low cost to the Government.' The facility at Willow Run, MI had been discounted in his recommendation, not because of the expense, but because AMC had already scheduled the facility for the medium bomber program.

During October 1950 AMC submitted a letter to Headquarters Continental Air Command in which AMC referred to plans to reactivate the Chicago plant for C-119 production. If the plan to reactivate the plant could be stabilized by 1 November 1950, it was stated that Fairchild would like to occupy part of the facility immediately.

On 25 October 1950, Gen Cook recommended that Fairchild be issued a contract to open the Chicago facility on 1 December that year. On 1 December he reaffirmed his position, stating that, while Plant No 8 was considered to be unsatisfactory and would cost $15,000,000 to reopen, about half of the costs could be charged to the MDAP program.

Three days later General Cook discussed the matter with Lt Gen K B Wolfe, AMC Commander. General Wolfe disagreed with Cook because of the undesirable labor market in Chicago, and stated that he wanted to establish additional production at Marietta, Georgia.

Later that day, Generals Cook, Bradley, and Johnson met with other AMC personnel to discuss the proposed FY 51 procurements. During this meeting, it was decided that 24 C-119s would be built by Fairchild at either Chicago or Birmingham, AL. Gen Cook announced that he planned to discuss the C-119 program with Fairchild.

On 8 December 1950, Headquarters USAF issued Procurement Directive 51-77 directing AMC to initiate procurement of 36 C-119s at Hagerstown and 113 C-119s at a yet to be determined facility.

On 11 December 1950, Headquarters USAF directed AMC to open a new production line for the C-119, stating that AMC was authorized '...to proceed with those steps which in its judgment are necessary to increase potential for all-out production of all components on any programmed aircraft. These steps may include, but are not limited to, the opening of duplicate sources, over-tooling, extra shifts, and additional subcontracting.' This message gave AMC a free hand in awarding a contract to whatever producer it chose. For the past two months, AMC had been recommending that Fairchild produce the aircraft at both Hagerstown and at a yet to be determined facility.

In November 1951, the order for C-119Gs with spares, tooling, and ground support equipment was increased to 193 aircraft; 50 of which were scheduled for Mutual Defense Assistance Pact (MDAP). On 18 February 1952, the order was revised to decrease the C-119Gs to 143, increase the MDAP aircraft to 62, and

C-119C, s/n 49-162, was delivered in this pristine condition with its nose number 162 applied. Note the open cowl flaps and black anti-corrosion paint on the underside of the boom only, indicating that the aircraft was powered by the twin-stacked R-4360 engines. Black anti-corrosion paint was also applied to the full length of the belly, starting at the nose gear doors. W J Balogh via MSgt D W Menard

Things did not always go well! Here C-119C-15-FA s/n 49-162, of the 50th TCS, 314th TCG, has bent her booms on landing at Taegu, in October 1950. The pilot, Capt Ralph S Saunders, flew 70 combat missions in Korea, went on to become a major general in the USAF, and was Commander of the Aerospace Rescue and Recovery Service from 1974 until his retirement in 1979. The right side of the ship carries some nice nose art that appears in color in Chapter 7. The aircraft was repaired and flown out. Note the scaffolding beneath the boom joint forward of the national insignia. In the background are an F-51 Mustang, F-80 Shooting Star and T-6 Texan. Subsequently this ship served with an Air Resupply and Communications unit. A Nelson via MSgt D W Menard

add 45 C-119Gs for the RCAF. By June 1952, there were 451 C-119s in this contract, as signed by Maj Gen K E Webber. The total price for the aircraft was $80,200,017 – each aircraft having a unit price of $259,171. The contract allowed Fairchild an 8% profit for the first 188 aircraft and 8.5% for the remaining 263.

Two test aircraft were ordered on 18 September 1950: a YC-119D and a YC-119E, that would be equipped with a detachable pod. These aircraft were production line modifications of the standard C-119C. The YC-119D was to be powered with Prattt & Whitney R-4360-20W engines, while the YC-119E was to have Wright R-3350-30Ws. On 26 June 1951, the YC-119D was canceled, and the YC-119E was placed on hold pending flight test data and evaluation of the YC-119H – a long-wing version of the basic Flying Boxcar. Then, on 7 November 1952, Headquarters AMC recommended cancellation of the YC-119E and that the airplane be built as a C-119F. Brig Gen W G Baine, from the AMC Procurement Division, approved a supplemental fixed-price contract calling for two additional C-119Gs (at a cost of $713,99) to replace the canceled YC-119D and YC-119E aircraft.

Fairchild had delivered 78 aircraft by 31 December 1952, which included eight for the RCAF and four for MDAP. The C-119Gs were delayed by five months due to difficulties encountered with the Aeroproducts propellers.

Another contract was let (on 22 August 1952) for 87 C-119Gs, spares, tools, ground support equipment, and a mobile training unit. The total cost of this contract was $30,516,000, with deliveries to be completed between March 1954 and February 1955. On 31 October 1952, the August contract was expanded with a new contract for 26 additional C-119s in FY 53.

Kaiser – A Second Source
During the morning of 5 December 1950, the Kaiser-Frazer Corporation secured a loan for $25,000,000 from the Reconstruction and Finance Corporation. Then Henry and Edgar Kaiser met for lunch with Under Secretary of the Air Force John A McCone with whom the Kaisers conferred about getting into the aircraft business. Under Secretary McCone called Gen Wolfe into his office where Wolfe suggested using Willow Run for the C-119 production. Later that afternoon, Col Lee W Fulton, from AMC's Procurement and Production Division, was called to General Wolfe's office, where instruction was given for Col Fulton to accompany the Kaisers to Hagerstown on the following day. Col Fulton was instructed to: '...negotiate with Fairchild management regarding turning over to Kaiser-Frazer Corporation information, plans, and other aids which would be necessary for the development of a proposal by Kaiser for the production of C-119 airplanes at the Willow Run plant.' There is no conclusive record to show that General Wolfe stated to Fairchild during the telephone conversation on the afternoon of 5 December 1950 that Kaiser would definitely be the second source for C-119s or that Kaiser wanted the data just to submit a proposal.

When Col Fulton and the Kaisers arrived at Hagerstown on the following day, the Fairchild representatives were somewhat shocked and reluctant to share the requisite data. A Fairchild vice president asked what effect a Kaiser proposal would have on their proposal for using the Chicago plant, a proposal already presented to AMC. When Col Fulton called General Wolfe for clarification, Gen Wolfe stated: '...the Willow Run proposal had nothing to do with the Chicago proposal, that they were to be considered as two separate things.'

On 15 December 1950, Under Secretary McCone met with key USAF and AMC personnel at Wright-Patterson AFB. In response to a question by Under Secretary McCone and Lt Gen Benjamin W Chidlaw, AMC Commanding General, said that if speed was essential, it would be better to obtain second sources by splitting off from parent organizations. Otherwise, the generals believed that it would be more advantageous to expand the base among other organizations. While Under Secretary McCone favored giving the contract to another existing company, Air Force Chief of Staff Gen Hoyt Vandenberg believed the contract should be awarded Fairchild for production at Marietta, GA. Gen Wolfe's objection to awarding the contract to Kaiser was based upon his belief that the plant could be used for building larger aircraft. General Chidlaw stated that while Fairchild might object to Kaiser being named a second source, conversely, Kaiser might object to Fairchild being established as a second source at Marietta. He went on to say that the Air Force should use companies whose non-defense production had been reduced. In the end, Under Secretary McCone stated that he assumed it would be proper to make arrangements for putting the C-119 production into Willow Run.

Justification for awarding the C-119 contract to Kaiser instead of Fairchild fell into several categories:
- Since Kaiser had cut its civilian production by 50%, the C-119 contract was expected to keep Kaiser's skilled labor force intact and in use.
- The trained management and working force at Chicago was not as large as that in the Detroit area.
- While the Chicago facility had a production potential for 150 aircraft per month, Willow Run had a potential for 265 per month.
- The decision to use the Willow Run facility was in line with Gen George C Marshall's policy in broadening the base, which was officially announced on 18 December 1950.
- There was some fear of losing the Willow Run facility to another service (that is, Army tank production).
- Another source stated that the Reconstruction and Finance Corporation wanted to assure collection on a portion of its loan to Kaiser, but this could have been a red herring.

On 19 December 1950, 113 C-119s for the USAF and 21 MDAP C-119Cs were ordered from Kaiser at a cost of $122,882,184. On the same day, a contract letter for $10,000,000 for facilities refurbishment was issued to Kaiser.

The Willow Run plant had been used by Ford during World War Two to produce B-24s. After the war, Kaiser first leased the facility (worth $88,500) and later on 1 December 1948, purchased it for $15,000,000. A caveat in the purchase allowed the Government to recapture the rights to the facility under the National Security Clause. As was the case in all recapture clauses, the company in place had the first right of refusal to build whatever the government directed at that location. Therefore, the Government was obligated to offer Kaiser the opportunity to produce C-119s once it was decided to use the Willow Run facility for such production, unless it could be shown that Kaiser did not have the capability. To show Kaiser incompetent would have been very difficult at that time. With award of the contract, Kaiser reconverted around 2,300,000 of the 4,700,000ft^2 of plant for C-119 production. The remainder was retained for automotive production.

Even though Fairchild was extremely displeased with the second source directives and raised objections to Under Secretary McCone, Fairchild's president Richard Boutelle promised to cooperate with Kaiser in the interest of national defense. On 2 January 1951, Mr Boutelle called on Under Secretary McCone and stated that he did not believe that AMC had recommended that Kaiser be awarded the second source contract. Mr McCone replied that '...everyone (was) in attendance when the decision was reached,' (most likely referring to the 15 December 1950 meeting). While McCone suggested that all were in agreement, he failed to inform Mr Boutelle that General Vandenberg wanted to award the contract to Fairchild.

When Mr Boutelle met with Henry Kaiser, he refused to hand over the required data, citing its classified nature. General Wolfe immediately had a release sent to Fairchild thereby giving Mr Boutelle no further reason to renege.

On 22 December 1950, Kaiser was given a contract to build 36 C-119Cs, with spares, tools, and ground support equipment. On 26 February 1951, this order was increased to 130 C-119s and 58 R4Q-2s and the $2,000,000 contract was increased to $7,110,000. On 9 August 1951, the contract was again changed to a fixed-price contract for 130 C-117Fs and 58 R4Q-2s at a total cost of $72,955,414. This contract was signed by General Bradley. Included in the contract was $4,267,170 to cover work to be performed by Fairchild under the Technical Assistance Agreement with Kaiser for 1951, plus an estimated $2,000,000 for 1952 follow-on assistance.

After securing a contract to build C-119s at Willow Run, Henry and Edgar Kaiser called upon General Cook on 10 May 1951, to advise him that they had just purchased a 49% interest in the Chase Aircraft Company five days earlier. Chase had recently developed the C-123 Provider, which the USAF was considering as a follow-on to the C-119. The Kaisers stated that they wished to build the C-123s at

Fairchild was so extremely proud of the C-119's airdrop capabilities at the Chosin Reservoir during December 1950, that it released this advertisement. Fairchild

their Willow Run plant. Upon learning of the Chase purchase by Kaiser, Fairchild's representatives, including ex-Senator Millard Tydings of Maryland, went to see Under Secretary McCone to voice their objections. They believed that Fairchild was teaching Kaiser the aircraft business in a field in which the C-123 was the chief competitor to the C-119. They recommended that Kaiser be given the C-123 program and that Fairchild be given all of the C-119 production.

Later in May 1951, Headquarters USAF revised the C-119 program. Kaiser was slated to build a limited number of C-119s before transitioning into the C-123, and C-119 production (by Fairchild) would be transferred to Chicago. The limited number of Kaiser C-119s was to be a production run of 200 aircraft. Headquarters AMC planned to award a contract to Fairchild for 50 (peaking at 60) C-119s per month at Chicago and 35 per month in Hagerstown.

The contract was amended on 13 September 1951 to increase the funds to be obligated or expended to $18,000,000. Changes in the contract resulted in the purchase of 165 C-119Gs for the USAF and another 28 for MDAP. Because Aeroproducts propellers were to be used, the aircraft were designated as C-119Fs.

Concerns arose over the state of inactive portions of Plant No 8 in Chicago. The main manufacturing area at Plant No 8 was permanently occupied and controlled by the Air Defense Command. The Procurement Directorate recommended that all surplus tools at Willow Run be shipped to Chicago immediately. A second problem involved joint AMC-ADC jurisdiction of the plant in Chicago. This stalemate left AMC and Fairchild hamstrung in their attempts to occupy the plant. Because of the state of disrepair of unused portions of the plant, Fairchild could not afford to insure the

facility due to fire risk. Subsequently, ADC had agreed to consider moving to accommodate Fairchild activities. AMC believed that $850,000 would resolve the fire issues, but the fire underwriters disagreed and estimated $2,250,000. The issue became moot when AMC decided that the extra protection afforded by six separate buildings would not be justified by the cost.

On 11 January 1952, Headquarters USAF directed AMC to terminate the Chicago program because of a major reduction in C-119 requirements. Four days later, Gen Bradley informed the Industrial Resources Division that: '…the termination be accomplished in an orderly fashion towards complete renovation of the Chicago facility if it is feasible to do so.' He further suggested that the Industrial Resources Division examine the situation to determine if the plant might be able to be kept on a standby basis.

Kaiser had been contracted to produce additional tooling for the Chicago plant. This issue was not addressed by the Headquarters USAF directive to terminate the Chicago program. On its own initiative, AMC directed Kaiser to ship all completed tools requested by Fairchild to Hagerstown and to complete any tooling in work. All of the ordered tools were completed. On 27 March 1952, the Air Force Plant Representative at Chicago was authorized to ship the tools required by Fairchild in Hagerstown and to store the remaining tools at Willow Run. On 7 May, the representative was instructed to store the extra tooling at Chicago. Then, on 2 June, he was ordered to ship the extra tooling to Hayes Aircraft in Birmingham, AL where it would be used in the C-119 reconditioning program.

POLITICAL POTBOILER

On 21 May 1952, when plans for the use of the Chicago facility were finally concluded, Representative T P Sheehan, Congressman from the Illinois 11th District, wrote Gen Edwin W Rawlings, then AMC commander, requesting information on the termination and the future of the plant. He was informed that changing requirements as a result of the Korean War and general international situation dictated that C-119 production be reduced. The letter went on to state that because Kaiser was far closer than the Chicago plant to producing the airplanes, Headquarters AMC had decided to terminate the less advanced Fairchild program in Chicago. While this issue was swiftly and quietly put to bed, a furious battle was brewing on Capitol Hill.

Congressional Cauldron

An explosion erupted on the floor of the House of Representatives on 21 May 1952, when Representative Alvin O'Konski of Wisconsin, under the cloak of Congressional immunity, delivered a verbal assault on both Henry Kaiser and AMC. He referred to Mr Kaiser as a bloodsucker and charged him with swindling the Government by charging two to three times more than Fairchild for each C-119. In addition, he charged that Kaiser owed $13,590,000 of the $15,000,000 loan for the Willow Run facility. O'Konski accused former Under Secretary of the Air Force John A McCone with influence peddling to enhance Kaiser's financial position. He went on to state that both McCone and the Reconstruction Finance Corporation stood up for Kaiser to keep the company from becoming insolvent. O'Konski's harangued with a call for an investigation of the Kaiser-Government relationships.

Henry Kaiser made a sworn statement refuting O'Konski's charges and the statement was read into the Congressional Record on 17 June 1952. Kaiser came to Congress to refute the allegations and the result was that O'Konski apologized for not checking his facts before going public. Representative O'Konski agreed to give equal publicity to Kaiser's rebuttal. Kaiser issued an 85-page rebuttal to the media with a statement marked 'from the office of' O'Konski. There was a statement that O'Konski was 'entirely satisfied' after reading the rebuttal and that it 'completely refutes all the charges I made.' Kaiser went on to say that because O'Konski had agreed that he would make such a statement on the floor of Congress, they released the document. Later that day, Congressman O'Konski could not be located for comment. However, both O'Konski's retraction and the report were presented on the floor of Congress by Louisiana Representative James Morrison. O'Konski suddenly appeared on the Washington scene and protested that he had not issued the retraction. On the following day, Kaiser reinforced their position, stating that 'O'Konski definitely wrote the news release… retracting false charges which the congressman had recently made against the Kaiser companies and its executives. Any statement by Congressman O'Konski to the contrary is just as untrue and insincere as his original erroneous charges.'

Then, on 15 August, Representative O'Konski attempted to tear Kaiser's statement apart paragraph by paragraph. Concurrently, the House Armed Services Committee began hearings on the Kaiser contracts. In the end, the Committee found that the entire issue centered around opening second sources for supply, and cooled its fervor for further investigation. However, Senator Styles Bridges (R-NH) stated that this was an argument against Kaiser, because the Air Force was not getting the planes as cheaply as possible. The senator contended that the USAF was paying $1,200,000 per airplane from Kaiser versus $260,000 from Fairchild. He recommended that the Senate Appropriations Committee review the Kaiser contracts prior to passing on the Air Force FY 54 funding requests. In addition, Senator Bridges arranged for the Senate Preparedness Subcommittee to investigate the matter, despite the fact that the House Armed Services Committee had recommended dropping it.

Between December 1952 and May 1953, investigators for the Senate Preparedness Subcommittee gathered information for the Kaiser investigation. One of the investigators informed Edgar Kaiser during a visit to Willow Run that: 'I have told Senator Bridges that I can find nothing wrong with your dealings with the Air Force – no collusion, fraudulent action, or acts of unethical dealings.'

On the morning of 2 June 1953, the Senate hearings began. Senator Bridges announced that he planned on hearing testimony by former Under Secretary McCone (and by Generals Cook, Bradley, and Wolfe. At the conclusion of John McCone's testimony, General Cook was called upon. Senator Bridges referred to a 23 October 1950, letter in which Gen Cook had recommended awarding the second production facility to Fairchild, and asked why he had changed his mind between the date of the letter and 15 December 1950. Apparently the senator did not know, and Gen Cook did not volunteer the information, that on 1 December 1950, he (Cook) had reaffirmed his 23 October 1950 recommendation, or that as late as 4 December 1950 Gen Cook had informed Gen Wolf that he believed Fairchild should operate the Chicago site for additional C-119 production.

Senator Bridges continued his interrogation of Gen Cook, complaining that Cook should have remembered more of the transactions, which had taken place some two and a half years earlier. Gen Cook, when pressed for specific answers, frequently asked for permission to check the record and to submit the answers at a later time – a common procedure permitted by Congressional committees. Chief Counsel James Anton charged that the general had exhibited a lack of knowledge or an unwillingness to give it. On 5 June, the hearings were adjourned for four days to allow the committee to study the testimony. Henry Kaiser asked for a public hearing so that he could present his side of the case.

The hearings resumed on 23 June 1952, with both Henry Kaiser and his son Edgar defending their records. Edgar Kaiser suggested that Chief Counsel Anton was attempting to crucify him. During the second day of hearings, all debates became moot because the Air Force had terminated the Kaiser C-119 and C-123 programs, stating that the cancellation was 'independent of the present Senate hearings now in progress.' The Senate hearings were then recessed until 'some future date.'

CONCLUSION

Despite all of the wrangling and shifts in dynamics due the exigencies of the times, the C-82 Packet and C-119 Flying Boxcar have their niches in the annals of military aviation. Regardless of the trials and tribulations encountered during their procurement and production phases, both aircraft met the ever-changing requirements environment: perhaps more through blind luck than engineering prowess on the part of Fairchild, and more as a testament to Yankee ingenuity on the part of both the flight crews and the maintainers.

Chapter 4

C-119 Description

The Fairchild C-119 is a twin-engined, twin-boom, high wing, land monoplane of all metal construction, designed for use as a cargo carrier, troop/paratroop transport with an aerial supply delivery system, an air evacuation aircraft, and a cargo drop airplane with provisions for the delivery of both heavy and light equipment and supplies. A retractable tricycle landing gear system with a steerable nosewheel is installed. The four-bladed, constant speed, reversible-pitch propellers are driven by a pair of supercharged Pratt & Whitney R-4360 engines. The twin booms and empennage are of sufficient height above the ground to permit ease of loading of large objects through the open cargo doors at the aft end of the fuselage.

C-119 Principal Dimensions

Wingspan	109ft 3¼in
Fuselage length	60ft 6⅝in
Overall length	86ft 5¾in
Height	27ft 6in

The cargo compartment has a rectangular cross-section that permits the carrying of a wide variety of equipment, while the tricycle landing gear affords a level floor to facilitate loading. The floor height is four feet above the ground – truck-bed height. Large clamshell doors swing outboard through an arc of 90° offering complete clearance for loading. Paratroop doors located within the clamshell doors could be opened in flight for troop drops. For heavy cargo drops, the clamshell doors would be removed so that the cargo could be extracted through the large opening.

C-119 Cargo Compartment Dimensions

Height	8ft 0in
Width	9ft 2in
Length	36ft 11in
Cargo Floor Area	353ft²

Mission Configurations

The C-119 Flying Boxcar could be configured for any of four missions.

Cargo Carrier: The C-119C is capable of carrying the following items: 75mm howitzers, 37mm guns, 40mm anti-aircraft guns and carriages, 2½-ton 6x6 trucks, large and small aircraft engines and cradles, propellers, and a wide variety of other military equipment. Through the use of special ramps and load-distributing devices on the cargo floor, the aircraft could carry 75mm guns and half tracks, and 155mm howitzers.

Troop Transport: Equipped with 20 folding seats along the left side of the aircraft and 22 seats along the right side, the airplane could transport 42 troops or paratroops with their equipment. An additional 20 troops could be carried if seats were installed along the center of the cargo compartment, giving a total capacity of 62 troops.

Equipment Drop: The airplanes were equipped with an electrically operated, automatic, aerial delivery system that was capable of dropping twenty 500 lb bundles in eight to ten seconds through paratainer doors in the floor at the forward end of the cargo compartment. Heavy and bulky equipment was

These engine mechanics were working on the No 2 R-4360 engine on C-119C-13-FA, s/n 51-2572. Note the offset cylinder banks that offered a modicum of cooling for the rear cylinders. The black cooling shrouds that covered the cylinders from front to rear also improved cooling airflow. These shrouds may be seen on the platforms of the two workstands. Also note now the removal of the three primary cowl panels afforded access for engine maintenance. USAF

Performance Comparisons

	C-47	C-46	C-82A	C-119G
Empty Weight (lb)	18,200	30,000	31,498	39,000
Gross Weight (lb)	26,000	45,000	54,000	64,000
Payload (lb)	10,000	10,000	20,000	32,000
Max Speed (mph)	234 @ 10,000ft	270 @ 15,000ft	248 @ 17,000ft	253 @ 17,900ft
Cruise Speed (mph)	150	173 @ 10,000	216 @ 10,000	162 @ 5,000ft
Initial rate of climb (fpm)	104	574	730	852
Service Ceiling (ft)	24,000	24,500	21,200	21,580
Range (statute miles)	1,600	1,200	1,920	1,415
Accommodations				
troops	27	50	42	42/62
litters	24		3	35

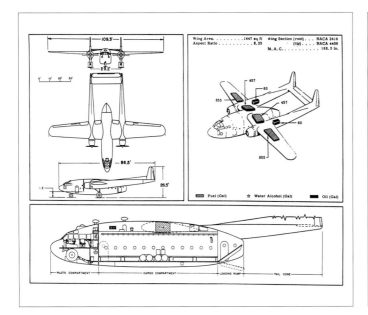
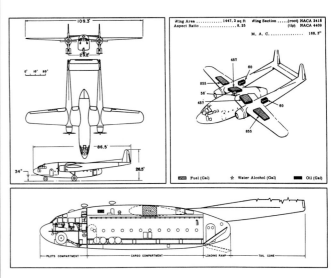

Above left: **This inboard profile for the C-119B reveals its salient internal features, including: retracted nose landing gear, flightdeck, main cargo compartment with troop O_2 bottles located in the middle of the fuselage, and loading ramp.**

Above: **This inboard profile for the C-119C reveals its salient internal features that were similar to the C-119B, except that the troop O_2 bottles were moved to the forward cabin.**

Left: **This inboard profile for the C-119G is in error in that it retained the large single nosewheel tire. The drawing reveals erected web troop seats along the sidewall, cargo tiedown in the center, and erected litters.**

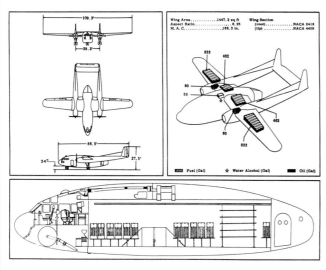

Below left: **Load varieties for the C-119.**

Below: **The C-119's fuselage housed these pieces of equipment:**

1. Driftmeter
2. Navigator's/Radio Operator's worktable
3. Lavatory equipment
4. Radio equipment
5. Electrical inverter
6. Hydraulic equipment
7. APP equipment
8. Anti-icing heaters
9. Monorail
10. Automatic pilot servo motors
11. Wing flap mechanism
12. Life raft compartment
13. Crew oxygen containers
14. CO_2 fire extinguisher
15. Paratroop door
16. Troop oxygen walk-around unit
17. Litter installation
18. Troop seats
19. Oxygen filler valve
20. Automatic pilot equipment
21. Troop oxygen cylinders
22. A-2 fire extinguisher
23. Main entrance ladder
24. Crew oxygen walk-around units
25. Pilot's seats
26. Rudder pedals

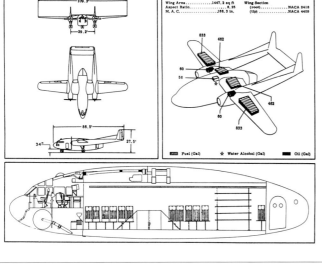
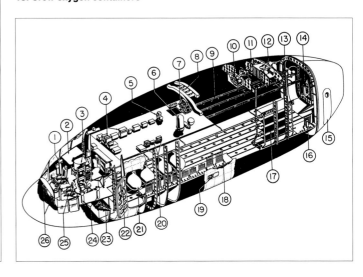

He ain't no customs man! This technical sergeant was inspecting the flight control cables located within the left boom. Four oxygen cylinders were located overhead along with the hot air anti-icing duct for the empennage. Via Air Force Association

The overall size and capaciousness of the interior of the C-119 main cabin is apparent in this view. The troop seats were stowed along the sides of the cabin. The rails above the seats provided the upper support for the web seat backs. A fire bottle is visible in the upper left. The tiedown rings may be seen in the floor. Padded insulation panels in the overhead provided a modicum of sound attenuation. Unfortunately, during heavy rains or under conditions of high humidity, water was known to come cascading through the edges of these panels. Entry to the cockpit as gained through the opening to the left of the forward bulkhead. Access to the nose gear compartment was gained through the panel by the officer's knee. A urinal and chemical toilet was located in the lavatory compartment on the right of the forward bulkhead. The officer was inspecting a portion of the paratainer system. USAF 40991 A C

extracted by parachute for delivery out the aft end of the aircraft when the clamshell doors were removed.

Air Evacuation: As an air ambulance, the aircraft was equipped with 35 litters – 20 on the left and 15 on the right side of the cargo compartment. Seven tiers, five litters high, were supported by stanchions and web straps. While 35 was the maximum number of litters that could be carried, during emergency conditions the airplanes could be configured to carry 76 troops – 62 seated and 14 litter patients with four medical attendants.

The main differences between the C-119B, C-119C, C-119F, C-119G, C-119J, and C-119L series airplanes are presented in the table below.

Structures

The structural design concepts of the C-82 Packet (as described in Chapter 1) were carried forward to the C-119 Flying Boxcar. The fuselage was an all-metal, semimonocoque structure constructed of alclad frames, longitudinal stringers, longitudinal and transverse beams covered by alclad skins. The booms were an all-metal, semimonocoque structure constructed with hydro-pressed frames, hat-section stringers, and light aluminum alloy skins. The wings were all-metal, cantilever structures consisting of a center section, outer panels, and tips.

Engines

The Pratt & Whitney R-4360-20-WA is an air cooled, reciprocating powerplant rated at 3,250bhp (dry) and 3,500bhp (wet) at sea level under standard day conditions at 2,700rpm. Nicknamed the 'corn cob', the engine has 28 cylinders arranged radially in four rows of seven cylinders each. A total of 56 spark plugs are installed on each engine. Each row is offset to provide maximum cooling. Seven channel-shaped baffles were designed to provide cooling air to each row of cylinders. A single-stage, variable-speed supercharger, driven by a hydraulic coupling, is controlled by an automatic power control unit that operates as a carburetor throttle valve and regulates blower speed as required so as to maintain the selected manifold pressure. A torquemeter system, connected to the propeller reduction gear, measures the torque output at the propeller shaft and presents this information on a torquemeter in the cockpit.

The engines are equipped with an automatic power control unit that functions to automatically maintain manifold pressures up to the engine critical altitude as selected by throttle position regardless of changes in rpm, altitude, or airspeed. The system operates through hydraulic control of the carburetor throttle valve and blower speed. Above the critical altitude for lower blower operation, the automatic power control unit changes the speed of the blower by controlling the flow of oil to the hydraulic coupling between the crankshaft and the impeller.

Component	C-119B	C-119C*	C-119F	C-119G	C-119J	C-119L
Engines	R-4360-20	R-4360-20WA	R-3350-85/-89/-89A	R-3350-85/-89/-89A/-89B	R-3350-89B	R-3350
Water injection	No	Yes	Yes	Yes	Yes	Yes
Horizontal stabilizer tips†	Yes	Some	No	No	No	No
Wing flaps	Electric	Electric or Hydraulic‡	Hydraulic	Hydraulic	Hydraulic	Hydraulic
Landing gear	Electric	Electric or Hydraulic‡	Hydraulic	Hydraulic	Hydraulic	Hydraulic
Propellers	Hamilton Standard 2H17Q3-26R	Hamilton Standard 2H17Q3-26R§ 2J17G3-26R	Hamilton Standard A644FN-C2	Aeroproducts A644FN-C2	Aeroproducts F40K-1-198-18MZ	Hamilton Standard (three-bladed) 43H60
Cargo doors	clamshell	clamshell	clamshell	clamshell	Flight operable (beavertail)	Optional

* The C-119CF was essentially a C-119C with hydraulically actuated landing gear and flaps; † Horizontal stabilizer tips were installed on airplanes 49-119 thru 49-199 only; ‡ C-119Cs 49-119 thru 51-2584 were electric, while 51-2587 thru 51-8273 were hydraulic; § This change in propellers occurred with C-119C-22-FA, s/n 51-2532.

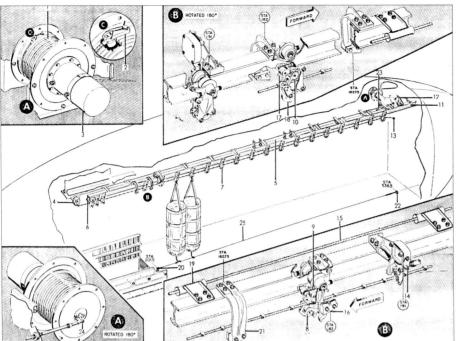

The paratainer aerial delivery system.

1. Cable drum
2. Cable securing link
3. Actuator
4. Forward pulley
5. Monorail
6. Forward stop
7. Trollies
8. Bundle release mechanism
9. Locking plunger
10. Cable fork arm
11. Rear stop
12. Aft pulley
13. Cable ball
14. Limit switch
15. Drive cable
16. No 2 trigger
17. Locking plunger
18. Bundle hook
19. Cable guide tube
20. Anchor cable forward attachment
21. No 1 trigger
22. Anchor cable aft attachment
23. Clutch control unit
24. Cable drum clutch lever
25. Anchor cable

This view reveals the details of the interior of the clamshell doors, with the lightening holes in the frame, padded insulation, portholes with their blackout curtains, and the troop door. A maintenance ladder to gain access to the upper portion of the aircraft while on the ground was stowed above the erected web troop seats. One of the insulated panels was opened at the aft inboard corner. Note how the two loading ramps were placed together to permit safer access and egress for the visiting Civil Air Patrol Cadets.
A T Lloyd

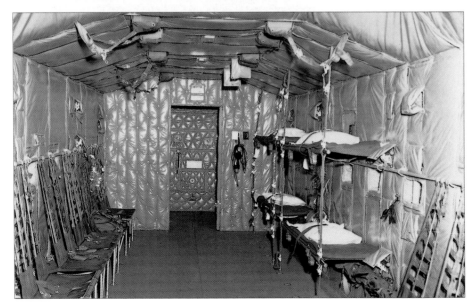

Some MC-119Js were equipped with a plush aeromedical evacuation module that insulated the cabin from noise and temperature. This module was originally designed for VIP use and served operationally with both the Indian and Italian air forces. This view is looking forwards – the cabin forward bulkhead may be seen ahead of the module doorway. Note the access panel to the nose gear in the lower portion of the forward bulkhead. Standard web troop seats were erected on the left and right foreground, while four litters were installed on their stanchions in the forward right side of the module.
Via Mel Duncan

Some airplanes were equipped with R-4360-20WD engines that were basically the same as the R-4360-20WA, except that the automatic control unit had been replaced by a solenoid valve that controlled the flow of engine oil to the blower hydraulic couplings. Now the supercharger was no longer a low and variable speed blower, but a two-stage blower (low and high).

Beginning with the C-119F, the airplanes were equipped with Wright R-3350-89B turbo-compound engines. These engines have three blow-down turbines located 120° apart around the circumference of the engine. While similar to a turbosupercharger, the turbines use kinetic energy rather that the pressure of the engine exhaust and, instead of driving a supercharger that provides ram air to the tops of the carbure-

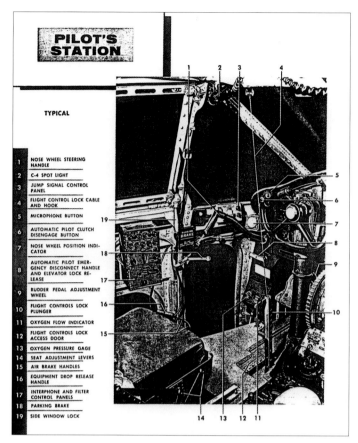

Pilot's cockpit arrangement.

Co-pilot's cockpit arrangement.

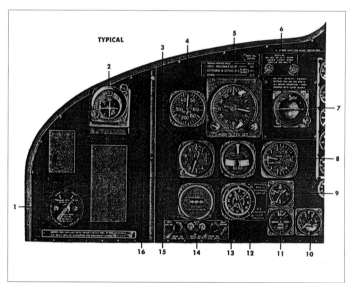

Pilot's instrument panel.

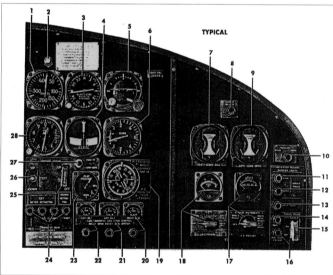

Co-pilot's instrument panel.

tor, they are geared directly to the crankshaft drive gear through a system of Zerol bevel gears. A fluid coupling transfers power to the crankshaft drive gear. The turbines have no separate controls since they operate at a constant ratio of 6.52:1 to the crankshaft speed. When the engine developed Maximum Except Take Off (METO) Power at 2,600rpm, the turbines turn at a speed of 16,950rpm. At maximum power, each turbine develops approximately 120bhp. By recovering a portion of the exhaust gas energy, the turbines permit higher horsepower at lower fuel consumption. An armored exhaust hood is installed on each turbine. Each engine is equipped with a two-speed supercharger, water injection system, fuel metering system with impeller fuel injection, torquemeter, and low tension ignition system. At take-off, each engine could develop 3,250bhp at 2,900rpm (dry) and 3,500bhp at 2,900rpm with water injection.

Power could be increased for take-off through use of the water injection system. A water-alcohol mixture was contained in a 56-gallon tank located in the wing center section. A 28-volt DC boost pump was energized to supply the water-alcohol mixture to the engines. The manifold pressure could be boosted to 45 inches of mercury (Hg) through use of this system. With a full tank of water, both engines would be supplied for about 16 minutes with the engines operating at maximum power. In the event of an engine failure, the water flow to the dead engine would automatically cease, while flow to the running engine would continue.

Propeller Systems

The C-119Bs and C-119Cs through the C-119-C-21-FAs were equipped with 15ft diameter,

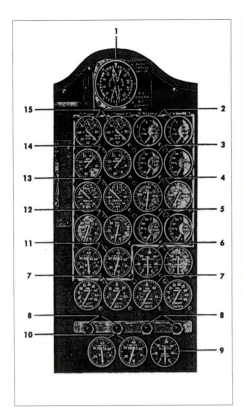

Left: **Engine instrument panel.**

Above: **Walking on top of a C-119 fuselage required extreme care. The black stripes delineate the walkway. The horizontal red stripe was part of the prop warning line. The horseshoe antenna in the foreground was for the instrument landing system. Behind the prop warning line was a fairing for an ADF antenna. Further back was an HF radio mast. Four fuselage air vents and four APU compartment exhaust vents followed. An LF radio wire is also visible.** F D Horkey

four-bladed Hamilton Standard 2H17Q3-26R hydromatic full feathering, constant speed, reversible propellers. Beginning with C-119C-22-FA, serial number 51-2532, the aircraft were equipped with Hamilton Standard 2J17G3-26R hydromatic full feathering, constant speed, reversible propellers. The latter propellers were also installed on the C-119Fs.

C-119Gs were equipped with 15ft diameter four-bladed Aeroproducts A644FN-C2 full feathering, constant-speed, reversible propellers. Aeroproducts was a division of General Motors. There were several incidents and accidents that resulted from uncommanded propeller reversal – sometimes in flight. Through the investigation the root cause was traced to a regulator in the propeller system. A technical Order was issued for C-119s with these Aeroproducts propellers to have the reverse feature locked out until a design change and retrofit could be implemented. This limitation was in effect for about six months during the mid-1950s.

The C-119Ls were created by retrofitting 22 C-119Gs with three-bladed Hamilton Standard 43H60 hydromatic propellers that were full feathering with reversible pitch. These propellers had had a non-rotating integral oil control (IOC) incorporating an independent oil system, mounted between the engine nose section and the propeller. An emergency oil replenishing system was provided to replace oil lost from the IOC with engine nose section oil. A 28-volt DC boot type electric heating element was installed along the leading edge of each prop blade for deicing. The Hamilton Standard 43H60 hydromatic propellers came from Lockheed C-121 Constellations that had been relegated to the boneyard at Davis-Monthan AFB, AZ. This change resulted in a 20% improvement in climb and a 7% gain in cruise performance.

Fuel System

A pair of fuel systems is employed to service each engine. The two systems are interconnected by a crossflow system that permits operating either engine from either fuel source. The aircraft is equipped with four fuel tanks: left and right inboard, each with a 464-gallon capacity, and a left and right outboard, each with an 864-gallon capacity. While this was the maximum capacity, the total useable fuel was 2,624 gallons or 15,744 lb. For extended range operations a pair of auxiliary fuel tanks could be installed on the cargo compartment floor affording an additional 1,020 gallons or 6,120 lb of useable fuel. Refueling is accomplished through overwing filler ports.

Flight Controls

The primary flight controls are independent mechanically operated systems consisting of the ailerons, elevators, and rudders. Aerodynamic boost devices, known as control tabs, are incorporated into each system so as to reduce the pilot's workload.

The ailerons are split into inboard and outboard segments. Flettner tabs are incorporated into the inboard ailerons to assist in moving the controls. The right inboard aileron have a trim tab that is used to make adjustments that affected the lateral balance of the airplane.

The elevator is full-span across the aft edge of the horizontal stabilizer. An elevator spring tab, operating automatically with control column movement, assisted the pilot in making control movements in flight.

Dual rudders are hinged to the aft spar of the vertical stabilizers. Spring tabs, located at the bottom trailing edge of the rudders, are employed to reduce the control forces.

The ailerons, elevator, rudders, and tabs consisted of an aluminum monocoque structure covered by fabric. Such surfaces offered excellent feel for the pilots and reduced weight.

Slotted wing flaps are located on the outboard wing panel and the wing center section. The flaps are hydraulically actuated and electrically controlled.

Electrical System

The aircraft is equipped with a 28-volt DC electrical system powered by a battery, a pair of engine-driven 28-volt DC generators, or an auxiliary powerplant. The 115-volt AC system is powered by the 28-volt DC system driving 115-volt, 400 cycle single-phase and three-phase inverters. The 24-volt, 34 ampere-hour aircraft battery is located under the cargo compartment floor just aft of the rear spar frame and is accessible from the outside of the aircraft through a hinged panel. Each engine is equipped with a 300-ampere, engine-driven, wide-speed range, direct current generator mounted on the accessory drive section of the engine. A Solar auxiliary powerplant (APP) is located on the A-deck behind the cockpit and consists of a 28-volt, 200-ampere generator driven by an internal combustion engine. If external power is not available, the APP is be capable of starting the engines and supplying power for ground checks.

Communications & Electronic Equipment

The C-119 was equipped with a variety of communication and electronic equipment for intercommunication, communication, navigation, and identification. The table below summarizes the communications & electronic equipment installed on the C-119.

Landing Gear System

The tricycle landing gear system consists of a pair of main gear that retract into the booms aft of the engines and a steerable nose gear that retracts into the forward nose beneath the cockpit. The nose gear is steerable through 60° either side of center. The main gear is equipped with Type II nylon cord 15.10-20, 14-ply rated tires. Initially the nose gear was fitted with a single wheel, that was known for its shimmy problems. At times the shimmy was so bad that the pilots could not read their instruments because of panel vibration and radio boxes were known to have punched their way through the fuselage skin. All C-119Fs and subsequent series were equipped with dual nosewheels. The dual nosewheels were also retrofitted on a number of C-119Cs.

Normal gear operation was accomplished electrically on all early aircraft. A hydraulic system was installed on some late aircraft in the C-series giving them the designation of C-119CF. With all subsequent series aircraft, the landing gear is hydraulically operated.

The nose gear steering system permits the gear to traverse a 32ft radius on a paved surface, with the wingtip describing a 70ft arc. The pilot has a nose gear steering handle to control the position of the nose gear on the ground. At take-off, a centering device prevents the gear from being cocked on landing.

Cargo Handling Equipment

A block and tackle fitting was employed to load equipment. A pulley was attached to a tie down fitting at the forward end of the cargo compartment. By pulling aft, the block and tackle would provide a 3,160 lb pulling force thereby permitting the loading of a 13,000 lb wheeled vehicle up the ramps. Should the cable be routed out the forward entry door, this force would be reduced to a 1,850 lb pulling force permitting the loading of a 7,650 lb wheeled vehicle up the ramps.

A total of 78 cargo tie-down fittings were installed in the cargo compartment floor, spaced to provide a variety of tie-down options. A pair of cargo tie-down kits were also carried on the airplane. These were employed in securing the cargo to the tie-down fittings. One kit contained 28 x 10,000 lb devices, while the other had 20 x 5,000 lb devices.

Two treaded light metal loading ramps with a 9,400 lb per ramp limit were carried to facilitate loading wheeled cargo through the aft cargo doors. These ramps could be stowed beneath the troop seats along each side of the aircraft when troops were not being carried. If troops were carried, the ramps were lashed to the center of the floor. If the center seats were installed, the ramps were removed from the airplane.

A cargo loading roller, located at the aft edge of the floor at the centerline, was used to assist in easing cargo into the aircraft. In addition, four metal skid strips, extending the length of the cargo compartment, facilitated loading of bulky cargo and prevented scuffing of the cargo floor.

A 28-volt DC electrically operated aerial delivery system was employed on the airplanes to drop cargo while the airplane was in flight. The cargo was stowed in special containers called paratainers or paracans that were attached to trolleys rolling along a monorail extending down the center of the cargo compartment ceiling. A canvas duck guide curtain formed a channel for the paratainers to preclude swaying as they traveled to the drop point above the opening in the cargo compartment floor. Static lines were used to open the parachutes as the paratainers departed the airplane. A jumpmaster's panel (either fixed on the center post of the clamshell doors or portable, depending upon the aircraft) was used to control the paratainer delivery system.

The C-119Js were equipped with flight-operable doors in lieu of the clamshell doors. They were also known as beavertail doors. These doors consisted of two major components –

Description	Army/Navy Specification	C-119B	C-119C	C-119F	C-119G	AC-119G	AC-119K
VHF Command Radio	AN/ARC-3	X					
VHF Command Radio	AN/ARC-3 or -27		X				
UHF/VHF Command Radio	AN/ARC-27			X	X	X	X
UHF Radio	AN/ARC-136					X	X
UHF/VHF Transciever	Wilcox 807A					X	X
FM	FM-622A (2)					X	X
Liaison Radio Set	AN/ARC-8	X		X	X	X	
Liaison Radio Set	AN/ARC-8 or -25A		X				
UHF Transciever	Collins 618T-3					X	X
LORAN	AN/APN-9	X		X	X		
LORAN	AN/APN-9 or AN/ARC-21		X				
LORAN S-Band	AN/APN-70					X	
LORAN	AN/APN-70B						X
Radio Compass	AN/ARN-6					X	X
Radio Compass	AN/APN-7	X		X	X		
Radio Compass	AN/ARN-6 or -7		X				
Omni-Range	AN/ARN-14					X	X
Localizer	RC-103A	X					
VOR Receiver	RC-103A or AN/ARN-14		X				
Glide Path Receiver	AN/ARN-5A	X					
Glide Path Receiver	AN/ARN-5B or -18		X				
TACAN Receiver	AN/ARN-16			X	X		
Glide Path Receiver	AN/ARN-18				X		
Interphone	AN/AIC-3	X					X
Interphone	AN/AIC-3 or -8		X	X	X		
Intercom	AN/AIC-10					X	
Intercom	AN/AIC-10A						X
Interphone (Glider)	AN/AIA-1A	X	X				
Marker Beacon	RC-193A or AN/ARN-12	X					
Marker Beacon	AN/ARN-12 or AN/APN-34		X				
Marker Beacon	AN/ARN-12			X	X	X	X
Radio Altimeter	AN/APN-1	X		X	X		
Radar Altimiter	AN/APN-1 or -42		X				
Navigation Radar	AN/APN-12	X	X	X	X		
Weather Radar	AN/APS-42*		X	X	X		
IFF	SCR-695B	X	X*				
L-Band IFF Transponder	AN/APX-6		X	X	X		
L-Band IFF Transponder	AN.APX-25					X	X
Emergency Keyer	AN/ARA-26			X	X		
Direction Finder	AN/ARA-25					X	
UHF Ranging	AN/ARQ-25					X	
Radar Altimeter	AN/APN-22					X	
TACAN	AN/ARN-21					X	X
Speech Encryption	TSEC/KY-8					X	X
Homing & Warning Radar	AN/APR-25						X
Doppler Radar	AN/APN-147						X
Terrain Avoidance Radar	AN/APQ-136						X
Emergency Radio	AN/CRT-3						X

* Provisions only.

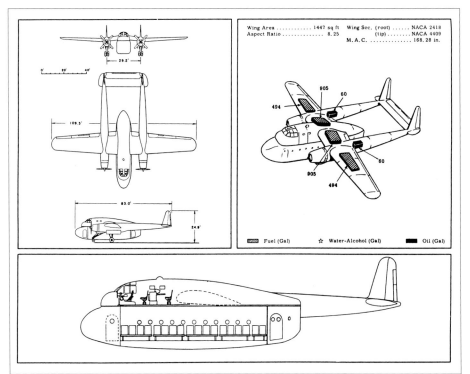

This inboard profile for the XC-120 reveals its salient internal features. The entire crew compartment is located high in the main fuselage, while the detachable pod is shown configured for troop transport.

The XC-120 lifts off with an experimental welded slab-sided prototype pack mounted under the fuselage. Via P M Bowers

Without its pack, the XC-120 Packplane had the stance of an insect. W J Balogh via MSgt D W Menard

a hinged hood, that faired out the top and sides of the aft end of the fuselage, and a floor that faired out the bottom of the aft end of the fuselage. This could be retracted within the hood, thus forming a capacious opening larger than the vertical cross-section area at any station within the aircraft's cargo compartment. Both the hood and floor were hydraulically actuated and electrically controlled. When in flight, the hood and door enclosed the aft end of the fuselage. The flight operable doors were not for use by paratroops. The beavertail doors were for use with an aerial retrieval system. However, they could be used for emergency jettison or bailout. Performance of the C-119Js was similar to that of the C-119Gs.

Under Contract AF36(600)-2199, 106 beavertail doors were built by Fairchild; while only 50 C-119Fs and 18 C-119Gs were modified to the C-119J configuration. The aircraft were modified in accordance with TO 1C-119-530, dated 15 June 1955. Subsequently, the C-119Fs with the beavertail doors were modified by TO 1C-119F-504 to replace the Hamilton Standard propellers with Aeroproducts props; thereby bringing them to the C-119G standard.

Emergency Egress

From the beginning, emergency egress from the C-119 was intended to be via the troop doors located within the clamshell doors. Experience showed that, with a cargo load, the crew may not have been able to get past the cargo in time to successfully bail out of a crippled airplane. A better means was required.

An emergency egress hatch was cut into the cockpit floor behind the pilot's seat. The exterior skin was cut to offer a door. The two were interconnected with a chute between the cockpit floor and the airplane exterior. The exterior door was slaved to the hatch in the cockpit floor. When the floor panel was lifted past a prescribed point, the exterior panel would fall away from the aircraft belly, thereby permitting the crew in the forward part of the airplane a rapid means of egress in flight.

Early on, the exterior doors departed the aircraft without explanation. On at least one occasion, while the C-119s were making mass take-offs, the tower saw a belly door depart one aircraft and called the formation to inform them of the door departure. Crewmen on other aircraft in the formation dutifully lifted the floor hatch to inspect for departure of the exterior

This right side view of the XC-120 shows the landing gear and the ADF antennas under the left boom. W J Balogh via MSgt D W Menard

Left side view of the XC-120 with support pogos under the ventral fins. W J Balogh via MSgt D W Menard

Details of the front end of the XC-120 are revealed in this view. The strut cover for the forward gear was attached to the strut. USAF 36833AC

A tractor pushed the pack, with its removable dollies, under the XC-120. The tractor operator took directions from a guide walking at the side of the tractor. A mechanic riding in the top of the pod also provided guidance and later attached the pod to the plane. Via P M Bowers

panel. Alas, there was a rain of exterior doors from all of the aircraft. The story was aptly captured by Col Bob Stevens, USAF (Ret) in his *There I Was* cartoon series.

Ditching

Ditching was considered to be an absolute effort of last resort. The crew was instructed that if at all possible they should bail out. The high wings placed the bulk of the aircraft in the water from the start. The aircraft's non-watertight fuselage had a tendency for the nose to roll under and break away. If the nose gear was lowered, there was an even greater tendency for the nose to tuck under.

During testing, a C-119 was ditched. The clamshell doors separated from the aircraft and a wall of water careened forward, filling the cargo compartment. The aircraft sank before the initial spray of the impact dissipated. While in ground training a film of this test was shown to anyone who flew as a crew member, the Airplane Flight Manual had a paragraph on ditching that stated DON'T.

New Model C-119s

Both the YC-119D and YC-119E were terminated before any prototypes were built.

With the C-119Fs, the electrically operated landing gear was replaced with a hydraulically operated system and Wright R-3350-85 turbo-compound engines were installed in lieu of the Pratt & Whitney R-4360s. The horsepower ratings for the two engines were similar. The higher horsepower on the R-3350s was made possible through the use of power recovery turbines on each of the three exhaust stacks. With the R-4360s, two exhaust stacks were located at the four and eight o'clock positions of the cowls. With the R-3350s, an additional stack was added at the twelve o'clock position. To further improve directional stability and engine-out performance, ventral fins were reinstituted. These fins were flattened on the bottom in order to improve ground clearance during take-off rotation and landing flare. Early production C-119Fs were delivered without the ventral fins, but they were subsequently retrofitted. A dual nosewheel replaced the former single wheel

Fairchild C-82 & C-119 39

beginning with the C-119Fs. This series made its maiden flight in December 1952.

A total of 247 C-119Fs was manufactured. Fairchild produced 141 for the USAF and 35 for the Royal Canadian Air Force, while Kaiser built the remaining 71 aircraft. Under the Mutual Defense Assistance Pact (MDAP), a total of 88 of these aircraft were delivered to Belgium, Italy, and Norway. Fairchild also produced 50 identical airplanes for the USMC that were designated R4Q-2s.

The final production version of the Flying Boxcar was the C-119G. These aircraft differed from their predecessors in having Aeroproducts propellers in lieu of the formerly installed Hamilton Standard props. Early problems with the new Aeroproducts prop governors resulted in a delay of initial deliveries of the C-119Gs. A total of 25 C-119Gs was delivered to the Indian Air Force. Production of the 480 airplanes in this series was completed in October 1955.

CONVERSIONS

Fairchild ventured into five additional cargo versions of the basic C-119 aircraft. Two were one-off test conversions; whereas the remaining three resulted in further operational applications.

XC-120 Packplane

An extremely strange machine emerged from the C-119 when one was converted into the one and only XC-120 Packplane. On 19 April 1948, Supplemental Agreement No 1 to the C-119B procurement contract called for the production-line conversion of aircraft s/n 48-330 into the Packplane. The aircraft retained the original wing and empennage and added a revised cockpit and upper fuselage. The landing gear was a four-legged affair that retracted into the booms. This airframe was flyable with or without the detachable pod. Multi-mission pods were conceived for use as cargo or troop carriers or an air-deliverable field hospital. This ungainly looking machine first flew on 11 August 1950 with its pack and 29 August 1950 without its pack. The aircraft had a 24,000 lb payload for cargo. The XC-120 was operated by a standard crew of five.

The sole purpose of this aircraft was to test the practicability of cargo pack carrying aircraft. A glider tow attachment fitting was installed on the aft end of the pack.

Possible XC-120 Personnel Loads

Airborne Operations	Troops	66
Aeromedical Evacuation	Litters	34
	Attendants	4

C-119H Skyvan

The C-119H Skyvan was an attempt to correct the chronic performance and stability problems with the Flying Boxcar. Air Materiel Command requested Fairchild to investigate the problems. Fairchild submitted a proposal for a design that would reduce wing loading to permit safe operation at lower airspeeds, correct the stability problems, improve the take-off and climb characteristics, and increase the structural strength of the airplane. The booms were lengthened, the wing was changed, control surfaces were enlarged, the fuselage was strengthened, and the fuel tanks were to be carried externally. This new airframe was designed to carry a 16,000 lb payload on a 1,000-mile radius resupply mission with all performance except cruising speed exceeding that of its predecessors. It was anticipated

A standard cargo/troop carrier pack was attached to the XC-120. W J Balogh via MSgt D W Menard

The XC-120 was carrying a Blood Donor Unit pod for the USAF Medical Service as part of the test program. N E Taylor via MSgt D W Menard

The sole XC-120, 48-330, in flight without its pod. Via P M Bowers

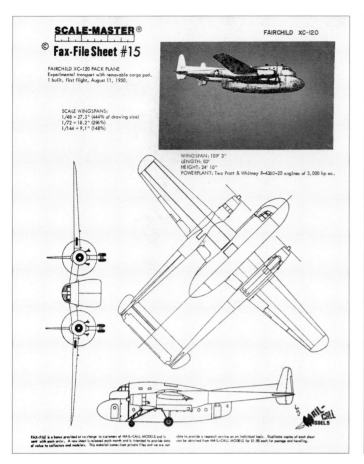
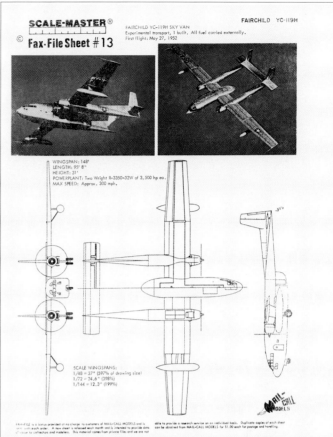

Above: **Three-view of the XC-120.** Fax-File by L S Jones

Above right: **Three-view of the YC-119H.** Fax-File by L S Jones

Right: **The YC-119H retracts its gear on take-off in front of a pair of its predecessors. An instrumentation probe was installed in the left wingtip.** Fairchild 12-440 via R Woodling

that a 12% loss in cruise speed would result from the changes.

Upon reviewing the engineering and wind tunnel test data, Air Materiel Command (AMC) recommended proceeding with the production of 195 C-119Hs even before the prototype had been built and tested. A new plant in Chicago was to produce these airplanes. A month later, AMC did an about face and terminated the production program until the testing had been completed. The new plan, generated about four months prior to first flight, was to have 151 of these airplanes built in Hagerstown, MD.

The prototype airplane, s/n 51-2585, was built at Hagerstown. A new wing, spanning 148ft, had a 40% increase in area. A pair of Wright R-3350-85 engines powered the airplane. The gross weight was increased from 74,000 lb to 86,000 lb. When test flown in May 1952, the airplane showed a marked improvement in controllability and some improvement in its take-off and landing characteristics. Problems in longitudinal stability and emergency aileron control became apparent. The C-119H flew about 20 knots slower than the C-119C and had good single-engine performance at an 80,000 lb gross weight.

The C-119H weighed approximately 51,000 lb empty; this being almost 5,000 lb greater than Fairchild's estimate. This discrepancy was determined to be partially the result of an aluminum shortage that had led Fairchild to substitute steel parts on the airplane (3:1 weight difference). Consequently, the aircraft was tail heavy. Fairchild's immediate solution was to add a 1,000 lb lead weight in the nose; thereby allowing the aircraft to enter the flight test program and once again reducing its payload.

The C-119H also had the interesting aspect of being one of a few aircraft participating in the early program to replace aluminum parts with magnesium parts. This was a design study program and apparently none of these parts were ever installed on the aircraft.

Fairchild had also proposed a four-engined follow-on to the C-119H. While the USAF was considering the four-engined Lockheed C-130 Hercules as a replacement for the C-119 in October 1952, it was suggested that the C-119H be converted into a four-engined testbed and be considered as a potential interim airlifter until the C-130s were available. With the demise of the C-119H program came an end to the

All of the fuel for the YC-119H was carried in the external tanks. A large-chord main strut and a pair of inboard struts supported each fuel tank. Fairchild via P M Bowers

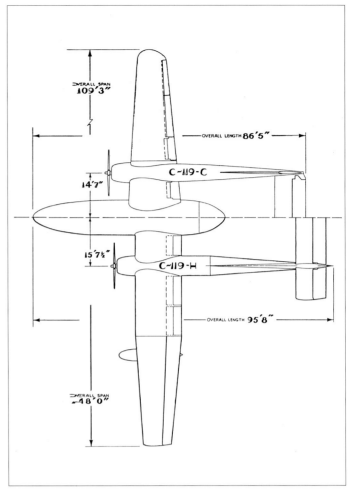

Comparative views of the C-119C and YC-119H. Fairchild via R Woodling

production of any new Boxcar airframe series; however, several other conversions were made.

The C-119H featured these design simplifications that would have improved manufacturing and maintenance:
- Three-piece cowl
- Simplified flap mechanism geometry
- Package heater eliminated long ducts
- Minimum filleting simplified manufacturing
- Added a mechanical trim tab
- Fuel system – reduction of parts, improved maintenance and servicing
- Constant section center panel and nacelle
- Straight-taper booms
- Four-bolt boom-stabilizer attachment
- Four-bolt fin-to-stabilizer attachment
- Internal match angle boom-to-nacelle attachment
- External match angle wing center section-to-outer panel attachment

C-119J

The C-119J or MC-119J was a conversion to replace the clamshell doors with a flight-operable beavertail door. Known as Fairchild Model 203, the conversions were made under Letter Contract AF36(600)-2199. A total of 52 C-119Fs and 15 C-119Gs were modified into the C-119J configuration in 1955. In addition, a total of 106 door assemblies were produced, Use of these doors precluded the need for removal of the standard clamshell doors for special airborne recovery operations. The MC-designation was briefly used to identify those aircraft employed in the aeromedical evacuation role.

C-119K

A single aircraft, s/n 53-3142, was converted into the YC-119K configuration with the addition of the General Electric engines mounted singly in pods beneath the wings. This prototype aircraft served as a testbed for the jet installation on the AC-119K gunships. Subsequently it was the support ship for the USAF *Thunderbirds* flight demonstration team. In addition, five other C-119Gs were converted to the C-119K configuration with the installation of the jet engines and an anti-skid system for improved braking.

C-119L

The C-119L was the end of the line in the Boxcar series of aircraft. A total of 22 C-119Gs were modified into this configuration. Over the years, the existing hydraulic propellers experienced problems with leakage. When the oil was lost, the pilot was unable to control the pitch of the propeller that could result in a runaway prop. A solution was at hand in the late 1960s when three-bladed Hamilton Standard hydromatic full feathering, reversible pitch propellers from Lockheed C-121s retired at Davis-Monthan AFB were retrofitted.

The last C-119Ls in the inventory were assigned to the 129th SOS (CA-ANG), 130th SOS (WV-ANG), and the 143rd SOS (RI-ANG). These aircraft were retired to MASDC between 27 March and 27 September 1975.

RC-119L

The RC-119L was the reconnaissance version of the Flying Boxcar. Little is known about these aircraft, except that, when flown for this mission, the clamshell doors were removed and a pallet-mounted camera was installed in the aft fuselage. Only known RC-119Ls are shown below:

Serial	Remarks
53-3160	Transferred to the Royal Moroccan Air Force.
53-3181	Assigned to the 302nd TAW (AFRes). To AMARC on 4 March 1973. To Dross Metals for reclamation on 14 September 1973. Transferred to RoCAF. Destroyed in a ground fire on 1 June 1996.

Above: **YC-119K, 53-3142, in its colorful flight test markings at Fairchild. This picture was taken at Dulles International Airport, on 16 August 1969.** Frank McSorley via MSgt D W Menard

Below: **When SAC had considered employing the C-119s for rescuing aircrews from behind enemy lines, RATO was tested as a means of getting the aircraft out of extremely short fields. For this test, the aircraft was equipped with two banks of three RATO bottles per side. With this arrangement, the aircraft gained an additional 12,000 lb of thrust.** USAF 40540 A C

AC-119 Gunships

In addition, two different gunship conversions were made to 52 C-119Gs. Twenty-six aircraft were converted to the AC-119G Shadow ships with four 7.62mm miniguns, a flare launcher, and armor plating. They carried a crew of ten. Another 26 aircraft were converted to AC-119K Stinger ships, similar to the AC-119Gs, with the addition of a pair of 20mm cannon, FLIR, terrain avoidance radar, beacon tracking radar, three-bladed Hamilton Standard propellers, and a pair of 2,850-lbst J85-GE-17 podded engines. These aircraft are described in Chapter 16.

C-119 Turboprop Conversion

By the early-to-mid 1960s, the USAF was interested in pursuing a turboprop conversion for the C-119 due to an increasingly apparent critical requirement for a short to medium range, high-capability, twin engined cargo aircraft. Such an aircraft was needed for internal airlift support in limited war areas such as Southeast Asia. Aeronautical Systems Division (ASD) at Wright-Patterson AFB, OH contracted for a study that would modernize the C-119 with minimum capital expenditure, maximum utilization of spares and support equipment currently in the inventory, and at minimum crew and maintenance personnel indoctrination.

ASD contracted with three companies for the study. This feasibility study was to determine if Allison T56-A-7 turboprop engines could be retrofitted on C-119C/G/J aircraft. Delivery of a flying prototype was anticipated in 180 days at a cost of $520,000. A reduction to $350,000 and 120 days could be achieved if the Allison Quick-Engine Change (QEC) kits were provided by the government.

These companies teamed together for the ASD turboprop C-119 feasibility study.

Company	Expertise
Skyways Inc (Sherman Oaks, CA)	Engineering & technical data development.
On Mark Engineering Co (Glendale, CA)	Douglas A-26 Invader executive conversions. Developed and produced the Pregnant Guppy & Super Guppy Stratocruiser conversions. Full FAA design, manufacturing authority.
SECDO (Encino, CA)	Aeronautical engineering – structural and aerodynamic.

The T-56 engine was already in the USAF inventory with the Lockheed C-130. If the existing Convair 540 turboprop QEC was utilized, there would be a step in the lower contour of the nacelle. Alternatively, a deeper, lower contour could be developed to better accommodate the larger C-119 nacelle diameter. A new semimonocoque transition plug would be fabricated to move the C-119 firewall forward. An aft fairing extension would be built to smooth the airflow from the higher QEC nacelle to the top of the C-119 nacelle. A new exhaust duct would be installed over the top of the wing, exiting at the wing trailing edge to preclude damage to the landing gear. No changes would be required for the landing gear. Stainless steel doublers would be added to the wing to prevent heat damage from the exhaust duct. The higher exhaust duct necessitated raising the engine thrust center line by about two feet. The air inlet would be above the propeller hub, thereby minimizing foreign object damage. A pair of Aeroproducts Model A6441FM-294 hydro-mechanical propellers would complete the power package. The QEC installation moved the C-119 propeller plane forward by about three feet.

The QEC installation would result in a reduction of engine weight, however the turboprop would have a higher fuel consumption. While no changes would be made to the prototype, it was recommended that additional fuel capacity be provided for any production aircraft. The study would include an analysis of the structural effects of additional fuel tanks.

Installation of the 2,000-lb lighter T56 engine would garner the following improvements:

- Markedly improved single-engine performance
- Decreased take-off distances
- Improved speed performance
- Improved climb rate
- Significantly improved reliability
- Improved maintainability, reduced maintenance index
- Increased cargo capacity due to reduced engine weight

No records could be found that this proposal went beyond the design phase.

CONCLUSION

The C-119s were eventually phased out of the USAF inventory and replaced by the Fairchild (formerly Chase-designed) C-123 Provider and the pre-eminently successful Lockheed C-130 Hercules. This marked the end of American twin-boomed endloading aircraft.

The basic design of the C-119 Flying Boxcar offered a lot of growth potential. While it had more than its share of growing pains, it proved to be a stalwart airlifter serving both the United States and its allies for several decades. In addition, it was capable of being modified for several unintended, at times rather unique, missions. In these respects, it proved its investment value to the American taxpayer.

Flying Boxcar Specifications

	C-119B	C-119C	C-119F	C-119G	AC-119G	AC-119K
Dimensions						
Wing Span	109ft 3½in	109ft 3½in	109ft 3½in	109ft 3½in	109ft 3½in	109ft 3½in
Length	86ft 6in	86ft 6in	86ft 6in	86ft 6in	86ft 6in	86ft 6in
Height	26ft 6in	26ft 6in	26ft 6in	26ft 6in	26ft 6in	26ft 6in
Wing Area	1,447ft²	1,447ft²	1,447ft²	1,447ft²	1,447ft²	1,447ft²
Weights (figures in pounds)						
Empty	38,329	39,942	39,118	40,758	52,407	60,277
Basic	39,912	40,300	40,476	41,170	58,433	68,450
Design	64,000	64,000	64,000	64,000	64,000	64,000
Combat*	47,952	49,350	49,368	49,368	60,374	70,102
Max TOW†	68,700	73,150	77,700	72,700	69,100	77,000
Max TOW‡	–	66,600	72,000	68,300	64,900	77,000
Max landing§	68,700	72,300	77,000	72,700	77,000	77,000
Powerplant					C-119L¶	
Engine	P&W R-4360-20	P&W R-4360-20WA or Wright R-3350-85	Wright R-3350-89A or Wright R-3350-85	Wright R-3350-85	Wright R-3350-85	Wright R-3350-85
Supercharger	1 Stage, Var. Speed	1 Stage, Var. Speed	2 Stage, 2 Speed	2 Stage, 2 Speed	2 Stage, 2 Speed	2 Stage, 2 Speed
Propeller (full-feathering, constant-speed, reversible)	Hamilton Standard Hydromatic	Hamilton Standard Hydromatic	Hamilton Standard Hydromatic	Aeroproducts Hydromatic	Hamilton Standard (three-bladed)	Aeroproducts Hydromatic or Hamilton Standard (three-bladed)
Propeller Diameter	15ft	15ft	15ft	15ft	15ft	15ft
Fluids (figures in gallons)						
Wings, Inboard (2 tanks)	1,710	1,710	1,666	1,666	1,598	1,598
Wings, Outboard (2 tanks)	914	914	924	924	890	890
Total	2,624	2,624	2,590	2,590	2,488	2,488
Auxiliary tanks	–	2 x 506	2 x 506	2 or 4 x 506	–	–
Oil	120	120	120	120	120	120
Water/Alcohol	–	56	57	56	57	57

* For Basic Mission; † Overload Limited by Performance; ‡ Normal Limited by Performance; § Limited by Max Taxi Weight;
¶ The data given under the heading of powerplants in this column in this column are for the C-119L only and not the AC-119G

Chapter 5

C-119 Flight Testing

In addition to the standard flight tests performed by the manufacturer, the USAF ran a number of tests on the C-119 at Edwards AFB, CA. These tests were conducted to verify the manufacturer's test data and to ensure operational suitability of the aircraft for the Air Force. Tests were performed on the first of a series of the C-119 built by both Fairchild and Kaiser. Phase IV tests were for USAF verification of the manufacturer's data. Later flight test programs were flown with the C-119s as part of ongoing development programs.

Phase IV Tests

Phase IV Performance and Cooling flight tests were conducted on Fairchild-built C-119F-1-FA, s/n 51-8089 between 24 February and 11 September 1953. A major facet of these tests was to disclose any differences between the R-4360-20WA and R-3350-85 engines. The results of this test were used in preparation of the Standard Aircraft Characteristics Charts and Appendix I of the Pilot's Handbook of Operating Instructions. While preliminary estimates called for 90 hours of flight testing, a total 105:10 hours were required for the 41 flights. The flight test pilot was Maj Val E Prahl and the test engineer was Willie L Allen.

Between 18 November 1952 and 1 May 1953, a partial Phase IV flight test was conducted using a Kaiser-built C-119F, s/n 51-8098, to obtain data on the R-3350 engines. Upon its arrival from Willow Run, MI, the aircraft was instrumented for testing. Extensive rewiring of the electrical system was required before the aircraft was considered safe for flight one engine was removed and was instrumented for cooling tests. The purpose of the test program was to verify aircraft performance and handling characteristics, engine cooling, and to check handbook data.

Tests on both 51-8089 and 51-8098 were conducted at weights ranging between 53,900 and 72,800 lb. The center of gravity positions ranged between 20 and 30% of the mean aerodynamic chord (MAC). The long-range ferry tanks had been removed for these tests.

The tests revealed that the flying and handling characteristics of the C-119F were normal and satisfactory with one exception – the single-engine minimum control speed to assure directional control was undesirably high at 112 knots indicated airspeed (IAS). The rudder force was excessive when compared to the light aileron and elevator forces. Cooling for the R-3350s was satisfactory at all airspeeds. With water-alcohol injection the available take-off brake horsepower was less than that in the manufacturer's estimates. Because the measured maximum fuel capacity was less than the manufacturer's estimate, the combat radius of the aircraft was 13% less that predicted. Because the take-off speeds proved to be 35% lower than the manufacturer's estimates, the take-off distance and 50ft obstacle clearance at 72,800 lb gross weight proved to be 37% less in actuality. The service ceiling at 72,800 lb gross weight was approximately 14% higher than estimated, and at 64,000 lb. The ceiling was 13% higher.

The Phase IV tests also revealed a problem with the aerial delivery system. Vibrations experienced during taxi and in flight resulted in the

Right: **The Air Research & Development Command (ARDC) used C-119F-FA, s/n 51-2586 in the parachute tests conducted in 1956. The forward fuselage had a white top with a scalloped Insignia Blue cheatline extending from the prop warning line, around the nose, and down to the nosewheel well. Centered on the nose was an insignia with the last three digits of the tail number under the marking. The Air Force Flight Test Center (AFFTC) insignia appeared within the Insignia Blue chevron on the fin. An ARDC logo was applied to the nose of the airplane.** Edwards AFB Historian

Below right: **ARDC operated C-119F-FA, s/n 51-8046, in this pristine overall natural metal finish. A beavertail door had been installed. The empennage appears to have been painted Insignia Red, with natural metal cutouts for the tail number and tail markings. The inboard surfaces of the dorsal fins appear to have been painted in either black or Insignia Blue. While the U.S. AIR FORCE and TROOP CARRIER markings were carried on the forward fuselage, an ARDC insignia was applied to the forward fuselage aft of the drop windows. Below and aft of that insignia is what looks like the Catch a Falling Star insignia (See Chapter 13). In addition, the red and black on white tail markings were applied.** Edwards AFB Historian

monorail system locking pins becoming disengaged. As a result, the trolleys were free to roll unless restrained by an adjacent trolley. On two occasions during the tests, a free-wheeling trolley would roll forward and contact the paratainer release resulting in the suspended ballast dropping onto the paratainer door causing damage. A more positive locking system was recommended.

Other Phase IV Test findings included:

- The elevator trim wheel was easily turned and was so located that the pilot's knee could inadvertently turn the wheel. An adjustable friction lock was recommended.

- The nosewheel steering was not positive. System modification to assure positive steering at all gross weights was recommended.

- The flight control lock was unsatisfactory, in that, when released, the controls could remain locked. It was recommended that the lock be spring-loaded to the *unlock* position. (This condition had resulted in several emergency landings in operational units.)

It was recommended that the rudder control force be decreased and directional control be improved so as to permit single-engine operation below 112 knots IAS.

Problems experienced with engine maintenance on the R-3350s was initially attributed to a lack of experience level of the mechanics supporting the Phase IV tests; however, a USAF investigation into engine service life and maintenance was recommended.

Partial Phase IV flight tests were performed at Edwards AFB, on C-119G-1-FA, s/n 51-8053, between June 1953 and June 1954. Capt Richard C Kennan Jr was the Project Pilot, and 1Lt John R Wallis was the Test Engineer. These tests indicated that the climb performance of the C-119G was superior to that of the C-119F, but that the engine cooling was less effective though satisfactory. These tests were conducted in 16 flights totaling 31:50 hours. Gross weights between 53,000 and 74,000 lb were used during these tests. The major difference between the C-119F and the C-119G was the propellers. The Hamilton Standard propellers had been replaced by Aeroproducts props. While the single-engine directional control had improved over the C-119F, it was still unsatisfactory below 107 knots IAS. The aircraft was grounded between 21 September and 12 November 1953 by a general grounding order resulting from propeller malfunctions. Subsequent modifications to the propeller control system were accomplished to change the low pitch blade angle stop and to block out the reverse pitch capability. Propeller synchronization was accomplished manually by the pilot because the prop governor was unable to maintain selected rpm settings. The resulting noise beat

Above: **This Kaiser-built C-119F, s/n 51-8117, had flown with the 314th TCW before going to Edwards AFB for the 1955 heavy weight tests.** Edwards AFB Historian

Below: **C-119J 51-8050, was equipped with the flight operable beavertail doors. Insignia Red Arctic trim was applied to the airplane. This picture dates from 11 September 1958.** Edwards AFB Historian

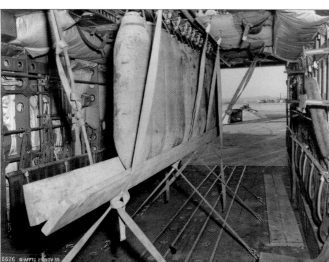

Dummy bombs were suspended from the paratainer system and secured with 2x6s and web straps for the heavy weight testing conducted on 51-8117. The picture dates from 23 November 1955. USAF via D C Leisy

This shark fin was mounted aft of the cowl flaps as a simple piece of flight instrumentation gear. The crew would observe the position of the cowl flaps relative to the shark fin to work their drag polar tests. USAF via D C Leisy

Fairchild's jet-assisted demonstrator, YC-119K s/n 53-3142, was marked in a bold red, white, and blue scheme that predated the US Bicentennial celebration by several years. The picture was taken at Dulles International Airport on 18 August 1969. Frank McSorley via MSgt D W Menard

In 1951, tow tests were performed by Fairchild utilizing a C-119 and a Chase YC-122 glider. The C-119 was carrying the ARDC logo. P M Bowers

produced extreme crew discomfort. It was recommended that the propellers be reworked as soon as possible so that the reversing capability could be used. It was further recommended that the propeller regulator be redesigned to eliminate rpm fluctuations, and a better method of prop synchronization be developed.

C-119H Testing

Capt John W Konrad was assigned as the USAF Project Pilot for the C-119H in June 1952. He was assisted by Bill F Owens, the Project Engineer. Phase II tests were to be conducted at Hagerstown, MD. The two arrived at Fairchild only to experience a lengthy delay as the manufacturer worked out an unexpected problem with the aerodynamic characteristics of the aircraft caused by the elevator spring tab. By 18 July 1952, the problem was resolved and the aircraft was accepted for flight. Between then and 5 August, 34 flights were conducted, totaling 64 hours and 30 minutes.

Research and Development

The 6511th Parachute Development Test Group, at Edwards AFB, performed a variety of tests ranging from live jumps to cargo drops between 1 January and 30 June 1953. During these tests they utilized 12 different types of aircraft from both USAF and US Navy inventories. One of these aircraft was a C-119 that flew 57 missions and conducted 227 drops during this period.

A 10,000-lb capacity, load-bearing platform with airbag decelerators was developed by the group during the second half of 1953. The system incorporated a side rail installation in the C-119 and was self-restrained and incorporated a release control for the pilot instead of a kicker as used during the Korean War.

Heavy Weight Tests

Heavy weight tests were conducted on C-119G, s/n 51-8117, between 18 November 1955 and 28 January 1956. Maj Jones P Seigler was the Project Pilot, and 1Lt David C Leisy was the Project Engineer. The test was designed to determine the maximum gross weight at which a rate of climb of 100ft per minute could be obtained using single engine military power (with water injection) with the gear and flaps retracted.

The aircraft was modified to incorporate the following instruments on the pilots' panels: sensitive airspeed indicators, sensitive altimeters, and sensitive tachometers. A sensitive free air temperature indicator was added to the pilot's radio console. Readings from these gauges were taken by Lt Leisy, seated in the radio operator's seat, and an enlisted technician in the navigator's seat. In addition, a shark fin was installed behind the cowl flaps so that the cowl flap opening could be visually determined from the cockpit. Precise cowl flap openings were required for both engine cooling and airspeed calibration.

Thirty-one test flights totaling 34:30 hours flying time were conducted. Because these flights had to be flown below the critical altitude of the engines in order to utilize maximum power, flights totaling five and ten hours, respectively, were flown from Point Mugu and El Centro Naval Air Stations to take advantage of the low elevation of the airfields and the surrounding terrain. Initially, the Air Force had requested the use of Los Angeles International Airport, but this permission was not granted by Air Traffic Control. The remaining tests were flown at Edwards AFB.

These heavy weight tests were conducted using similar conditions to those utilized in the limited Phase IV tests for the C-119G. The exceptions were that R-3350-89 engines were used in lieu of the R-3350-85 engines, and dual, instead of single nose gear wheels were installed. Cargo loads were simulated with up to 20 dummy bombs, weighing a total of 10,163 lb, suspended from the aerial delivery system while an additional 5,675 lb of lead weights were secured to the cargo floor.

During the 15th test, conducted on 8 December 1955, the aircraft was being flown at 69,500 lb gross weight at a 2,700ft altitude with the cargo doors installed. A series of sawtooth climbs were being attempted at an altitude of 2,500ft. The right engine failed at the point in time that the left engine was being feathered. A cylinder head temperature of 60°C was being indicated on the left engine. The right engine was feathered and normal rated power was applied to the left engine. During this emergency, a loss of 400ft in altitude was incurred as the aircraft was diverted on a 20-mile leg to Los Angeles International Airport without a further loss in altitude. The entire flight lasted 40 minutes. After replacement of the right engine, an engine calibration run on 14 December revealed that insufficient power was being developed in order to continue the tests. A second replacement engine was installed and testing was resumed on 20 December.

Testing continued on 5 January 1956, when a 25-minute engine calibration flight was conducted. On the following day, testing was halted after 40 minutes due to air turbulence. A full 2:20-hour flight was conducted on 7 January. The clamshell doors were removed, and testing continued later in the day. The flight was again terminated after 20 minutes because of turbulence. These tests were resumed and two flights lasting 1:35 and 1:05 hours were flown on the following day.

The clamshell doors were reinstalled for testing on 9 January. After 25 minutes the flight was terminated due to roughness in the right engine.

As a result of the tests it was determined that the C-119G could not sustain the single engine gross weights as published in the current flight

EC-119C-19-FA, s/n 50-135, was modified for the tandem landing gear tests. Note the sailor inspecting the nose, and the pogos under the aft fuselage. A camera pod is mounted under the aft fuselage. In the background was a T-6 Texan and an L-19 Bird Dog. Fairchild via George Cully

Fairchild developed a rough field landing gear for the C-119. These illustrations show the aft bogie being employed on normal runways and the front wheel assembly for rough runways, gear features, and design criteria.

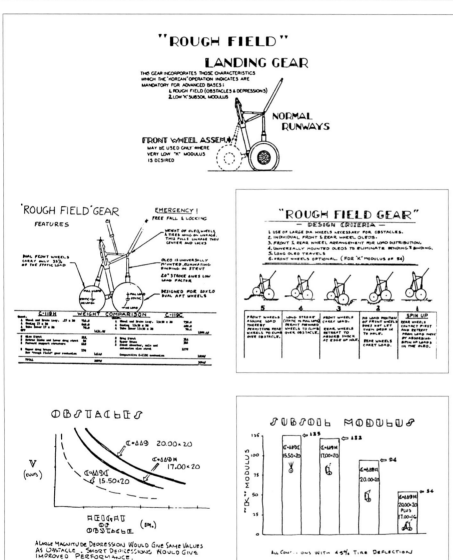

Large Capacity Spray System Tests

A report dated August 1953 from the Air Force Armament Center, Eglin AFB, FL described an evaluation for a production model of a large capacity spray system for both the B-29 and C-119. Only the C-119 aspects of the tests are covered herein. The test program was initiated on 15 December 1952, with program support provided by:
- Special Weapons Branch, Armament Laboratories, Wright Air Development Center, Wright-Patterson AFB, OH
- Biological Laboratories, Research and Engineering Command, US Army Chemical Corps, Camp Detrick, MD

The tests were designed to evaluate the handling, installation, and performance characteristics of a production model of the large-capacity bomb bay spray tank designed for carrying and dispensing anticrop chemicals. The agent was a mixture of three parts Agent A, undiluted technical grade butyl 2,4-dichlorophenoxyacetate, and one part Agent B, 2,4,5-trichlorophenoxyacetate. Consideration was given to the effects of various wind and temperature conditions on the spray pattern.

Hayes Aircraft Corporation, Birmingham, AL designed the 1,000-gallon capacity aluminum tank, self-priming centrifugal pump, and connecting plumbing for installation in the cargo compartment of a C-119 to specifications provided by the Army Chemical Corps and the Air Force Research and Development Command. A small gasoline-powered engine drove the centrifugal pump. Controls installed on either end of the tank facilitated system operation. Four detachable castering wheels permitted the unit to be towed and maneuvered into the aircraft. The system was designated MC-1.

The C-119 cargo compartment was modified to accept the tank cradle, and a hole was cut into the bottom of the fuselage to permit operation of the dump valve. Another 2in diameter hole was cut into the right clamshell door to permit the nozzle assembly to extend outside of the aircraft. Lastly, an exhaust port was cut into the side of the fuselage for the gasoline-driven engine.

Hayes Aircraft also modified a Model 900 Heating and Transfer Unit from an E3R2 Incendiary Oil Mixing and Transfer Unit for use with the MC-1 system. The unit was designed to transfer a viscous fluid from drums, tanks, or other containers through a heating chamber into the spray tank.

manuals. At sea level, the maximum weights that would permit a 100ft per minute rate of climb with the gear and flaps up at 3,500bhp were: 72,600lb with the cargo doors on and 69,700lb with the doors removed.

Tandem Gear Tests

As with most transport aircraft, the C-119 was restricted to operating from prepared airfields. To permit soft-field operations, Fairchild began experimenting with a tandem main landing gear system that would increase the aircraft's footprint. These tests were conducted in 1951.

The new twin axle truck was installed on the main gear. Each axle had a pair of wheels with tires of a smaller diameter that those on the standard C-119. The gear doors were modified with cutouts that permitted the wheels to partially extend into the slipstream. The tandem gear installation never went into production.

A pair of 16mm GSAP cameras equipped with 35mm focal length lenses were installed on the aircraft. One was located in the tail position about 4ft above the spray nozzles to record the spray pattern. The second camera was mounted in the left tailboom to record the spray pattern as liquid departed the nozzles. Switches for operating the cameras were located in the cargo compartment aft of the spray tank.

During the test, a crew of six men expended 36 manhours to install the single tank and its ancillary equipment in the C-119.

Eleven successful spray tests were flown using the B-29, while another three were flown with the C-119. The aircraft were flown at altitudes of 1,000ft, 1,500ft, and 2,000ft. After analyzing that data, the test force recommended:

- Replacing the gasoline driven engine with an electric pump because of exhaust fumes, daily maintenance requirements, and pressure-surging of the discharge lines.
- Continued contact between the agent and tank insulation blanket resulted in deterioration of the neoprene coating on the blanket, although the insulating qualities of the blanket were satisfactory.
- The location of the spray nozzle on the C-119 clamshell doors resulted in excessive deposits of the agent on the aircraft skin. While extending the nozzle boom 12in aft of the fuselage markedly reduced the impingement, it did not completely eliminate the condition. A retractable spray nozzle boom was recommended for future operations.
- Tests showed that the Heating and Transfer Unit was not completely satisfactory for loading and heating the agent.

Subsequently the Air Force procured 100 MC-1 systems and placed them in storage along with the defoliant agent in Spokane, Washington. While never employed operationally with the C-119, these tests paved the way for Operation *Ranch Hand* in which Fairchild C-123 Providers performed defoliation operations in Southeast Asia using a variety of chemicals, including Agent Orange.

By way of note, a fleet of six UC-123Bs was employed in Southeast Asia on 28 November 1961. Projections for future requirements indicated a need for a 40% increase in defoliation capability. While the USAF could not dedicate 32 of their aircraft to this mission, consideration was given to transferring the mission to the Republic of Vietnam Air Force (VNAF) using some of their C-119s. Operation *Ranch Hand* already required the UC-123s to be painted in VNAF markings and carry a Vietnamese crew member aboard for each mission. USAF staff personnel in the theater determined that the only way this mission could be completely transferred to the VNAF would be if the aircrews could overcome their fear of ground fire at the low altitudes required to fly the mission profile. VNAF requirements at the time would have taken eight C-119s and 21 experienced aircrews out of the already strained VNAF airlift capabilities.

AC-119 Tests

The Limited Performance and Stability and Control tests were completed on the AC-119G on 23 January 1969. The aircraft was de-instrumented and returned to Fairchild at St Augustine, FL, on 29 January. The AC-119K arrived at Edwards AFB for tests on 19 June 1969, for similar testing.

Tactical Air Command's Special Operations Forces conducted other tests at Eglin AFB, FL. These included tests of the night observation system (NOS), fire control system, illumination systems, flare launcher, cabin smoke removal system, and overall aircraft performance. A total of 25 test missions was flown between 9 and 30 June 1968. Recommendations for a 200ft per minute rate of climb on one engine could not be met. The C-119 still could only muster a 100ft per minute rate of climb. A weight reduction program was instituted. One development that resulted from the program was a pilot-operated flare launcher that weighted 1,000 lb with the flares. In an emergency, the launcher could be jettisoned to reduce weight during a critical phase of flight. As a result, the AC-119G was capable of achieving a 150ft per minute rate of climb.

AIR FORCE RESERVE FLIGHT TESTS

It should be noted that the Air Force Reserve Component ranks are filled with members who had prior Regular Air Force experience and long tenure with them on a single aircraft. Such background made them well-qualified to perform late-program testing. Two examples are the Alamo Slingshot and the Free-Fall Delivery system.

Alamo Slingshot

Members of the 433rd TCW stationed at Kelly AFB, TX devised a system that would markedly improve aerial delivery operations. Maj George H Slover, a TAC advisor to the 433rd, was responsible for the concept and development of the new system. His proposal became a test identified as TAC Test 67-5Q. While the crews were able to determine the Computed Air Release Point (CARP), the exact timing of parachute performance was proving troublesome during drops. They were using two parachutes – an extraction chute and a main cargo chute. The conventional method called for the extraction chute to pull the cargo out of the aircraft, and a cargo chute to subsequently deploy to carry the load to the ground.

With the guidance of Maj Slover, members of the 433rd TCW developed a new delivery system known as the Alamo Slingshot based on a child's stick and rubber band slingshot. The Wing devised a system employing a bridle consisting of a 3,000-lb test cable looped around with the two ends terminating in the overhead monorail trolley at the top of the cargo compartment, located well forward of the cargo packages. Using a standard load with Army 2,250-lb A-22 containers, the navigator would precisely control the release of the trolley through the monorail salvo button that would drive the trolley forwards and propel the load out of the back of the aircraft. The web strap securing the cargo was released a split second before the sling launched its load. The pilot chute (activated by the monorail system) would release and pull out the cargo chute. The average deployment time for a single load was four seconds. A full load of six pallets could be ejected in 4.75 seconds. The Alamo Slingshot reduced the average CARP from 210 yards to 73 yards over conventional drop methods. Multiple releases over a given drop zone could be accomplished within three minutes (the time required for a procedure turn). The concepts developed with this system were subsequently employed on the C-119, C-123, and C-130 aircraft.

Free-Fall Delivery Tests

The introduction of the C-119 into the war in Southeast Asia, and the probability of a requirement for free-fall delivery of supplies led the 434th Troop Carrier Wing (TCW), AFRes, Bakalar AFB, IN, to suggest testing of a free-fall system for the C-119.

TAC Test 68-208, Free-Fall Delivery, C-119 Aircraft, was conducted by members of the 434th TCW between September and December 1968. The tests were conducted to develop aircrew procedures, ballistics data, and determine the drop zone size for use with free-fall deliveries from C-119 aircraft. Maj Paul A Dehmer Jr, was the test manager.

The ballistics data published in TAC Test 67-5Q for the C-130 was found to be inapplicable to the C-119. The horizontal distance and time of fall from a C-119 were consistently shorter than that for the C-130. Because there was no apparent reason for this disparity, TAC Test 68-208 included the C-130.

The three phases of the free-fall drop tests were:

Phase I   36 C-119 drops conducted at Bakalar AFB, IN in September 1968.
Phase II   3 C-130 drops at NAF El Centro, CA, DOD test range with theodolite capability.
Phase III   12 C-119 drops on the Fort Bragg Reservation on 10 December 1968.

The average exit time for a single 1,800-lb A-22 container was 1.5 seconds. The maximum deviation was about 0.3 second. The tests revealed that the existing 60 x 200-yard drop zone (DZ) for single loads be increased to 60 x 250 yards for the C-119. The point of impact should be located 125 yards from the leading edge of the DZ. The additional DZ length required for each succeeding container in a stick should be increased from 25 to 50 yards. The tests proved the C-130 data to be correct, and provided different data for the C-119.

CONCLUSIONS

While the Regular Air Force performed the requisite syllabus of acceptance flight tests, the Air Force Reserve proved itself to be equally capable in developing and performing follow-on tests that further enhanced the capabilities not only of the C-119, but of other tactical aircraft.

Chapter 6

Air Resupply Drop Procedures

The concept of supplying military units through airdrops was pioneered during World War One, and developed into a consistently reliable alternative during World War Two in virtually all theaters of the war. However, it was not until the Korean War, with its peculiar logistical problems, that we would experience the greatest airdrop resupply operation in history.

Air Drop Resupply Requirements
The need for an airdrop resupply system emerged during the Korean War because of poor communications, both road networks and rail facilities. Of even greater significance was the lack of adequate surface routes between forward airfields and the actual front lines. Poor weather, enemy interdiction and the rugged Korean terrain all had their impact on the rapid forward movement of ammunition; petroleum, oil, and lubricants (POL); and rations. Enemy action and winter conditions often rendered the available roads impassable.

The enemy was clever enough to stay away from the few major routes and forced US troops to fight in difficult off-road terrain. They would encircle US troops and deny them a way out without airlift.

Techniques developed within the Zone of Interior prior to the Korean War, utilizing C-82 Packets and then C-119 Flying Boxcars, proved that airdrops could replace the glider. Anything that could be carried in a glider could be parachuted. Air dropping could be accomplished with less vulnerability to hostile fire and loss of lives and equipment.

Air Drop Preparations
Working in concert the 314th Troop Carrier Group at Smyrna AFB, TN and the 2348th Quartermaster Airborne Supply and Packaging Company, which was attached to the 187th Airborne Regimental Combat Team (RCT), developed the techniques for packaging, loading, and dropping supplies.

Special parcels were built up on 4ft x 4ft plywood pallets. These pallets would then be trucked to the flight line and loaded onto the aircraft. A floor-mounted roller system within the aircraft facilitated both loading and dropping of the pallets. Steel cables and nylon web straps with hooks were used to secure the pallets to the tie-down rings in the aircraft floor. The clamshell doors were removed from the aircraft for these operations. However, with the doors removed, the aircraft's range was severely hampered and crew conditions, particularly in winter, were marginal at best.

Air Drop Techniques
At a point 20 minutes from the drop zone, kickers would remove the steel cables and allow the load to be secured solely by the nylon web straps. When the aircraft reached the drop zone, the pilot would signal the kickers through an alarm bell system. At this time, the kicker, who stood forward of the cargo, would actuate a newly developed bomb shackle release device that permitted the entire cargo load to depart the aircraft in approximately 3.5 seconds. Parachutes would extract each bundle. The plywood pallets would break away from the bundles as they hit the slipstream. While few Korean drop zones permitted anything greater than single ships in trail, a 9-ship formation could drop almost 50 tons of cargo in 3.5 minutes.

Above left: **This formation of C-119s from Hamilton AFB, CA are preparing for a drop. Note the absence of clamshell doors on four of the aircraft, while the top rear C-119 has beavertail doors installed. A paratrooper is surveying the situation from the rear of aircraft s/n 53-3158.**

Left: **A palletized jeep and trailer have just been extracted from aircraft s/n 53-3158.**

The C-119s could drop their entire load in a single pass and execute a rapid climb-out through mountain passes, thereby reducing vulnerability to ground fire; while C-46s and C-47s, with their side cargo doors, would have to make several passes to drop an entire load.

In order to accomplish the airdrops, the C-119s had to be slowed to 115 knots indicated airspeed (IAS) because the existing cargo parachutes would not withstand the opening shock at higher speeds. A damaged chute could cause the bundle to fall at a faster rate, thereby increasing the risk of damage. In addition, higher drop speeds would scatter the bundles over a greater area. At 115 knots IAS, the aircraft was flying just a few knots above stalling speed, yet it was passing the drop zone at a rate of 60 yards per second. To slow the C-119 from its cruising speed of 160 knots to its drop speed took approximately 90 seconds, during which time it traveled approximately three miles.

The optimum drop altitude was determined to be between 600 and 800ft above ground level. At lower altitudes the parachutes would not have had adequate time to open. During the Korean War this drop altitude was often achieved far below the surrounding rugged mountain peaks.

Selection of a drop zone (DZ) by troops on the ground was critical to the success of the mission. To ensure that most of the cargo would land in the desired spot, the DZ had to be at least 500 yards in length. When 30 or more aircraft approached the same DZ, the cargo tended to pile up at the center exposing it to damage from subsequent drops. Therefore, it was recommended that staggered DZs be established.

A DZ was identified by a **T** laid out on the ground. The stem of the **T** was placed in line with the heading of the incoming aircraft. Its crossbar was placed perpendicular to the stem at the end away from the approach. The **T** was made up of eight 3ft x 15ft pieces of brightly colored fabric. Airborne units placed the **T** at the beginning of the DZ, while non-airborne units placed the **T** at the center. Consideration was given to the size, shape, and terrain of the DZ; wind velocity and direction; approaches to and exits from the DZ; and proximity to the unit requesting the drop. To preclude drops to the wrong units, a code letter was applied in addition to the **T**. To prevent a last minute scramble in laying out the DZ, this task was to be performed at least 30 minutes prior to the scheduled arrival of the aircraft that could be early due to winds enroute.

Above: **Paratroops are exiting the rear of aircraft s/n 53-3501. The two paratroops that are high reveal why the C-119 had such an upsweep to the tailbooms.**

Below: **An explosive charge separated the pallet harness from the parachute lines to prevent the wind from catching the chutes and dragging the equipment across the ground.**

An average 5-ton load could have required as many as 104 G-9 18ft diameter and 50 G-1 24ft diameter parachutes. When so many parachutes were simultaneously in neighboring airspace, a saturation condition occurs. As the chutes steal the air from each other, the bundles oscillate violently. When this happened, the shroud lines would become entangled between chutes resulting in streamers, thus allowing the bundles to free-fall. With adequate advanced notice on the DZ, packers could load a double-section thereby permitting the kicker to drop the first half on signal, count to two, and release the second half of the load. This staggering of the drop greatly reduced losses due to streamering. A double-section load provided a 120-yard separation in the drop.

Parachute Maintenance and Rigging
During World War Two, parachutes were sewn from silk – hence the term 'hitting the silk'. Later, parachutes are made of nylon or rayon depending upon their use. Their 1950 cost to the government ranged between $5 and $2,000 each. Lives of the paratroops and the integrity of their supplies depended upon the proper care and maintenance of the parachutes. During the Korean War, the Army Quartermaster Corps was responsible for the maintenance and rigging of all parachutes employed in airdrops. Initially this mission was assigned to the 2348th Quartermaster Airborne Supply and Packaging Detachment. This unit was subsequently redesignated the 8081st Quartermaster Airborne Supply and Packaging Company. Members of the 8081st were responsible for:
- Detailed inspections of the parachutes and harnesses
- Drying and dehumidifying the canopies
- Making requisite repairs
- Storage of serviceable parachutes and equipment
- Pallet and paratainer build-up
- Aircraft loading
- Flying as kickers on drop missions

Shops for the 8081st had over 100 sewing machines capable of performing a wide variety of different stitches. Special tables were employed for inspections and packing of the parachutes. Serviceable parachutes and equipment were stored in a painstaking, but necessary, manner. Four layers of waterproof material protected the equipment from mold and mildew. The chutes were then packed in crates stored in a warehouse with dehumidifiers and temperature control.

Members of the 8081st were responsible for ensuring that the correct load was placed aboard each aircraft so that it could be dropped to the proper DZ. They ensured proper parachute attachment to each cargo load. These personnel worked throughout the night to ensure that the aircraft were properly loaded and ready for the flight crews in the morning.

Personnel from the 8081st were innovators in developing specialized packaging and deliver systems for unusual and outsized cargo. Such innovations included:
- Color-coded parachutes for specific types of cargo
- Floor-level roller conveyor system for installation in the C-119 cargo compartments
- Bomb-shackle release systems to ensure rapid, uniform drops
- 55-gallon drum delivery capability
- Plywood platforms with frangible materials to reduce impact damage

US Army Quartermaster School
The dropping of paratroops and their equipment to establish an airhead was developed and fully exploited during World War Two. Sustained ground operations by the airborne forces were bolstered by aerial resupply. It was not until the Korean War that America had a heavy drop capability. Early training was conducted using C-82s, followed by C-119s. It was the members of the 8081st that wrote the book in heavy drop operations.

Between 1946 and 1953, a series of joint Army-Air Force field exercises and maneuvers tested the equipment and procedures that led to an awesome capability.

The table below identifies the most significant joint Army-Air Force airdrop exercises conducted between 1946 and 1952.

Date	Exercise	Location	Aircraft	Units
Oct 1946-Apr 1947	Task Force Frigid	Ladd Field, AK	C-82	
Nov 1947- Feb 1948	Snowdrop	Pine Camp, NY		
Nov 1947-Jan 1948	Yukon	Fairbanks, AK	C-82	62nd TCG
Feb-Mar 1950	Portex	Vieques Island, PR		
Apr-May 1950	Swarmer	Camp Mackall, Fort Bragg, NC	C-119	314th TCW
Jul-Aug 1951	Southern Pine	Fort Bragg, NC	C-119	375th & 443rd TCW
Dec 1951-Feb 1952	Snowfall	Camp Drum, NY	C-119	435th & 436th TCW
Mar-Apr 1952	Long Horn	Fort Hood, TX	C-119	8 wings

The US Army Quartermaster School at Fort Lee, VA, instituted a quartermaster airborne course of instruction that opened in 1950 and continued through until the end of the Korean War.

The purpose of the course was:

'Training in inspection, packing, repairing, and maintenance of personnel and cargo parachutes and aerial supply equipment, loading and securing cargo in aircraft, ejection of cargo in flight, and recovery of parachutes and aerial supply equipment.'

Prior to 1950 there had never been any instruction given in the maintenance, packing, and rigging of 100ft diameter cargo parachutes. In May 1951, the school curriculum included a 12-week, 528-hour parachute, rigging and aerial delivery course. The 140-hour aerial supply portion of the course included these elements:

Subject	Hours
Air Transportability Subjects	28
Free Drop Techniques and the 2,200-lb Container	4
Heavy Cargo Parachute Packing	32
Heavy Equipment Drop Techniques	76

Rigger's Pledge

I will keep constantly in mind that until men grow wings their parachutes must be dependable.

I will pack every parachute as though I am to jump with it myself, and will stand ready to jump with any parachute which I have certified as properly packed.

I will remember always that the other man's life is as dear to him as mine is to me.

I will never resort to guesswork, as I know that chance is a fool's gold and that I, a rigger, cannot depend on it.

I will never pass over any defect, nor neglect any repair, no matter how small, as I know that omissions and mistakes in the rigging of a parachute may cost a life.

I will keep all parachute equipment entrusted to my care in the best possible condition, remembering always that little things left undone cause major troubles.

I will never sign my name to a parachute inspection or packing certificate unless I have personally performed or directly supervised every step, and am entirely satisfied with all the work.

I will never let the idea that a piece of work is 'good enough' make me a potential murderer through a careless mistake oversight, for I know there can be no compromise with perfection.

I will keep always a wholehearted respect for my vocation, regarding it as a high profession rather than a day-to-day task, and will keep in mind constantly my grave responsibility.

I will be sure – always.

Chapter 7

Boxcars in Korea

After VJ-Day things remained relatively tranquil in the Pacific, at least as far as the United States was concerned, although the French were involved in combat operations in French Indochina. On Sunday, 25 June 1950, the weather along the 38th Parallel dividing North from South Korea was overcast and rainy. At 0400 hours the Red North Korean Army launched a sudden all-out attack against the Republic of Korea. While the Republic of Korea (ROK) had feared aggression from the North and had built a series of field fortifications along the 38th Parallel, their lightly armed troops were no match for the advancing Communist troops. By 0600 hours, columns of North Korean infantry, supported by Soviet-built T-34 tanks, advanced toward Kaesong in the west and Chunchon in central Korea. Along the east coast, south of Kangnung, a disheveled, but effective force of junks and small boats deposited North Korean troops ashore. The Communist forces had completely overrun the ROK forces. The US Korean Military Advisory Group (KMAG) working with ROK forces had seen similar incursions by Communist troops at isolated sites in the past; therefore this advance was not immediately reported. By 0900 hours, KMAG was in a position to better assess the situation and determine that the Communist forces were bent on armed subjugation of the Republic of Korea. By 0945 hours, the word was given to the commander of District 8 of the Office of Special Investigation who in turn relayed the message to the Far East Air Forces (FEAF). This message was immediately relayed to all FEAF bases. It was not until 1130 hours, when Gen Earl E Partridge, FEAF commander, arrived in his office in Nagoya, did he learn of the developments. Instantly he understood the gravity of the situation, but was limited in his actions. Insofar as Korea was concerned, FEAF was tasked solely with the minor mission of providing for the safety of American nationals, and only then at the request of the American ambassador in Korea.

A Fifth Air Force operation plan for such contingencies had been issued on 1 March 1950. General Partridge issued orders to stage airplanes from the 374th Troop Carrier Wing (TCW) at Tachikawa near Tokyo to Itazuke because it was closer to Korea. He further warned the 374th that they were not to transgress Korean air space until ordered to do so. Such orders had to originate from Gen Douglas MacArthur. The 374th TCW was the only airlift wing assigned to the Fifth Air Force at that time. By early September 1950, it was attached to the 1st Troop Carrier Task Force (Provisional), renamed FEAF Combat Cargo Command (Provisional) on 10 September. The wing operated a variety of aircraft. Three troop carrier wings and two troop carrier groups, operating C-46, C-47, C-54, C-119 and C-124 aircraft, were assigned to the theater.

When an urgent call for a wing for a C-47 came from Korea, it was only a matter of minutes before it had been loaded into a C-119 Flying Boxcar of the US Far East Air Forces, 315th Air Division (Combat Cargo), in Japan. The crew who would make the aerial delivery were, left to right: Capt Richard E Knie, SSgt James Castain, Sgt Everett Leonard, and 1Lt Randall Wood. The photograph dates from May 1951. Note the interesting admixture of uniforms. Capt Knie was wearing fatigue pants and a long johns top with leather work gloves. SSgt Castain wore his fatigues with the jacket out of his pants. Sgt Leonard wore a flight suit as did Lt Wood. The man to the extreme right wears a fur-collared flight jacket over his flight suit. Both Capt Knie and Lt Wood wore their *Mae West* life preservers for the overwater flight. Note Sgt Leonard's shoulder-holstered side arm. USAF PRT 7417

As the war broke out in Korea, the 21st Troop Carrier Squadron (TCS), operating C-54 Skymasters from Clark AFB in the Philippines, was directed to fly all of its aircraft to Tachikawa AB, Japan where the planes, aircrews, and maintenance personnel were transferred to other squadrons within the 374th TCW. Then the 21st TCS gained all 11 C-47s that were available from other units. This transfer occurred on 29 June 1950. Aircrews for the 21st TCS were drawn from pilots who had been flying desks in a myriad of administrative jobs. The 21st TCS immediately began assisting in the evacuations of civilians from Korea, earning them the name *Kyushu Gypsies*. Their first mission was to evacuate civilian personnel and families from US offices in Seoul. They were unique in that they operated their C-47s not only for routine missions, but on airland and airevac flights into and out of extremely small airfields. While the C-119s to come required relatively well prepared airfields, the C-47s could operate from almost any flat field.

South Korean President Syngman Rhee overestimated the ROK Army's capabilities when he only asked the American ambassador to request that ten F-51 Mustangs equipped with rockets be turned over to the ROK Air Force no later than the following morning. He also requested heavier artillery pieces. Shortly thereafter the United States and other United

C-119C-15-FA, s/n 49-164, from the 50th TCS, 314th TCG, undergoing maintenance in an engine dock. O J Baird

It was originally intended to equip the first 20 C-119Bs with bladder tanks having a 2,798-gallon fuel capacity. A scheduled vacation at the US Rubber Company precluded their availability. Gen K B Wolfe, from Air Materiel Command, reversed the plan on 12 July 1950. Rather than stop the production line, the planned self-sealing tanks were installed. Fairchild calculated that with the self-sealing tanks and a 1,005-gallon auxiliary tank, the aircraft would have a range of approximately 3,000 statute miles. However, performance figures developed by the 314th TCW showed the range to be 2,688 statute miles. Previous experience with Fairchild led the Air Force to use the 314th TCW's calculations.

The 314th TCW evaluated the fuel burn on five C-119Bs under various conditions, the results are shown in the table below.

The averages resulting from these tests were:
- Average maximum range (no reserve remaining) – 2,100 statute miles
- Average fuel per hour cruise (not including take-off and climb) – 241 gallons/hour
- Average airspeed (true) – 192mph
- Manifold Pressure – 38in with rpm adjustment at 2 hour intervals – 1,850/1,750/1,650/1,550rpm
- Average gross take-off weight – 66,000 lb

Nations became involved in the Korean Police Action. When the need for US ground forces became a necessity, so did the requirement for additional airlift. Maj Gen (later Lt Gen) William H Tunner, former Air Transport Command *Hump* and Berlin Airlift commander, was assigned to FEAF as Deputy Commander Military Air Transport Service (MATS) where he would temporarily serve to organize a major airlift in Korea.

The C-119 was an untried airplane at the time, and, while it had great potential, Maj Gen Tunner was a bit apprehensive about the fact that he would have a large number of them assigned to his units when all of the bugs had not been worked out of the airplane. Gen Tunner called George Hatcher, a former ATC colonel from World War Two who was now an engineer with Fairchild. Hatcher was made an offer to return to active duty in the grade of colonel and serve as Tunner's engineering officer. The offer was accepted and Gen Tunner immediately had orders cut.

Deployment Plans
Plans for deploying C-119 Flying Boxcars to Korea were quite tedious and presented a number of challenges for ferrying a heavy, twin-engined transport from the ZI to Japan.

Aircraft	Gross Wt	Altitude	Range	Fuel/hr	Fuel Remaining	Flt Time	Remarks
49-111	66,000 lb	5,000ft	1,500 st mi	1,400 lb	4,800 lb	8:25	
49-109	65,800 lb	6,000ft	1,500 st mi	1,520 lb	5,400 lb	7:45	
48-348	66,000 lb	7,000ft	1,500 st mi	1,435 lb	4,500 lb	8:25	
48-103	66,000 lb	10,000ft	1,500 st mi	1,600 lb	3,600 lb	8:00	
49-119	66,177 lb	10,000ft	1,500 st mi	2,915 lb	Unknown	1:58	Carburetor trouble increased fuel burn

This left side view of the nose of aircraft 48-144 reveals its blue/white quartered nose markings, indicating that the ship is from the 62nd TCS, 314th TCG. The ship also boldly displayed its name *REAM SUPREME* and the 'divine digit'. Because the USAF was undergoing a transition from its former Army roots, there was no such thing as uniform – here the crew are wearing the World War Two officers' 'pinks and greens' covered by a raincoat and a field cap; next is the new USAF blue uniform and wheel cap with requisite 50-mission crush, brown leather flying jacket, and capeskin flying gloves; and lastly, a standard issue set of Army olive drab uniform with Ike jacket, Army field cap, and a green nylon flying jacket with a fur collar. O J Baird

The right side of the nose of ship 49-144 carries this girl and the name *TUCSAN CHEE-CHEE*. The name in fractured Japanese means much, or a lot of, breasts. Note yellow chop marks surrounding the nose art. The blue scarves were from the squadron color. Here the pilot is wearing a flight suit that actually is a set of mechanic's coveralls. He is carrying a side arm in a shoulder holster, and an Army-issue wheel cap with a 50-mission crush. O J Baird

C-119B Range (computed with zero wind)

Main Fuel Tank (self-sealing tanks)	2,624
Auxiliary Fuel Tank (3 @ 335 gallons)	1,005
Total	**3,629**
Total Fuel (3,629 gallons @ 6 lb/gal)	21,774
Less Trapped Fuel (218 gallons)	-218
Gallons available	**21,556**

The following two routes were planned (all distances in statute miles):

Northern Route

Fairfield-Suisun AFB, CA to McChord AFB, WA	610
McChord AFB, WA to Elmendorf AFB, AK	1,425
Elmendorf AFB, AK to Shemya AFB, AK	1,630
Shemya AFB to Misawa AB, Japan	1,738
Misawa AB, Japan to Tokyo	366
Total	**5,769**

Southern Route

Fairfield-Suisun AFB, CA to Hickam AFB, HI	2,400
Hickam AFB, HI to Wake AFB	2,324
Wake AFB to Iwo Jima AB	1,662
Iwo Jima AB to Tokyo	750
Total	**7,136**

Route Differences

Via Hickam AFB, HI to Japan	7,136
Via Shemya AFB to Japan	5,769
Difference	**1,367**

Longest Leg	Distance	Reserve (no wind)
Via Hickam AFB, HI	2,400	288
Via Shemya AFB, AK	1,738	950
Difference	**662**	**662**

It was concluded that the northern route via Shemya AFB, AK, offered the greatest safety by providing a much greater fuel reserve and emergency landing fields along most of the route.

Boxcar Mobilization

The 314th TCG, based at Sewart AFB near Smyrna, TN, was equipped with C-119s and regularly supported the 187th Airborne Regimental Combat Team (RCT), based at Camp Campbell, KY. Both of these units were assigned to Korea. The 314th TCG was to be available to FEAF by 15 August 1950 with 64 C-119s. Under the command of Colonel Hoyt Prindle, the personnel and equipment of the 314th TCG flew across the Pacific arriving at Tachikawa Air Base. They immediately redeployed to Ashiya Air Base in southern Japan. Initially, their mission was to lift 2,700 paratroopers. However, it was not long thereafter when the Department of the Army notified the USAF of a requirement to airlift 3,500 paratroops and their heavy equipment. This requirement would necessitate use of 140 of the C-119s, or their equivalents, when only 64 had been dispatched. Headquarters USAF agreed to provide 96 of the Flying Boxcars, but FEAF would have to provide the remainder of the aircraft. While the Fifth Air Force had already converted the 21st TCS, 374th TCG, to C-47s equipped for paratroop operations, the remainder of the requirement took some doing. C-46 aircraft were obtained from throughout FEAF and the pilots were drawn from desk jobs within the command.

The first missions for the C-119s were airlifting trucks from Tachikawa AB, Japan to Taegu AB, South Korea. This airlift began on 11 August 1950.

Above: *REAM SUPREME* just after take-off, revealing transitional markings. The quartered nose was new, whereas the Insignia Blue stripes behind the cockpit window were old. The No 1 engine cowl appears to have been a replacement, sans color, and a blue scallop to the rear. The vertical tail is painted in its squadron colors. While the dorsal fins are added to the booms, the original horizontal stabilizer tip extensions remain. I P Ingrassia via MSgt D W Menard

Below: Paratroops from the 187th RCT prepare to board C-119s from the 314th TCG. In the foreground is C-119B-FA, s/n 48-328, to the rear is *Marian*, C-119. Note the *Mae Wests* that are being donned by the paratroops for their overwater flight. Fully loaded, each paratrooper carried over 80 lb of gear. USAF via NASM 4A-37941

Inchon Invasion

Gen Douglas MacArthur had planned an invasion at Inchon that would take place on 21 September. In the meantime tactical air strikes were used to hold the advancing Communist forces at bay. When it was learned that the 187th RCT would not arrive in time to support the Inchon invasion, Gen MacArthur decided to make the invasion an amphibious assault. Upon their arrival in the theater, the 187th would be made available for an airlanding or paratroop assault in Korea.

This right side view of *Marian* reveals its transitional markings with the original diagonal tail stripes and broad red bands. The nose carries the red/white quartered markings for the 50th TCS, 314th TCG. In addition, the main gear wheel hub caps are painted red. O J Baird

Airborne troops board these C-119s from the 403rd TCG under the watchful eye of a pair of officers in their ¾-ton truck. Behind the troops is C-119C-13-FA, s/n 49-135, with its ferocious face on the clamshell doors. USAF 79638 A C

If there was nose art, then why not tail art? Enterprising troops painted a face on the clamshell doors of this 314th TCG airplane. Note the horizontal stabilizer tip extensions on these aircraft and the retrofitted dorsal fillets on top of the booms that date this photograph to some time after mid-1951. NASM 4A26111

***REAM SUPREME*, C-119C-14-FA s/n 49-144, was being loaded with a special platform that was used to drop the treadway bridge to the 1st Marine Division and the 7th Infantry Division troops who were surrounded at the Chosin Reservoir.** USAF 78487AC

In June the retreating ROK forces had destroyed the Han River bridge at Seoul. A complete pontoon bridge was to have been brought to Korea for the Inchon invasion so that the Han River bridge could be replaced. This bridge had been left behind in Japan and its loss was not discovered until the offloading began at Inchon. The solution was to airlift the bridge in C-119s – the only airplane capable of the airlift. Components of the 50-ton, 740ft long, floating bridge were flown to Kimpo aboard 70 C-119s. It was then trucked to the Seoul Municipal Airport where it was quickly assembled by the combat engineers. On 30 September 1950, 3,034 vehicles crossed the bridge. Gen MacArthur was first to cross the bridge when he symbolically led the offensive northward. His forces not only reached the 38th Parallel but, with approval from President Harry S Truman and the Joint Chiefs of Staff, had moved into North Korea. An operation that had begun as an effort to defend South Korea had now become an attempt also to liberate North Korea.

Airlift Requirements

Gen MacArthur told FEAF that his ground forces would require between 700 and 1,000 tons of airlifted supplies daily for an indefinite period. Hence, Gen Tunner wanted to have the 64 C-119s served by double crews and additional maintenance personnel, thus enabling each aircraft to fly 200 hours per month. However, it was soon found that parts (always to be a chronic problem) and engine shortages would only permit a utilization rate of 100 hours per month. Therefore, on 10 September, Gen Tunner requested an additional 32 C-119s in order to sustain the required operations tempo.

First Paratroop Assault

The shortage of C-119s in the theater led Gen Tunner to make two proposals to the 187th. Either 87 C-119s and 40 C-47s could be used for

Maggie was C-119C-15-FA, s/n 49-158, from the 50th TCS, 314th TCG, carries the squadron insignia over the forward entry door. Seen here is a ¾-ton flightline vehicle painted yellow, and six USAF officers headed out on an R&R adventure with their B-4 bags and summer khakis. The ramp was created by use of pierced steel planking. O J Baird

Paratroops from the 187th RCT exited C-119B-FA, s/n 48-337, flown by the 50th TCS, 314th TCG on a practice mission over Korea. Their equipment was also dropped through the paratainer doors. Remnants of the former diagonal stripes on the fins were replaced by colored fin tops and the split nose markings were added. USAF AF 363-4

By the time this photograph was taken in May 1951, the 314th TCG had adopted the additional lightning bolt for their markings. The lightning bolt was red on this aircraft, for the 50th TCS. Here *Le Audra* is shown with her record of 75 combat sorties. Note the nose markings of the seven league boots and group motto: *Viri Veniente* – Men Will Come. USAF 80079AC

a single drop mission, or all of the C-119s could perform the drop in two days. The 187th opted for the single drop mission. On 18 October, Gen Tunner ordered the 314th TCG's C-119s and the 21st TCS's C-47s down for maintenance.

The take-off was scheduled for dawn on 20 October 1950. The paratroops assigned to the 187th RCT were rousted from bed at midnight and fed a combat breakfast consisting of soggy pancakes and cold coffee. They then assembled around the aircraft and awaited the boarding order. Numerous weather delays due to rain slipped the boarding time to 1100 hours.

The first aircraft took off at noon and headed for the Sukchon-Sunchon drop zone. The airlift force flew out of Kimpo in tight formation with an escort of Fifth Air Force F-51 Mustangs. They flew over the Yellow Sea and turned inland for the drop zone. Gen Tunner, flying alongside the formation served as the airborne mission commander. In another airplane, Gen MacArthur flew to observe the operation. At 1355 hours the airborne force turned on its drop leg. At 1401 hours the paratroops stood up and hooked up. Four minutes later the first stick was dropped on DZ William south of Sukchon. Within one hour, 71 C-119s and 40 C-47s dropped 2,860 paratroops and 301.2 tons of equipment at the two drop zones. High-tension lines missed on the aerial reconnaissance photographs posed a minimal problem since the power had been turned off. In comparison with other combat jumps, the casualties were light – only one paratrooper was killed and another 36 sustained injuries. Brig Gen Frank S Bowen, 187th RCT commander, stated that, 'There has not been a better combat jump.' He did caution that in the future the spacing between the drop airplanes should be increased so that the large 100ft diameter cargo parachutes would not steal the air from each other. With regard to equipment losses, the following statistics apply: 2 out of 12 howitzers, 4 out of 28 jeeps,

Left: *Jo-Jo*, C-119C-13-FA, s/n 49-132, carried her nose art on both sides of the nose. The name *Frances* was painted beneath the cockpit windows. She is shown here taxying out after off-loading supplies that would later be trucked to the front. To the rear is C-119C-14-FA, s/n 49-143. These aircraft served with the 314th TCG. Both flight crews and men from the 6127th Air Terminal Group performed miracles during the 10-day supply lift in May-June 1950. The 1,100 tons of artillery shells delivered daily into two airstrips by the C-46s, C-54s, and C-119s provided the margin for victory against the Chinese at this point during the war. USAF C-1228-3

Below left: *Jo-Jo* displays 77 airland resupply missions and four airborne assaults with numerous air resupply drops for each. The names *Marlie* and *Helen* are applied beneath the cockpit windows. SSgt Jack J Minton was her proud crew chief. USAF

and 2 of 4 ¾-ton trucks were lost. One of the damaged howitzers was repaired in the field. Gen Bowen attributed the materiel losses to the inexperience of his packers. The D-Day commitment for the airdrop included: ¾-ton trucks, 90mm anti-tank weapons, ¼-ton trucks, 105mm Howitzers, M-55 anti-aircraft multiple mounts, ¼-ton trailers, 6,000-lb load-bearing platforms, gasoline, water, 105mm and 90mm ammunition, .30, .45 and .50-caliber ammunition, grenades, 3.5-inch rockets, signal supplies, medical supplies and rations.

The 187th RCT fought throughout the afternoon and night and was able to secure the high ground overlooking the drop zones. At 1000 hours on the second day, 40 C-119s delivered an additional 1,093 paratroopers and 106.8 tons of supplies. Resupply missions were flown during the following two days when an additional 184 tons were dropped in 31 C-119 sorties. During three days of operations the 187th engaged a force of about 6,000 North Korean troops, killed over 2,700 of them, and captured another 3,000. They were less successful in their second objective – that of rescuing American POWs. The North Koreans had moved them northward by train.

Twin Nifties, C-119B-FA, s/n 48-327, was flown by Capt Hank Hoefs and Lt Ora J Baird, of the 50th TCS, 314th TCG. This picture was taken at Ashiya AB, Japan in 1950. O J Baird

C-119C, s/n 49-162, of the 50th TCS, 314th TCG, carried the name *RED-TAIL* and this nose art. A J Reveley via MSgt D W Menard

The 50th TCS Maintenance Officer, Capt Hank Hoefs, took time out from his inspection of Capt Ralph S Saunders' aircraft, C-119C15-FA s/n 49-162 of the 50th TCS, 314th TCG, to pose for this picture. The tailbooms of the early C-119s were inherently weak. The size and shape of the stabilizer tip extensions are evident in this view. See Chapter 3 for another photo of this aircraft.
O J Baird

Hot to Trot was a C-119B-FA, s/n 48-343, assigned to the 62nd TCS, 314th TCG. The aircraft was dropping supplies to UN troops at Chungjiu when this picture was taken in late 1950. Note the steep climbout of the aircraft in the background. USAF +78758AC

On 24 October, Combat Cargo Command aircraft delivered a record 1,182 tons of freight to Pyongyang, marking the largest single-day airlift into any one airfield to date during the Korean War. This record was surpassed on the following day. The C-119 airdrops continued concurrently with the airland resupply efforts.

A group of friendly forces was cut off at Unsan and nine C-119s dropped 28.5 tons of ammunition, fuel, and oil on 26 October. This relief mission allowed the troops to rejoin the main force.

Through the efforts of Combat Cargo Command's airlift, the US Eighth Army was able to advance from the Pusan perimeter to almost the Yalu River along the Chinese border in record time thereby marking this as one of the swiftest advances of any ground force in history. While enemy guerrilla forces erected roadblocks on surface supply lines, their efforts were negated by C-47s and C-46s landing at forward airfields with crucial loads as C-119s dropped supplies from overhead.

One of the lessons learned was that the circular error at the drop zone could be cut almost in half by hanging the C-119s just above the stall. With the nose-high attitude, the cargo was aided by gravity as it exited the aircraft and landed in a smaller area.

The Sukchon-Sunchon drop marked the first combat jump during the Korean War, the first combat jump from C-119 Flying Boxcars, and the first successful combat heavy equipment drop.

Parachute Requirements

The availability of parachutes and equipment in the theater in the quantities required was critical. In addition, there was no adequate supply of parachutes and equipment in the ZI that could be used for replacements. Parachute costs added up in a hurry when one considers that a T-7 personnel chute cost $265 and a large cargo chute cost $2,200. Supply containers cost an additional $120 each.

Senior members of the 2348th Quartermaster Airborne Air Supply & Packaging Detachment (later redesignated the 8081st) were well aware of the costs and availability. On D-Day +1 one officer and 30 men (15 each from the 2348th and a Quartermaster Parachute Maintenance Company) were tasked with recovering parachutes and associated equipment from the Sukchon-Sunchon drop zone. The team was able to recover about 80% of the personnel chutes and most of the cargo chutes. The losses incurred were traceable to a lack of supply discipline on the part of the airborne troops. These personnel had cut up a number of personnel parachutes for souvenirs and to make scarves. In addition, lack of training resulted in the paratroops cutting the tie-down and suspension webbing from the heavy-drop platforms instead of using the quick-release devices provided by the riggers for that purpose. Loss of any portion of the suspension or tie-down system rendered the equipment useless. Subsequently a platoon of 60 men from the 8081st was organized to perform equipment recovery after an airdrop.

Miracle at Chosin

All was quiet as the 1st Marine Division and the US Army's 7th Infantry Division secured positions in the northernmost regions of North Korea. US intelligence and the White House claimed that they would be home for Christmas; however the troops in the field had uneasy feelings because of their personal observations. The Communist Chinese entered the fray early on in the Korean War. Suddenly there was a respite. The Chinese assessed the situation and then attacked at weakest point in the Allied line – the undermanned ROK Army. Combat cargo planes were called in to resupply both ROK and American forces.

Senior General Sung Shin-lun, who had been one of Mao Tse-tung's best field commanders, led the Chinese IX Field Army that consisted of 12 divisions. He had the 79th and 89th Divisions waiting entrenched in the ridges and mountain tops ringing Yudam-ni, along the path of the slowly advancing Marines. Many of the seasoned Chinese troops had 15 years of combat experience and had little respect for America's fighting ability. The Chinese troops were cloaked in white uniforms that were invisible against the new snow. With the eerie wail of their bugles echoing off the mountainsides, the hordes of Chinese descended upon our troops.

The US Eighth Army began to fall back in the face of the advancing Chinese on 26 November 1950. However, Maj Gen Edward M

Above: *California Ferry* was assigned to the *Flying Jennies*, 63rd TCS, 403rd TCG. USAF

Above right: *Ratchet* was C-119C-24-FA, s/n 49-124 assigned to the 314th TCG. The dust churned up on the Korean airfields found its way into every nook and cranny of the C-119s, tripling the workload of the maintenance personnel. This picture dates from January 1951. NASM 4A26112

Below: C-119C-16-FA, s/n 49-176, from the 50th TCS, 314th TCG, returned from a mission with its No 2 engine caged. Presumably the engine was shut down on the return leg when the aircraft was empty. Single-engine performance was not a strong point of the Flying Boxcar. O J Baird

Above: Crewmen from the 64th TCS, 403rd TCG were performing overwing refueling on C-119C-13-FA, s/n 49-128. The dorsal fillets had been retrofitted on this aircraft and served as a billboard to display the *Packet Rats* squadron name. To the rear were a VB-17 and an SB-29. V Lunning

Almond, commander of the US Army X Corps expected the Marines to advance as if nothing had happened.

The exhausted Marines had fought heated battles on 27 November. With temperatures at -20°F, the Marines had to keep moving lest the sweat in their shoepacks virtually turned to ice and their fingers stuck to their triggers. The Chinese kept coming all night, hoping to break the Marines' resolve. But, the Marines held out and at dawn they counterattacked. One Chinese platoon suffered 60% losses within 10 minutes, and their survivors fled down the hill. Maj Gen Almond thought this was a minor spoiling action and continued in his belief that his X Corps could advance all the way to the Yalu River.

A force of 20,000 men from the 1st Marine Division and the 7th Infantry Division had secured the Chosen hydroelectric plants and a reservoir in the snow-covered mountains northwest of Hamhung in November 1950. Then six divisions of the Chinese Communist Third Field Army began to sever the escape routes behind the 5th and 7th Regiments of the 1st Marine Division and elements of the Army's 31st and 32nd Regiment, 1st Battalion, 7th Infantry Division. Around 1,100 Army personnel from each regiment had just relieved the Marines on the east side of the Chosin Reservoir when the Chinese attacked. They were overrun and the survivors walked or crawled into the Marine lines around Hagaru-ni. Close air support was provided by United Nations tactical aviation units.

The name *Chosin* resulted from the Japanese maps our forces used. Chosin is Japanese for reservoir. The Korean name for this location is Changjin.

C-47s from the 21st TCS *Kyushu Gypsy* unit flew overtime missions on 28 November to drop 10 tons of ammunition to the Marines at Yudam-ni and 16 tons to the Army at Sinhung-ni. By noon the following day, a request for 400 tons of supplies for the beleaguered troops could not be fulfilled by the *Kyushu Gypsies* because it by far exceeded their capabilities. In fact, the entire FEAF Combat Cargo Command's airdrop system could only handle 70 tons per day. This limitation was the result of the Army's packaging capabilities. The 2348th Quartermaster Airborne Air Supply and Packaging Company at Ashiya augmented its operation with Japanese

Close-up of the right side nose art on *Ready 'n' Waiting* C-119C-22-FA, s/n 51-2561. Her co-pilot was 2Lt H Jordan Jr, and A2C R L Burns the radio operator in 1952/53 when this picture was taken. J Coin via MSgt D W Menard

When the *Red Devils* pranged C-119C-21-FA, s/n 50-166, at Pusan, the enterprising members of the 35th FIS, flying F-80s, commandeered the hulk and converted it into their officers' snack bar. O J Baird

employees so that they could have a 24-hour-a-day operation. A detachment of the 2348th was deployed to Yon-Po Airfield along with a detachment of C-119s. The Quartermaster personnel trained the Marines how to load the C-119s. While FEAF Combat Cargo Command geared up for a 250-ton-per-day capability, a reduced-scale resupply effort was conducted around the Chosin Reservoir. By 3 December, the air-resupply operation got into high gear and the remnants of the Marine and Army units were able to regroup. They were cut off to the front and the rear. However, they were able to smooth out an airstrip that could be used by the 21st TCS's C-47s. The *Gooney Birds* flew 250 sorties and brought in 273.9 tons of supplies and airlifted out 4,689 sick and wounded troops. In addition, the 1st Marine Air Wing flew 56 of the total sorties and the Royal Hellenic Air Force's detachment flew 30 sorties. The 801st Medical Evacuation Squadron provided medical care throughout the operation. Their efforts not only saved lives, but boosted the morale and combat effectiveness of the 1st Marine Division.

One inexperienced rigger made an error in releasing the load and fell out of a C-119 that was flying south of the Chosin Reservoir at an altitude of 8,000ft. He landed in enemy territory, lost his weapons and helmet, but managed to walk out to Yon-Po on the following day. There, he caught the same aircraft for a flight back to Japan. This example only highlighted the requirement for trained personnel.

John J Kustura graduated from Parks College in Cahokia, IL and received a commission as a second lieutenant in the USAF. He arrived in Korea without a job. The requirement for kickers was so great, that he was quickly trained for the job and sent out on combat missions. Because the job was not befitting of an officer, Lt Kustura was subsequently reassigned as an instructor.

Col Hoyt Pringle was Gen Tunner's liaison officer with Maj Gen Almond's X Corps. The situation in the field was deteriorating rapidly. Already 800-1,000 casualties had been sustained by Army and Marine forces in the Chosin Reservoir area. Col Pringle hurriedly scribbled a note to Gen Tunner describing the situation and emphasizing the urgency for immediate aerial resupply. The message arrived at Tunner's headquarters by courier and the General was awakened just past midnight on 1 December. Tunner called his staff together and placed Brig Gen Robert D 'Red' Foreman in charge of the relief operation. Within an hour after Gen Tunner had been awakened, crews were rousted from their quarters and every C-47 in Japan and Korea was ready to go. The C-119s followed. The aircraft were loaded with rations, winter equipment, small arms, and ammunition. Flying Boxcars were in the area by noon, seeking pockets of troops who eagerly awaited their drops.

On the morning of 5 December, Gen Tunner flew to Hagaru-ri in a C-47 to confer with Marine Maj Gen Oliver P Smith. A formation of C-119s appeared overhead and began disgorging their cargo. Parachutes in red, blue, green, yellow, and white identified the contents of the parcel. One parachute failed to open and the load crashed into the compound, causing Gen Smith to complain about the chute failures and the fact that several of his Marines had been injured and killed by these missiles. Gen Tunner apologized but stated that every effort was made to reduce such happenings, and their success rate was quite high. He went on to make an offer for an air evacuation of the encircled Marines. This offer was countered with a request for the continuation of the airdrops and to fly in Marine replacements. Gen Smith intended to fight his way out. Two days later the Marines were able to break out of Hagaru-ri and link up with the 1st Regiment moving in from Koto-ri. The Chinese then blew up the apron to a bridge crossing a 1,500ft-deep Su-dong Gorge, thus cutting off the escape route for the

At least ten C-119s from the 64th TCS, 403rd TCG are lined up on the ramp at Chitose AB, Japan. V Lunning

The 63rd TCS, 403rd TCG flew this delightful damsel, C-119C-23-FA s/n 51-2563, with her red/white nose rings, checkered nose gear strut doors, and tail stripes, in addition to the Insignia Red Arctic markings. The main gear wheel hub caps were also painted red. The aircraft went on to serve with the French in Indochina (See Chapter 8). V Lunning

C-119C-23-FA, s/n 51-2572, carried this large piece of nose art on her right side. The aircraft had Insignia Red Arctic trim and the red/white markings for the 63rd TCS, 403rd TCG. Note how this aircraft had striped nose gear doors and four red arcs on the nosewheel. V Lunning

Marines. Maj Gen Almond believed the only way out for the Marines would be to abandon their equipment and get out on foot. Lt Col John Partridge, commander of the 1st Engineering Battalion, briefed Gen Smith with a most unusual request – he wanted eight spans of an M-2 treadway bridge, complete with plywood planking, to be airdropped to his forces.

A treadway bridge had never before been airdropped. Each span, when packaged for dropping, weighed in at an even two tons and measured 18ft (length) and 7ft 6in (width). At Yon-Po, one of the bridge sections was test-dropped using six G-1 24-ft diameter parachutes. The test was a failure and time was running out. The requested eight spans were loaded onto eight C-119s. However this time a pair of large G-5 48-ft diameter chutes were attached to the ends of the spans. On the morning of 7 December, the eight C-119s departed Yon-Po for Koto-ri. Upon reaching an altitude of 1,000ft, the loads were re-rigged so that about seven feet of the bridge section extended aft of the aircraft to shorten the drop time and reduce the size of the drop zone circular error. The drop zone was approximately 300 yards in length. By shifting the load aft, the drop time was reduced from four seconds to less than two seconds. The eight aircraft let down through the mountains to an altitude of 800ft in a trail formation to drop the bridge spans on an unmarked 300ft-wide drop zone. One span was damaged and another fell into the hands of the enemy. A few more supplies were dropped, and late in the afternoon of 8 December, a 3rd Infantry Division task force from Hungham broke into Koto-ri. After 13 days of isolation the 1st Marine Division and remnants of the 31st and 32nd Infantry Regiments were able to escape across the only bridge in the world to be airdropped. By nightfall, some 265 tons of equipment dropped by almost 14,000 parachutes had been supplied to the troops at Koto-ri. Despite frigid weather, adverse terrain, and combat conditions, the units got out with most of their equipment. These intrepid Marines and soldiers were dubbed the *Chosin Few*.

Senior General Sung Shin-lun's forces suffered massive losses. According to Chinese documents, they suffered 37,500 casualties, including 25,000 dead. Consequently his entire IX Army Group had to be withdrawn from the Chinese order of battle.

During this 13-day operation, 313 C-119 sorties and 37 C-47 sorties had dropped a total of 1,580.3 tons of equipment and supplies to the beleaguered troops on the ground. The breakage rates were high due to the hardness of the frozen ground. While some of the drop zones were missed due to the adverse terrain and some of the supplies were dropped into enemy hands, the air resupply operation was a success. Gen Smith stated, 'Without the extra ammunition many more friendly troops would have been killed. There can be no doubt that the supplies received by this method proved to be the margin necessary to sustain adequately the operations of the division during this period.' For the actions at the Chosin Reservoir between 28 November and 10 December 1950 by the 314th TCG, 21st TCS, and the 801st Medical Air Evacuation Squadron, these units were awarded the Distinguished Unit Citation, the first such USAF awards presented to units in the Korean War.

Major Pullout

After the rescue at the Chosin Reservoir, the entire US Army X Corps began seriously working out the details for a wholesale evacuation. These plans were started on 11 December. This operation could have been accomplished in ten days through water lift, but there was no guarantee that ten days remained before their positions would be overrun by the Chinese. Maj Gen Almond planned on using airlift to its fullest. While the Yon-Po Airfield could be used for much of the traffic, an auxiliary airstrip was made on the beach at Hungnam.

An all-out airlift was begun on 14 December and lasted until 0900 hours on 17 December when the airfield could no longer be held against Chinese infiltrators. Throughout these four days FEAF's Combat Cargo Command flew a 24-hour-a-day operation, during which the planes took off at five-minute intervals. During this time the Command flew 393 sorties from Yon-Po airlifting 3,891 passengers, 228 patients, and 2,088.6 tons of cargo.

Flying conditions were tedious due to the adverse weather. The flight crews were not able to rest and had to assist in loading their airplanes in order to speed their turnarounds. The fatigue and tension actually developed into illnesses that ultimately required the hospitalization of a number of pilots. Ground crews also were put to the test. Four C-119s were grounded at Yon-Po for mechanical reasons. If not repaired, they would have to have been destroyed. One had a broken elevator replaced and another was flown out with an inoperative fuel pump. Two engines were pulled from an airplane at Ashiya and flown into Yon-Po to be installed on a third C-119 so that it could be flown out. The fourth airplane experienced a failed scavenge pump at the last minute and had to be destroyed by the retreating troops.

Carolina Baby was painted on the right side of the nose of C-119B-12-FA, s/n 49-113. The yellow corners and words 'CUT HERE FOR EMERGENCY RESCUE' appeared forward of the nose number. O J Baird

The left side of aircraft 49-113 carried this interesting piece of nose art that roughly translates into *40 Men and 8 Horses*. The ship was assigned to the 61st TCS, 314th TCG. Written in script, the pilot was 1st Lt John C Parish Jr, and the crew chief was SSgt William A Roscoe. O J Baird

US Army X Corps Support

In January 1951, the US Army X Corps located in the central sector of Korea was seriously engaged with the North Korean II and V Corps as they headed toward Wonju, a major road junction city in a mountain basin of the area. The US Army 2nd Division's advance was held up by snow-clogged and guerrilla-infested supply lines. Air support was being provided by planes from the US aircraft carriers *Leyte*, *Philippine Sea*, and *Valley Forge*. Combat Cargo Command's help was needed. The 21st TCS landed their C-47s at Wonju, providing 115 tons of cargo. C-119s from the 314th TCG dropped another 460 tons of supplies to the 2nd Division. Maj Gen Robert B McClure, 2nd Division's commander, commended both cargo units for their help.

During the first 24 days of January, Combat Cargo Command's C-46s, C-47s, and C-54s airlanded 5,041 tons of materiel and men for the Fifth Air Force and another 7,445 tons for the Eighth Army. On their return trips they evacuated 10,489 combat casualties. This quantity of airlanded material was still insufficient to meet the needs of the X Corps, requiring an additional 406 C-119 sorties dropping another 2,007 tons of cargo.

Operation Thunderbolt

Gen Matthew B Ridgway, Eighth Army commander, assigned the American I and IX Corps to Operation *Thunderbolt* on 25 January 1951. This was a reconnaissance mission designed to advance past the Han River. The Fifth Air Force provided close air support. The reconnaissance force moved northward against a Communist screening force provided by two divisions of the Chinese 50th Army. Next Gen Ridgway sent the US Third Army into action and converted the operation into a full-scale attack.

By 13 February the Communist forces had captured Hoengsong and then focused their attention on Chipyong-ni, another mountain-surrounded village northwest of Wonju. Chipyong-ni was then held by elements of the US Army 2nd Infantry Division. Should the town be taken, which was at the hinge between the US IX and X Corps, the entire Eighth Army would be endangered.

The US Army 23rd Infantry Regiment and a French battalion were soon surrounded at Chipyong-ni and the 2nd Division was then given the highest priority in air support. The Fifth Air Force provided fighter support. C-119s from the 314th TCG dropped 87 loads of gasoline, ammunition, and rations.

After the battle, X Corps commander, Maj Gen Edward M Almond, said, 'Our air support and our flying ammunition into the circle of defenses, about half mile in diameter, sustained those men in that position, and they held it.'

Operation Killer

Gen Matthew B Ridgway initiated Operation *Killer* on 21 February 1951, in a move designed to cut off and destroy the enemy troops who had penetrated into South Korea. The United Nations attack caught the Communists off guard and the supporting air strikes dealt heavy losses to the overextended enemy forces. The early spring rains and thawing took their toll and made a mess of lines of communications for the US Army IX and X Corps. The C-119s from the 314th TCG made every effort to support the troops in central Korea. Between 23 and 28 February 256 C-119 sorties were employed to drop 1,358 tons of supplies to the ground forces north of Wonju.

Viva La France

Between 14 and 16 February 1951, the Chinese had a French battalion surrounded in a one square mile area near Chipyong-ni. C-119s from the 314th TCG were subjected to heavy automatic weapons ground fire during these three days as they dropped nearly 400 tons of ammunition and weapons. One night 20 C-119s made deliveries to the French. A weather plane reported the advance of a violent snow storm as the Boxcars approached at dusk, but the crews bore on knowing the urgency of the situation. The weather plane pilot spotted the burning gasoline-soaked rag markers for the drop zone and circled the area with his landing lights on, heedless of the ground fire to assist the C-119s in their mission. The airdrop was a success and the French used the ammunition to fight their way out of the trap with the assistance of an advancing Allied armored column.

Munsan Mayhem

The initial drop of the 187th RCT into Munsan was staged from Taegu, Korea, where the unit was located. The fighters that normally operated out of Taegu were temporarily relocated during the airlift operation. Troops were airlifted from Taegu to Munsan by 80 C-119s and 55 C-46s. All of the 187th's heavy equipment located at Taegu was airlifted back to Ashiya where it was packed and rigged for the airdrop. A last minute requirement for the 1st Battalion necessitated a C-119 to return to Ashiya for three additional radio jeeps that were delivered to Taegu and integrated into the drop sequence. Dust on the airfield forced following aircraft to take off in the blind until they cleared the airfield.

The 187th RCT jumped into Munsan northwest of Seoul on 23 March. During the initial airdrop, 27 jeeps and trailers, a pair of weapons carriers, twelve 75mm howitzers, four 105mm howitzers, two large trailers, and fifteen 600-lb load-bearing platforms were delivered to the 187th. Immediately thereafter, more than 500 tons of ammunition, gasoline, food, and other supplies were parachuted to them. After two days of heated battle with the Chinese and even with daily air resupply, one unit from the 187th had not eaten for 24 hours and was down to a mere three rounds of ammunition per man. An airdrop came just in time to save the unit.

During the initial attack on Munsan, one of the C-119s had made a successful drop and on the return trip an engine caught fire. Five of the crew bailed out, but the pilot and co-pilot were caught in the fireball that destroyed the aircraft. It was believed that the aircraft was struck by ground fire. The crew chief, who had taken his

Skivy Girl was the name applied to the right side of the nose of C-119C-23-FA, s/n 51-2558, from the 50th TCS, 314th TCG. Note the retracted curtains for the aft two cockpit windows, and the yellow life raft package stowed against the window. O J Baird

"Jewel" was the name applied to the right side of C-119B-FA, s/n 48-334, from the 65th TCS, 403rd TCG, as she sat on the frosty ramp at K-47. The ship was retrofitted with the dorsal fins and the squadron name *Blue Tail Flies* was applied. V Lunning

dog *Rivets* on every mission, carried the dog in his arms as he jumped. The dog had been promoted through the rank of sergeant, and had even been awarded the Air Medal.

Another C-119 was hit badly during the drop at Munsan and was returning home in formation with smoking, and finally burning, engines. Five of the seven-man crew managed to bail out. A psychological warfare C-47 from the *Kyushu Gypsy* squadron spotted the downed C-119 and proceeded to circle the area broadcasting for the status of the downed crewmen. For three hours the C-47 circled the area until a rescue helicopter made it to the downed personnel. While not saving any critically injured airmen, the *Gooney Bird* was appreciated for its timely morale efforts.

Wear and Tear

During the month of March, Combat Cargo Command dropped more than 2,300 tons of supplies to a large number of units. Some of the drops were made in single or two-ship runs. Most of the units supplied were American; however, ROK and other UN organizations also benefited from the airdrops. Determining the proper drop zone was difficult at best. The crews had to by-pass units that had received a drop on the previous day even though they were adjacent to those who were to receive their drop. This task was particularly difficult when dealing with supply-hungry units, especially from the ROK Army who would lay out the **T** markers whenever they spotted supply planes. In addition, the enemy would attempt to lay out similar panels. The cargo carriers frequently relied on radio communication to verify a drop zone.

The C-119s from the 314th had experienced severe wear and tear since their deployment to FEAF in August 1950. By April 1951, 75 Flying Boxcars were grounded for mechanical reasons. This was to have been a 60-day TDY, but turned into a seven-month visit. On several occasions, engines were reported to have dropped off the C-119s with disastrous results. Severe shortages in engines and spare parts along with the rugged operating conditions led to a major deterioration in the airworthiness of the Flying Boxcars that regularly flew in an over-grossed condition. The airplanes were grounded while the mechanics and other specialists from throughout Combat Cargo Command worked on them. Of particular concern were the propellers. The airdrop mission was temporarily turned over to the 437th TCG's C-46s. On 23 April the C-119s had been refurbished and placed back on flying status.

High-Altitude Drop

During the latter part of May 1951, heavy equipment drops were assigned to the 314th TCG. On 24 May, they dropped 38 tons at Sango-ri. The following day they dropped 150 tons to the 187th RCT and 2nd Infantry Division at Ua-Yong-ni. During the next three days the C-119s dropped 100 additional tons to ROK forces at Kap-Tun-ni and Sanggang-ni.

Eight C-119s made one of the highest altitude drops near a 5,400ft mountain top. Under the command of Col William H Delacy, the Boxcars circled the mountain for over an hour as US fighter bombers struck the enemy positions with napalm, fragmentation bombs, and rockets. A total of 35 tons of ammunition and supplies was dropped. According to Col Delacy, 'We worked our way through low hanging clouds and heavy smoke from the napalm and got 100% results from our drop.'

More that 500 tons of supplies were dropped on 31 May and 1 June. The recipients were the 1st Marine Division, 7th US Division, and the 2nd ROK Division near Chunchon and Chang-ni. Engineers were building a new airstrip. Despite heavy enemy ground fire and dangerous mountainous terrain coupled with poor visibility from low hanging clouds, the drops were completed.

Operation *Ripper*

Brig Gen John P Henebry had taken over command of the 315th Air Division from Gen Tunner on 8 February 1951. Gen Henebry looked forward to an airborne operation from the day he assumed command. The 187th Regimental Combat Team was being readied for a jump into Chunchon, when, on 21 March, the 1st Cavalry's armored columns drove into the city without much difficulty. The US forces in Chunchon were a mere eight miles from the 38th Parallel.

On 21 March, the 187th RCT had been staged at Taegu along with 80 C-119s from the 314th TCG awaiting a drop into Chunchon. With the city's capture, the mission was scrubbed. However, Gen Ridgway envisioned expanding Operation *Ripper*. The Communist forces had withdrawn from Seoul and Gen Ridgway wanted to pursue them with the US Army I Corps attacking at the Imjin River. Then he wanted the 187th to jump into Munsan-ni, a village lying across the Seoul-Kaesong highway, so that they could trap the fleeing enemy forces on the morning of 23 March.

This new mission was named Operation *Tomahawk*. Reconnaissance and intelligence assessment showed that approximately 12,000 North Korean troops were in the vicinity of Munsan-ni and the mission had to be timed perfectly. To ease their planning, Gen Henebry and the 187th commander, Brig Gen Frank S Bowen, opted to use the same sequence and loading originally planned for the jump at Chunchon. General Bowen wanted his troops on the ground at two drop zones simultaneously.

Two wings of B-26 Invaders began softening up the enemy using airbursting 500-lb bombs and low-level strafing attacks. The 452nd BW sent 32 B-26s to a target just north of Seoul, while the 3rd BW dispatched 24 Invaders to targets near the drop zone. The 35th FG sent 16 F-51 Mustangs as an escort for the troop carrier aircraft. By the end of the day, 72 C-119s had dropped 2,011 paratroops and 204 tons of supplies and equipment, while 48 C-46s dropped an additional 1,436 paratroops and 15.5 tons of signal equipment, ammunition, and food. In the low-level jump, the 187th sustained 84 jump casualties, 40 of which soon returned to duty. Eighteen paratroops were wounded and one man was killed in enemy action. The 314th's

C-119s came through with five aircraft slightly damaged by small arms fire. Another Boxcar apparently sustained greater damage and, on the return trip to Taegu, burst into flames. Five of the crew bailed out; however, the pilot and co-pilot died in the ensuing explosion.

Captured North Korean troops indicated that they had begun to move out as early as 21 March when they had learned that the 187th would be coming. While the Communists employed a number of espionage agents in South Korea, especially around airfields, it is believed that they saw the large concentration of troop carrier aircraft parked at Taegu and sent out a general alarm. The 187th killed approximately 200 enemy troops and captured 87 as a result of their jump. Another 24 troops were captured within the 187th's perimeter. The Communist forces consisted of the second-rate North Korean 19th Division.

Without profitable results, the 187th moved due east to capture the high ground behind the enemy troops that were resisting the US 3rd Division's advance up the road from Seoul to Yonchon. Without a supply line from Seoul, the 187th had to rely on a continued airdrop resupply. On 24 March, support was started with 36 C-119s dropping 40 additional troops and 187.7 tons of supplies. An additional 65.8 tons were dropped by 12 Flying Boxcars on 26 and 27 March. During the last two days of the operation things were pretty grim for the 187th. Many of the troops had not eaten for 36 hours and one artillery battery was down to five rounds of ammunition. General Bowen praised the air support by saying, 'The D+3 supply drop was as near perfect as anyone could imagine. We recovered 95% of the supplies.'

Aching Back Missions

As had been done several times before in Korea, the 502nd Tactical Control Group (TacCG) had built radio stations on mountain tops to give navigational assistance to the UN aircraft plying the skies of Korea during the war. In November 1951, they took a particularly challenging mountain top. The new site was located at 4,900ft atop a mountain in the central sector near the frontline. There were no roads or trails to the top. Loose rock posed an avalanche threat. There were areas with slippery slopes.

Troop carrier C-119s in their vee-of-vees formation fly over C-119C-17-FA, s/n 49-195, from the *Packet Rats*, 65th TCS, 403rd TCG during their going home ceremonies. The ship on the ground carries Insignia Red Arctic markings in addition to the green and white nose and tail trim. Because of difficulties with the vee-of-vees formations, they were discontinued after the Korean War. USAF Museum A1/C-119C/pho/18

C-119B-10-FA, s/n 49-102, operated with the 36th TCS, 314th TCG, seen here with its nose art, Insignia Blue nose with blue stripes aft of the nose and cockpit windows, and on the vertical tail. In addition, the cowl rings are Insignia Yellow. This aircraft has both the horizontal stabilizer tip extensions, and the retrofitted dorsal fins. USAF K6962

Lastly, heavy fighting had taken place and the site was littered with mines left by both sides.

More than 150 Korean *chogie boys*, or bearers, were employed in getting the 502nd TacCG initially established on the peak. This 10-day effort during good weather resulted in numerous injuries, including several broken legs, two broken arms, and a broken back. The *chogie boys* brought radio equipment, generators, and the original tents up the mountain.

The 502nd TacCG approached FEAF Combat Cargo for assistance until adequate roads could be built and normal ground resupply was able to support the unit. The result was the *Aching Back* missions named in honor of the *chogie boys* who still would have been hauling supplies up the mountain.

The three essentials dropped by the C-119s were gasoline, C-rations and water. For the first *Aching Back* mission, six C-119s from the 314th TCG flown by seasoned crews were employed. In place of the traditional T-panels, the members of the 502nd TacCG used smoke pots to mark the drop zone. For security reasons, the smoke pots were lit only after they had been alerted that the C-119s were on their way. The first mission was flown with excellent weather. While the clouds blanketed the valleys below, the peak was miraculously clear. Normally the *Aching Back* crews had to circumnavigate heavy cloud cover to find the peak. The smoke pots marked the drop zone in a small saddle atop the mountain. The pilots of the Flying Boxcars circled the mountain assessing the wind direction and speed to plan their drops. Five-ton loads of supplies rolled out of each aircraft and were lowered on brilliantly colored parachutes. The first mission was so successful that 95% of the cargo fell into the drop zone.

Just because the drop was successful did not mean that the recipients would get all of the loot! During the first night, Turkish soldiers guarding the mountain top heard rattling in the bushes. The next day it was learned that Red guerrilla troops had skulked away with some of the gasoline and rations. After that incident, a security perimeter was established after each drop until the supplies could be relocated into

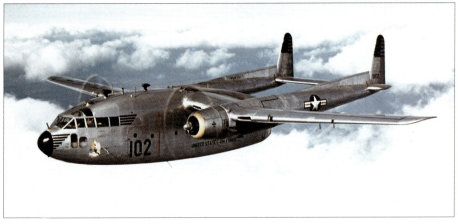

C-119C-16-FA, s/n 49-172, from the 61st TCS, 314th TCG, carries its *Green Hornets* designator on the retrofitted dorsal fins. The aircraft is dropping the last of its paratainers.
USAF 81650 A C

a barbed wire compound. The guards had orders to shoot anyone not authorized to handle the materials.

The supplies sustained more than 100 people on the mountain top including Turkish soldiers, the *chogie boys*, and members of the USAF 605th Tactical Control Squadron.

Dispersal encountered during the first drop was countered in subsequent missions when only half a load was dropped on each pass. Despite all of the adverse conditions, the aircrews consistently dropped 90-95% of their load within the drop zone during their weekly resupply missions.

Bundle recovery for the recipients was no small chore. They constantly had to direct the bundles away from the radio antennas, tents, and buildings. The main Quonset hut was holed several times by errant 55-gallon drums swaying beneath the parachutes.

While the weather was forecast as good when the C-119s departed Ashiya AB, it was not unusual for the mountain peak to become socked in by the time the aircraft arrived in the area. Crews then would circle until they reached a critical fuel state in hopes of being able to drop their load. If the weather did not lift, they would head for the nearest suitable airfield and await a change in the weather – sometimes taking several days.

The only known building to be airdropped was flown in a C-119 during one of the *Aching Back* missions. The building was an outhouse constructed from plywood pallets. It had a door with a window. A requisite crescent moon was applied as was the name *Li'L Abner*.

June Quagmire

The rains in June 1951 turned the Eighth Army's communications lines into quagmires. Airdrops were essential to the support of the US Army I Corps and the ROK Army I Corps. The C-119s had to thread their way through a maze of mountain peaks in order to make their drops on often inadequately marked drop zones. Many of the drops were made at 800ft altitudes. Disaster struck on 3 June when a C-119 formation was searching for a drop zone in the ROK Army 5th Division's area. The Boxcars flew through a barrage of friendly artillery fire resulting in the loss of two aircraft. Consequently, Gen Henebry ordered that the troop carrier aircraft would not enter a drop zone prior to establishing radio contact with a *Mosquito* controller or a tactical air control party on the ground. In addition, he sent a team of officers to the front to brief the ground units on what constituted a drop zone.

Awards

The 314th TCG was awarded the Distinguished Unit Citation for its actions during the period of 28 November to 10 December 1950, and the Republic of Korea Presidential Unit Citation for the period 1 July 1951 to 27 July 1953.

More Boxcars Needed

The USAF supply system could not keep up the demands of the 314th TCG. The in-service rate plummeted and more C-119s were lost. From the beginning, the 314th never possessed enough aircraft to lift the 187th in one drop. To rectify the situation, a major reorganization of the troop carrier units took place in October 1951. Initially the 314th operated with four squadrons of C-119s. The new plan called for two groups with three squadrons each. One squadron from the 314th TCG was returned to the ZI in a paper move; its airplanes remaining for the new group. Also at this time the operating units were redesignated from groups to wings.

The 403rd TCW, an Air Force Reserve unit at Portland, Oregon, was called to active duty on 1 April 1951, and traded their C-46s and C-47s for C-119s. Personnel from the 403rd transferred to Ashiya and initially shared the aircraft with the veteran 314th TCW. The new Table of Organization & Equipment (TO&E) called for three squadrons and 48 aircraft per wing. Col Maurice F Casey Jr (former commander of the 435th TCG, Miami International Airport, Florida), assumed command of the 403rd on 15 May 1952, shortly after their arrival in Japan. His task was formidable.

Of the 71 C-119s in the unit, only 28 were in commission during June; and none were really considered safe for flying. This deplorable state of affairs caused FEAF to demand remedial action. Matters came to a head, and Air Materiel Command prodded delinquent suppliers to provide the necessary spare parts and to expedite deliveries to Japan. From the ZI, Tactical Air Command provided a number of newer and serviceable C-119s to FEAF, thereby permitting the 403rd to return some of their hangar queens to a newly opened repair depot in Birmingham, Alabama. This depot was operated by Hayes Aircraft. Col Casey, on 2 September, announced Operation *Get Ready* that had a goal for having 75% of the wing's aircraft operational. His maintenance personnel came through with a 60.2% in commission rate in September thereby allowing the wing to participate in its first mission.

Operation *Snowball* was flown between 1 and 3 October 1951. During this operation, 315th Air Division C-119s experimentally dropped 55-gallon drums filled with napalm behind enemy lines.

The Reserve 403rd TCW was relieved from federal service on 1 January 1953. At that time they had 46 of the original C-119s that had deployed to Korea in 1950. Problems with the C-119 had led the airplane to be restricted from carrying passengers and only permitted to perform cargo drops and the carriage of paratroopers. The 403rd TCW was replaced by the 483rd TCW that benefited from the improved logistics system. The 483rd TCW received its initial allocation of 96 replacement C-119s in April 1953. As a result of the improved logistics system, the 483rd was able to attain a 67.2% in-commission rate during the first half of 1953, and by June, this had risen to 78.8%.

Operation *Feint*

Maj Gen Trapnell was reassigned to French Indochina as Commander of the US Military Advisory and Assistance Group (MAAG) which was helping the French and Vietnamese in building resistance to the ever-growing Viet Minh forces. Brig Gen William C Westmoreland became the new 187th RCT commander. The unit was out of practice in paratroop operations –

not having jumped since before the Kojedo airlift. Retraining was in order.

On the first day, the 315th TCW provided C-46s for a battalion-sized drop. The aircraft arrived the night before and were loaded. Early in the morning the C-46s departed with nearly 1,000 paratroopers. An earlier aircraft had dropped a pathfinder team into a fertile valley. The members of the 187th RCT broke into various groups to work out their particular portion of the exercise. Winds on the second day precluded any jump activity and the planned exercises were canceled. On the third day, C-119s from the 483rd TCW flew a similar mission with a pathfinder and a second battalion-load of paratroops. That afternoon a formation of six C-119s dropped heavy equipment to the troops on the ground. The fourth day brought another battalion of paratroops aboard C-46s, and nine C-119s dropped administrative personnel from the 187th RCT. After completing the training exercises, the members of the 187th were sealed into a barbed wire cantonment for two days. All local personnel had been evacuated from the area and no visitors were allowed. The rumor mill began in earnest – this had all the makings of another major airborne assault.

Neither the men of the 187th RCT nor the aircrews from the 315th TCW knew that this was all part of a joint-service ruse to draw the enemy out into the open where they could be dispatched by strategic bombers and tactical fighters from FEAF and Navy and Marine fighter and fighter-bomber aircraft.

Brig Gen Westmoreland spoke informally to each of his battalions stating that they had been ordered back to Japan for joint training with the 315th AD. Well after dark on the next day, C-46s from the 315th TCW, 483rd TCW C-119s, and a pair of C-124s from the 374th TCW began airlifting the entire 187th RCT back to Japan.

On 15 October 1952, all the elements of a major assault were present. FEAF bombers had hammered the east coast of Korea north of the battle line. This was followed by a naval bombardment from the sea. The 403rd TCW dispatched 32 C-119s from Ashiya without members of the 187th RCT in an airborne feint. The airborne mission commander was Maj Gen McCarty. As the formation approached the battle line at an altitude of 2,000ft, they witnessed fighting on the ground. Controllers from the mobile Radar Bomb Scoring sites ordered a cessation of artillery fire to allow the formation to pass safely. They flew in tight formation as they headed toward Chorwon at a drop altitude of 800ft. Just before the aircraft crossed into enemy territory, the C-119s turned back to land at Taegu. Coupled with this air operation was a simulated amphibious assault made by the 8th Cavalry Regiment at Kojo. When the boats came within 4,000 yards of the beach, they turned back to the troop transports.

When the C-119s landed at Taegu, they were loaded with the remaining 800 paratroops of the 187th RCT for their airlift back to Ashiya. The paratroops were then taken by road to their bases at Beppu and Kumamoto in 50-truck convoys provided by the 483rd Motor Pool Squadron.

The actual results of Operation *Feint* were not publicized. Whether it had an impact on the war is unknown; however it did prove that Combat Cargo had the ability to respond swiftly to the ever-changing requirements.

Hip Pocket

During June 1953, peace negotiations were being conducted at Panmunjom. It became apparent that, even while these negotiations were being conducted, the Communists were planning another all-out offensive. All commanders within the UN Command began to prepare for the worst. On 21 June, Gen Mark W Clark ordered the 315th Air Division to move the 187th Airborne Regimental Combat Team from southern Japan to central Korea. At this time the C-124 Globemaster IIs were grounded and the 315th had to rely on 53 C-46 and 249 C-119 sorties. On 23 June they airlifted the 187th to Korea, moving 3,252 paratroops and 1,770.6 tons of cargo. During the day the flights arrived at Chunchon and at night they came into Seoul Airport with the aid of the ground-control-approach equipment. To further bolster the Eighth Army's forces, the 315th Air Division airlifted the 19th and 34th RCTs of the 24th Infantry Division from central Japan to southern Korea. Faced with bad weather, the flights left Misawa and Tachikawa, flew to Pusan or Taegu, refueled and changed crews at Ashiya, and then returned to reload at Misawa or Tachikawa. Between 28 June and 2 July, the 315th Air Division moved 898 soldiers and 284.2 tons of cargo from Misawa and 3,039 troops and 943.27 tons of cargo from Tachikawa. The forces were in place.

A series of large-scale bombing operations began on 10 July. Bad weather had hampered interdiction attacks, but the UN line held. On 12 July an RF-80 mission found the Communists concentrated along lines held by the US Army IX Corps and the ROK Army's II Corps in the Kumhwa River valley in central Korea. Then, on the night of 13/14 July, Chinese divisions began attacking the right flank of the US IX Corps and initiated an assault that forced the ROK Army II Corps to retreat. Joint air strikes from the Fifth Air Force, Bomber Command, and the Navy's Task Force 77 began extensive operations. By 20 July the UN lines were intact and the crisis had ended. To gain a few miles of territory, the Communists lost more than 72,000 troops – the equivalent of nine divisions from the five armies that were involved in the attack. On 19 July, Gen Mark W Clark was in a position to state that a truce, short of the administrative details, had been reached.

Nocturnal Bogie

One night a bogie was spotted by the ground-based radar in Japan. The aircraft was headed for them out of Korea and a pair of F-94s was launched for an intercept. The lead Starfire locked onto the target with its radar and proceeded to make a visual identification. The ground-controlled-intercept (GCI) controller asked if they had found the target. 'Yup,' came the reply. 'Do you know what it is?' queried the controller. 'Yup,' came the reply again. 'Can you tell us what it is?' asked the controller. 'I don't know if I want to,' responded the F-94 driver. In front of him was a solo C-119, apparently returning from a heavy equipment drop without its clamshell doors. The aft cabin was fully illuminated by the interior lights, and inside a kicker was calmly sweeping out the aircraft.

KOREAN EPILOGUE

It was through the combined efforts of all Allied forces – air, sea, and land that led to the ultimate treaty signing at Panmunjom. The troop carrier units assigned to FEAF played a major role in the outcome of the Korean War, and the C-119 Flying Boxcar pulled its weight – oftentimes over-grossed. The greatest detriment to the C-119 operations was the lack of logistical support. The aircraft, crews, and maintainers proved that they could provide support anywhere in the theater.

This formation of C-119s from the *Green Hornets*, 61st TCS, 314th TCG is over Korea. In the lead is C-119C-14-FA, s/n 49-146. This picture dates from February 1953. USAF 82152 A C

Chapter 8

The French in Indochina

For ten long years, between January 1946 and July 1956, the French fought to regain control of French Indochina after World War Two. Six air transport groups from France's *Armée de l'Air* participated in the operations using a variety of aircraft including: the Douglas C-47, Junkers Ju 52, Nord 2501 Noratlas, and Fairchild C-119. The C-119s served between May 1953 and August 1954.

Services Rendered
The French government came to the United States with a request for C-119s that could fly tanks and heavy equipment into Laos in support of the French Foreign Legion. On 23 April 1953, Secretary of State John Foster Dulles went to the White House to discuss the plan with President Dwight D Eisenhower. It was the belief of the French that having the C-119s would mean the difference between holding or losing Laos. The French had wanted American military crews to operate the airplanes. This was unacceptable to the United States; however an answer lay with Gen Claire Chennault's airline known as Civil Air Transport, or CAT, which was operating in Asia. Brig Gen Chester E McCarty, who had led the 403rd Troop Carrier Wing (TCW) during the Korean War, went on to command the 315th Air Division (Combat Cargo) in Japan between 1953-1954. In addition, he was in charge of USAF airlift operations in support of the French in Indochina, including the massive airdrops at Dien Bien Phu.

With the end of the Korean War in sight, the United States was able to provide the French with some C-119s from the 314th and 403rd TCWs operating out of Japan. In anticipation of this loan, selected crews from the *Anjou*, *Béarn*, and *Franche-Comté* air transport groups in the *Armée de l'Air* began training with the United States Air Force Europe's (USAFE) 317th TCW at Neubiberg, West Germany, in early 1953. After completing training the French returned to Indochina as a new unit known as *Détachement C-119*. The unit was supported by US technicians and advisors from CAT. Operation *Squaw* became the codename for CAT's support of the French in Indochina during 1953. A total of six C-119s were loaned for the operation. The selected CAT crews went to the Philippines for an intensive 72-hour ground school and flight familiarization in the C-119 that was conducted by members of the 483rd TCW. All US markings were replaced by French insignia. In addition to the CAT crews, 18 USAF mechanics in civilian clothes were sent to Indochina to provide ground support. These six Flying Boxcars left Clark AFB in the Philippines on 5 May 1953.

Initial Operations
Initially the *Détachement C-119* was based at Hanoi-Gia Lam, but it was soon learned that the runway was not strong enough to support the heavy aircraft. They moved to Haiphong-Cat Bi that was more suitable for their operations. As part of Operation *Castor*, troops from the Franco-Vietnamese army began to occupy the valley near Dien Bien Phu. The C-119s supported these troops with airdrops of heavy cargo.

French Operations
During Operation *Squaw*, both CAT and French crews flew the C-119s in air resupply missions. The C-119s proved more effective than the C-47s because of their capacity and quick drop capabilities. The French employment of the airplanes was most extravagant. They flew some supplies, but also furniture, ice cream, and champagne. It was soon concluded that the French should not have use of the C-119s on a long-term basis because of their general irresponsibility.

While the French crews were already flying arduous missions dropping cargo over Dien Bien Phu, the French high command gave them an additional and most unusual assignment. The C-119s were to become bombers dropping napalm in support of the *Gascogne* and *Tunisie* bombardment groups operating the Douglas B-26 Invaders. A liaison officer from the USAF arranged for a single C-119 with a French crew to participate in a test drop of napalm on a small village outside of Haiphong. This mission alienated the CAT crews and most of them left Indochina. Operation *Squaw* was terminated on 16 July 1953.

Operation *Squaw II*
The battle for Dien Bien Phu began in earnest when French paratroops occupied the city on 20 November 1953. Large quantities of barbed wire and heavy equipment became a major requirement. In response to the French request for support, the USAF instituted Project *Ironage* on 5 December. This time 12 C-119s would be made available by the 315th AD. Aircraft from the 483rd TCW were flown to Cat Bi where a detachment from the 483rd looked after the C-119s. A provisional maintenance squadron was established at the base. In addition, the 8081st Quartermaster Airborne Supply and Packaging Company sent a detachment to Cat Bi to perform requisite packing, rigging, load-

C-119C-23-FA, s/n 51-2571, taxiing at Cat Bi airfield. The Insignia Red Arctic paint was retained along with the green and white markings of the *Packet Rats*, the 65th TCS, 403rd TCG. USAF

These C-119C-23-FAs were lined up at Cat Bi in the spring of 1954. The first ship was s/n 49-187 from the 403rd TCG, the third and fourth aircraft were s/n 51-2562 and s/n 51-2572, respectively, from the 314th TCG. USAF

C-119C-23-FA, s/n 51-2557, formerly of the *Packet Rats*, was being loaded at Cat Bi in April 1954. USAF

C-119C-22-FA, s/n 51-2536, previously had flown with the *Flying Jennies*, 63rd TCS. 403rd TCG. The hole beneath the cockpit window came from a 37mm round which almost caused the loss of Paul R Holden's arm. USAF

ing, and equipment maintenance to support the French operations. Between 7 and 21 December, the aircraft dropped 1,070 tons of equipment, including 105mm howitzer ammunition, tent stakes, and barbed wire. The C-119 support was scheduled to cease by Christmas, but the Viet Minh committed four divisions to the area and the aircraft remained. By mid-January 1954 the French air resupply operation required 20 C-119 and 50 C-47 sorties per day. By the end of January another 2,500 tons of priority cargo were dropped into Dien Bien Phu. During Operation *Iron Age*, C-119s based at Cat Bi flew 965 sorties and dropped around 5,700 tons of equipment and supplies.

When a requirement for a 17,000-lb bulldozer for the French engineers arose at Dien Bien Phu, French parachute packers at Cat Bi prepared the machine for the drop. Both French aircrews and packers at that base were reasonably fluent in English. As the drop unfolded, the small extraction chute began dragging an almost 9,000ft² main chute from the C-119. While the main chute appeared to open normally, the bulldozer began working its way loose from its rigging after the opening shock of the parachute. The bulldozer nosed over and plunged some 10ft into a rice paddy. The machine was destroyed. It was believed that an error occurred when converting figures from English to metric. Another C-119 with a bulldozer returned to base.

A second attempt was made during which the 5,000-lb blade was dropped as a separate load. The main bulldozer, now weighing a mere 12,000 lb, was strapped to a steel plate with protruding planking to prevent the load from tilting upon landing. In addition, lead weights were added to the underside of the bulldozer to lower its center of gravity. A string of 21 smaller, multi-colored parachutes lowered the bulldozer gently to earth. French paratroopers cheered as the monstrous load floated to the ground. This drop, flown by American crews, was successful. According to Col Maurice F Casey, 483rd TCW commander, this was the heaviest single load ever dropped in the Far East.

By mid-April 1954, the 816th TCS, 483rd TCW, moved to Clark AFB, Philippines, with 15 C-119s, tasked with making six round trips daily to Indochina. The 1,000-mile leg from Clark to Haiphong could be flown in about six hours. At Clark, cargo handling personnel worked double shifts breaking down the loads for separate destinations in Indochina, preparing the documentation, and loading the aircraft.

The French could muster 70 C-47s of their own for the air resupply mission. Insofar as the C-119s were concerned, the French had 22 crews that were trained by the 317th TCW in Europe, but they could find only 10 crews at any one time. Pilot fatigue mounted and once again the French had to request support from CAT. In early January 1954, 21 CAT check pilots were sent to Ashiya AB, Japan for training in the C-119. A contract was signed on 3 March 1954, calling for 24 CAT pilots to fly the 12 C-119s, which were loaned and maintained by the USAF, in French markings, and for the exclusive benefit of the Expeditionary Corps. The CAT crews would be expected to fly all requested logistical support missions at the direction of military authorities, with the exclusion of any combat missions. The dropping of bombs or napalm would never be required. Thus began Operation *Squaw II*. The French had agreed to pay CAT $60 per flying hour and guaranteed at least 60 hours per month. The CAT crews shared an operations building with the French who also flew the C-119s.

Communications was always a problem. The CAT pilots did not speak French and many of the drop zone controllers spoke no English. Consequently, almost half of the supplies were dropped outside of the drop zone, thus providing assistance to the enemy. A solution was at hand when the French-speaking operations manager of CAT, Frank Guberlet, was ordered to the base at Haiphong. Guberlet attended the French operations briefings and provided a translation to the CAT crews. At one point, it was thought that Guberlet would have to fly on the missions to act as an interpreter, but through his briefings and the use of English-speaking drop zone controllers, he was spared the duty. Guberlet also negotiated for improved air support by French F6F Hellcat pilots flying off the French carrier *Arromanches*.

Lt Gen Henri Navarre, newly arrived commander of the French Union Forces, believed that the French should establish an air head deep in the enemy occupied western portion of North Vietnam, and force them to fight in the open. Despite much opposition from Maj Gen René Cogny, commander of the all-French forces in North Vietnam, Brig Gen Jean Dechaux, the commander of the tactical air group known as *Catac Nord*, and Col Jean-Louis Nicot, commanding officer for all air transport in the French Expeditionary Corps, the die was cast. Having been there before, the French selected Dien Bien Phu, a wide flat plain with surrounding hills. He wanted to place troops in the surrounding hills and establish a main base in the valley. The French had left an airfield they had previously constructed in the valley. Col Christian Marie Ferdinand de Croix de Castres was named on-site commander. What Gen Navarre failed to do was take into account the voracity and ingenuity of his enemy. Gen Vo Nguyen Giap ordered his troops to assault the surrounding mountain peaks one at a time. Then his troops dragged anti-aircraft guns to the mountain tops. Resupply was conducted by a marathon line of people-powered carts and bicycles that carried the supplies to the base of the mountains. The civilians carried the ammunition and supplies up the slopes in baskets. Scattered resupply drops to the French fell into the hands of General Giap's troops. The ammunition was hauled up to the mountain peaks and used against the French. With the Communist forces holding the high ground, the end was inevitable.

A pair of C-119s drop supplies to French forces in Indochina. In the foreground is C-119C-17-FA, s/n 49-186, carrying the markings from the *Blue Tail Flies*, 64th TCS, 403rd TCG. The squadron name appears on the dorsal fillet. Blue and white stripes are applied to the fins, nose, and nose gear doors. The cowl rings are blue. A French roundel replaces the USAF star and bar on the booms and wings. Via *Aerospace Historian* Magazine

While the C-119s were employed primarily in support of Dien Bien Phu, they also airlifted supplies to the French garrison at Luang Prabang, and made twice weekly courier missions between Cat Bi and Saigon. While officially denied, USAF aircrews flew C-119s to Dien Bien Phu for the French. Sometimes the crews actually landed there. On 10 March 1954, Maj Thomas Yarbrough flew out of Dien Bien Phu, making him the last USAF pilot to do so. He departed as a heavy artillery barrage began in advance of a major ground assault by the Viet Minh three days later. Major Yarbrough commanded the C-119 detachment at Cat Bi, serving in that capacity between February and May 1954.

Last Stand at Dien Bien Phu

The city of Dien Bien Phu sits in a mountain bowl. Its valley floor is at an altitude of approximately 2,000ft, with the surrounding mountains rising to 6,000ft. Of topographical interest were the 10 conical peaks, resembling huge ant hills, that dotted the area giving the enemy a marked advantage. While the French positions were located in the valley floor, the Communist Viet Minh held the mountains, ringed with anti-aircraft guns. Although the defenders had a number of strongpoints in the hills, they had stripped them of trees to build their fortifications. A C-119 was shot down on 11 March while approaching the airfield. On 13 March 1954, the siege at Dien Bien Phu went full-scale. On the following day, Communist artillery effectively closed the airfield at Dien Bien Phu, destroying seven Grumman F8F Bearcats, two C-47s, one C-119, and two Sikorsky H-19 Chickasaw helicopters that were on the ground. To the northeast of the airfield, strongpoint *Beatrice* fell to the Viet Minh. A reinforcing battalion was dropped into Dien Bien Phu on the following day. By 17 March, two more strongpoints fell. Resupply operations became increasingly more hazardous because the Communists had more than 100 37mm guns in the area. These anti-aircraft guns now controlled the approach to the airfield.

Between 13 March and 7 May 1954, more than 7,000 tons of equipment were dropped to the French garrison at Dien Bien Phu. While 2,000 tons were dropped by the C-47, the remaining 5,000 tons were dropped by the C-119s. CAT crews flew 682 airdrop missions in support of the battle at Dien Bien Phu. It was estimated that the garrison would have run out of supplies by mid-April had it not been for the C-119s.

The French had achieved reasonable results using C-47s to drop napalm on enemy positions and asked the United States if they could use the C-119s for the same purpose. In a desperate attempt to turn the tide of battle, the C-119s were employed as bombers on 23 March. The clamshell doors were removed and the aircraft were loaded with napalm. Six tons of napalm were dropped on the Viet Minh gun emplacements; however the rain-soaked forests refused to burn. One C-119, carrying 4,000 gallons of napalm in 55-gallon drums crashed on take-off from Cat Bi on 23 March.

Seven C-47s were shot down by 27 March, resulting in the French dropping from 8,000ft during the day and 1,500-2,000ft at night. The side cargo doors of the C-47s necessitated numerous passes resulting in greater exposure to ground fire.

The C-119s could drop seven tons in a single pass with near perfect accuracy. Consequently, they were never exposed to the anti-aircraft fire for more than three minutes. It was only during the last week of the battle that they too were forced to higher altitudes. The planes were flown by CAT pilots during the day and French crews at night. Because of the high level of C-47 traffic, the C-119s were limited to two half-hour periods per day over the drop zone. In order to increase the drop altitude from 8,000-10,000ft, retain accuracy, and limit dispersal, the French developed a parachute deployment delay system. A piece of refueling hose hobbled the parachute until the parachute reached a lower altitude. Then, an exploding charge with a time-delay fuse allowed the parachute to deploy. This system was then adopted by members of the 8081st Quartermaster Airborne Supply and Packaging Company at Cat Bi for use on all airdrops during the last two weeks of the campaign. While crews believed that they could place cargo pallets within a 330 square yard area, ground forces could only retrieve about one-third of the loads.

The arrogance, frustration and desperation of Col de Castres were born out in his 4 May 1954 communiqué: 'When the Air Force talks to me about the risks encountered by the aircrews, while every man here faces infinitely larger risks, there cannot be any double standards. Air drops must henceforth begin at 200ft instead of 2,300ft. The considerable intervals between each plane flying night drop mission has ridiculous results. Quantities which are dropped already represent only a fraction of what I request. That situation cannot go on much longer.'

C-119 Losses

Nearly every aircraft showed scars from the battle. One aircraft, flown by Hugh H Hicks, was hit by 37mm fire that shredded the fuselage, punctured both engine nacelles, and caused the loss of aileron trim tab control. He managed to complete the drop and return safely to Cat Bi. In another instance, a C-119 flown by Thomas C Sailer had its tailboom and rudders riddled by 37mm fire and yet managed to return to base.

Capt Paul R Holden, CAT's director of operations, elected to fly in the right seat of C-119C, s/n 51-2536, on 24 April 1954. A new co-pilot, Wallace A Buford occupied the left seat on this mission. Anti-aircraft fire filled the skies as the aircraft approached the drop zone at Dien Bien Phu. The aircraft was bracketed and a 37mm round went through a tailboom without exploding. Another round entered the cockpit at the right side. It exploded, causing damage to the upper part of the cockpit and severely wounded Holden. Buford, a veteran of the Korean War, completed the drop and returned to Cat Bi. French doctors insisted on amputating Holden's arm, but he opted to be evacuated to an American military hospital at Clark AB, Philippines. USAF doctors saved the arm, allowing Holden to return to duty several months later.

During April 1954, the 483rd TCW C-119s supplying Dien Bien Phu flew 477 sorties, during which 19 of the aircraft received flak damage.

Earthquake McGoon – A Legend

James B McGovern Jr, was born in Elizabeth, New Jersey, on 4 February 1922. After graduation from high school he became an aircraft mechanic through schooling at the Casey Jones School of Aeronautics. Later he went to work at the Wright Aircraft Engineering Company in Patterson, New Jersey, where he operated an engine test stand. He enlisted in the Army's Aviation Cadet program, earned his wings and was commissioned. By November 1944, he was flying P-51 Mustangs with the 23rd FG in the China-Burma-India Theater. He bagged a pair of Japanese fighters on 20 January 1945. After the war he remained in China flying C-47s with the 322nd TCS where he gained 475 hours of multi-engine time. McGovern separated from the service on 12 April 1947, and joined CAT as a co-pilot earning $560 per month. In April 1948 he was promoted to captain garnering $850 per month for 60 hours of flying time and an additional $10 per hour for overtime. He generally logged over 100 hours per month; thereby earning in excess of $1,200 per month – not bad for a bachelor in post-war China.

McGovern was 5ft 10in tall and weighed between 225 and 300 lb. Tales of his prowess in drinking, fighting, and womanizing led to him becoming equated with Al Capp's cartoon character *Earthquake McGoon*. He also had a soft side to him – he laughed easily with his friends and was most at ease with children. CAT's Manila station manager, Al Kindt, once published a poem depicting this legendary individual.

> The rumor is growing apace
> Of a behemoth creature who flies in the skies
> With a lecherous smile on his face.
> His three hundred pounds shake the earth when he walks,
> Yet soars with the grace of a loon.
> Through all the Far East the fabulous beast
> Is known as *Earthquake* McGoon.

C-119C-17-FA, s/n 49-186, returned to Cat Bi with severe damage. The right propeller was feathered and the left prop was severely bent.
Via *Aerospace Historian* Magazine

Indolence was McGovern's greatest failing. He dressed in gaudy clothes and flew without the necessary equipment – navigation charts and let-down procedures. He was continuously being written up on his check rides for miraculously finding his airfields without the requisite equipment. While sloppy in his flying procedures, he was not known for shirking responsibility for a worthy cause. He never turned down a dangerous mission. He served as an inspiration to others in his unit with his prowess.

On 4 December 1949, his accident-free luck ran out when he was tasked with flying a deported woman and her child from China. While approaching Kunming he was unable to pick up reliable ADF signals, due to the night-time distortions, and had to alter course for Hainan. The C-47 ran out of gas and he made a forced landing on a sandbar in a river in Kwangsi Province, about 100 miles from Hainan. McGovern was captured by the communists and interned at the Great Asia Hotel in Nanking. On 31 May 1950, a bearded, disheveled, and disgruntled McGovern appeared in Hong Kong. He went home on leave.

Earthquake McGoon returned to Asia in time to participate in Operation *Squaw II*. While outwardly his demeanor had not changed, his stint in a communist prison had matured him. His lackadaisical attitude prevailed, until he was drawn into a conversation about communism and a sober philosopher emerged.

On 6 May 1954, flying with Wallace A Buford, McGovern approached Dien Bien Phu with an artillery piece. They were in *Bird Two* in a flight of six. It was McGovern's 45th mission, and he was determined to make the drop count. As they approached the drop zone flying C-119C, s/n 49-149, a curtain of flak was thrown up around the aircraft. Shrapnel hit the left engine and it shuddered. Instinctively, McGovern feathered the damaged engine. The tail was riddled by enemy fire. McGovern was unable to maintain altitude and had to restart the dead engine. Steve Kusak, in an accompanying C-119, advised McGovern to jump and await a helicopter pickup. McGovern elected to stay with the aircraft so as not have to risk walking out as he had once before. Kusak directed McGovern towards a narrow, winding river where a belly landing might be attempted. On the approach to the river McGovern ran out of altitude and radioed Kusak, 'Looks like this is it, son.' A wingtip caught the ground sending the aircraft into a double flip. The aircraft exploded and McGovern and Buford were lost along with the two French kickers.

The loss of *Earthquake* McGoon shook the CAT crews badly. They talked about a shutdown in protest, but rain canceled the missions for 7 May, and on the 8th, Dien Bien Phu fell, thereby preventing a confrontation between the crews and their management.

EPILOGUE

According to the Fairchild tech rep in the Far East, G T Ewart, the C-119s were subjected to more anti-aircraft fire than had been experienced in Korea. The flak was said to have been as dense as that over the German Ruhr valley during World War Two.

Aircraft s/n 49-184 returned with 60% of the right rudder missing. The left vertical stabilizer was full of holes, as was the right side of the horizontal stabilizer and the entire elevator. In addition, the left boom was riddled.

Aircraft s/n 51-2552 returned with 90% of the left inboard flap shot away. A 36-inch diameter hole was made in the nacelle near the flap. The left oil tank and left main gear tires were hit by flak. The entire left boom was riddled by flak. The left rudder and tab cables were badly damaged. Only two strands of cable were still intact on each cable assembly. One blade on the left propeller was severely damaged.

Of the 35 C-119 Flying Boxcars loaned to the French for their operations in Indochina, remarkably only two were lost to enemy fire. These aircraft, drawn from the US units in Korea, went to Clark AB in the Philippines, where the US national insignia and USAF were painted out and replaced with the French national insignia. The US troop carrier group and squadron markings were retained along with any nose art that was on the airplanes. At the end of their service with the French the C-119s were returned to the US, again through Clark AB.

Of the 35 aircraft to have served with the *Détachement C-119* in Indochina the known serial numbers are given in the table below.

The major complaint of the CAT crews was the complexity of the C-119, insofar as maintenance was concerned. From a flying standpoint, the aircraft could deliver more cargo quicker than any of its predecessors. However, the French were so impressed with the payload and quick on-load/off-load capabilities of the C-119 and its heavy-load drop capability, along with its resiliency to battle damage, that their next venture in a military cargo airplane resulted in the Nord 2501 Noratlas that has a marked resemblance to the venerable Flying Boxcar.

The battle for Dien Bien Phu lasted 170 days – the longest engagement fought by the French Expeditionary Corps in the Far East. The last 57 days were the most furious. By March 1954, the ranks of Col de Castries' grew to some 16,000 men consisting of members of the French Foreign Legion, troops from the French colonies in North Africa, and loyal Vietnamese. At least 2,200 of Col de Castries' troops died during the battle, while Gen Vo Nguyen Giap's force of some 50,000 soldiers suffered around 23,000 casualties and 8,000 dead.

With the withdrawal of the French from Indochina, the country was divided into North and South Vietnam; with the North being controlled by the Communists and the South by a pro-Western government. By 1963 American involvement grew in South Vietnam, leading Soviet Premier Nikita Khruschev to remark to a US official: 'If you want to, go ahead and fight in the jungles of Vietnam…The French fought there for seven years and still had to quit in the end. Perhaps the Americans will be able to stick it out for a little longer, but eventually they will have to quit, too.'

Once again the C-119s would return to the region as described in Chapters 16 and 20.

Fairchild was extremely proud that the C-119s continued to soldier on in Southeast Asia in support of the French at Dien Bien Phu and produced this full-page advertisement in *Aviation Week* Magazine.

Series	Serial	USAF Unit	Name / Remarks
C-119B	49-116	403rd TCG/64th TCS	
C-119B	49-131	403rd TCG	
C-119B	49-137		
C-119B	49-139	314th TCG	
C-119B	49-144	314th TCG/50th TCS	Ream Supreme/TUCSON Chee-Chee
C-119B	49-149	314th TCG/61st TCS	Shot down over Dien Bien Phu on 6 May 1954. Capt James B McGovern, aka *Earthquake* McGoon, and Buford A Wallace killed in crash landing.
C-119B	49-152		
C-119B	49-165		
C-119B	49-183		
C-119B	49-184		Lost 60% of right rudder due to AA fire.
C-119B	49-185	403rd TCG	
C-119B	49-186	403rd TCG/64th TCS	
C-119B	49-187	403rd TCG/64th TCS	
C-119C	51-2536	403rd TCS/63rd TCS	Capt Paul R Holden, CAT director of operations almost lost his right arm due to AA fire on 24 April 1954.
C-119C	51-2537	314th TCG/61st TCS	
C-119C	51-2539	403rd TCG/64th TCS	Oriental Beauty
C-119C	51-2541		
C-119C	51-2543		Kansas City Kitty
C-119C	51-2545	403rd TCG/61st TCS	
C-119C	51-2546		
C-119C	51-2540		
C-119C	51-2552	403rd TCG/64th TCS	Lost 90% or left inboard flap due to AA fire.
C-119C	51-2557	403rd TCG/65th TCS	
C-119C	51-2562	314th TCG	
C-119C	51-2563	403rd TCG/63rd TCS	(Nose art)
C-119C	51-2571	403rd TCG/65th TCS	
C-119C	51-2572	403rd TCG/63rd TCS	Rose Marie
C-119C	51-2573	314th TCG/50th TCS	
C-119C	51-2575	314th TCG/61st TCS	
C-119C	51-2577	314th TCG	

Chapter 9

European Operations

As an outgrowth of the Marshall Plan, the North Atlantic Treaty Organization (NATO) was formed on 4 April 1949. The Brussels Pact, signed on 17 March 1948, stated that if one of the signatories was attacked in Europe the other members would provide all requisite military and other assistance. These signatories were Britain, Belgium, France, Luxembourg, and the Netherlands.

In the United States Senate, the Vandenberg Resolution was agreed to on 11 June 1948. It called for United States participation in regional and other collective security arrangements outside the Western Hemisphere under United Nations auspices and led to talks with European nations for a military defense alliance across the Atlantic Ocean.

Twelve nations met in Washington, DC to sign such a military alliance agreement. They included the signatories of the Brussels Pact and added Canada, Denmark, Iceland, Italy, Norway, Portugal, and the United States. In a Senate vote of 82 to 13, the United States accepted this collective security agreement on 21 July 1949. Ironically a similar concept had been rejected after World War One. Article V of the North Atlantic Treaty stated that attacking one member of the alliance would be perceived as attacking all of them.

Airlift within Europe would become an integral part of NATO operations within the collective bargaining unit. The first USAF C-119 Flying Boxcars to operate in Europe were from the 433rd TCW, a USAF Reserve unit from the Cleveland, OH area that was activated in 1950. They were followed by the Regular Air Force 317th Troop Carrier Wing (TCW) that was reactivated in 1952. Other NATO nations also provided airlift support, many using aircraft obtained from the United States.

60th TCW In Europe

The 60th TCW had operated C-82s in Europe between 1949 and 1951. They gained C-119s in 1951 then C-54s. In 1953 the wing began taking on C-119s that they operated until 1958. Initially based at Rhein-Main AB, the 60th TCW provided airlift for troops and cargo throughout Europe, North Africa, and the Middle East. It also provided training to the 433rd TCW between August 1951 and July 1952, and the 312th TCW from July 1952 through March 1953.

The 60th TCW operated Kaiser-built C-119s. C-119F-KMs had a serial number range of 51-8098 through 51-8168, whereas the C-119G-KMs ranged between 53-8069 and 53-8156. Having aircraft from these two production batches in the same wing caused confusion with similar nose numbers. To solve this problem, the 60th began using smaller nose numbers utilizing the last four digits of the tail number.

Mutual Defense Assistance Act

The Mutual Defense Assistance Act was passed on 21 September 1949. It provided military aid to the NATO allies. Known as the Mutual Defense Assistance Program (MDAP), emphasis was placed on training and the furnishing of equipment. The MDAP remained in existence until 1954 when it was renamed the Military Assistance Program (MAP). For the USAF in particular, that was backed by *America's Arsenal of Democracy*, allied nations were supplied with used aircraft and equipment, and the requisite training for its maintenance and operation. This program permitted the American industry to develop newer weapons systems for the United States while providing continuity of compatibility with its allies.

C-119C, 50-167, was delivered from the factory to the 433rd TCG at Greenville AFB, SC, and served with the wing while on active duty at Rhine-Main AB, West Germany. The natural metal props indicate that the airplane was subject to the prop-crack surveillance program. When the wing was inactivated, the aircraft was turned over to the 314th TCW at Neubiberg AB, West Germany. Subsequently, the aircraft served with the 4750th Air Defense Wing, 3345th Technical Training Wing, 328th Fighter Group, 4900th Air Base Group, 3565th Pilot Training Wing, 4756th Air Defense Fighter Wing, 446th Troop Carrier Wing (AFRES), and was retired to MASDC on 17 February 1966. Via V D Seely

These 433rd TCG C-1119s, including ship 50-121, were taking on a load of French paratroops at Rhein-Main AB, West Germany in 1952. USAF Rhein-Main photo 287.G via C N Valentine

C-119C-20-FA, s/n 50-149, displayed its red and green squadron colors on the nose and tail, red cowl rings. The aircraft was also assigned to the 433rd TCG. C N Valentine

C-119C-20-FA, s/n 50-148, was assigned to the 433rd TCG. The 67th TCS insignia was carried beneath the drop windows. British Ministry of Supply Ref No W1192/6 via C N Valentine

Jayhawker was a C-119C assigned to the 433rd TCG. This view reveals the details of the crew boarding ladder. C N Valentine

Activation of *The Royal Ohio*

Known as *The Royal Ohio* because of the composition mainly of Ohioans, the 433rd TCW with its four squadrons, 67th, 68th, 69th and 70th TCSs, trained at the Cleveland Municipal Airport, OH. On 15 October 1950, the 433rd TCW was activated and deployed to Greenville AFB, SC. Three of the four squadrons were activated and the resources of the 70th TCS were redistributed amongst the activated squadrons. At Greenville, they transitioned into C-119s that began arriving in late November. Training continued until 5 July 1951, and then they redeployed to Germany. Led by a former United Air Lines captain, Col Harry W Hopp, they took the wing to Westover AFB, MA, where they obtained one MATS navigator per aircraft in order to make the Atlantic crossing. Their route took them to Harmon AFB, Newfoundland, Keflavik, Iceland, Bluie West 1, and RAF Burtonwood. For the last leg, they flew in the troop carrier vee-of-vees formation to Rhein-Main AB. Lt Gen Lauris Norstad, Commander of US Air Forces Europe (USAFE), personally greeted

'*KANAKA*' was another 433rd TCG C-119C. It was photographed at Udine, Italy in 1951 during one of their regular deployments with Army forces from West Germany. C N Valentine

The 433rd TCG operated C-119C-21-FA, s/n 50-168. The aircraft carried its red and white squadron colors. Lee Davis

the air echelon of the 433rd TCW upon their arrival. General Norstad was also on hand when the ground echelon of 1,183 officers and airmen arrived at Bremerhaven aboard the SS *General Sturgis*. The 433rd remained at Rhein-Main AB until they were inactivated on 14 July 1952. The motto of the 433rd was, 'If we can't deliver it…you're better off without it.'

Major NATO Exercise

In the fall of 1951, the 433rd along with the 60th participated in a massive NATO exercise. While the 433rd was equipped with C-119s, the 60th continued operating their well-worn C-82s along with some C-119s. Troops from Belgium, Canada, Denmark, France, Great Britain, Iceland, Italy, Luxembourg, the Netherlands, Norway, Portugal, and the United States were involved in this exercise.

Scheduled Cargo

Lt Gen William H Tunner, who had formed the Combat Cargo Command in Japan in order to cope with the Korean Conflict, took over command of USAFE from Lt Gen Norstad in July 1953. In addition to commanding US Air Forces in Europe, the USAFE commander also was responsible for the air forces of the NATO nations. To his dismay, Gen Tunner found that the maintenance and supply of his USAF units and those of the MDAP nations relied upon traditional ground transport lines. The in-commission rate for USAFE tactical aircraft fell to 80%, and as low as 50% in some instances, due to a lack of parts. At one point, this totaled 225 aircraft. Sizing up the situation, Lieutenant General Tunner ordered troop carrier aircraft in the 322nd Air Division (AD) to fill the pipeline with the needed critical spares. By November 1953, he had established the Air Logistics Service that would initially fly 1,000 tons of cargo per month throughout his command. Within a year this figure had risen to 3,600 tons per month.

The Air Logistics Service (ALS) had major trunk lines and feeder lines in its system. Eighty-four per cent of the cargo carried was of a priority nature required to keep the fighter units operational. The other 16% was filler that would take up the remaining capacity of the aircraft. By using the ALS, a saving of $345,000,000 was realized because this amount in added resources at the fighter units was not required to maintain the same level of readiness. In addition, $500,000 per year was saved over the use of ground transportation that exposed the materials to greater damage and pilfering. A new palletized cargo system was developed which greatly reduced the aircraft loading times.

The ALS routes covered 16,000 miles; C-119s operating over these routes covered 260,000 miles per month. They operated 58 flights per week utilizing 18 aircraft per day. Orders would be cut and a C-119 and crew would depart on a two-week circuit of the system. The trunk routes stopped at RAF Burtonwood, England; Chateauroux AB, France; Rhein-Main AB, West Germany; Erding AB, West Germany; Bordeaux AB, France; Madrid, Spain; Nouasseur AB, French Morocco; and Wheelus AB, Libya. Feeder routes covered the area between Rhein-Main and Chateauroux with stops at Hahn, Bitburg, and Landstuhl ABs in West Germany; and Toul-Rosières, Chaumont, and Laon ABs in France. ALS routes were also flown by C-119s in the Belgian and Italian air forces. Later the Norwegians obtained the Flying Boxcars and joined the Air Logistics Service. The MDAP routes ran from the Danish capital Copenhagen; through Amsterdam in Holland; Brussels, Belgium; Chateauroux, France; Rome, Italy; Athens, Greece; and Eskisehir, Turkey. Another MDAP leg operated between the Erding AB in West Germany, and Rome.

Six USAF fighter-bomber wings, a pair of pilotless bomber squadrons, eight fighter-interceptor squadrons, the three C-119 wings, strategic bases in North Africa, the MDAP units of NATO, and the Army Aviation units in West Germany all benefited from the Air Logistics Service.

Prior to the establishment of the ALS, an average of 45 days was required for a unit to obtain requisitioned parts. With the advent of the airlift service the flow time was cut to about 28 days. At the end of the line was Turkey,

This C-119G-36-FA, s/n 53-7845, was assigned to the 22nd AD. Photographed at Traub AB, France in June 1959, the aircraft was taxying past a pair of RAF 2 Sqn Supermarine Swifts. Note the departing FOLLOW ME truck in the background.
MSgt D W Menard

where an average flow time that had been 150 days was reduced to 15-20 days. Priority items that had taken 16 days before the ALS had been initiated was reduced to 6 days.

Air Logistics Service Units

The 60th TCW operated its C-82s until 1953. While some C-119s were in their inventory in 1951, it was not until 1953 that they were solely equipped with this aircraft. The 60th moved from Rhein-Main AB, West Germany, to Dreux AB, France, (38 miles west of Paris) on 15 October 1955. They remained at Dreux until 25 September 1958, when they were inactivated. Two of the 60th TCW's squadrons, the 11th and 12th, were reassigned directly to the 322nd AD upon the inactivation of the wing. The 60th TCW provided training for the 433rd TCW between August 1951 and July 1952. They later provided training to the 317th TCW between July 1952 and March 1953.

The 317th TCW was activated on 14 July 1952, at Rhein-Main AB, West Germany, under the command of Col Lucion N Powell. The component squadrons of the 317th TCW were: 39th, 40th and 41st TCSs. On 17 April 1953, the wing moved to Neubiberg AB, West Germany, where they provided training for the French who would borrow 35 C-119s from Combat Cargo Command in Japan for their operations in French Indochina (see Chapter 8). From 17 April 1957, the 60th operated out of Evreux-Fauville AB, France, until their inactivation on 25 September 1958. The base was located 65 miles northwest of Paris.

The 465th TCW was activated on 25 August 1953, replacing the 313th TCW at Mitchel AFB, NY, and operated in a training status until 2 April 1954, when they took up residence at Toul-Rosières AB, France, under the command of Col Earl W Worley. The component squadrons of the 465th TCW were: 780th, 781st, and 782nd TCSs. They moved to Evreux (later Evreux-Fauville) AB, France, on 23 May 1955. The 465th TCW participated in USAFE operations until their inactivation on 8 July 1957.

MDAP C-119s came from the 20th Transport Squadron, 15th Transport Wing, Royal Belgian Air Force; and 2, 50, and 98 Gruppi (Squadrons), 46ª Aerobrigata, Transport Wing 1, Italian Air Force. In 1957, No 335 Squadron, Royal Belgian Air Force began operations with the Flying Boxcar.

465th TCW Deployment

The aircraft were flown across the Atlantic, while the support personnel and heavy equipment went by sea in November 1953. An advanced party from 465th Maintenance Squadron went to Toul-Rosières AB aboard the USS *Patch*, while the main body sailed aboard the USS *General Bunker*, arriving on 3 April 1954. The media, led by Walter Winchell, stated on a Sunday radio broadcast that the Soviets had predicted that the trans-Atlantic deployment of the 465th TCW would end in disaster with half of the aircraft crashing because of crew inexperience, unreliable aircraft, weather, and the like. What the Soviets had forgotten and what the media may never learn is that most Reservists have prior active duty experience and with minimum effort can be notified for such deployments that are completed with aplomb.

The 465th TCG Headquarters and the 780th TCS were assigned to Toul-Rosières AB, France, while the 781st went to Wiesbaden AB, West Germany. The 782nd TCS was to bed down at Neubiberg AB, West Germany because the French were unable to accommodate the entire wing in such short order. Those stationed at Toul-Rosières AB spent a miserable winter and spring in 1954 living in tents and wading through mud.

Operation *Brown Jug*

In this scenario, the *Blue Forces* had made an amphibious assault and occupied parts of the Island of Zealand in Denmark. Their mission was to capture Copenhagen, 200 miles to the north. The *Orange Forces* made a feeble attempt at defending their positions, while the *Blue Forces* enjoyed air superiority.

For this exercise, 50 C-119s from the 322nd AD staged out of RAF Jever, 20 miles west of Bremerhaven, West Germany. They flew a tight low-level formation out over the North Sea. On board were 1,500 paratroops from the US 11th Airborne Division based at Stuttgart, West Germany. A single C-119 arrived 15 minutes ahead of the main formation. Thirteen men from the 322nd AD Combat Control Team jumped with 300 lb of radar, radio, and other communications equipment. The Combat Control Team set up immediately and began relaying weather, wind, and terrain information to the incoming force. Within minutes the sky was filled with paratroops. This airborne assault sent the *Blue Forces* into a full retreat.

Flood Relief

During early February 1953, Holland was struck by the most disastrous flood in modern history. The worst North Sea storm in 250 years had laid to waste 500,000 acres of farmland. During the second day the Dutch Army, Navy, Government School of Aviation, and KLM Royal Dutch Airlines began rescue operations. On the following day, Allied forces arrived with over 260 aircraft to participate in this humanitarian

Ship 53-7845 was taxying past a C-124 at Traub AB, France in July 1959. Note the down elevator and extended flaps. MSgt D W Menard

operation. C-119s from the 41st TCS, 317th TCW flew in the operations. They dropped numerous sand bags while flying formation with KLM's C-47s. Crews on the ground eagerly awaited the bags so that they could fill them to stem the flooding. In some instances filled sand bags were dropped directly on the dikes, requiring only some rearrangement by the ground parties. Inflated life rafts were also dropped to the stranded people. Parcels of bread were dropped from extremely low altitudes. On 5 February, 1,178 people were rescued. By the end of the operation, 2,200 lives had been saved.

Mid-Air Collision

During the late afternoon of 15 May 1953, a formation of 18 C-119s from the 60th TCG, 10th TCS, based at Rhein-Main, was near the city of Weinheim, some 12 miles from Mannheim while participating in a fly-by for General of the Army Dwight D Eisenhower on his departure as Commander, Supreme Allied Headquarters-Europe (SHAPE). A reporter from the Stars and Stripes newspaper reported the incident. The Flying Boxcars were at an altitude of 5,000ft. A formation of 12 F-84E Thunderjets from the 36th Fighter Bomber Wing, stationed at Bitburg, was flying above the C-119s around 1700 hours. Suddenly one of the F-84s fell out of the formation and headed for the C-119s. The F-84 struck one C-119 head on and careened into a second transport. One of the C-119s crashed into a farmer's field, making a 15ft-deep crater. At least two crewmen who had parachuted from the C-119 were taken to the local hospital at Weinheim for treatment, as was the fighter pilot. At least two of the personnel aboard the transport perished.

This profile shot reveals the markings on C-119-CF-70-FA, s/n 51-8252, assigned to the 47th BG (M) Base Flight at RAF Sculthorpe. This picture was taken at RAF Greenham Common in May 1956. The aircraft displays its black-edged fin stripe and wedges emanating from the 47th BG insignia on the nose. Via MSgt D W Menard

A US Army officer and his jeep driver were in the vicinity and described the event. One formation of C-119s came out of the east and circled to the north, then around to the east. A second formation of C-119s came out of the east and turned south. The flight of jets appeared from the east about 20 seconds later, and circled southwest. It appeared as if the first two echelons of fighters pulled up and over the formation of transports; however the remainder of the F-84s scrambled in all directions. One of the jets hit two C-119s in a cell of three, damaging one and causing another to burst into flames and crash. Plumes of black smoke followed the stricken C-119 and F-84 to the ground. C-119s s/n 51-8235 and 51-8242 were lost. Three of the crew members aboard these aircraft died.

A further consequence of this incident was that the remaining C-119G-FA, s/n 51-8259, returned to Rhein-Main with a square hole aft of the fuselage nose on the left side and ahead of the large drop window, and a rectangular hole beneath the nose number. The blue nose on the C-119 indicated that it was from the 60th TCW, 10th TCS.

Another Major Accident

The 60th TCW experienced another major accident on 11 August 1955, when a pair of C-119s from the 10th TCS collided over West Germany. Two brand new C-119s, s/n 53-3222 and 53-7841, collided while flying formation, resulting in the loss of 66 men – 11 aircrew and 55 Army engineers. As a result of this accident, the Air Force initiated a policy that transport aircraft cannot fly in close formation, except in wartime, unless the passengers are airborne personnel equipped with parachutes.

322nd Air Division (AD)

The 322nd Air Division (Combat Cargo) was activated at Wiesbaden AB, West Germany on 1 March 1954, and relocated to Ramstein AB, West Germany, on 22 March 1954. The headquarters was again moved to Evreux-Fauville AB, France, on 12 August 1955. During this time frame the 322nd AD was assigned to the United States Air Forces in Europe (USAFE). C-119s were assigned to the unit between 1954 and 1958.

The mission of the 322nd AD was to airlift personnel, cargo, and mail within USAFE. With the inception of the intra-theater Air Logistics Service (ALS), instituted by Lt Gen Tunner, the air movement of high priority cargo was assumed by the 322nd AD. Initially these operations were conducted within France and Germany. When MATS withdrew its intra-theater airlift operation in May 1954, the 322nd AD assumed operations in an area exceeding that of the entire United States. The 322nd AD supported numerous humanitarian aid missions to Iran, Morocco, Pakistan, and Turkey, in addition to performing their routine ALS mission. In Project Bali-Hai, the 322nd AD provided airlift of French troops from bases in France to Indochina.

These three C-119CF-70-FAs were assigned to the 47th BG (M). On the left is the nose of s/n 51-8253, showing the scars from its former nose number. In the center is s/n 51-8265. To the right was s/n 51-8247, whit the black-edged white fin stripes and group insignia on the nose. J Therrell

When a medical emergency arose at Chaumont AB, France, there was no time to dispatch a pressurized MC-131 Samaritan to fly the mission. However, a C-119 was pressed into service and an ambulance, replete with patient and medical team, flew the mission. There was sufficient oxygen aboard the aircraft to support the patient during the flight.

The operations tempo for the troop carrier units continued to rise. In addition to flying the ALS routes, they were tasked with providing airlift for paratroop training by the US Seventh Army in Europe, and the British airborne forces in England. To augment the troop carrier units stationed in Europe, C-119s from rotational squadrons deployed from the ZI.

When tactical fighter units deployed to Wheelus AB, Libya for gunnery training, C-119s from the 322nd AD flew spare parts, ammunition, and ground support equipment from the various USAFE bases. As many as 12-15 Flying Boxcars were employed for each fighter deployment. These missions averaged nine hours in length, making for extremely long crew duty days.

Operation Blue Bat
Communist-backed insurrections flourished in Third World countries during the Cold War. Lebanon was just another example during these times. The political instability in the country lead to armed rebellion in May 1958 when well-equipped Muslim rebels took control of much of the country and demanded removal of Camile Chamoun, the Christian President. The situation turned into a stalemate when Chamoun refused to resign. The Iraqi government was overthrown on 14 July, leading President Chamoun to call immediately for military assistance from Britain, France, and the United States. Several months earlier, the United States stated that it would come to the aid of any nation asking for assistance to quell armed aggression. When President Chamoun asked for help, it was readily forthcoming because the United States did not want to lose any Allied nation to Communism. Under the codename Operation Blue Bat, President Dwight D Eisenhower ordered the US Sixth Fleet to land US Marines in Lebanon at 1500 hours the next day.

It must have been quite a spectacle to see the Marines make an amphibious assault on the beaches of Beirut amidst a bevy of bikini-clad swimmers! Shortly thereafter the Marines had secured the Beirut International Airport, and the city on the following day. They met no resistance.

On 15 July, the 322nd AD directed that some C-124s and 32 C-130s from the 317th TCW stationed at Evreux-Fauville AB, France; and 19 C-119s from the 60th TCW based at Dreux AB, France fly to Fürstenfeldbruck and Erding ABs in West Germany. On the following day the began airlifting the US Army's Task Force Alpha, consisting of 1,749 paratroops and their equipment from there to Adana, Turkey. Task Force Alpha was ready to deploy on 17 July. Congestion on the airfield in Beirut kept the troops from arriving until 19 July. Task Force Bravo remained on 24-hour alert in West Germany while the support personnel in Task Force Charlie followed directly behind Task Force Alpha. During this 12-day deployment, aircraft of the 322nd AD flew 418 accident-free sorties.

During the first two weeks of August, aircraft from the 322nd AD airlifted Task Force Delta to the theater. In this deployment, 4,411 support personnel and an Honest John missile battery were brought to Lebanon. At the conclusion of this last major airlift for Operation Blue Bat, the 322nd AD had accrued 13,997 flying hours and airlifted more than 8,200 tons without incident.

Concurrently, TAC deployed F-100 Super Sabres from the ZI, with the initial package arriving in 12½ hours. A TAC reconnaissance wing was also deployed from the ZI. In addition, a pair of ZI-based MATS troop carrier wings equipped with C-130s participated in the airlift.

Operation Blue Bat was concluded on 24 October 1958. Lessons learned during this operation revealed inadequacies in the current battle plans, and paved the way for the Composite Air Strike Force and today's Air Expeditionary Force. Participants in Operation Blue Bat were eligible for the Armed Forces Expeditionary Medal and the units were awarded the Armed Forces Expeditionary Streamer.

End of an Era
Funding became tight and by the end of 1959, USAFE efforts were markedly reduced accordingly. This was the C-119 drawdown schedule in Europe:

Date	Unit	Base
14 Jul 1952	433rd TCW	Rhein-Main AB, West Germany
8 Jul 1957	465th TCW	Evreux-Fauville AB, France
25 Sep 1958	60th TCW	Dreux AB, France
25 Sep 1958	317th TCW	Evreux-Fauville AB, France
8 Jan 1961	322nd AD	Dreux AB, France

OVERVIEW

C-119s from the troop carrier units in Europe performed yeoman service for USAFE's tactical units and other NATO forces, and humanitarian relief missions. Dedicated ground crews and support personnel worked around the clock to keep the aircraft flying. The aircrews made the aircraft perform any time of the day or night, during challenging European weather conditions, all while complying with a myriad of international regulations.

Chapter 10

Zone of Interior C-119 Operations

Tactical Air Command (TAC) had eight troop carrier groups equipped with C-119s within the Zone of Interior (ZI) between 1949 and 1958. To meet the emerging requirements of the Cold War, the USAF underwent numerous organizational changes. It should be noted that during this period there was a transition from group to wing. While the group was the operational unit with its component troop carrier squadrons, the wings came into being during the mid 1950s. This organizational change kept the tactical squadrons under the operational group, and the balance of the wing's organizations provided the requisite administrative and heavy maintenance support.

Tactical Air Command (TAC) had eight troop carrier groups equipped with C-119s within the Zone of Interior (ZI) between 1949 and 1958. These are shown in the table on this page.

64th Troop Carrier Group

During the summer of 1953, the 64th Troop Carrier Group (TCG) transitioned from the C-82 to the C-119. By September, the conversion was complete. The group flew 30 missions during August that year, of which 11 were joint missions with the 82nd Airborne Division. During these joint maneuvers the 64th TCG dropped 5,513 paratroops, bundled supplies, supplies in *parapacks*, and heavy equipment.

Operation *Dogsled* was conducted between 1 July and 7 September 1953, and involved the aerial delivery of equipment and supplies to Thule AB, Greenland. During Operation *Dogsled* the 64th TCG used 12 C-119s to fly 662 sorties and drop over 4,000 tons of material without incurring any losses to equipment or personnel. The unit's efforts garnered them a letter of appreciation from the commander of the 6612th Air Base Group at Thule, with endorsements from the commanders of the Northeast Air Command, TAC, Eighteenth Air Force and the 64th TCW.

Between 1 January and 21 July 1953, the 64th TCG flew 919 sorties, accruing 3,626:30 flying hours. During this period the group transported 3,522 passengers over 1,527,419 passenger miles. A total of 4,692 paratroops were flown 550,271 air miles. In addition, the unit performed 87 heavy equipment drops totaling 286.6 tons; and another 40 tons of cargo were dropped. This was all part of the group's train-

C-119F-36-FA, s/n 52-3137, from the 464th TCG reveals its upper surface markings and Insignia Red Arctic trim as it drones along. F D Horkey

TAC's TCGs equipped with C-119s within the Zone of Interior 1949-1958

Unit	Base	Dates	Remarks
64th TCG	Donaldson AFB, SC	30 Nov 1953 to 21 Jul 1954	Inactivated
313th TCG	Mitchel AFB, NY	1 Feb 1953 to 2 Oct 1953	Moved
	Sewart AFB, TN	2 Oct 1953 to 8 Jun 1955	Inactivated
314th TCG	Smyrna/Sewart AFB, TN	Oct 1949 to 1957	Relocated to Ashiya AB, Japan
316th TCG	Smyrna/Sewart AFB, TN	1952 to 15 Nov 1954	Relocated to Ashiya AB, Japan
443rd TCG	Donaldson AFB, SC	Feb 1952 to 1 Feb 1953	Inactivated
463rd TCG	Memphis Mun Apt, TN	16 Jan 1953 to 24 Aug 1954	Moved
	Ardmore AFB, OK	24 Aug 1954 to 25 Sep 1957	Group inactivated. Wing transitioned to C-123s & C-130s
464th TCG	Lawson AFB, GA	1 Feb 1953-16 Feb 1954	Moved.
	Pope AFB, NC	16 Feb 1954 to 11 Nov 1958	Group inactivated. Wing transitioned into C-123s in 1955.
465th TCG	Donaldson AFB, SC	1 Feb 1953 to Nov 1953	Relocated to Toul/Rosières AB. France

ing and higher headquarters-directed missions during this period.

During TACAIR 54-7, the 64th TCG supported the 464th TCG between 26 and 30 April 1954. The 64th flew 192 sorties, dropped 365.8 tons of heavy equipment. An additional 502.77 tons of cargo and 347 military personnel were also airlifted.

Eighteenth Air Force

Headquarters USAF established the Eighteenth Air Force (Troop Carrier) on 7 March 1951. It was organized and activated at Donaldson AFB, SC on 28 March 1951, and assigned to TAC. Maj Gen Robert W Douglass Jr, was the first commander. It was then redesignated Eighteenth Air Force on 26 June 1951.

The Eighteenth Air Force subsequently gained other combat units in addition to troop carrier wings. Headquarters Eighteenth Air Force was moved to Waco, TX on 1 September 1957, then on 1 January 1958, the Twelfth Air Force absorbed all of the resources of the Eighteenth Air Force.

The table on the following page shows the C-119-equipped troop carrier wings which reported to the Eighteenth Air Force:

314th Troop Carrier Wing

After World War Two, the 314th TCG operated C-47s from Albrook Field and Curundu Heights in the Canal Zone until October 1948. During this period the group was assigned to the Caribbean Air Command. The unit was redes-

C-119-equipped TCWs reporting to the Eighteenth Air Force

Wing	Base	Dates	Remarks
313th TCW	Mitchel AFB, NY	1 Feb to 25 Aug 1953	Inactivated. Replaced by the 465th TCW
314th TCW	Sewart AFB, TN	1 Jun 1951 to 1 Sep 1957	Transferred to Ninth AF
443rd TCW	Donaldson AFB, SC	1 Jun 1951 to 8 Jan 1953	Transferred to MATS
456th TCW	Miami Int'l Apt, FL	1 Dec 1952 to 25 Jul 1953	Relocated to Charleston AFB, SC.
	Charleston AFB, SC	25 Jul 1953 to 10 Nov 1955	Trained Indian AF crews in the C-119 between Aug 1953 and Jan 1954. Attached to 1st AD (Meteorological Survey) SAC 22 Apr 1955 to 26 Mar 1956.
	Shirio AB, Japan	10 Nov 1955 to 10 May 1956	Aircraft and personnel dispersed to other units. Six
	Ardmore AFB, OK	25 May to 9 Jul 1956	aircraft and crews transferred to AF Systems Command.
463rd TCW	Sewart AFB, TN	16 Jan 1956 to 1 Sep 1957	Transitioned to some C-123s in 1956 and C-130s in 1957.
464th TCW	Lawson AFB, GA	1 Feb 1953 to 21 Sep 1953	Began transition into C-123 in 1955. Continued with
	Pope AFB, NC	21 Sep 1953 to 1 Sep 1957	C-119s until 1958.
465th TCW	Mitchel AFB, NY	25 Aug 1953 to 1 Apr 1954	Transferred Twelfth AF and attached to 322nd AD (USAFE) at Toul-Rosières AB, France.

Above: **Paratroops resting in the sun prior to boarding C-119G-1-FA, s/n 52-5899, assigned to the 464th TCG.** F D Horkey

Below: **The paratroops saddled up and headed to the forward door of aircraft s/n 52-5899. The 464th insignia is applied to the left side of the nose. The green trim indicate that the aircraft is assigned to the 778th TCS; however the replacement yellow prop hub came from the 779th TCS. Note how the paratroops blithely walked through the prop arc – truly a safety violation, for one never knows when there is sufficient residual fuel in the cylinders and adequate heat to cause ignition resulting in a snap rotation of the blades!** F D Horkey

ignated the 314th Troop Carrier Wing (Heavy), detached to US Air Forces in Europe (USAFE), and operated C-54 Skymasters during the Berlin Airlift. The unit was detached to USAFE between 1 and 29 July 1948. Its tactical units were the 20th and 334th TCSs. The 314th TCW was assigned to the Airlift Task Force (Provisional) between 29 July and 19 October 1948. The squadrons were replaced by the 50th and 62nd Troop Carrier Squadrons (TCSs) in October 1949. The inactivated 61st TCS was redesignated the 61st Troop Carrier Squadron on 20 September 1949, and activated within the 314th TCG on 17 October 1949. The group was redesignated 314th TCG (Medium), and assigned to the newly formed 314th Troop Carrier Wing (TCW) at Smyrna AFB, GA on 1 November 1948. C-82s entered the unit's inventory at this time.

The 314th TCW replaced its C-82 Packets with C-119B Flying Boxcars during October 1949. The wing had a full schedule the following year while learning to operate and maintain the new aircraft.

C-119s from the 314th TCG dropped 2,014 paratroops from the 82nd Airborne Division during the night of 13 March 1949. This was one of the largest night airdrops in history.

Using innovative techniques, C-119s from the 314th TCG worked in conjunction with the Army's Artillery School at Fort Sill, OK in experiments and exercises for airdropping field artillery pieces. This exercise was successfully completed on 18 March 1950.

Exercise *Swarmer*

A giant joint Army/USAF exercise was conducted over North Carolina, South Carolina, and Virginia between 24 April and 8 May 1950. While the units had trained individually in the past, this was the first time they all participated in the same exercise. In what was named Exercise *Swarmer*, paratroops were dropped to seize an airhead, then expand it to permit transports to land with reinforcing troops. The forces on the ground were to be resupplied by air while surrounded by hostile forces. The exercise called for all-weather capability and assumed air superiority, but not air supremacy.

The reason behind Exercise *Swarmer* was that many people within the Pentagon believed that the only traditional method for attack, through an invasion via beachheads, was now obsolete because of atomic bombs. Those with an air sense, believed that airheads could be chosen with more flexibility than beachheads.

The overall exercise was under the command of Lt Gen Lauris Norstad, USAF Vice Chief of Staff for Operations, while Brig Gen Willard R Wolfinbarger, Tactical Air Division, Continental Air Command Commander, headed the Air Task Force for Exercise *Swarmer*.

C-119s from the 314th TCG dropped some 4,000 paratroops during Exercise *Swarmer*. In addition, they successfully airdropped 105mm artillery pieces for the first time in history.

For the first time, C-119s were employed to bring in 2½-ton 6x6 trucks that were fully loaded. Army personnel were able to drive the trucks off the aircraft and head for the front. Whereas MATS C-47s and C-54s were only capable of carrying jeeps, two of these trucks could be carried in a C-119. Army field commanders were not enamored with having their ground troops unload the aircraft after they landed. This led to the idea of having trained personnel akin to Navy beachmasters be responsible for the unloading of the aircraft. This concept evolved into the aerial port program.

Exercise *Swarmer* proved that troop carrier and strategic air transport elements could work in concert. Each complemented the other with its capabilities. That said, much work was ahead to resolve a number of deficiencies in command and control, and distribution of duties during such joint operations.

Sewart Air Force Base

On 25 March 1950, Smyrna AFB, TN was renamed Sewart AFB in honor of Tennessee-born Maj Allen J Sewart Jr, who was killed in action in the Pacific during World War Two. For the dedication ceremony, C-119s from the 314th TCG performed a flyover.

Smyrna/Sewart AFB remained home for the 314th TCW from 1 November 1948 to about 15 January 1966. The base also was home to the 316th TCW between 4 November 1949 and 15 November 1954.

Korean War Mobilization

While the 314th TCW remained at Sewart AFB, the flying organizations – 314th TCG and its 50th, 61st and 62nd TCS departed for Ashiya AB, Japan on 4 September 1950. The 37th TCS from the 316th TCG joined the 314th TCG at Ashiya on 29 November 1950.

When the 314th TCG was assigned to FEAF Troop Carrier Command it had the strength shown in this table.

Unit	Officers	Airmen
Headquarters	13	28
50th TCS	67	155
61st TCS	67	155
62nd TCS	43	138
37th TCS	43	138
Total	**233**	**614**

Operations of the above units are covered in Chapter 7 describing the Korean War.

C-119G-35-FA, s/n 52-2997, from the 773rd TCS, 463 TCG, appears to have been undergoing part of a fleet campaign propeller inspection program. The dolly holds two props. Note the buckets on the dolly that held the prop hubs. E T Allen

C-119F, s/n 51-8008, from the 773rd TCS, 463 TCG, is undergoing a complete change of the No 1 engine. The mobile crane is used to lift the R-3350 'power egg' from its transportation dolly and swing it into place for installation. E T Allen

314th TCW at Sewart AFB

Throughout the Korean War, the 314th TCW remained at Sewart AFB, TN. While its three squadrons were in Japan, the wing operated with the 36th and 75th TCSs that remained at Sewart AFB during this period. The wing flew a variety of aircraft as it developed new concepts for airborne and airland assault missions.

These aircraft were assigned to the 314th TCW from 1948 and later:

C-82	1948 to 1951	YH-12	1951
C-47	1948 to 1953	H-19	1952 to 1955
CG-15	1949 to 1951	C-46	1952
CG-18	1949 to 1951	L-5	1952 to 1953
C-119	1949 to 1957	L-16	1952 to 1953
C-45	1949 to 1951	L-20	1952 to 1954
	1954 to 1955	H-21	1955 to 1959
TC-46	1950	C-123	1956 to 1957
YC-122	1950 to 1954	C-130	1956 to Present

The 321st TCS was reactivated and assigned to the 314th TCW on 8 June 1955.

Exercise *Southern Pine*

A joint Army/Air Force training maneuver, known as Exercise *Southern Pine*, was conducted in the vicinity of Fort Bragg, NC between 9 July and 27 August 1951. Airlift operations were performed by the Troop Carrier Command (Prov), which had been activated on 1 March 1951, expressly for this exercise.

The 2nd Forward Medical Air Evacuation Flight was assigned to the Eighteenth Air Force and attached to the 314th TCW on 6 July. Command and control for the USAF medical units participating in Exercise *Southern Pine* was provided by the Troop Carrier Medical Group (Prov) which was activated at Laurinburg-Maxton, NC on 3 August. The Troop Carrier Medical Group (Prov) moved to Donaldson AFB, SC on 4 September and was discontinued on 25

C-119G-1-FA, s/n 51-8090, was flown by the 313th TCG, stationed at Sewart AFB, TN. The spaciousness of the cockpit is readily discernible in this view. Via MSgt D W Menard

November 1951. The 1st Aeromedical Group was activated at Donaldson on 26 November 1951, and attached to the 375th TCW; while its operational control remained with the Commanding General, Eighteenth Air Force.

The Air Cargo Supply Squadron (Prov) was organized on 20 July 1951, as an experimental unit to train personnel in aircraft loading techniques for Exercise *Southern Pine*. On 1 November 1951, the unit was redesignated the Aerial Port Operations Squadron (Prov). The unit was attached to the 443rd TCW for control, administration, and logistical support. These predecessors resulted in the activation of the 1st Aerial Port Operations Squadron at Donaldson AFB on 11 January 1952.

Operation *Snowfall*

On 4 December 1951, the Troop Carrier Air Division (Prov) was organized at Mitchel AFB, NY for supervision of Operation *Snowfall* that was a joint Army/Air Force exercise conducted in the Camp Drum area of New York state. C-119s from the 435th and 514th TCWs, along with C-124s from the 62nd TCW airlifted some 10,000 personnel, flew over 4,000 miles, and dropped 6,400 paratroops. Operation *Snowfall* was conducted in January and February 1952.

Operation *Snow Shoe II*

A joint defense exercise, dubbed Operation *Snow Shoe II*, was conducted within Northeast Air Command and Alaska between March and May 1952. C-119s from the 316th and 435th TCWs and C-124s from the 62nd TCW participated in airlifting Army personnel and equipment.

Exercise *Long Horn*

The most extensive post-World War Two Army-Air Force joint maneuver to date, known as Exercise *Long Horn*, was conducted between 25 March and 11 April 1952. The exercise involved the airlift of the 31st Infantry Division from Fort Jackson, SC to Temple, TX. Eight of the troop carrier wings assigned to the Eighteenth Air Force flew 8,941 troops and 523.3 tons of equipment over 269,700 air miles. Upon completion of the maneuver, the division was airlifted to Camp Atterbury, Indiana.

Exercise *Test Drop*

In order to determine if World War Two troop carrier techniques were still applicable in the post-war era, an extensive test program known as Exercise *Test Drop* was conducted between June 1952 and July 1953. Introduction of the C-119 and C-124 prompted the field study that included evaluation of formations, navigational aids, the Joint Operations Center, use of the Chase C-122 Avitruc (forerunner of the Fairchild C-123 Provider), and evaluation of drop techniques. A series of 10 tests was conducted. Evaluation of the results evolved into the Computed Air Release Point (CARP) system of paradropping personnel and equipment. The CARP system was officially adopted by the Eighteenth Air Force on 8 May 1953.

USAFE Support

Between 19 October 1954 and 3 May 1955, the 776th TCS, 464th TCW was deployed to Rhein-Main AB, Germany to support the 322nd AD. They were followed by the 778th TCS that deployed between 25 April and 6 November 1955.

During October 1955, the 62nd TCS deployed 12 C-119s to Dreux AB, France to support USAFE operations for a period of six months. The detachment was under the command of Lt Col William F Kellerher.

FEAF Ferry Operations

During August 1952 crews from both the 62nd and 314th TCWs supported MATS by ferrying C-119s to FEAF for the Korean War.

During May 1953, under Operation *Boxcar*, crews from the 64th and 465th TCWs ferried C-119s to Japan from the ZI and returned war-weary Flying Boxcars from Japan to repair depots within the ZI.

1952-1956
Troop Carrier Support Missions

Operation *Redbird* was conducted between 1 and 31 October 1952, using C-119s from the 514th and 516th TCWs and C-124s from the 62nd TCW. During this operation, the aircraft moved 893,293 lb of cargo and 1,242 personnel when SAC's 55th SRW moved from Ramey AFB, Puerto Rico to Forbes AFB, KS.

These C-119s from the Eighteenth Air Force were engaged in a heavy equipment drop while participating in TACAIR 54-7. Various stages of the extraction process may be seen in this picture. Flying in a tight vee formation, these C-119s are engaged in a heavy equipment drop. C-119C-25-FA, s/n 51-2592, has just disgorged a palletized composite load consisting of a howitzer with a trailer stacked onto it. The sky is filled with pilot and cargo chutes in various stages of deployment. USAF

Another joint Army/Air Force exercise was conducted between 15 January and 4 February 1953 in the Camp Drum area of upstate New York. Dubbed Exercise *Coldspot*, aircraft from the Eighteenth Air Force dropped over 9,000 paratroops and airlifted another 10,931 for the operation.

TACAIR 54-2, named Exercise *Ski Jump*, was conducted between 4 and 26 March 1954. Three C-119s from the 463rd TCW airdropped 30 tons of equipment to the 511th Regimental Combat Team (RCT) of the 11th Airborne Division during their cold weather maneuvers at Camp Hale, CO.

Beginning on 20 April 1954, TACAIR 54-7 opened with C-124s from the 62nd and 64th TCWs airlifting members of the 145th RCT from Alexandria, LA to Pope AFB, NC as a prelude to the Army's Operation *Flashburn* – the Army's first simulated atomic maneuver. All units of the Eighteenth Air Force were committed to TACAIR 54-7 that was designed to test and train its tactical air units in all phases of operations. The exercise included 80 C-124s and 500 C-119s for dropping 9,000 paratroops from the 82nd Airborne Division at Fort Bragg. Crews from the Eighteenth Air Force flew a total of 1,453 aerial resupply and troop carrier sorties.

During Operation *Spearhead*, which was TACAIR 54-8 conducted between 3 and 19 May 1954, 17 C-119s from the 463rd TCW airdropped 99 tons of cargo at Fort Hood to the 1st Armored Division as part of a joint Army/Air Force maneuver.

Operation *Shockwave* was conducted between 2 and 11 December 1954, when C-119s from the 456th and 463rd TCWs airlifted 356 tons of equipment and 2,500 infantrymen from the 296th RCT from Ramey AFB to NAS Roosevelt Roads in Puerto Rico.

During February 1955, four C-119s from the 463rd TCW participated in a series of atomic tests in Nevada during Operation *Teapot*.

Between 5 November-8 December 1955, the 314th TCW participated in Exercise *Sage Brush*, a large Army/Air Force maneuver in Louisiana. The 321st TCS was deployed to England AFB, a TAC base that was home to the 366th TFW. A follow-on operation known as Exercise *Red Arrow* was conducted between 17 and 19 November 1956. C-124s from the 61st TCG airlifted some 14,000 Army troops from Fort Riley, KS to six forward operating locations where C-119s and C-123s continued the lift to areas strategically located around the combat zone.

ALASKAN OPERATIONS

A number of C-82 and C-119 units went TDY to Alaska in support of paratroop training operations. In addition, some units provided combat support to the Alaskan Air Command. Between 1948 and 1950, the 57th Fighter Wing at Elmendorf AFB, had a total of four C-82 troop carrier squadrons provide combat support. Three of the squadrons; the 4th, 7th, and 8th TCSs, came from the 62nd TCG at McChord AFB, WA. The 37th TCS came from the 316th TCG at Greenville AAB, SC, and Smyrna AFB, TN.

Exercise *Warm Wind* was conducted between 27 October and 10 December 1952. C-119s from the 435th TCW, augmented by the 64th, 314th, and 433rd TCWs, accomplished one of the largest peacetime airlifts to date when they flew the entire 503rd RCT to Alaska. During this exercise both airlift and airdrop missions of personnel and equipment were conducted.

TACAIR 55-3 was designated Exercise *Snowbird* and was designed to test the combat capability of troop carrier and airborne units during extremely cold conditions in January 1955. A total of 50 C-124s from the 62nd and 63rd TCWs and 100 C-119s from the 313th, 314th, and 456th TCWs went to Alaska during the dead of winter where they dropped paratroops from the 503rd RCT.

Exercise *Ember Dawn* was conducted in the summer of 1969. C-119s from the 933rd and

These C-119s from the 314th TCG were deployed to England AFB, LA for Operation *Sagebrush*. Paratroops were loaded into the C-119s for an airdrop. Beneath the tail of C-119-36-FA, s/n 53-3215, is an airborne instructor, with the red hat, who was checking the parachute harness on one of the troops. Three USAF flight crew members sit in their blue flight suits that were extant for the period. Behind the crewmen was a pair of clamshell doors from the aircraft in the foreground, that is being rigged for a heavy equipment drop. USAF

The ramp at Elmendorf AFB, AK was packed with 30 Flying Boxcars from the 314th TCG that were participating in Exercise *Snowbird* when photographed on 23 January 1955. The aircraft had brought troops from the 503rd RCT from Fort Campbell, KY for this joint Army/Air Force winter maneuver. USAF JAAFIO-55-18

During Exercise *Snowbird*, this 314th TCG aircraft stopped at Whitehorse, Yukon Territory. Refueling a C-119 in the Arctic was no easy task. Access to the top of the aircraft was gained through the astrodome. The crewman standing on the fuselage is holding a camera. Snow blowers were constantly clearing the airfield.
USAF AACPH-55-12

934th TAG and the 433rd TAW, Air Force Reserve participated.

Potent Lesson

During one of the early deployments to Alaska, a severe lesson in airplane operations was learned. The C-119 was equipped with an oil diluter system for use during extremely low temperatures. Basically, the system introduced aviation gasoline into the oil tanks so as to reduce its viscosity. In practice, this system was rarely used. The severe temperatures encountered in Alaska proved the need for this system; however, it was to be employed at specified intervals. During this deployment five aircraft were lost due to engine failures, these being caused by severe engine overheating. Investigation revealed that when the oil diluter system was not consistently employed, the oil lines tended to coke up because of slow oil movement and the high temperatures encountered during normal engine operation. When the system was needed on this particular mission, the aviation gasoline not only diluted the oil in the tanks; it caused the caked-on oil to break away from their lines and choking the oil flow to the engines, resulting in severe overtemperatures. A directive was issued which required flight crews to use the oil diluter system regularly and the problem was corrected.

Assigned C-119s

The only C-119 unit assigned to Alaskan Air Command was the 5039th Air Transport Squadron (ATS) based at Elmendorf AFB. This unit operated these aircraft between July 1955 and late 1957, when the C-123 was introduced. During the last six months of 1955, a few of the eventual ten C-119s were in the unit. A year of schedule revisions and depot modifications resulted in the first two aircraft arriving in July. Three more came in August and one each in November and December. A shortage of parts and a lack of qualified pilots prevented the C-119s from taking over the combat support role from the venerable C-47.

The 5039th ATS experienced low in-commission and utilization rates of a little more than 100 hours per month in the first six months:

	Jul	Aug	Sep	Oct	Nov	Dec
Aircraft on hand	2	5	5	5	7	7
Hours available	483	1,675	3,300	3,720	4,464	5,173
Hours in-commission	0	787	1,222	1,426	1,375	1,572
Hours flown	23	67	141	128	152	138
In-Commission rate	0	47%	37%	38%	31%	30%
Utilization rate	0	8.7%	11.5%	9.0%	11.0%	8.8%

By 1 March 1956, the entire complement of ten C-119s was in the inventory of the 5039th ATS. With the improvement in the weather, the utilization rate increased and they achieved 338 of the 400-hour objective. As the parts shortages and crew deficiencies were overcome, the in-commission rate rose to 60% and above.

During the second half of 1956, operation of the C-119s was reasonable. These operational statistics reveal the performance of the 3039th ATS between January-June and July-December 1956:

Dates	In-Commission Rate (Average)	Actual Flying Avg per Month	Utilization of Acft Assigned
Jan-Jun	52.00%	276 hours	65 hours
Jul-Dec	47.0%*	310 hours	97 hours

* This reduced figure was due to an extremely poor showing during the month of December.

The 5039th ATS provided logistical support to remote radar sites. In addition, they provided yeoman service in bringing POL to land-locked Sparrevohn. This was one of a few aircraft control and warning stations that could not be supplied by water transportation.

Even though the performance of the C-119 improved in Alaska, it was not the proper cargo airplane for the theater. It was marginal in mountain performance (engine-out) and operation from gravel strips. The first C-123s to replace the C-119s arrived on 27 October 1957.

OVERVIEW

C-119s assigned to units of the Eighteenth Air Force proved their worth in joint exercises with the Army and developing airlift/airdrop techniques for both cargo and personnel. Innovative personnel within the command proved effective methods for such operations in the future.

These four Flying Boxcars were performing a run-up prior to taking off for the Talkeetna area for a mass airdrop during Exercise *Snowbird*.
USAF JAAFIO-55-95

Chapter 11

Miscellaneous USAF Packet & Boxcar Operations

In addition to providing tactical airlift, troop carrier support, and humanitarian effort, C-119 Flying Boxcars continued in operation with the Regular Air Force in the Far East Air Forces long after the Korean War, and served as base flight aircraft with several commands. Examples of these various operations are provided.

HUMANITARIAN AIRLIFT OPERATIONS

Traditionally the military is known for its combat operations; however its training and equipment are also employed for humanitarian missions. Within the Zone of Interior (ZI) or Continental United States (CONUS) these missions may be requested by the governors of states that have been hit by natural disasters. Internationally, requests for humanitarian operations may be asked for by heads of state or come at the direction of the State Department to further American influence in that part of the world. Direct use of humanitarian airlift can reduce strife within a sovereign state, and/or reduce the temptation of a neighboring power to take over the devastated nation.

Both the C-82 Packets and C-119 Flying Boxcars were employed in numerous domestic and international relief efforts. For the period of service for the C-82s and C-119s from the Regular Air Force, Air National Guard, and Air Force Reserve units flew the humanitarian missions shown in the accompanying table above. Such a high proportion of these missions being flown by the C-82s and C-119s is a testament to basic capabilities of the aircraft, and the dedicated maintenance and operational capabilities of the units involved.

Humanitarian Airlift Operations flown by C-82s and C-119s

Location	Period	Total Missions	C-82/C-119 Missions	Percentage
North America	17 Sep 1947 to 2 Mar 1971	47	28	60%
Latin America	16 Jan 1949 to 3 May 1963	18	6	33%
Europe	26 Jun 1948 to Dec 1959	17	10	59%
Africa	Sep 1947 to 1 Mar 1960	9	5	55%
Southwest Asia	Mar 1952 to 19 Dec 1959	10	8	80%
East Asia	Aug 1950 to Sep 1955	7	3	43%
Pacific & Australia	Dec 1951 to 4 Aug 1957	18	6	33%
Total		**126**	**66**	**52%**

C-119G-36-FA, s/n 53-7861, was photographed on landing at Yokota AB, Japan on 17 March 1960. The aircraft was assigned to the 421st TCS, 6102nd ABG. Note the squadron insignia on the vertical tail and the Aussie *Roo* zap on the forward fuselage. T Matsuzaki via D Remington

FAR EAST AIR FORCES

After the Korean War, two C-119-equipped troop carrier wings remained assigned to the 315th Air Division (Combat Cargo). Both the 374th Troop Carrier Wing (TCW) and 483rd TCW were stationed at Tachikawa AB in Japan. The latter had more units assigned/attached than any other wing, as depicted in Appendix 4.

The 483rd TCW provided training and logistical support for the C-119s loaned to *Détachement C-119* from France's *Armée de l'Air* during the battle for Dien Bien Phu (see Chapter 7).

Major Accident

On 30 March 1956, C-119G 53-3150 from the 817th TCS, 483rd TCW, took off from Ashiya AB, Japan on a routine support mission to Kimpo AB (K-9), Korea. The take-off began at 0741 hours. Runway 30 (300° heading) was in use. The 6,000ft long concrete runway had a 100ft long pierced steel planking (PSP) overrun, 10ft of turf, terminating with a fairly steep, relatively smooth undulating slope to the perimeter road 150ft from and 20ft below the end of the overrun. The field elevation is 106ft above mean sea level. The aircraft was equipped with reversible Aeroproducts C1 propellers; however the reversing feature was inactivated at the time of this flight. In fact, the propellers were locked out of reverse for a period of about six months because several uncommanded instances of the propellers going into reverse, including in flight, had occurred.

Weather conditions at the time of take-off

Ceiling	600ft Broken
Visibility	5 Miles
Wind	NNE at 14 Knots
Temperature	50°
Dew Point	50°
Altimeter Setting	3007
Other Weather Conditions	Rain and Ground Fog

Above: **This 483rd TCW C-119 was undergoing an engine change in 1955 at Yokota AB, Japan. Note the scars above the 'U.S. AIR FORCE' from the 'TROOP CARRIER' markings. The main cabin windows are masked over. In addition to the cowl panels, the main gear doors are removed to afford ease of access. An engine specialist is on a stand working within the No 2 nacelle. The three turbosupercharger exhausts reveal that this was an R-3350 engine. Note the ever-present flightline fire bottle. Of special interest are the chalk markings on the two lower Aeroproducts prop blades, both in English and Japanese – 'ENG PICKLED DO NOT MOVE PROP'.** USAF 88710A C

Personnel onboard the aircraft at the time of the accident.

Personnel	Crew Duty	Organizational Assignment
1Lt Robert A Stancliffe	Pilot	315th AD, 483rd TCW, 483rd TCG
Capt Albert H Swanson	Co-pilot	315th AD, 483rd TCW, 483rd TCG
TSgt Bruno J Kaminski	Flight Engineer	315th AD, 483rd TCW, 483rd TCG
A1C Jaye C Colling	Radio Operator	315th AD, 483rd TCW, 483rd TCG
Capt Daniel D Steiker	Passenger	Fifth AF, 6147th TACCG
1Lt Edward G Orgon	Passenger	Fifth AF, 6147th TACCG
A3C James A Bernett	Passenger	315th AD, 7th Aerial Port Sqn

The pilot briefed the crew prior to take-off and included directions on a rejected take-off. Power was applied to the engines and the take-off began normally. At a speed of 70 knots, the right engine torquemeter began fluctuating, then dropped to about two-thirds the normal reading. At this time the pilot elected to abort the take-off with about 3,500ft of runway remaining. He began applying brakes, but there was no discernible slowing of the aircraft. Then the co-pilot began applying brakes to no effect. Next, the pilot attempted to ground loop the aircraft to the right by applying full right rudder and brakes. The aircraft was unresponsive. At approximately 200ft from the end of the runway, the pilot called to the co-pilot to retract the gear. As the aircraft crossed the PSP overrun, the gear began to retract. The nose gear retracted as the aircraft cleared the PSP, the nose settled and contact with the turf caused the nose gear doors to depart. The left main gear retracted and the aircraft dropped on its left side. When the aircraft came stopped 55ft past the overrun and at the nose was just over the lip of the slope, the right gear began to retract.

The aircraft came to rest in a nose-down attitude with the cockpit twisted from the aft cabin. The cockpit crew escaped through the navigator's astrodome, while the passengers egressed through the left troop door. There were no per-

These seven C-119s from the 483rd TCW were photographed on the ramp at Don Muang Airport during Operation *Firm Link* on 15 February 1956. USAF K7346

C-119C-20-FA, s/n 50-155, was assigned to the 21st TCS, 483rd TCW, when photographed at Tachikawa AB, Japan in 1957. The aircraft sports red lightning bolts on the nose and ventral fin. The squadron insignia is applied to the vertical fin. Roger Johnson via MSgt D W Menard

One of several C-82s that were assigned to the All Weather Flying Center based at Clinton County AFB, OH during the mid-1940s. J Vollemeck

The USAF *Thunderbirds* operated C-119F-KM, s/n 51-8146, when photographed in 1956. She was later flown by the USAF Reserves and retired to MASDC. P M Bowers

Of the three C-119s operated by the *Thunderbirds*, only 51-8146 carried the unit paint scheme. A R Krieger via MSgt D W Menard

sonnel injuries; however the aircraft was destroyed at a cost of $593,922.

The DD Form 365F, Weight and Balance Clearance Form, showed the allowable gross weight for the take-off was 68,000 lb, and the allowable load was 16,832 lb. While weight was not a factor in this accident, it may well have led to the new operating limitations published by the 483rd TCW later that year.

New Operating Limitations Published

Safety was a major consideration to the 483rd TCW, and on 7 December 1956, Col Marvin W Heath, wing Director of Operations, issued a letter rescinding the C-119G Allowable Gross Weights published on 5 December 1956, and the 483rd TCW Standard Operating Procedure Number 3. These were replaced by charts and data published in the flight handbook for the C-119G, and safety supplements thereto.

Published data for Normal Limited by Performance Maximum Take-off Gross Weights for the C-119 are displayed below:

	C-119C	C-119F	C-119G
Max take-off weight	66,600 lb	72,000 lb	68,300 lb
Max overload TOW	73,140 lb	77,700 lb	72,700 lb

Utilizing the average temperature and dew point at Tachikawa AB for the past eight years, the 315th Air Division computed new numbers to be used for planning purposes for missions flown from the Islands of Japan and Korea.

For planning purposes, weight limitations for C-119s operating within the 315th AD were divided into these six periods:

Period	Allowable	Gross Weight
January and February	16,000 lb	69,400 lb
March and December	15,700 lb	69,100 lb
April and November	14,600 lb	68,000 lb
May and October	14,400 lb	67,800 lb
June and September	12,200 lb	65,600 lb
July and August	11,100 lb	64,500 lb

This data was utilized by 483rd TCW mission planners for forecasting future unit operations until the C-119s were removed from the inventory in the theater in 1959.

Operation *Firm Link*

As an outgrowth of the Marshal Plan, the North Atlantic Treaty Organization (NATO) was formulated on 4 April 1949. A similar origination was created in Southeast Asia, known as the Southeast Asia Treaty Organization (SEATO). This alliance was organized in 1954 to fill the void of France's departure from what had been French Indochina (see Chapter 8). It was headquartered in Bangkok, Thailand. The alliance consisted of: Australia, Great Britain, France, New Zealand, Pakistan, the Philippines, Thailand and the United States.

SEATO conducted annual maneuvers utilizing forces of member nations for training and as a show of force to deter Communist insurgency in the region. Between 15-18 February 1956, SEATO conducted Operation *Firm Link*. Designed to demonstrate the mobility and effectiveness of SEATO armed forces in the event of an emergency in Southeast Asia. During this show of force, elements of these nations participated: Australia, Great Britain, New Zealand, the Philippines, Thailand.

During Operation *Firm Link*, C-119s and C-124s from the 315th Air Division (Combat Cargo), Far East Air Forces, hauled paratroops and their equipment from Ashiya AB, Japan to Don Muang Airport in Thailand. They brought in everything from vehicles to field kitchens. While on this deployment, the C-119s performed paratroop and heavy equipment drops. Dignitaries from various SEATO nations were seated in a grandstand where they observed the airdrops. One of these individuals was Brig Gen Russell L Waldron, Commander of the 315th Air Division (Combat Cargo).

AIR DEFENSE COMMAND

In addition to the Douglas C-47 Skytrain and Convair T-29/C-131 Samaritan, Air Defense Command (ADC) used a number of C-119s as support aircraft for their fighter interceptor squadrons throughout the CONUS.

ADC units that are known to have operated the C-119 are the 4440th ADG, Langley AFB, VA; 4600th ABW, Peterson AFB, CO; 4750th ADFW, Yuma AFB, AZ; and the 4750th ADF at Tyndall AFB, FL.

ALL WEATHER FLYING CENTER

The All Weather Flying Center (AWFC) was dedicated to researching flight safety in all sorts of meteorological conditions. It developed and tested aircraft and associated equipment under extreme weather conditions. Established at Clinton County AAF, OH in June 1945, under Headquarters Air Technical Service Command, the unit moved to Lockbourne AAF, OH in October 1945. On 9 March 1946 the unit returned to Clinton County AAF (later AFB) where it was operated by the All Weather Flying Division of the Air Materiel Command. With the closure of Clinton County AFB, the AWFC moved to Wright-Patterson AFB, OH in October 1949.

The AWFC developed air traffic control and instrument landing equipment and procedures to permit operations under all types of meteorological conditions. One of their more famous missions was performed under Project *Thunderstorm* in which aircraft penetrated thunderstorms to gather operational data using Northrop P-61 Black Widows and F-15 Reporters. During 1948, daily flights utilizing C-54s were made between Clinton County AFB and Andrews Field, MD. The C-54's cockpit windows were covered with colored plastic and the pilot wore glasses that precluded outside vision, thereby simulating instrument conditions on a daily basis. In addition, a B-29 was employed for cosmic ray research.

The AWFC operated a variety of aircraft, including several C-82s, in the unit's resplendent markings. The C-82s were used for logistical support – hauling radar trailers and prototype electronic equipment to remote sites for AWFC testing. Some of the sites were: Andrews AFB, MD; National Airport, DC; Pinecastle AFB, FL; Selfridge AAFB, MI; and Smoky Hill AFB, KS.

Known C-82s in the AWFC inventory were 44-22968 and 44-22989

STRATEGIC AIR COMMAND

Strategic Air Command (SAC) operated both C-82s and C-119s that were assigned to various bomb groups for logistical support. These aircraft were allocated to the base flight and also served to provide flight time to staff personnel. According to SAC records these aircraft were in service between 1948 and 1952: 1948, 11; 1949, 4; 1950, 4; 1951, 4; 1952, 4.

The larger number of C-82s in SAC's inventory in 1948 may result from the fact that the 7th Geodetic Squadron was assigned to the 55th Strategic Reconnaissance Wing at Ramey AFB, Puerto Rico during this period.

A little-known SAC unit was the East Reconnaissance Group (Provisional) that was employed in the photomapping of Greenland between 25 June 1946 and 27 March 1947. This unit operated one C-82 to haul men and materiel to Ellesmere Island to build a weather station. Using a pair of ski-equipped C-47s and the C-82, the unit delivered 250 tons of cargo within two weeks. These aircraft, crewed by volunteers from Shaw Field, SC, landed on ice close to the shore.

SAC also employed some C-119s during the mid-1950s as base support aircraft for hauling the cantankerous R-4360 engines powering their fleet of Convair B-36 Peacemakers, Boeing B-50 Superfortresses, and Boeing KC-97 Stratofreighters.

During the famous SAC Bombing and Navigation Competitions, the C-119s were employed to haul everything including the kitchen sink. The aircraft brought in tool boxes for the mechanics, spare parts, field kitchens, and the all important motor scooters for local transportation.

In addition, SAC utilized an entire wing of C-119s in Project *Drag Net* (see Chapter 13).

C-119C-15-FA, s/n 49-159, had the dual nose gear retrofitted. Carrying the SAC *Milky Way* band, this aircraft was assigned to the 28th BW, Ellsworth AFB, SD, between 31 August 1952 and December 1957. Fifteenth Air Force Historian

C-119G-84-KM, s/n 53-8072, was assigned to ATC when photographed at Randolph AFB, TX, on 28 September 1955. In lieu of the CQ buzz number, the aircraft carried the last two digits of the tail number on the nose. Note the ATC insignia with RANDOLPH AFB above on the forward fuselage. G S Williams

C-119G-84-KM, s/n 53-8073, was assigned to the 3499th MTD when it was photographed at Chanute AFB, IL, in February 1956. MSgt D W Menard

Peter M Bowers built a replica of the Curtiss Pusher and demonstrated the aircraft at a number of airshows during the late 1950s and early 1960s. On several occasions the aircraft was loaded onto a USAF transport for military airshows around the country. Here it is being loaded on C-119J-84-KM, 51-8140. P M Bowers

AIR TRAINING COMMAND

Air Training Command (ATC) had C-119s assigned to several specialized units. The 3560th Pilot Training Wing, based at Webb AFB, TX used the aircraft to train flight crews. Technical training wings employed the aircraft as instructional airframes for training mechanics.

These ATC units operated the C-82s: the 3345th TTW, Chanute AFB, IL; 3415th TTW, Lowry AFB, CO; 3499th TTW (Mobile), various bases; and the 3750th TTW, Sheppard AFB, TX.

The Air Force Flight Demonstration Team (*Thunderbirds*) briefly operated three different C-119s as a support aircraft. Only one of these Flying Boxcars had the *Thunderbird* paint scheme applied.

AIR SHOW SUPPORT

Two C-82s were known to have served with the name *Nose for News – Packet Press Room*. The Air Force would dispatch the aircraft to various airshows for use by traveling media personnel. Its main deck cabin was outfitted with tables, chairs, lights, and typewriters.

During the 1950s it was not unusual to see a C-119 bring in support personnel and equipment for the stars of the show.

On several occasions famous engineer/author Peter M Bowers had his Curtiss Pusher replica airlifted to various airshows across the country. There, the jaunty and witty aviator would dazzle the audiences and performers alike with his replicated vintage flying machine.

NACA/NASA C-82 Packets

The National Advisory Committee for Aeronautics (NACA)/National Aeronautics and Space Administration (NASA) operated C-82A 44-23056 between 31 August 1947 and 7 February 1961. The aircraft carried NACA/NASA Fleet Number 107. It operated from the NACA/NASA Ames Facility at NAS Moffett, CA. In addition to being used as a utility aircraft, this C-82 flew a limited number of gust load research flights. The aircraft was retired to MASDC at Davis-Monthan AFB, AZ.

In addition, NACA employed several C-82s at their Lewis Research Center in Cleveland, OH during the 1950s. One test program involved full-scale crashworthiness fire investigations on piston-powered aircraft, while the others dealt with the origin and prevention of crash fires in turbojet aircraft.

In the first series of tests, the crashes were designed to simulate a take-off accident in which the aircraft failed to become airborne; struck an embankment, shearing off the propellers and landing gear; striking trees or poles, rupturing fuel tanks, then sliding along the ground to a standstill. In addition to flammability tests, g-force effects on dummies were also tested. Both C-46 and C-82 aircraft were provided by the USAF for these tests. Walter Kidde & Company built a fire suppression system to meet USAF requirements. The system incorporated these features:

- Fuel shut-off valve on each firewall and in the tubing between each carburetor metering section and fuel injection nozzle; and an oil shutoff valve on each firewall.
- A storage and plumbing system in each nacelle for discharging carbon dioxide into the diffuser housing of the engine induction system.
- A storage and plumbing system in each nacelle for spraying a coolant on the hot exhaust collector ring and heat exchangers.
- A switching arrangement for disconnecting the aircraft batteries and generators from the electrical power system.

The second series of tests were designed to simulate either take-off or landing accidents in which there was a high probability of human survival. C-82s were modified with the addition of both J35 and J47 turbojets that were pylon-mounted on a wing. The C-82s were accelerated to a speed of around 90 miles per hour along a 1,700ft runway. A crash abutment at the end of the runway was arranged to rip off the landing gear, while a pair of poles on each side of the wing tore open the fuel tanks containing 1,000 gallons of JP4 jet fuel. The test conclusions were that it was highly improbable that a jet engine would separate and become a fire hazard in any crash that would be survivable for the crew.

OVERVIEW

The size and capabilities permitted use of both the C-82 Packet and C-119 Flying Boxcar in a variety of missions for which they were not originally designed. While necessity is the mother of invention on the part of the operators, it was the basic design of the aircraft that permitted its previous unplanned and varied usage.

In this view, the NACA wing has been removed from the nose and the NASA emblem applied to the forward fuselage, as a result of the organization changing its name. NACA

This rear three quarter view of NASA C-82 reveals the scalloped cheatline, NASA on the tail without the wing, and the NASA 107 registry. NASA

Chapter 12

Military Air Transport Service

Between 1946 and 1957, the Military Air Transport Service (MATS) operated a few C-82s and C-119s in their ancillary services. C-82s were assigned to Air Rescue Service (ARS) and several squadrons within the Airways and Air Communications Service (AACS). C-119s were operated by AACS, a ferrying squadron, and the Air Resupply & Communications Service (AR&CS). Distribution of these aircraft within MATS is contained in the table to the right.

Distribution of C-82s and C-119s within MATS

C-82	1946	1947	1948	1949	1950	1951	1952	1953	1954
ARS		4	6	11	18	18	14		
MATS	1	6	7	16	25	24	22	8	1

C-119	1951	1952	1953	1954	1955	1956	1957
AR&CS		12	12	12	12	12	
MATS	10	7	8	12	12	13	8

AIR RESCUE SERVICE

Between 1947 and 1952, the Air Rescue Service (ARS) employed up to 18 C-82s. During November-December 1946, the aircraft were used on two occasions to transport a Sikorsky R-5 helicopter long distances for their subsequent use in rescue operations.

In January 1949, a severe blizzard paralyzed the central and western states, isolating rural residents and livestock. During Operation *Haylift* and Operation *Snowbound*, ARS C-47s and C-82s dropped 525 cases of C-rations, over 20,000 lb of food, 10,000 lb of coal, and 25,000 lb of cattle feed for the snowbound inhabitants.

One C-82 was assigned to each of these ARS units:

Unit	Base
1st ARS	MacDill AFB, FL
	Albrook AFB, CZ
4th ARS, Flt A	Hamilton AFB, CA
4th ARS, Flt B	March AFB, CA
5th ARS	MacDill AFB, FL
	Westover AFB, MA
6th ARS	Westover AFB, MA
	Pepperell AFB, Newfoundland
7th ARS	Wheelus AB, Libya
9th ARS, Flt D/58th ARS	Wheelus AB, Libya
41st ARS	Hamilton AFB, CA
66th ARS	RAF Manston, England
67th ARS	RAF Sculthorpe
2151st RU	Lowry AFB, CO
2156th TTU	MacDill AFB, FL
	Palm Beach Airport, FL

ARS = Air Rescue Squadron; Flt = Flight; RU = Rescue Unit; TTU = Technical Training Unit

C-82s in Air Rescue Service were found to be generally unreliable and, with only a few aircraft of that type in a given unit, a lack of spares only exacerbated the situation. Hence, these aircraft mainly served in a support role.

Air Rescue Service operated this C-82A, s/n 44-22978. The yellow and black ARS markings are applied to the nose, waist, wingtips, and booms. The buzz number appears both on the nose and under the left wing. A protective boot with streamers is installed over the pitot probe on the nose. The two bungee cords extending from the clamshell doors to the tail were used to hold and subsequently remove the elevator control locks. W J Balogh via MSgt D W Menard

MATS FERRYING SQUADRON

The 1739th Ferrying Squadron was activated on 1 July 1952, as a result of Military Air Transport Service (MATS) General Order 92. The 3075th Aircraft Ferrying Squadron, based at Tinker AFB, Oklahoma, was redesignated the 1739th Ferrying Squadron, 1708th Ferrying Wing, Continental Division, MATS, with this order. In August 1952, the unit relocated to Amarillo AFB, TX, with its cadre of 26 officers and 23 airmen. Within three years, the squadron grew to 117 officers and 135 airmen. While at Amarillo, the 1739th was a tenant on a base controlled by the 3320th Technical Training Wing, Technical Training Air Force, Air Training Command. The 1708th Ferrying Wing was headquartered at Kelly AFB, TX. Also under control of the 1708th were the 1737th Ferrying Squadron at Dover AFB, DL, and the 1738th Ferrying Squadron at Long Beach Municipal Airport, CA. As a division of labor, the 1737th and 1738th squadrons specialized in the movement of single-engined aircraft; whereas the 1739th concentrated on multi-engined aircraft and helicopters, although early in their career they flew all types of aircraft.

Between 1 July 1952 and 31 December 1955, the 1739th Ferrying Squadron had delivered a total of 3,308 aircraft, 979 of which were to foreign destinations. No less than 27 different aircraft types were delivered by the squadron. During 1955, the 1739th delivered a total of 322 C-119s – 150 domestic and 172 foreign. The aircraft were delivered to both USAF and friendly foreign governments throughout the free world. The destinations included: Africa, Alaska, Canada, Central America, Europe, the Far East, Greenland, Iceland, the Middle East,

Assigned to the 5th ARS, C-82A-FA, s/n 44-22982, was photographed on the ramp at MacDill AFB, FL. The entire lower surface of the booms and leading edges of the ventral fins is painted with black anti-corrosion paint. Rescue markings consist of the large black-edged block on the forward fuselage, boom bands, and large panel spanning from the outboard edges of the nacelles across the top of the fuselage. 'RESCUE' is applied on top of the fuselage along with the last three digits of the tail number. A B-29 from the 307th BG is in the hangar. USAF

and South America. In statistical terms, in any given 24-hour period, the 1739th had delivered 1.8 aircraft to domestic destinations, while simultaneously delivering another 0.77 aircraft to foreign destinations. During this time frame, the squadron was led by three commanders – Lt Col Charles R Fitch (28 August 1954 to 4 January 1954), Lt Col Russell Gray (4 January 1954 to 11 March 1955), and Lt Col John K Thompson (11 March 1955 to 31 December 1955).

In order to maintain proficiency in the wide variety of aircraft flown by the unit, an intensive training program was in continuous operation for both pilots and flight engineers. Most crews were checked out in several different aircraft at the same time. In some instances, they were current in as many as eight different types. It was not unusual for a crew to deliver a C-119 to Europe, bring a C-47 back to the ZI, and then deliver a B-29 to another stateside base. While trips of 30-40 days were not uncommon for the squadron crews, an average of 25 days was the norm. Not all of the aircraft were factory- or depot-new. On the contrary, many of the aircraft were being returned to ZI depots for overhaul.

Between July 1952 and July 1955, the 1739th Ferrying Squadron had a perfect safety record. There were; however, several near accidents. For example, on 16 January 1954, Capt James T Beck and his crew, flying a C-119, lost an engine, dropped 9,000ft, but managed to fly on for 6:57 hours and make a safe landing at Kindley AFB, Bermuda. For superior flying skill in averting a major accident, Capt Beck was given an award for safety in military aviation.

Another C-119 lost an engine while over water at night. The crew bailed out and spent the night at sea. The radio operator did not know how to swim but a crew member threw him out of the troop door as the crew exited the airplane. The radio operator was the sole casualty. During the following day, the crew was picked up by a US Navy destroyer.

The 1st ARS, Flight A, operated C-82A, s/n 45-57734, out of Albrook AFB, Canal Zone. This aircraft does not carry the standard ARS black and yellow bands on the nose, waist, booms, and wingtips. However, the identifying markings on the fuselage are in black and yellow. It is interesting to note that the Insignia Red Arctic trim appears on the empennage, less rudders and elevators; and the wingtips appear to be devoid of the red paint. 'USAF' appears under the left wing. Twenty-Third AF Historian

Mission to India

Crew Control assigned the crew; passports and visas were confirmed along with the inevitable shot records. The crew was briefed on the latest procedures and directives as well as foreign NOTAMS (Notice to Airmen). After clearing the squadron and drawing personal equipment, the crew was ready to depart early the next morning. The first leg was to Hagerstown, MD, in order to pick up a new airplane from the factory. Normally the crews would fly commercially, but in this instance, a C-54 being ferried to Germany would provide the airlift.

The flight crew then 'bought' the new C-119 from Fairchild by checking the paperwork and inspecting the aircraft. The following day the aircraft was flown to Dover AFB, DL for its international clearance. Two approaches were flown, one by the pilot and a second by the co-pilot. These were Ground Controlled Approaches (GCAs). At Dover, a MATS navigator and radio operator were added to the crew. In addition, overwater survival gear was placed aboard the aircraft.

The weather was checked and a 1700 hour departure was made. After five hours of flying, Harmon AB, Newfoundland, was reached. There, the weather had deteriorated to a 1,000ft ceiling with three miles of visibility that was further reduced to half a mile in snow showers. Consequently, a GCA was executed. By the time the flight plan was closed, it was 0100 hours. After checking the weather for the next day, the crew turned in for the night.

A 1500 hour departure was planned and the crew had a scheduled wake-up call that allowed them to be at Base Operations by 1300 hours. The weather was studied and departure preparations were made. The ferry tanks were filled along with the main fuel tanks. An oil leak found in the No 1 engine resulted in a 2-hour delay. Once airborne, the route was direct to Prestwick AB, Scotland, via Bluie-West 1 at the southern tip of Greenland and Keflavik AB, Iceland. Shortly after passing BW-1, the Aurora Borealis lit up the sky presenting a scene known only to a few mortals. At the cruising altitude of 9,000ft, the outside air temperature was -15°C (about -5°F). The overwater leg was made in a single 10-hour flight. At Prestwick, Transient Maintenance took 24 hours for a post-flight inspection. Maintenance requirements for the aircraft dictated such an inspection after every 15 hours of flight for the C-119.

An 0900 hour departure was made for Wheelus AB, Libya. There was a brief overwa-

ARS C-82A, s/n 45-57737, as she appeared at an open house at Selfridge AFB, MI in 1950. The aircraft was probably assigned to the 5th ARS at Westover AFB, MA. A jeep and rescue radio trailer are also part of the display. The black and yellow ARS bands appear around the booms. A control lock is installed at each end of the elevator. W J Balogh via MSgt D W Menard

ter leg across the English Channel. France was departed at Marseilles, and once again the C-119 was over water. At Wheelus, the crew took a delay while a leaking hydraulic system was repaired.

At noon on the following day, the C-119 headed across the North African desert, past Cairo, Egypt, and landed at RAF Nicosia, Cyprus.

At 1100 hours on the next day it was off to Dhahran AB, Saudi Arabia. The crew arrived after dark and had to clear customs.

A check of the weather for New Delhi, India, revealed that it was too bad to schedule a departure for the next day. An 0800 departure was made on the following day. After a 6-hour delay New Delhi was reached after some eight hours of flying. The crew landed at Palam AB, India. After clearing customs and the local health authorities, the crew met with personnel from the Indian Air Force. The aircraft was delivered to its final destination within India on the following day where the crew officially 'sold' the aircraft and its paperwork to the customer.

The next morning the crew took a train to New Delhi and made arrangements for a commercial airline flight back to the United States. They traveled home in civilian clothes. Upon arriving back at Amarillo AFB, they were given three days of crew rest before they would be eligible for another trip.

Assigned Aircraft

Four aircraft types (usually a total of six aircraft) were permanently assigned to the the 1739th Ferrying Squadron: 2 B-26 Invaders, 2 C-119 Flying Boxcars, 1 C-47 Skytrain and 1 C-54 Skymaster.

These C-119Gs were 53-8097 and 53-7896 and were replete with a white cap and blue cheatline, a MATS insignia on the booms, and Continental Division band on the fins.

AIRWAYS & COMMUNICATIONS SERVICE

Between 1955 and 1959, the AACS operated a few C-82s and C-119s to support installation, maintenance, and flight checking of equipment employed in navigation aids and communications facilities. The 1800th AACS Wing, Tinker AFB, Oklahoma first requested the C-82s in 1949. Three C-82s were acquired by the wing during the first quarter of 1950. By 1953, the wing had four C-82s. By June 1954, the inventory dropped to two C-82s, and by 1955 none were assigned. Records indicate that four, and possibly as many as six C-119s were in the AACS inventory between 1954 and 1958. The first C-119 came into the inventory during June 1954. It is believed that the C-119 assigned to the 1855th Flight Check Flight was not employed in facilities checking, but rather for mission logistical support only.

The AACS units operated these aircraft from the indicated bases:

Unit	Base	Aircraft
1st AACS I&M Sqn	Tinker AFB, OK	C-82A
3rd MCS (Mobile)	Tinker AFB, OK	C-119C
1881st EIS	Tinker AFB, OK	C-119C
1884th EIS	Erding AB, West Germany	C-119C
1885th FCF	Elmendorf AFB, AK	C-119C

AACS	Airways and Communications Squadron
EIS	Electronics Installation Squadron
FCF	Flight Check Flight
I&M Sqn	Installation & Maintenance Squadron
MCS	Mobile Communications Squadron

The 1st AACS Installation & Maintenance Squadron at Tinker AFB, OK was inactivated on 16 March 1955 and the 1881st AACS Installation & Maintenance Squadron was activated on the same date. The unit was subsequently redesignated the 1881st Installation & Maintenance Group on 15 July 1955, and inactivated on 1 November 1957.

The 156th AACS Squadron (Installation & Maintenance) was organized at Friesing AB, West Germany on 1 June 1948. It was redesignated the 1854th Installation & Maintenance Squadron on 1 October 1948, then the 4th AACS Installation & Maintenance Squadron on 24 June 1950. The squadron moved to Erding AB, West Germany in June 1954, and was redesignated the 1884th AACS Installation & Maintenance Squadron on 4 March 1955. In 1956, the squadron moved to Bordeaux AB, France. It was redesignated the 1884th AACS Installation & Maintenance Group on 18 January 1955, and inactivated on 18 December 1957.

The 1850th AACS Mobile Communications Squadron at Tinker AFB was redesignated the 3rd ACCS Squadron (Mobile) during October 1952, and then the 3rd Mobile Communications Squadron.

The 1855th Flight (Facilities Checking) was organized at Elmendorf AFB, AK on 1 November 1954. Subsequently the unit was redesignated the 1885th AACS Facilities Checking Flight.

AIR RESUPPLY & COMMUNICATIONS

Special operations have their lineage back to World War Two when bombardment units flew unique missions in psychological warfare. These

The ARS formerly operated C-82A, s/n 44-23029. Still wearing the remnants of its former markings, the aircraft gained civil registry N4829V and was owned by M&F, Inc. W J Balogh via MSgt D W Menard

This C-119C-25-FA, s/n 51-2587, was one of two assigned to the 1739th Ferrying Squadron. The aircraft carries stencil-style 587 nose numbers and Insignia Red Arctic markings only on the empennage. Wendel Loyd

C-82A-20-FA, s/n 44-23031, with the remnants of its MATS markings, became civil registered N4833V. This aircraft had served with Airways & Communications Service before being bought by New Frontier Airlift Corp. R Besecker via N E Taylor

flights were conducted usually at night, during bad weather, and in single-ship sorties. They dropped leaflets and/or agents. Most famous of these units was the 801st BG (Provisional)/ 492nd BG. Known as the *Carpetbaggers*, they flew all-black B-24 Liberators out of Harrington, England. The unit returned to the United States during July and August, stopping at Sioux Falls AAF, SD, before going on to Kirtland Field, NM, where it was inactivated on 17 August 1945. They were awarded the Distinguished Unit Citation for action over Germany and German-occupied territory between 20 March and 25 April 1945, and the French *Croix de Guerre* with Palm.

The mission was re-established and the successor organizations, known as Air Resupply & Communications Wings, were created during the 1951-1952 time frame. They were officially tasked with psychological warfare and unconventional operations. The three wings, 580th, 581st, and 582nd AR&CWs, were activated at Mountain Home AFB, ID, on 16 April, 23 July 1951, and 24 September 1952, respectively. The units operated as wings until September-October 1953, when they were downgraded to groups and continued operations until October 1956, when they were inactivated. Their lineage is carried on to today by the USAF Special Operations Groups and Wings assigned to the Air Force Special Operations Command, headquartered at Hurlburt Field, FL.

Reporting lines for the AR&C units were purposefully obfuscated for security reasons. On paper, the AR&CWs reported to the Air Resupply & Communications Service, that in turn reported to the Military Air Transport Service, while in fact they were the operational arm of the Psychological Warfare Division, Directorate of Plans, HQ USAF.

Combat Crew Training

Training requirements for the Korean War strained the resources of TAC's Troop Carrier Command. On 4 June 1951, an additional requirement for Combat Crew Training was presented to TAC by MATS on behalf of the AR&CWs being formed. An agreement was reached that provided for eight AR&CW crews who would form the initial cadre of instructors for their own training program. Due to shortages in aircraft, MATS would have to furnish one of its own aircraft for the training.

While the headquarters for the 314th TCW remained at Sewart AFB, TN during the Korean War, its operational unit, the 314th TCG, was deployed to the Far East. The 316th TCG was stationed at Sewart and attached to the 314th TCW during this period and was tasked with the training of AR&CW crews. As of May 1951, the 316th TCG was through-putting 40 pilots and 20 aircraft maintenance technicians per month to meet TAC's requirements. To accommodate the MATS requirement, one AR&CW crew would replace one of the TAC crews in class.

Student pilots had to be current in a multi-engined transport and possess a valid instrument card that would not expire during the course of training.

At the beginning of each month, 14 airmen and 4 officers from MATS would start class. Of these students, two pilots and one aerial engineer would be given the compete CCTS class, including flying time. The remaining MATS students received only the ground school portion of the training.

The 60 days of ground school covered 40 hours in the maintenance training unit, 40 hours of instruments and regulations, and 47 hours on a variety of short subjects.

The three wings were each equipped with a variety of aircraft: 10 B-29 Superfortresses, 4 C-119 Flying Boxcars and 4 SA-16 Albatrosses.

In addition, one or two aircraft of other types found their way in to the unit inventories. The 580th had the Douglas C-47 Skytrain, and the 581st was equipped with the Sikorsky H-19, Douglas C-54 Skymaster, and Douglas C-118 Liftmaster.

The three ARC&W wings operated out of these bases:

Wing	Base
580th	Wheelus Field, Libya
581st	Clark AB, Philippines
582nd	Great Falls AFB, MT & RAF Molesworth, England

The 582nd AR&CW had the distinction of conducting limited operations in support of the French in Indochina during 1953.

Albanian Infiltration

Albania was established as a kingdom in 1928, with 60% of the population Muslim and 40% Christian (Roman Catholic and Orthodox). Of greater importance was the dialect spoken and tribal membership. Albania had been occupied by the Italians in 1939, and was followed by the Germans during September 1943 when the Italians tried switching sides in the war. A Stalinist government was established in the cities after World War Two under Enver Hoxha. Both the Americans and British believed the country was ripe for revolution and backed their exiled King Zog I (Ahmed Bey). Several failed attempts were made to penetrate Albania by British forces. While the British lost interest, the Americans formed a training camp in Munich for a group known as *Company 4000*. This force was parachuted into southeast Albania on 19 November 1950. Radio traffic confirmed a successful insertion. Additional parachute drops of smaller units were made until 31 December 1953. However, these units were compromised by the infamous British double agent Kim Philby. Subsequently the Allied force was captured, tried and executed. Their equipment was captured and employed for several years to confuse the Americans.

In an attempt to 'roll back the Iron Curtain,' as President Harry S Truman stated, the United States supported a number of agents in Albania, Poland, and the Ukraine through the 582nd Air Resupply & Communications Wing. The wing moved from Wiesbaden AB, West Germany to RAF Molesworth in February 1953 to support these operations.

AR&CW C-119s

Flying Boxcars flew a variety of support missions for the three wings. They were employed as unit supply and personnel carriers. With the clamshell doors installed, they would be used to drop small quantities of supplies to agents in the field.

Chapter 13

Drag Net and Later Projects

Aerial reconnaissance requirements can result in some interesting innovations through use of a variety of resources. Manned reconnaissance can prove hazardous to aircrew members – hence the phrase 'unarmed and unafraid'. In an interesting development of ideas came the combination of high-altitude balloon-borne reconnaissance packages, use of worldwide air currents, and an entirely new use for the C-119 Flying Boxcar.

Project *Grayback*/Project *Gentrix*

Project *Grayback* was the initial classified codename for the overall air recovery program for capturing high-altitude balloon-borne equipment. The Air Research and Development Command began work on the program in 1949. Subsequently the classified codename was changed to Project *Gentrix*. The unclassified codename for the overall program was Project *C-119L*. The logistics phase of the program was known as Project *Grand Union*, while Project *Drag Net* was the recovery phase. Operational suitability testing was conducted under Project *Moby Dick Hi*.

After World War Two, the US Navy's Office of Naval Research had developed balloons for scientific high-altitude research relative to cosmic rays under *Sky Hook*. While most pre-World War Two balloons were made from rubberized fabric, the newer ones were fabricated from polyethylene that had been developed during the war. The Air Force recognized a requirement to learn more about weather conditions at higher altitudes because its newest and planned aircraft would operate in these environments. The Navy's balloons held the key. The new USAF program was known as *Moby Dick*.

As the Iron Curtain closed around Eastern Europe and the Soviet Union, there became an urgent requirement for current intelligence about that vast and poorly charted portion of the earth. Shared technology between *Sky Hook* and *Moby Dick Hi*, led to Project *Gopher* where balloons would be launched from Western Europe, overfly and photograph the Soviet Union from altitudes not achievable by their interceptors, and be recovered over the western Pacific Ocean. During October 1950 Project *Grandson* was implemented with 1-A priority.

The Equipment Lab at the Wright Air Development Center (WADC) conducted feasibility testing of mid-air recovery systems at El Centro, CA. For these tests, a C-119 was equipped with a winch and a grapnelling hook on a trailing cable. During these tests, 15 parachutes were dropped and 12 were successfully contacted; however, not all were captured. On one occasion, the grapnell hook bounded upwards and imbedded itself in the aircraft's elevator. More engineering work was required.

WADC contracted the All American Engineering Company to develop the recovery system for the C-119 under Project *Grayback*. The winch employed was the Model 80C, which was almost identical to the equipment used for glider pick-up and towing during World War Two. Capitalizing on the company's experience with airmail pickup, a system of two poles to hold hooks and a loop assembly in position to ensure positive parachute engagement and recovery was developed.

Kaiser-built C-119F-KM, 51-8119, was accepted into the USAF inventory on 31 January 1953 and delivered to TAC on 6 February. The aircraft was assigned to the 456th TCW at Charleston AFB, SC. Subsequently, the aircraft was converted into the C-119L configuration by Fairchild at Hagerstown, MD and returned to the 456th. The aircraft served with the wing at Shirio AB, Japan. She subsequently served with the 94th TCW, 357th TCS and the 902nd TCG. Replete with Insignia Red Arctic trim and red and white checkerboard markings on the ventral fins and nose, the aircraft was photographed on the 111th FIW, Pennsylvania Air National Guard, ramp at Philadelphia International Airport, on 2 November 1956. E M Sommerich via P M Bowers

Another view of 51-8119, showing the beavertail door. A pair of unusual antennas appear on top of the fuselage between the cabin air vents and the ILS antenna. These most likely were employed in the capsule snare operations.
E M Sommerich via P M Bowers

94 Fairchild C-82 & C-119

C-119F-FA, 51-8039, with its recovery gear extended through the open beavertail door. This aircraft was recovering a capsule from a *Discovery* satellite in November 1961, a use subsequent to Project *Drag Net*. This aircraft was later operated by the Air Defense Command, was retired to MASDC on 29 June 1972, and disposed of by Kolar, Inc, on 13 February 1976. USAF KE45238

Three aircraft, 51-8042, 51-8115 and 51-8038, assigned to the 6593rd Test Squadron. A pair of *Yagi* antennas were installed on the nose of these aircraft to assist in locating the targets to be snared. Aircraft 51-8042 had been retired to MASDC by 1968. USAF via B Burlingame

The distinctive beavertail door installed on 51-8039, operated by the 6593rd TS. USAF via B Burlingame

Two pallets were designed for the C-119. The forward pallet was called the winch deck, while the aft pallet was named the sheave deck. A Model 80C winch holding a 500ft long, ½-inch diameter steel cable was mounted to the winch deck. The sheave deck contained the mechanical equipment employed for the pickup operation and subsequent package recovery. Mounted to sheave deck were: the pole mounts, main sheave, aft rollers, and cable cutter. To preclude cable fouling and enhanced personnel safety, a trough with removable covers ran down the center of both pallets. The pickup poles were 34ft long and were fabricated from tubes of several different diameters welded together. The air-to-air loop assembly was made of a 110ft long, ½-inch diameter nylon rope with five hooks. A pair of transfer sheaves was attached to the aircraft's monorail system. These transfer sheaves held the transfer cable that would recover the object once it had been snared.

A cluster of four 24ft diameter parachutes was attached to the balloon packages. The apex of each parachute was attached to a ½-inch diameter, 105ft long drogue line, which in turn was connected to a specially reinforced 12ft diameter drogue chute. The nominal rate of descent for the balloon-borne packages was 1,200ft per minute.

A crew of five in the cargo bay of the C-119 was required for operation of the balloon recovery system. Close coordination between the back end crew and flightdeck crew was required to effect a successful capture.

Project *Drag Net*

Established as the 456th Troop Carrier Wing (Medium), Reserve, on 15 October 1952, the unit was activated on 1 December of that year and operated C-119s out of Miami International Airport. The 456th TCW participated in a number of tactical exercises both in the United States and overseas. Most of these operations were in conjunction with Army airborne forces.

On 1 March 1955, the 456th was reorganized. The tactical group and all of its support

Above: **Preparing for an aerial snatch, the recovery poles were extended through the beavertail doors of aircraft 51-8115. The recovery was accomplished by the engaging line that extended between the poles. Once engaged, a nylon line absorbed the shock and a high-powered winch reeled the capsule into the aircraft.** USAF via B Burlingame

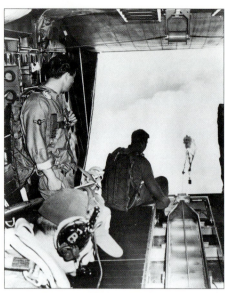

Above right: **Recovery personnel from the 6593rd TS in action. A3C Owen L Johnson and SSgt Lawrence G Bradley (kneeling) watch the nylon line as the winch slowly reels in the capsule.** USAF 161300AC

Below: **C-119G-FA, s/n 53-8050, in its faded dayglo orange trim, was in the midst of a surface recovery exercise off the coast of Hawaii. The pararescue team was departing the area.** USAF K1326

components were inactivated. At that time the wing assumed command of three tactical squadrons and three squadron-sized detachments. Each of the subordinate units was equipped with eight specially modified Flying Boxcars. These aircraft were configured and manned for independent operations. Between around 22 April 1955 and 26 March 1956, the 456th TCW was attached to and placed under the operational control of Strategic Air Command's 1st Air Division (Meteorological Survey). During this time, the unit participated in Project *Drag Net*, designated as a high-altitude meteorological research program. The Flying Boxcars were standard C-119Fs modified by the replacement of the clamshell doors with the flight-operable beavertail doors. A snare system was installed within the aft fuselage. This snare would be extended through the open beavertail door, enabling the aircraft to snatch balloon-borne instrument packages. The program called for modification of 50 C-119Fs for the mission.

The 1st Air Division (Meteorological Survey) was headquartered at Offutt AFB, NE and was under the command of Maj Gen William P Fisher.

Beginning in January 1955, flight crews and maintenance personnel from the 456th TCW went to the All American Engineering test base in Georgetown, DL for training on prototype equipment. A six-month training program was then established at Charleston AFB, SC. On 1 March 1955, aircraft and crews arrived at their new base. While crews underwent extensive training, the aircraft were modified for the new mission. During this phase, the aircraft were operating without their clamshell doors, resulting in an extensive drag penalty. With the doors removed and 3,524 gallons of fuel, the aircraft would gross about 70,494 lb at take-off and would be operating at 8,500-15,000 lb in excess of their safe single-engine operating weight limitations dependent upon free air temperature and dew point temperature at the time of take-off. The installation of beavertail doors lessened the overload condition at take-off and increased the possible radius of action. In addition, the aircraft had 1,000-gallon fuel tanks installed in the fuselage.

Because of the aircraft configuration after modification, the 456th TCW could not perform their own logistical support. Consequently, deployment of the wing relied on other organizations to provide the support aircraft. These support aircraft brought in a minimum of 30 days of support equipment and spare parts during the initial deployment and subsequently would provide sufficient logistical support for the 456th TCW to operate for 120-180 days. Depot aircraft would be available at all times for the airlift of short-notice priority parts and equipment.

Upon completion of training at Charleston AFB, SC, only fully qualified aircrews and maintenance personnel were permitted to deploy with the wing. On 2 August 1955, Col James L Daniel Jr, led an advanced party of the wing and Det 1, 746th TCS, from Charleston. The unit arrived at their new headquarters at Shiroi AB, Japan, four days later. Its headquarters at Charleston was closed on 16 October 1955, and reopened at Shiroi on 10 November 1955.

Other wing components were located at these bases:

744th TCS	Kadena AB, Okinawa
745th TCS	NAS Adak, Alaska
746th TCS	NAS Kodiak, Alaska
Det 1 744th TCS	Itazuke AB, Japan
Det 1 745th TCS	Misawa AB, Japan
Det 1 746th TCS	Johnson AB, Japan

The 456th TCW assumed operational control of the 6926th Radio Squadron, Mobile, in the forward area. The 6926th had these detachments:

This quarter view of C-119G-FA, s/n 53-8041, was taken on the ramp at Edwards AFB, CA on 8 September 1961. Note the blue nose ring, cowl ring, prop hub, and *Catch a Falling Star* insignia over the entry door. To the rear were a pair of T-33s. USAF KE15385

Det 1	Shiroi AB, Japan
Det 2	Northwest AB, Guam
Det 3	Wake Island
Det 4	Clark AB, Philippines
Det 5	Yonton AB, Japan
Det 6	Pyongtaek AB, Korea
Det 7	Chitose AB, Japan
Det 8	Midway Island
Det 9	Shemya AFB, Alaska
Det 10	Elmendorf AFB, Alaska

Balloons would be released from such places as Turkey, allowed to overfly the Soviet Union, and recovered. In conjunction with the 6926th Radio Squadron, the balloons would be tracked and the C-119s positioned for a recovery. When in position, the balloon would be released, allowing the instrument package to descend by parachute. Flying at altitudes of 30,000ft, the C-119 crew listened for directions from the ground-based radio tracking stations. When in range, the C-119 crew used a rotary dial telephone device to signal the release of the balloon and subsequent parachute deployment. The C-119 would descend over the parachute in a rather sporty maneuver, allowing the parachute to be snagged by the snare. The instrument package could then be pulled into the aircraft. It was not unusual for a pilot to miscalculate his approach, resulting in an airplane nose being enshrouded in the parachute or have the chute be chewed apart by a propeller. With a parachute-covered nose, the pilot would fly on instruments in search of his base. No aircraft losses were reported due to being wrapped up in a chute.

The aircraft usually flew in a loose trail formation. On one occasion the aircraft were operating near the Soviet coastline north of Japan. The second aircraft commander asked the lead ship if they knew where they were. 'Of course,' was the response. Then what was the island beneath them. The second lieutenant navigator had erred. Next, the second ship asked if they had the MiGs in sight. 'What MiGs?' The first fighter was spotted when it zoomed beneath the lead C-119. Using all of his piloting skill, coupled with a great deal of luck, the lead aircraft commander bent the throttles over the firewall and headed for the nearest cloudbank. Fighters were scrambled from Japan, but the action was over before they could arrive on station. That night in the officers' club there was a boastful aircraft commander stating that 'there he was with a pair of MiGs cornered but they refused to come within range of his .45!' If the truth were known, his flight suit was probably dropped off at the cleaners earlier that day.

If a package was missed, it would fall into the sea and float. The package was roughly the size of a 55-gallon drum. It had a hooked rod attached to the top end. The C-119 could then make a low approach over the water and snare the hooked rod to extract the package from the water. For practice, C-119 crews snared 55-gallon drums floating in the water. One day a C-119 crew was practising near Misawa AB when witnessed by a fighter pilot. The latter called the Misawa tower and informed them that he saw a C-119 practicing touch and goes in the water! Not one of the brighter fighter pilots.

During operational missions, crews from the 456th TCW would perform the capsule recovery. Upon landing, the recovered units would be accepted by an outside agency. Secure storage facilities were required at each operating base.

During the operational phase of Project *Drag Net* the aircrews flew regardless of the weather to meet their mission tasking. Maintenance crews often worked around the clock in preparation for the missions. During this period, the 456th TCW did not suffer the loss of a single aircraft or crew. For its actions in support of Project *Drag Net*, the 456th TCW was awarded the Air Force Outstanding Unit Award for the period 1 April 1955 through 20 March 1956.

The 456th TCW was released from its attachment to the 1st AD on 26 March 1956, and began returning to the United States on 10 May of that year. The wing arrived at Ardmore AFB, OK, on 25 May and was attached to the 463rd TCW. No operational missions were flown by the 456th while it was attached to the 463rd. On 9 July 1956, the 456th TCW, and its three squadrons and detachments, were phased out and inactivated. The 50 C-119s assigned to the wing were distributed throughout various troop carrier units. Six of the aircraft and crews were transferred to Air Force Systems Command where they continued their work.

Catch a Falling Star

Air Force Systems Command operations, similar to those conducted during Project *Drag Net*, were flown with C-119s between 21 August 1958 and 25 January 1962. These operations were conducted out of Hickam AFB, HI, by the 6593rd Test Squadron, under the command of Maj Joseph Nellor. Their mission was officially described as: 'to develop training and recovery techniques and employ these procedures in aerial and surface recovery of scientific components of the appropriate re-entry vehicles.'

These aircraft were modified to incorporate a pair of antennas in the nose and associated homing radios to assist in directing the aircraft to a descending capsule.

Nine C-119s were operated by the 6593rd Test Squadron. Three of the aircraft returned to the ZI in July 1961, followed by four more in November, and the final pair on 25 January 1962.

The aircraft assigned to the squadron and their arrival dates are shown below:

51-8037	19 Sep 1958	51-8045	18 Sep 1958
51-8038	4 Sep 1958	51-8049	11 Sep 1958
51-8039	21 Aug 1958	51-8050	8 Sep 1958
51-8042	29 Aug 1958	51-8115	25 Sep 1958
51-8043	27 Aug 1958		

Lockheed C-130 Hercules aircraft took over the *Catch a Falling Star* mission upon the retirement of the C-119 Flying Boxcars.

Discovery XIV Capture

The art of capturing airborne packages developed in 1952 remained an art in 1960. The crew of *Pelican 9*, under the command of Capt Harold E Mitchell, was assigned to the recovery of the *Discovery XIII* capsule. While the radio beacon for the off-course capsule was picked up by the crew, the capsule splashed down into the Pacific. The crew of *Pelican 9* spotted the capsule bobbing in the ocean and a Navy helicopter was vectored to the location. There a

The USAF Museum at Wright-Patterson AFB, OH, displays Capt Harold E Mitchell's C-119J-FA, s/n 51-8037, in which he made the USAF's first capture of a capsule from space. This aircraft has Gloss Insignia Red Arctic trim; whereas most of these aircraft had the dayglo orange scheme of the day. The 0 of the nose number has a natural metal edge. A partial white cap was applied to the aircraft and ends just ahead of the APP exhaust stacks on top of the fuselage. T Panopalis

This right side view of Capt Mitchell's aircraft reveals the beavertail doors and the aft end of the tapered black speed line. The window curtains have been drawn to protect the aircraft interior. This aircraft is still part of the outside display. To the rear is the museum's B-50. T Panopalis

A close-up of the nose of Capt Mitchell's C-119J-FA showing the aerial array. T Panopalis

frogman was able to right the capsule and secure a cable to it. Then the helicopter hauled the capsule back to the *USNS Haiti Victory*, T-AK-238 – a Greenville Victory Class Cargo Ship. The ship was reclassified as a Missile Range Instrumentation Ship and renamed *USNS Longview* (T-AGM-3) on 27 November 1960.

Discovery XIV was launched from Vandenberg AFB, CA on 18 August 1960, into a north-south polar orbit on top of a Thor booster rocket. After burnout of the Thor rocket engines, an Agena A shot the capsule into an orbit with a perigee of 116 miles and an apogee of 502 miles. The top speed attained by the capsule was 17,658mph. After 17 orbits, the satellite ejected from the Agena A booster, retrorockets were fired to slow the capsule, and it descended back into the earth's atmosphere. The first operational recovery mission occurred on 19 August 1960, when C-119 51-8037 from the 6593rd Test Squadron captured the re-entry capsule from *Discovery XIV* as it descended over the Pacific.

Because the Navy got the laurels for the recovery, Capt Mitchell and the crew of *Pelican 9* were assigned as the last backup sortie for the recovery of the *Discovery XIV* capsule. For this mission, the 6593rd Test Squadron launched six C-119Ls and a C-130. Their mission was to patrol a rectangular recovery box measuring 60 by 200 miles. *Pelican 9* and another C-119 were assigned patrol areas beyond the recovery box thereby extending the box by an additional 400 miles.

The crew of *Pelican 9* sighted the capsule some 360 miles southwest of Honolulu. They first sighted the billowing orange and white parachute from the *Discovery XIV* capsule while they flew at 16,000ft. The capsule was descending at about 1,500ft per minute. The trapeze was deployed and a pass was made. They missed by a mere six inches! Capt Mitchell wracked the aircraft around for another run, only to fail again. Determined to make the catch, Capt Mitchell hauled the aircraft around for yet another run. At 8,500ft they successfully snagged the capsule. The crew of *Pelican 9* called in to mission control to advise of their catch only to be told to stay off the radio because they were interfering with the recovery operation.

The capsule had flown for 27 hours and covered 450,000 miles through space. This was the first film capsule recovery from a satellite. The satellite had been launched the day before and placed into orbit. Photographs taken during this mission provided valuable intelligence data on the Soviet Union. This aircraft, s/n 51-8037, is currently on display at the USAF Museum at Wright-Patterson AFB, OH.

For their efforts the crew of *Pelican 9* was awarded individual Air Medals, and Capt Mitchell was presented with the Distinguished Flying Cross.

Capt Mitchell was a native of Bloomington, IN. His name would again surface relative to the AC-119 gunships in Southeast Asia (see Chapter 16).

Chapter 14

USAF Reserve C-119s

Air Force Reservists had to maintain the same levels of proficiency as their Regular Air Force counterparts in all phases of the troop carrier mission. Instructor pilots were encouraged to have new students study the aircrew training outline and be especially familiar with the chapter on airplane overview when a mobile training detachment course was not available. Flight crews had to be intimately familiar with Dash 1 flight manual technical order. Other areas of proficiency included:
- Troop Carrier Operations – General
- Arctic Survival
- Troop Carrier Operations During Nuclear Warfare
- Hazardous Cargo Loading
- Air Intelligence

When called to active duty, Regular Air Force forces and units being supported by the Reserve troop carrier units expected all personnel to become an integral part of any higher headquarters tasking.

The Air Force Reserve gained C-119s in two phases. One was when 19 Reserve wings were activated for the Korean War, and the second was in 1957 when the Reserve increased its troop carrier force to 45 troop carrier squadrons.

Korean War Call-Up

During the Korean War the 375th and 433rd Troop Carrier Wings (TCWs) from Cleveland, OH, and Pittsburgh, PA, respectively, were called to federal service on 15 October 1950. Both units transitioned from the Curtiss C-46 Commando: the 375th TCW into the C-82 and the 433rd into the C-119. Both units were assigned to Greenville, (later Donaldson) AFB, SC, where they supported the US Army Infantry School's airborne requirements out of Fort Benning, GA. On 14 July 1952, the 375th TCW was released from active duty and the unit returned to Pittsburgh where they resumed Reserve operations in the C-46. The 433rd TCW, at Hensley Field, TX, served TAC for several months before deploying to Rhein-Main AB, West Germany, to participate in tactical exercises and special missions between 5 August 1951 and 14 July 1952, when they were relieved from federal service and inactivated until 1955.

Another 17 Air Force Reserve troop carrier wings were also mobilized for the Korean War. Six of these wings remained within the ZI to augment Tactical Air Command's Eighteenth Air Force. Five of these wings transitioned into C-119s. The 403rd TCW, from Portland, OR, was sent to Korea on 14 April 1952, the 435th TCW, at Miami International Airport, FL, flew both the C-46 for crew training and the C-119 in support of Tactical Air Command (TAC) missions within the ZI between March 1951 and December 1952, when they were relieved from active duty and C-119 operations. The 514th TCW, at Mitchel AFB, NY, initially operated C-46s and then transitioned into C-119s on 31 December 1952, which they operated on active duty until 1 February 1953. The 516th TCW, at Memphis Municipal Airport, continued to operate their C-46s until 1952 when they changed to C-119s that they operated until the unit was replaced by the 463rd TCW on 16 January 1953.

While operational with the Eighteenth Air Force, the activated AFRES TCWs participated in routine training missions and several joint exercises, as shown in this table.

Name	Dates
Exercise *Southern Pine*	August 1951
Operation *Snowfall*	January to February 1952
Exercise *Long Horn*	March 1952

These C-119s from the 904th TCG, 336th TCS, Stewart AFB, NY participated in Operation *Pine Cone*, at Pope AFB, NC, in September 1956. In the foreground is C-119G-36-FA, s/n 53-78327.
USAF K324575

This C-119B-12-FA, s/n 49-111, as she appeared in post-Korean War configuration with a single nose gear, and no ventral fins on the tailbooms. Insignia Red Arctic trim appears only on the empennage. Note the scars from the former 'U.S. AIR FORCE' on the fuselage beneath the wings, and the new 'U.S. AIR FORCE' on the forward fuselage. This aircraft went on to serve with the 336th TCS, 904th TCG, Stewart AFB, NY.
H S Gann

Displaying the dayglo orange paint of the day, these C-119s from the 904th TCG, 336th TCS were parked on the ramp at Stewart AFB, NY. In the foreground is C-119B-12-FA, s/n 49-0111. The 0- indicated that the aircraft was over 10 years old, with retrofitted dorsal and ventral fins. The production outboard stabilizer tips were retained. Black-edged dayglo orange bands were applied to the booms. Black-edged red and white stripes were applied to the vertical tails. To the rear was C-119B-12-FA, s/n 49-0110, with a scalloped dayglo orange nose trim. A pair of blue chevrons appeared on the dayglo nose. It had been upgraded to the C-119G standard with dual nosewheels. Note the open astrodome hatches to assist in keeping the cockpits cool. USAF

The 435th TCW at Miami International Airport, was composed of both Reservists and Regular Air Force personnel who had seen service in the Korean War. In August 1952, the wing deployed four C-119s to Thule AB, Greenland, where they operated until 1 November 1952. The purpose of the deployment was to support the building of an airstrip and weather station that would become Nord AB, Greenland. The new base was then operated by Denmark. The 435th's aircraft were employed in heavy equipment drops. One piece of hardware needed for the construction was a road grader. It was too large to fit into a C-119; however a solution was at hand. One of the construction men was known as 'Blowtorch' Morgan because he always carried a blowtorch on his belt. The solution was to cut the road grader in half and load the parts into two aircraft. After the drop, 'Blowtorch' Morgan welded the two halves together, presumably using a more appropriate tool.

The 435th TCW, at Miami International Airport, FL, flew logistical support missions to Thule AB, Greenland while the base was being constructed between August and November 1952. Here, C-119G-FA, s/n 52-5910, shares the gravel ramp with an Air Rescue Service SA-16 Albatross. Maintenance is being performed on the No 2 R-3350 engine. In addition to the Arctic trim, note how far aft the black anti-corrosion paint was applied to the boom. Exhaust residue may be seen on the dorsal fin. Lt Col C D Bright

Operation *Sixteen Ton*

Between 22 June and 15 September 1956, the AFRES demonstrated its sustained operations capabilities for the first time in Operation *Sixteen Ton*. During this operation, AFRES crews flew 164 sorties, airlifting 856,715 lb of cargo in support of long-range navigation (LORAN) stations in the Caribbean. The LORAN sites provided navigational signals for both aircraft and ships. Twelve of the thirteen C-46 and C-119 AFRES units from CONAC's First, Tenth and

During the height of the Cuban Missile Crisis redeployment, the AFRES sent C-119CF-FA, s/n 52-5950, to Homestead AFB, FL, home of the 19th BMW, operating B-52s. While the 435th TCW, AFRES, operating C-119s was also stationed there, this was a transient aircraft that was being directed to a parking stall by this SAC 'FOLLOW ME' truck. Crews were pressed to their physical limits during this period. This night, the C-119 overran the truck that was tipped about 45° in the air by the plane. The aircraft's nose struck the 'FOLLOW ME' sign, while its belly hit the aft corner of the truck. There were no injuries, other that to the pilot's pride. There are no records of an accident report being filed. The crew probably stopped at the cleaners then hit the bar. Sheetmetal technicians would have repaired the aircraft, and the pickup would have mysteriously been dropped from the inventory. USAF via Reese Sias

C-119G-FA, s/n 52-5939, from the 97th TCS, 941st TCG, 446th TCW, stationed at Paine Field, WA, was configured for a heavy drop exercise. This ship was retired from service in 1971, returned to service in 1972, and re-retired in 1974.

C-119G-36-FA, s/n 53-3202, from the 97th TCS, was flying in the Seattle area. Note the double-stepped cheatline.

Assigned to the 314th TCS, 940th TCG, 349th TCW, at McClellan AFB, CA, C-119G-24-KM, s/n 53-8124, was photographed at Norton AFB, CA in the early 1960s. It was the subject of one of the airplanes in the Testors/Italaeri release of the C-119 model kit. The aircraft subsequently flew with ADC before being retired to MASDC in 1969. It was obtained by Kolar Inc, on 12 February 1976. H S Gann

Fourteenth Air Forces participated. The aircraft were under the operational control of the 2585th Air Reserve Flying Center. Each day between one and four aircraft departed NAS New York for Miami International airport. From there the aircraft flew to San Juan, Puerto Rico or San Salvador AFB, Bahamas.

Airlift Mission Assignments

During 1957 a major reshuffle occurred in the USAF airlift community. Military Air Transport Service (MATS) assumed control of all C-124s for strategic airlift. TAC retained the troop carrier mission using aging C-119s, C-123s and newly arriving C-130s. Gen O P Weyland, TAC Commander (1 April 1954 to 31 July 1959) protested about this redistribution but the action was cast in concrete. His successor, Gen Frank F 'Hank' Everest, now had to deal with meeting the Army's airlift requirements. Gen Everest had to testify before a Congressional subcommittee that TAC had the capability to provide the requisite 1,200 tactical aircraft to meet the Army's needs. To meet this formidable task, Gen Everest included TAC's 48 new C-130s and 720 C-119s that had not been transferred to the Reserve.

Air Force Reserve Troop Carrier Expansion

The Air Force Reserve troop carrier wings included 12 with C-46s and one with the C-119 by 1955. Tactical Air Command (TAC) observed that the AFRES units were sufficiently advanced to participate more regularly in Air Force operations and joint operations. TAC also recommended that Reserve units end their annual training encampment with a mass airdrop. In August 1956, the Reserve units showed their capability when they participated in Operation *Pine Cone*, a massive drop of Army paratroopers at Fort Bragg by both active and Reserve troop carrier units.

During the first half of 1955, Continental Air Command (CONAC) directed the detachment of AFRES squadrons from their parent wing to separate locations. This concept offered several advantages. Local communities were more likely to accept a single squadron rather than an entire wing; separate squadrons would ensure training of each squadron as the basic operating element of a wing; and location of separate squadrons within smaller population centers would facilitate recruiting and manning. CONAC's plan called for relocation of AFRES units at 59 locations throughout the ZI.

The first AFRES C-119 detachments are shown in this table:

Wing	Base	Squadron	Base
459th TCW	Andrews AFB, MD	757th TCS	Byrd Field, VA
403rd TCW	Portland, OR	65th TCS	Paine Field, WA
435th TCW	Miami, FL	78th TCS	Orlando, FL

In August 1957, the Air Force Reserve lost its entire fighter mission to the Air National Guard, thus making the Reserve a troop carrier/rescue force with 50 squadrons. In the event of mobilization, the 45 troop carrier squadrons would all be gained by TAC and flew the C-119 exclusively.

At the beginning of 1960, the Reserves had 15 troop carrier wings with 45 squadrons that were located at 35 airfields around the country. While three squadrons were equipped with the C-123, the C-119 remained the primary aircraft in the inventory. At its peak, in 1962, the Air Force Reserve operated 669 C-119s.

Between 1954 and 1972, the AFRES C-119 inventory was as shown:

1954	31	1959	622	1964	601	1969	190
1955	35	1960	653	1965	578	1970	120
1956	39	1961	614	1966	399	1971	34
1957	201	1962	669	1967	344	1972	13
1958	517	1963	616	1968	259		

This line-up of 733rd TCS aircraft reveals 10 C-119s assigned to the unit. There is a mixture of plain and Arctic-marked aircraft, but all have the AFRES insignia applied to the fins. 419th TFW/HO

Here C-119G-36-FA, s/n 53-8096, is captured in flight with its full-up unit markings and Arctic trim. The AFRES insignia appears on the fin. 419th TFW/HO

C-119G-36-FA, s/n 53-8106, is undergoing a practice radiological decontamination by the base fire department. 419th TFW/HO

The mission of the Reserve troop carrier units was: 'to provide air transportation for airborne forces, their equipment and supplies; provide medium-range movement of personnel, supplies, and equipment, including air evacuation within the theater of operation.'

Mission Transition

The transition of the Air Force Reserve unit stationed at Hill AFB, UT from a fighter-bomber squadron to a troop carrier squadron, occurred in 1957. It is used here as an example of how the Reserve units made the change.

The 313th TCS was assigned to the 349th TCG in June 1957 and was stationed at Hill AFB. Previously both the squadron and group had been a fighter-bomber organization equipped with F-84Gs. With the transition came the lumbering Curtiss C-46 Commandos. On 18 August 1957, the entire 313th TCS moved to Chico, CA with their eight C-46s to operate with other squadrons of the group. Eventually, the 313th TCS was stationed at Portland Airport, OR.

The 733rd TCS, previously stationed at Dobbins AFB, GA, was stood up at Hill AFB in October 1957 as part of the 452nd TCW. By early 1958, the unit began receiving C-119s and funds were allocated for construction of a new hangar. This hangar could accommodate up to four Flying Boxcars. The squadron's first two full-time Air Reserve Technicians were gained by the squadron in October 1958. By April 1959 the squadron was equipped with 16 C-119s and became the first unit in the Fourth Air Force to qualify new combat ready crews.

On 15 and 16 April 1959, 10 of the 733rd TCSs C-119s airlifted 200 paratroops from the 101st Airborne Division, and their equipment, from Hill AFB to a training site on the Wendover, Utah Range, in Operation *Utah Eagle I*. Col Benton M Clay, 733rd TCS Commander, stated: 'Operation *Utah Eagle I* was the most realistic simulated D-Day mission the 733rd performed and the experience and training gained were invaluable. The true effectiveness can be measured by the excellent participation, even though this exercise was conducted in mid-week. The mission was accomplished without man-days or overtime and a large percentage of squadron personnel performed duty in a non-pay status.'

Subsequently the 733rd TCS trained with the 82nd Airborne Division and the Utah ANG's special forces.

Exercise *Bright Star/Pine Cone III*

A major joint training exercise was conducted during August 1960 employing over 55,000 AFRES, ANG, and Army personnel in Exercise *Bright Star/Pine Cone III*. The operation included troop drops, air resupply, and aeromedical evacuation under combat conditions. Maj Gen Maurice A Preston, commander of the Nineteenth Air Force, TAC, was the overall exercise director. For the first time, ANG and AFRES generals commanded their own forces during an exercise. Brig Gen Donald L Strait, commander of the 108th TFW (NJ-ANG) led the F-84Fs from the 108th TFW, McGuire AFB, NJ, and RF-84Fs from the 117th TRW (AL-ANG) Birmingham, AL. These aircraft operated in conjunction with TAC F-100s. Brig Gen Rollin B Moore Jr, commander of the 349th TCW (AFRES), Hamilton AFB, CA, was in charge of all troop carrier operations during the exercise.

A total of 30,000 Army troops, of which 11,000 were airborne, from the XVII Airborne Corps Artillery, 82nd Airborne Division, 101st Airborne Division, a pair of engineering battalions, military police, and other combat and support elements were under the command of Lt Gen Herbert B Powell, commanding general of the Third Army.

These AFRES units participated in Exercise *Bright Star/Pine Cone III*.

Air Reserve Technician (ART) SSgt David G Kelly was also an accomplished artist. Here he is applying a Santa Claus to the nose of one of the 733rd TCS aircraft. 419th TFW/HO

ART David G Kelly also painted *Season's Greetings* on C-119G-36-FA, s/n 53-8136. Note the star insignia in the nose and the red and white prop tips. Such markings were applied each year when the unit flew a Christmas airdrop for the children on the local Navajo Indian reservations. 419th TFW/HO

Unit	Base	Aircraft
94th TCW	L G Hanscom Field, MA	C-119
302nd TCW	Lockbourne AFB, OH	C-119
403rd TCW	Selfridge AFB, MI	C-119
433rd TCW	Brooks AFB, TX	C-119
434th TCW	Bakalar AFB, IN	C-119
435th TCW	Homestead AFB, FL	C-119
440th TCW	Gen Billy Mitchell Field, WI	C-119
442nd TCW	Richards-Gebaur AFB, MO	C-119
445th TCW	Dobbins AFB, GA	C-123
446th TCW	Ellington AFB, TX	C-119
452nd TCW	Long Beach Mun Apt, CA	C-119
549th TCW	Andrews AFB, MD	C-119
512th TCW	NAS Willow Grove PA	C-119
514th TCW	Mitchel AFB, NY	C-119

In addition, six aerial port squadrons, two casualty staging squadrons, and an aeromedical evacuation group from the AFRES participated in the exercise.

During Exercise *Bright Star/Pine Cone III*, the AFRES troop carrier wings operated out of the following fields: Shaw AFB, SC; Myrtle Beach AFB, SC; Donaldson AFB, SC; North Auxiliary Airfield, SC; Charleston AFB, SC; Robins AFB, GA; Bush Field, GA; and Pope AFB, NC.

The scenario was to simulate a limited war situation where an allied nation was invaded by a neighboring state. The exercise took place in North and South Carolina. On 13 August 1960, in response to a plea for assistance from the *allied nation*, the 101st Airborne Division assembled at Fort Campbell, KY for air deployment by MATS and TAC aircraft. On the following day, the ANG tactical aircraft and 15 AFRES troop carrier wings were rushed to the theater. US Strategic Army Corps paratroops continued to assemble on 15 August.

Advancing *enemy* troops had taken over Pope International Airport on 16 August, and the *capitol city* of Fayettville had been evacuated. *Enemy* forces had also gained control of rail and road routes north of the city. MATS aircraft had airlifted more than 6,000 paratroops of the 101st Airborne Division and around 2,000 tons of equipment and supplies into staging areas. Lt Gen Thomas J Trapnell, XVIII Airborne Corps and Strategic Army Corps (STRAC) commander, was designated commander of the land forces in the theater.

Enemy forces had split the *allied* nation in two by 17 August. More than half of the 11,500-man invading army had been committed to the campaign.

By 18 August, some 600 AFRES troop carrier aircraft and 120 ANG aircraft had arrived in the theater. The fighters used air refueling to make their 3,000-mile trek, thereby simulating an actual deployment.

Enemy forces continued to make gains on the following day, as relief forces continued to stage. Fighters from the allied forces gained aerial supremacy. In addition, seven special activities sorties were flown by SA-16 Albatrosses, and three RB-57 Intruders brought back pictures of the battle zone.

On the morning of 20 August, TAC and ANG fighters had begun softening up the *invading* forces prior to the paratroop assault. Following closely behind the fighters were the troop carrier aircraft flown by AFRES crews. By noon some 6,600 paratroops from the 101st Airborne Division and 890 tons of equipment were dropped into the battle zone by C-119s, C-123s and C-130s.

Heavy ground fighting continued through 21 August. While the invading forces were temporarily repelled, they regained the initiative.

The weather on 22 August brought low ceilings and intermittent rain. Despite the conditions, more than 3,500 airborne troops deployed to bases near the war zone and were preparing to jump into the Fort Bragg-Camp Mackall area on the following morning. Airlift was to be provided by 93 C-119s making 180 sorties. In total, 7,573 paratroops and over 2,553 tons of equipment had been airlifted into the staging areas. Weather precluded paratroop operations on the following day.

Heavy ground fighting continued during the morning of 24 August. A break in the weather came in the middle of the day and troop carrier

C-119G-36-FA, s/n 53-3201, was assigned to the 935th TCG at Richards-Gebaur AFB, MO when photographed on 12 August 1972. The aircraft had a white cap and blue cheatline above the Aircraft Gray fuselage and empennage. An AFRES insignia is applied to the vertical fin and the AFRES identification is carried on the boom. Via N E Taylor

planes airdropped and airlanded 3,700 paratroops from the 82nd Airborne Division and 238 tons of equipment into the battle zone. Cross winds hampered operations in the airdrop areas. The AFRES employed 123 C-119s to drop the troops and equipment during a 2-hour break in the weather. While further assault operations were suspended, TAC and ANG fighters continued to control the area over the battle zone. The battle and exercise were over on 25 August.

During Exercise *Bright Star/Pine Cone III*, 10,519 paratroops from the 82nd and 101st Airborne Divisions, and other STRAC units, and 2,845 tons of equipment were carried by AFRES and TAC aircraft. The intense exercise provided vital experience and proved the capabilities of the citizen airmen within the AFRES. This exercise also changed the collective minds of the active duty US Army, who henceforth asked that AFRES troop carrier units provide weekend support for Army paratroop operations.

The Cuban Missile Crisis
By October 1962, the Reserve structure had changed slightly. There were 12 C-119 wings with 37 squadrons, a C-123 wing with three squadrons, and a pair of C-124 wings with five squadrons. These units would be gained by TAC in the event of a call-up. Six months prior to the Cuban mobilization, the C-119 and C-123 units began to augment TAC by providing about ten aircraft per day for TAC-directed missions.

The Western Hemisphere had been free of Communist domination until the overthrow of Cuba's government by Fidel Castro. The Soviets began nurturing this toehold in the Americas by providing economic aid and advisors. The United States suspected that the Soviets were bringing strategic missiles into Cuba.

The Cuban Missile Crisis was coming to a head. At 1732 hours (Eastern Daylight Savings Time), Friday, 12 October 1962, about an hour before normal quitting time, Maj Wesley C Brashear was on duty at the Continental Air Command (CONAC) command post. He took a telephone call from Maj Gen Stanley J Donovan, DCS/Operations at Headquarters TAC. TAC had an urgent requirement for the airlift of approximately 60 aircraft loads of number one priority from as yet undetermined points around the ZI. This airlift was to commence on Monday, 15 October. The specific mission requirements would be given on Saturday. The mission was classified secret. An assessment made by Maj Brashear showed that training over that weekend would have as many as 310 C-119s, 12 C-123s, and 15 C-124s available for such a mission. Lt Col W L Spenser, Reserve Chief of the Current Operations Division, called TAC Headquarters to determine if the mission was valid, and then committed the Reserve force to the operation.

TAC called the CONAC Command Post back with the mission requirements, and the Reserve mobilized five C-119 wings around the country. These wings were instructed to prepare for operational orders that would be given at 0800 hours on Saturday. When the operation was completed, a total of 80 (not the initially requested 60) C-119s flew 1,232 hours during the weekend, carrying 45 passengers and 361.5 tons of cargo to Naval Air Station Key West, and Homestead AFB, FL. The build-up in the southeastern states had begun.

These AFRES C-119 units were deployed to the southeastern United States for the Cuban Missile Crisis:

Unit	Base
302nd TCW	Clinton County AFB, Ohio
349th TCW	Hamilton AFB, California
434th TCW	Bakalar AFB, Indiana
446th TCW	Ellington AFB, Texas
452nd TCW	March AFB, California

When the crisis had passed, Gen Walter C Sweeney Jr, commander of TAC, sent his appreciation to the units, saying: '…The present deployment of personnel and supplies… has been a challenge which at times created what appeared to be insurmountable problem areas in the air transport field. As a result of the professional competence demonstrated throughout your entire command, we were able to resolve these problem areas swiftly and effectively. In every instance where it became necessary to seek the assistance of your Reserve force C-119 capability, your people came through with flying colors.'

Between 16 and 27 October, CONAC airlift support of TAC continued at a very high rate. While normally the Reserves provided 10 aircraft per day, they now had 25 supporting the daily airlift requirements. Air Force Reserve C-119, C-123s, and C-124s delivered an additional 332 passengers 342.2 tons of cargo to the Southeast between 20 and 27 October. In addition, they flew priority missions in support of Air Defense Command (ADC), Air Force Systems Command (AFSC), and Air Force Logistics Command (AFLC).

C-119F, s/n 51-2671, operated with the 73rd TCS, 434th TCW, at Scott AFB, IL when photographed in June 1963. A partial white cap was applied over the forward fuselage. An AFRES disk-style insignia appears on the fin. Note the Army L-19 in the background. Via N E Taylor

C-119G-36-FA, s/n 53-3186, from the 68th TAS, 433rd TAW, appeared at Elmendorf AFB, AK, on 6 July 1969. The Air Force Reserve insignia had been changed from a disk to a crest, and AFRES was added to the tailboom. An Air Force Outstanding Unit Award, earned for service between 1 July and 31 December 1964, is applied to the nose. The curtains are deployed beneath the cockpit overhead windows and the astrodome hatch is opened for ventilation.
N E Taylor

Newspapers and radio and television newscasts kept the American public abreast of the developments in the Cuban Crisis. As a result, it came as no surprise to the Reservists when one C-123 wing and seven C-119 troop carrier wings were given a no-notice recall at 0120 hours, 28 October 1962.

The status of the mobilized aircraft and aircrews from the Cuban Missile Crisis is shown in the table below.

The 403rd TCW experienced a unique happening during their mobilization. TAC had elected to impose a full Operational Readiness Inspection (ORI) on the unit. While they passed, it was only after a great deal of work. The TAC ORI team arrived at Selfridge AFB, MI on 13 November, announcing their intentions. The wing was just emerging from the great number of problems associated with the 28 October no-notice recall. They were in the midst of converting from CONAC to TAC directives. Most of the air base personnel who would normally have supported the wing directly if it had been operating independently as a Reserve unit, had been integrated into other Selfridge AFB functions. Getting them back for the ORI was no small job in itself. Since the wing had not received any mobility orders, it was a practical matter to give them as much training possible by integrating them with the regular base functions. Conflicts between the Reserve manpower authorizations and TAC's criteria caused another major problem. Despite these conflicts, during the time of the ORI the 403rd TCW managed to fly more missions than asked for during the inspection.

While not part of the call up, the 435th TCW was directed to move its C-119s from Homestead AFB, FL, on 23 October. Nine of the aircraft went to Miami International Airport, and another three each went to Broward County and West Palm Beach Airports for the night and then all were consolidated at Miami on the following day.

Mobilized were 14,220 personnel and 422 AFRES aircraft. During the Cuban Crisis, the Reserve troop carrier units airlifted 4,743,000 lb of cargo to bases in Florida. During the redeployment phase, they flew 274 additional sorties and moved 2,110,952 lb of cargo from Florida to all points throughout the ZI. While officially inactivated on 28 November 1962, a total of 442 AFRES aircrews, including 290 pilots, 64 navigators, and 88 flight engineers, voluntarily remained on active duty to assist the Regular Air Force personnel redeploy the materiel and personnel deployed to the Southeast for the crisis.

On 2 November, Adlai E Stevenson, US Ambassador to the United Nations, sent a letter to Anastas I Mikoyan, First Deputy Prime Minister of the Soviet Union, identifying certain 'offensive weapons' in Cuba and asking for their removal the complete list included the following items:
- Surface-to-air missiles, including those designed for use at sea, and including propellants and chemical compounds capable of being used to power missiles
- Bomber aircraft
- Bombs, air-to-surface rockets, and guided missiles
- Warheads for any of the above weapons
- Mechanical or electronic equipment to support or operate the above items such as communications, supply, and missile launching equipment, including Komar-class motor torpedo boats

On the same day, Soviet Prime Minister Nikita S Krushchev agreed to remove the IL-28 *Beagles* from Cuba. After discussing Krushchev's 14-page letter, the Executive Committee agreed to lift the quarantine of Cuba.

Afterwards it was surmised that the Soviets had planned on establishing the missile sites in Cuba to use as a threat in the event the United States was to counter a planned Soviet incursion into West Berlin. There was also speculation that the Soviets had planned on building a submarine base in Cuba.

An interesting outcome from these tense times was the Washington-Moscow Hotline, officially known as the *US-Direct Communications Link for Crisis Control*. The system was installed less than a year after the crisis. The United States and the Soviet Union signed an agreement for this vital communications link on 20 June 1963.

An editorial in the London *Times* credited the troop carrier units with a major role in breaking the Cuban Crisis deadlock. Titled, 'American Determination – Key to Success,' the editorial stated, 'Looking back over that fateful week, some officials are disposed to believe that the mobilization of 24 troop carrying squadrons finally persuaded Mr Krushchev that war would be inevitable if the missiles were not withdrawn.'

Regarding the mobilization, Gen Curtis E LeMay, Chief of Staff of the Air Force, wrote: 'As the recalled Air Force Reserve units return to inactive status, I wish to express to the members of the Air Force Reserve Forces the pride which the Air Force feels in their outstanding response to the Cuban Crisis, both those called to active duty and those serving without mobilization orders. Among the noteworthy unit and individual actions were the performance of the

Unit	Base	Aircraft Type	Aircraft Possessed	Aircraft Ready	Aircrews Authorized	Aircrews Ops Ready
94th TCW	L G Hanscom Field, MA	C-119G/J	54	39	66	33
302nd TCW	Clinton County AFB, OH	C-119C/G/J	52	39	66	28
349th TCW	Hamilton AFB, CA	C-119G	68	51	88	57
403rd TCW	Selfridge AFB, MI	C-119G/J	54	35	66	40
434th TCW	Bakalar AFB, IN	C-119G/J	57	42	66	37
440th TCW	Gen Billy Mitchell Field, WI	C-119C/J	37	27	44	34
445th TCW	Dobbins AFB, GA (C-123)	C-123	45	38	84	38
512th TCW	NAS Willow Grove, PA	C-119G/J	59	43	66	39
Total			426	314	546	306

The 83rd TCS, 437th TCW, operated C-119G-FA, s/n 52-5901, from O'Hare Airport, Chicago, IL in 1961. The wing insignia appears above the entry door. Insignia Red Arctic trim is applied to the aircraft. Flush ADF antenna fairings are installed on top of the airplane. A R Krieger via MSgt D W Menard

C-119G-FA, s/n 52-5951, was operated by the 313th TCS, 939th TAG, 349th TCW, from Portland International Airport, OR. A white cap and blue cheatline are applied to the fuselage. Anti-corrosive paint is applied to the belly, while the fuselage sides are natural metal. The cowlings are natural metal, but the booms are painted Aircraft Gray. An Air Force Outstanding Unit Award is carried on the nose. CAC is applied to the boom while the round AFRES insignia appears on the fin. A Swanberg via MSgt D W Menard

Troop Carrier Wings and Aerial Port Squadrons that reacted immediately to the call to active duty; the remaining Air Force Reserve and Air National Guard units of CONAC, TAC, and ADC that heightened their readiness; the aircraft dispersal and other services provided by Air Guard personnel; and the remarkable dedication of Air Force Reserve recovery units working around the clock on dispersal of SAC, TAC, and ADC elements… This demonstration of responsiveness of the Air Reserve Forces underlines the importance of maintaining and further supporting the readiness of this vital element of Air Force capability. Our nation can be proud of the professionalism and devotion to duty and country displayed by the Air Reserve Forces in augmenting our active forces in this crisis.'

Outstanding Performance

The 440th TCW, stationed at Gen Billy Mitchell Field, Milwaukee, WI, was recognized as the top AFRES unit for two consecutive years at the Air Force Association's 1963 and 1964 National Conventions. The award is based on the wing's tactical, administrative, and logistical efficiency with the winner being judged by CONAC from submissions by each of the AFRES regions.

The 1963 award was for the units overall performance as follows:
- In August 1961, the 440th TCW participated in one of the largest peacetime maneuvers known as Operation *Swift Strike*. The unit supplied 24 aircraft and flew 94 sorties in five days, dropping 1,325 paratroops and 253 tons of equipment.
- The 440th TCW had a stellar showing at the Troop Carrier Competition sponsored by the Air Force Association in Las Vegas in June 1962
- During July 1962 the wing dispatched 16 C-119s for Exercise *Big Sweep II* in Alaska where they airdropped paratroops and equipment of the 1st Battle Group, 23rd Infantry, from Fort Richardson, Alaska. In addition, they airlanded supplies on gravel airstrips at remote sites north of the Arctic Circle.

The 1964 award was for the units overall performance as follows:
- The 440th Maintenance Squadron was recognized for achieving the highest engine time at overhaul experienced with the R-4360-89 engine by either a Regular Air Force or AFRES unit.
- Dedicated maintenance personnel permitted the unit to achieve more flying hours than any other AFRES unit.
- Having the best supply department within CONAC for the past two years.
- During the Cuban Missile Crisis, the 440th led all eight recalled AFRES units in aircraft and aircrew operational readiness.
- Three out of four of the 440th Field Maintenance Squadron personnel sent to technical schools were honor graduates in the top 3% of the classes for the past two years.
- Aircrews scored high on written examinations where 85% is the passing grade. Their average test score was 96%.
- The wing newspaper garnered first place for CONAC units for the past two years.
- During a TAC ORI, the 440th TCW was recognized as the best AFRES unit evaluated, exceeding some Regular Air Force units.

900-Series Groups

Initially, each Reserve troop carrier squadron, regardless of location, reported to a parent troop carrier group with the same designator as the group's parent troop carrier wing. These groups were generally co-located with the parent wing. The group level was phased out around 1955; thereby having each squadron, regardless of location, reporting directly to the wing. The troop carrier squadrons are operational units and do not have integral support components such as aerial port, security, civil engineering, communications, consolidated aircraft maintenance, and supply. It was soon realized that these support functions could operate better at the local level providing more immediate and relevant service to the tactical squadrons.

Between December 1962 and January 1963, a plethora of 900-series groups were established at each base with an operating tactical squadron. Each 900-series group was assigned a tactical squadron and a number of support squadrons or flights. A listing of these groups may be found in Appendix 4.

Beehive Group

One aircraft lived up to its unit's name during mid-June 1964. C-119G-36-FA, s/n 53-3173, from the 945th TCG at Hill AFB gained some notoriety when a swarm of bees took over the cockpit. A local beekeeper had to be called in to remove the hive that had developed above the co-pilot's window.

Project *Drag Net* Mission

The 73rd TCS, 932nd TCG at Scott AFB, IL was equipped with a number of C-119Fs and

This aircraft, C-119G-36-FA, s/n 53-7869, was photographed at the Van Nuys, CA airport on 30 April 1961. Note the nose number 869A, indicating that there was another aircraft with the same last three digits. 'Remove before flight' tags hang from the pitot tube covers on the nose. Assigned to the 349th TCG, 314th TCS, based at McClellan AFB, CA. The aircraft carries the dayglo orange trim of the day, and a white cap demarked by an Insignia Blue cheatline that drops below the upper cockpit window line and runs aft around the clamshell doors. Note the red rotating beacon on top of the left vertical fin.
H S Gann

C-119Gs. Several of the aircraft were equipped with beavertail doors and equipment for the trapeze recovery of parachute-borne capsules and inflight recovery of objects from the surface. This secondary mission for the unit had been pioneered under Project *Drag Net* by SAC's 456th TCW during 1955 and 1956.

Operation *Power Pack*

In October 1963, a military junta headed by Col Elias Wessin had overthrown the administration of the elected president of the Dominican Republic, Juan Bosch. By 24 April 1965, the political unrest in the capitol city, Santo Domingo, had exploded into an active revolution. Acting president Donald Reid Cabral went into exile; however Wessin rallied the military to oppose the return of Bosch. President Lyndon B Johnson intervened by dispatching a contingent of US Marines to the island to protect the American Embassy and evacuate non-Dominican citizens who might be in jeopardy. One battalion of Marines was on an exercise in Puerto Rico at the time. They boarded ship and redeployed to the Dominican Republic. While the rebellion was initially done in the name of democracy, it had quickly been taken over by Communist conspirators.

The remainder of the 2nd Marine Division at Camp Lejune and the 2nd Marine Air Wing from Cherry Point flew to the Dominican Republic. In addition, the 82nd Airborne Division was flown in from Fort Bragg.

In order to support the American forces and to provide emergency relief supplies to the islanders, the United States also conducted a massive airlift operation. Air Force Reserve aircrews flew 1,844 sorties, accruing 16,859 hours, while carrying 5,436 passengers and 4,547 tons of cargo in the performance of Operation *Power Pack*. A total of 188 Reserve missions were flown to the island in support of MATS and TAC allowing these commands to continue their operations in Southeast Asia. While a few C-123s and C-124s participated in

C-119CF-FA, s/n 51-8019 from the 73rd TCS, came to rest in a farmer's field off the end of Runway 31 at Scott AFB, IL after a series of malfunctions during a post maintenance FCF. Pieces of the aircraft were left in its wake. Base Security, Crash Rescue, and maintenance vehicles are at the aircraft. A fuel truck is standing by to drain the remaining fuel from the broken aircraft. (See story on page 109). USAF

this operation, most of the missions were flown by the Reserve C-119s. The C-119s flew 1,708 missions; while the C-123s and C-124s flew 120 and 16, respectively. Because of the volunteer efforts of AFRES personnel, a recall of the units to active duty was not necessary. The airlift lasted from 30 April to 5 July 1965.

Offshore Missions

Operation *Power Pack* had demonstrated the overwater capabilities of the C-119. As a consequence they were tasked with providing similar support to MATS and TAC as the war in Southeast Asia escalated. In this support role, Reserve C-119s conducted 3,648 offshore missions, flying a total of 27,138 hours, while carrying 3,155 passengers and 8,418 tons of cargo. At its peak in 1966 and 1967, the C-119s flew 16 offshore missions per week from Dover AFB, DL; to Goose Bay, Labrador; and Argentia, Newfoundland; from Patrick AFB, FL; to Grand Turk in the Turks and Caicos Islands; and Argentia; from NAS Norfolk, VA; to Guantanamo Bay, Cuba; and Puerto Rico; in addition to many other places.

Until the C-119s left the Reserve inventory in March 1973, they flew in support of Military Airlift Command (MAC), the successor to MATS in January 1966, operations. This support of the Operation *Power Pack* and the offshore mission did not go without notice. In March 1966, Gen Howell M Estes, MAC commander, stated: '...Let me also take this opportunity to commend the real job the Air Force Reserve C-119s have been doing for us in the past six months. Their mission in support of MAC fulfilled a sizable portion of near offshore responsibilities and accounted for almost 100% support of the recent airlift requirements to the Dominican Republic.'

Reserve Training for the USAF

The 514th Tactical Airlift Wing had moved from the small congested base at Mitchel AFB, NY, to McGuire AFB, NJ, on 15 March 1961. In addition to normal Reserve training, the wing performed routine missions for the Military Air Transport Service (MATS) and then Military Airlift Command (MAC) after the USAF organization was redesignated. In addition, the 514th

Vee-three-ship formations were later replaced by the off-set in-trail (echelon left or right) formation. High density drops tended to steal air from adjacent parachutes. Only one of the three aircraft had Insignia Red Arctic trim. Note how the prop warning line wrapped completely under the bellies of these aircraft. USAF Reserve

TAW performed C-119 training for maintenance and flight crews from the South Vietnamese Air Force, and maintenance personnel from the Royal Hellenic Air Force between 10 August and 18 December 1967.

Combat crew training for active USAF personnel was initiated at Clinton County AFB, OH, on 1 April 1968. The Combat Crew Training Squadron (Provisional), was attached to the 302nd TAW for this function. They provided Phase I (transition) training on the AC-119G gunship for instructor crews and maintenance personnel, providing a pipeline of personnel for TAC's Special Air Warfare Center. On 1 July 1968, this provisional unit was redesignated as the 1st Combat Crew Training Squadron (CCTS). The unit was again redesignated as the 1st Tactical Airlift Training Squadron (TATS) on 1 January 1970, in keeping with TAC's policy that all its training squadrons be known as TATSs. When Clinton County AFB closed on 20 June 1971, the 1st TATS relocated to Lockbourne AFB, OH. Between 1969 and 1973, the 1st TATS had trained 2,490 flying personnel (451 pilots, 264 navigators, and 202 flight engineers) and 1,573 maintenance personnel. In addition to the gunship instruction they trained foreign nationals from Ethiopia, Jordan, Morocco, and South Vietnam. The 1st TATS had flown 14,159.8 accident-free hours while performing this training.

Springfield Shuffle

Reservists did not engage in whimsical flights of fancy; they trained under a variety of conditions. One Saturday a crew took a 73rd TCS C-119 up for a routine training mission. 'After a mid morning take-off they flew several navigational legs before calling the Illinois ANG at Springfield, IL to shoot some practice ground controlled approaches (GCAs) to the field. The unit operated Republic F-84F Thunderstreaks. GCAs were a normal part of military flying in which a ground controller, utilizing ground-based radar equipment, would literally talk a pilot down to the runway during adverse weather conditions. This was no easy task and took an extreme amount of faith on both the part of the flight crew and the controller – especially in the controller's equipment.

'Our C-119 made a number of low approaches over the Illinois countryside. It was in July 1963 and the thermals were performing marvelously. Each plot of farmer's field with its differing vegetation offered varying degrees of vertical air currents. A slight haze was produced by the dust from the fields. Trying to perform a smooth, consistent rate of descent to the end of the runway under these mid-day conditions was extremely taxing on the flight crew. Fortunately we had a minimum crew and everyone was able to occupy a seat in the capacious cockpit of the aircraft. The controller brought us down the glideslope at a more than acceptable rate; however he consistently placed us 500ft to the left or right of the runway centerline. Each approach became more unsettling – we flew as directed, but never hit the mark. Coupled with the heat and the thermals that buffeted the aircraft, the crew actually began to sweat and become queasy. Airsickness in seasoned flight crews is rare; but, given the proper conditions, no one is immune. Enough was enough and we called to break off the insanity. Suddenly a new voice came up on the radio – 'This is master sergeant ___, I had a student controller on. Would you please make another approach so that we can assure the equipment is functioning properly.' We obliged, albeit a bit green around the gills. The old master made the approach as smooth as a tailor threading a needle. We were on glide slope and on glide path, and had we landed it would have been on the numbers. The sergeant thanked us for the opportunity to check out his equipment and we were sure some special training resulted upon our departure.

'We lumbered back to Scott AFB in a sweaty and semi-dazed condition. The flight lunches remained unopened. After landing we taxied to the ramp and shut down. For ventilation, the cockpit windows were opened as was the navigators' blister. About a half an hour later the unstable crew gingerly stepped off the aircraft and headed for base operations. A Coke provided instant blood sugar and stabilized the queasy stomachs'.

Morale Airlifts

In addition to the AFRES strategic airlift missions, the Reservists flew a pair of morale airlifts – Operation *Christmas Star* in 1965 and Operation *Combat Leave* in 1966.

CONAC coordinated and conducted Operation *Christmas Star* during November and December 1965. Military units, civilian service organizations, and private citizens contributed Christmas gifts to US servicemen in Southeast Asia and Alaska. Of the 469.11 tons of cargo delivered during Operation *Christmas Star*, AFRES units accounted for 67.18 tons while the ANG delivered 401.93 tons with their larger Boeing MC-97 Stratofreighters.

Triggered by a massive labor strike against five major US airlines, CONAC began Operation *Combat Leave* that began on 9 July 1966. With servicemen enroute to or from Southeast Asia given priority, 122,863 servicemen were airlifted under this operation that lasted for 63 days. AFRES units employed C-119s, C-124, HC-97s, C-47, and a single HU-16 during Operation *Combat Leave*, when 6,638 hours and 2,774 missions were flown to airlift 44,917 passengers. While the AFRES flew 36.5% of these missions, the balance were performed by the ANG, MAC and TAC. During Operation *Combat Leave*, five AFRES air terminal squadrons (later redesignated aerial port squadrons) provided continuous support at Travis AFB, CA. This activity spawned employment of all 12 air terminal squadrons performing their annual training at MAC bases to help that command reduce its airlift backlog.

The AFRES Air Terminal Squadrons performed their training at these bases in support of Operation *Combat Leave*.

C-119G-36-FA, s/n 53-3157, from the 349th TCW, nicknamed the 'Golden Gate Wing', was photographed over a drop zone near Beale AFB, CA. Its only distinctive markings were the full white cap and the dayglo orange trim.
USAF 162703AC

C-119s from the 357th TCS, 512th TCW, at Shaw AFB, SC. In the foreground, replete with its dayglo orange nose and wing insignia, is C-119G-FA, s/n 52-5945. Next in line, with the dayglo trim but devoid of a white cap and wing insignia, is C-119G-36-FA, s/n 53-7839. The last two aircraft are C-119B-FA, s/n 48-325, and C-119CF-70-FA, s/n 51-8254; both aircraft had been upgraded to the C-119G standard.
363rd TFW Historian via N E Taylor

Number	Base
5	Travis AFB, CA
4	Hickam AFB, HI
2	McGuire AFB, NJ
1	Charleston AFB, SC

Class A Accident

C-119CF-FA, s/n 51-8019, had undergone its 22nd periodic inspection and was dispatched with a minimum crew for a Functional Check Flight (FCF) on 17 April 1966. The FCF was designed to check out the aircraft prior to release for normal operations. The aircraft was assigned to the 73rd TCS, 932nd TCG, 434th TCW, based at Scott AFB, Illinois.

Maj Leroy Kinzel instructed Capt Van McNeil to preflight the aircraft while he received the FCF data from Quality Control, filed the flight plan and computed the performance data. The gross weight at take-off was 55,006 lb.

The Start Engines, Taxi, and Runup Checklists were performed without any special note. Next, an uneventful take-off and climbout to the assigned FCF area were completed. The crew performed several checks at an altitude of 5,000ft with satisfactory results.

Subsequently Maj Kinzel feathered the No 2 engine as part of the FCF. With the right prop lever in the full feather, the prop required 16 seconds for feathering. When bringing the No 2 prop out of feather to full increase, then to low stop, the rpm was noted to reach 2,950, even at low stop, instead of governing achieving the required 1,200-1,400rpm. At this point Maj Kinzel elected to again feather and shut down the malfunctioning prop. Upon placing the prop in the full feather position, the errant prop did not go into full feather, but windmilled. Maj Kinzel then brought the lever out of the feather position and quickly moved it firmly back into full feather. The prop continued to windmill then settled into full feather in about four to five minutes.

Maj Kinzel declared an emergency and returned to Scott for immediate termination of the flight. He requested a straight-in approach to Runway 31. At 1040 hours CST the tower cleared the aircraft to Runway 31 and reported surface winds of 20 knots at 150°. The crew shut down the No 2 engine and descended from the FCF area direct to the field. Both Phase I and Phase II Descent Checklists were completed and followed by the Before Landing Checklist. During the descent the flaps were lowered to the take-off position of 15°. The landing gear was lowered between 5,000 and 4,000ft. It was 1042 hours when Maj Kinzel reported 3,000ft over Mancoutah, located 3.6 miles southeast of the leading edge of the runway, then called for 40° flaps. At 1043 the tower reported winds at 130°, variable to 150° at 20 knots. All instruments and indications were normal, albeit for the shutdown No 2 engine and feathered prop. A C-119 with an engine out was extremely difficult to handle and lost significant performance capability.

While approaching the perimeter of the field, the aircraft was flying between 1,000 and 1,500ft carrying an indicated airspeed of 130-135 knots. The second approach was slightly higher than normal with a 150-155 knot calibrated airspeed. Maj Kinzel estimated that the touchdown point would have been near the middle of the 7,037ft long runway. The runway had 1,000ft macadam overruns at each end. The throttle for the No 1 engine was nearly fully closed during the descent. The left main gear green indicating light was flickering on Capt McNeil's instrument panel. Maj Kinzel called for a go-around.

During the transition from a high rate of descent to level flight for go-around, the airspeed remained around 130-132 knots indicated. Capt McNeil raised the flaps from 40° to 20° and then reached for the gear up switch.

The aircraft struck the runway and slid off the end into a grassy field. A fire that ensued after impact was contained by base crash and rescue crews. Miraculously, the only injury was to SSgt John Brown. (See photo on page 107).

FCF crew assigned to C-119CF-FA, s/n 51-8019 on 17 April 1966.

Name	Assigned Duty	Rating
Maj Leroy A Kimzel	932nd Materiel Sqn Asst Maint Officer	Command Pilot
Capt Van D McNeil	73rd TCS Line Pilot	Pilot
SSgt John G Brown	73rd TCS Flt Mechanic	N/A

Reserve Bill of Rights

Until 1968, CONAC managed the Air Force Reserve field program. Public Law 90-168 established the new Air Force Reserve, as a Separate Operating Agency, on 1 August 1968, replacing CONAC. During its existence as a Separate

C-119G-FA, s/n 51-8059, flew with the AFRES and carried the AFOUA ribbon on the vertical tail. She was sent to Davis-Monthan AFB, AZ, on 12 December 1969, then to Kolar, Inc, in Tucson for scrap on 24 February 1976. H S Gann

Operating Agency, the Air Force Reserve was the largest and most diverse such organization. In 1997 the Reserve became a Major Air Command for the first time. Known as the Reserve Bill of Rights, the new law directed that management of the Air Force Reserve would be by key Reservists. The new organization, headquartered at Robins AFB, GA, was headed by Maj Gen Rollin B Moore Jr. Gen Moore had been the troop carrier commander of Exercise *Bright Star/Pine Cone III* in August 1960.

Exercise *Exotic Dancer II*

During May and June 1969, 97 C-119s and 57 C-124s from the AFRES participated in Exercise *Exotic Dancer II* in Puerto Rico, an operation conducted by the unified Atlantic Command (LANTCOM). Operations were conducted around-the-clock while living under field conditions. Tropical heat and rain added to the hardships.

Over 31,000 AFRES personnel from these units participated in the Exercise *Exotic Dancer II*.

Unit	Base	Aircraft
94th MAW	Hanscom AFB, MA	C-124
302nd TAW	Lockbourne AFB, OH	C-119
403rd TAW	Selfridge AFB, MI	C-119
433rd TAW	Kelly AFB, TX	C-119
440th TAW	Gen Mitchell Field, WI	C-119
442nd MAW	Richards-Gebaur AFB, MO	C-124
445th MAW	Dobbins AFB, GA	C-124
446th TAW	Ellington AFB, TX	C-119
459th MAW	Andrews AFB, MD	C-124
512th MAW	Carswell AFB, TX	C-124
514th MAW	McGuire AFB, NJ	C-119/C-124

The main force arrived in the maneuver area on D-Day, where a formation of 45 C-119s flawlessly dropped 70 tons of heavy equipment within the drop zone. Gen William W Momyer, TAC Commander, observed the D-Day drop and stated: 'The C-119 drop was tremendous. Its obvious to me that these Reserve Forces were really peaked for this exercise. The formation, the air discipline and the way that the cargo was put on the target was an outstanding display of professionalism.'

Admiral Ephraim P Holmes, USN, was the overall exercise commander. He too observed the significant part played by the AFRES and ANG personnel, stating: 'The efforts of the Air Force Reserve aircrews and support personnel were a major contribution to the success of the of Joint Exercise *Exotic Dancer II*. The heavy equipment airdrop was accomplished in an exemplary manner. The effort of your command in support of the deployment/redeployment phases was a most significant contribution.'

During the exercise, AFRES airlift crews were credited with accruing just under 3,700 flying hours, and airlifting more than 1,200 tons of cargo and 1,200 passengers.

The Puerto Rico ANG's 156th TFW employed 10 Lockheed F-104 Starfighters as the opposing force during the mock war. They flew 74 sorties and were credited with destroying the headquarters for the invading force, 28 fighters, and 10 ships. In addition they were credited with destroying or damaging some of the aircraft on the ground and anti-aircraft sites.

Exercise *Exotic Dancer II* provided realistic training with a unified force from the Army, Navy, Marine Corps, and Air Force. While no winner was declared, the joint operation experience proved invaluable.

OPERATIONAL SUCCESS

The Air Force Reserve is made up of many experienced prior service personnel. In addition, those in any given unit tend to remain for a greater number of years as opposed to the four or five-year active duty tour for an individual attending a technical school and then serving in an operational unit. The C-119 Flying Boxcars were in the Air Force Reserve inventory from 1951 until 1973 – longer than a career for many of the personnel. As a result, the maintenance technicians were better able to cope with the idiosyncrasies of the aircraft and the flight crews were better able to make the airplane perform. Consequently, the Reserves had a high degree of operational success with the aircraft.

The last C-119 Flying Boxcar left the Reserves on 3 March 1973. At its peak in December 1962, a total of 669 of the airplanes were in the Reserve inventory. During its 19 years with the Reserves, the C-119s had flown at least 1,282,360 hours. In the summer of 1960, an Air Force Reserve general officer led a force of over 500 C-119s into the war games known as Operation *Bright Star/Pine Cone III*. Beginning in 1962, Reserve C-119s supported the NASA space program. During the last five years of that the C-119s served with the Reserves, one squadron conducted Phase I transition training in the airplane for instructor crews and maintenance personnel of both the US regular and reserve forces as well as foreign nationals.

The C-119s and C-124s were phased out of the Reserve inventory and a new form of reserve operation came into being. This was the Associate program in which the Reserve personnel fly and maintain aircraft owned by co-located Regular Air Force units. The maintenance personnel work shoulder-to-shoulder with their active duty counterparts. Today, the flight crews are made up of all Regular Air Force, all Reserve, or a combination thereof all performing a common mission in airlift.

C-119C-20-FA, s/n 49-0157, operated with the Reserves and was retired to Davis-Monthan in 1968. The MASDC Reclamation Number, CJ112, appeared on the nose. Sealant was applied around the cockpit windows and door hinges. To the rear is a C-97. H S Gann

Chapter 15

Air National Guard Flying Boxcars

Air National Guard (ANG) units, assigned to the various states, traditionally were given fighter, fighter-bomber, or attack missions. A new mission was given to a number of ANG units in 1957, this being aeromedical transport. The aircraft provided for this mission were MC-119Js with the flight-operable doors. This mission lasted for five to six years until the C-119s were replaced by the quieter Lockheed C-121 Super Constellations.

Briefly, several ANG units served as troop carriers until they were redesignated as air commando/special operations units. These ANG squadrons flew the C-119C, C-119G, and C-119L series aircraft. Serving in these capacities, the C-119s were in the ANG inventory between 1958 and 1975.

The first ANG Flying Boxcar to retire to Davis-Monthan AFB, AZ, was a C-119J, serial number 53-3213, from the 102nd Aeromedical Transport Squadron, NY-ANG. The aircraft arrived on 31 August 1960. The last of these ANG aircraft to retire was C-119L, serial number 53-8154, from the 130th Special Operations Squadron, WV- ANG, on 27 September 1975. This airplane received a civil registry and became N4999P owned by Starbird Inc in Reno, NV.

AEROMEDICAL AIRLIFT

Rumors began during the mid-1950s, that some ANG fighter units would transition into transports; with the C-97 Stratofreighter being speculated as the most probable. The seasoned fighter pilots were appalled by the noise, size, and loss of several hundred knots of airspeed. Difficulties with the initial transition from fighters to the lumbering four-engined C-97s gave thought to making the change easier by using the C-119 as an interim aircraft. The old adage that 'fighter pilots can do anything' got a new meaning when high-time ANG fighter pilots began transitioning into the C-119. Some of the fighter pilots became airsick after several hours in the air and had to use the driftmeter in the floor to get their bearings. Another major stumbling block for the fighter pilots was the concept of crew coordination. With the WY-ANG, many of the older fighter pilots transferred to the CO-ANG that was flying North American F-86L Sabres at the time. This solved half of the problem. A blessing in disguise was the fact that the CO-ANG had a number of younger fighter pilots who were looking forward to building time to get with an airline. The latter group transferred to the Wyoming ANG and a multitude of problems were solved.

Nine of the 12 ANG units equipped with the C-119s operated between 1957 and 1963. These units transitioned from fighters to the C-119, resulting in an increase in manning for each of the flightcrew positions. An aeromedical airlift flight, consisting of one flight nurse and two medical technicians per aircrew, was also added to the unit. With the advent of the C-119s, the traditional 'weekend warrior' status of these units changed to where the crews could bid for particular missions that better suited them as individuals with their civilian jobs, yet had the added benefit of making the unit a year-round operation for augmenting the Regular Air Force. Live-patient training from the home bases was not performed because the C-119 was considered unsuitable for a peacetime mission.

156th Aeromedical Airlift Squadron

156th Aeromedical Airlift Squadron, NC-ANG, was based at the Douglas Municipal Airport. On 1 January 1961, the squadron gained its first C-119C. This new aeromedical evacuation mission necessitated an increase in manning

During April 1973, the ANG deployed C-119s to Robert Gray Army Air Field, TX for Exercise *Gallant Hand*, a joint forces operation. The ANG had to keep two sorties in the air for 24 hours per day on alert status. Note the Army Hueys that shared the ramp. USAF K54581

C-119L, s/n 53-3186, from the 143rd SOS, 143rd SOG, RI ANG, was undergoing engine maintenance in June 1973, at Providence, RI. An ANG *Minuteman* insignia was applied to the fins. The aircraft had previously served as a C-119G with the 68th TAS, 433rd TAW, AFRES. She was retired in June 1975. T Panopalis

C-119L-FA, s/n 53-8073, also was assigned to the 143rd SOS, RI ANG. The aircraft has a full white cap that extends aft from the lower cockpit line, joggles down at the prop warning line, and wraps around the clamshell doors. Aircraft Gray paint is applied aft of the prop warning line on the fuselage, booms, and empennage; while the forward lower fuselage is in natural metal. Note how the black antiglare panel extends aft and down to surround the drop windows. Such a paint scheme could only help for performing clandestine night drop operations. A Navy A-4 Skyhawk from Replacement Air Group CVG-6 shared the ramp. *Via T Panapolis*

In contrast to aircraft 53-8073 is C-119L 53-7837 with its overall Aircraft Gray and white cap finish. The lower in-spar wing surfaces are painted black. Entire 'power eggs' from C-121 Constellations replaced the former R-3350 engine package on these aircraft. To the rear is an EA-3D from Replacement Air Group CVG-6. *Via T Panapolis*

Operated by the 129th SOS, CA ANG, C-119G-84-KM, s/n 53-8069, was taxying at Hayward, CA. It has a natural metal finish, white cap, stepped cheatline, and gray anti-corrosion finish on the belly. The 129th SOG insignia appears above the entry door. *Lt Col J J Craddick*

Converted to a C-119L, s/n 53-8076 had last served with the 129th SOS, CA ANG, based at Hayward, CA, before retiring to MASDC in March 1975. The aircraft has a white cap, silver painted lower fuselage, and Aircraft Gray applied to the booms and empennage. An ANG *Minuteman* insignia and CALIF are applied to the fins. She became N8506A. *T H Brewer*

to 800 personnel. An accelerated recruiting campaign garnered the squadron 30 nurses and 60 aeromedical technicians. In 1962 the unit constructed nurses' quarters and a new training hospital to perform its new mission.

The C-119 was not the right airplane for this mission, and in 1962 the squadron began transitioning into Lockheed C-121 Super Constellations. The last C-119 was phased out in that year.

167th Aeromedical Transport Squadron
Previously known as the 167th Tactical Fighter Squadron, equipped with F-86Hs, the unit was redesignated the 167th Aeromedical Transport Squadron (ATS) on 1 April 1961. The 167th ATS was assigned to the WV-ANG and was stationed at Martinsburg, WV. With its new aeromedical role, there was a mass exodus of fighter pilots. However, the unit added 22 maintenance personnel, 16 flight nurses, and 31 aeromedical technicians to their unit manning. In addition to the aeromedical mission, the squadron was tasked with routine cargo operations. The USAF dispatched a mobile training unit to the base to assist the 167th in their transition. Training was completed within three months.

The average reciprocating engine was overhauled around ten times during its service life. Engine reliability must be watched at two ends of the time spectrum. High time engines tend to fail because of inherent wear of the internal

C-119G-36-FA, s/n 53-7865, from the 129th SOS, was photographed at Van Nuys, CA on 4 July 1971. While the fuselage is in natural metal finish with a white cap, the booms and empennage are painted Aircraft Gray. The aircraft carries the ANG *Minuteman* insignia and CALIF on the vertical fins. Barely visible is the 129th SOS insignia aft of the cockpit. It shares the ramp with one of the unit's U-10D Helio Couriers, s/n 66-15348; an Army T-41 Mescalero, s/n 65-5252; a Navy S-2; and a C-118. The Boxcar was subsequently converted into a C-119L, and later retired to MASDC on 5 March 1979. Still later, the aircraft gained civil registry N850W and was operated by J D Gifford & Associates, Anchorage, AK. P Bergagnini via D Remington

C-119G-36-FA, s/n 53-3216, from the 129th SOS, 129th SOG, CA ANG, was at Offutt AFB, NE in May 1977. An ANG *Minuteman* insignia and 'CALIF' were applied to the fins. She was retired from service and became N8504Y, operated by Stebbins Community Service, Stebbins, AK. T H Brewer

C-119L, s/n 53-8142, from the 129th SOS, was photographed on 5 October 1973 at Hayward, CA. The dual ADF football antennas on top of the fuselage had been replaced with faired antennas. An additional UHF blade antenna is also installed. A mechanic's toolbox is parked next to the entry door. The aircraft is painted in overall Aircraft Gray. A stepped cheatline separates the white cap from the gray. The nose is natural metal. This aircraft was retired to MASDC on 22 January 1976, and subsequently gained civil registry N8504X for operations with Northern Pacific Transport. In the background is C-119L, s/n 52-5836. L Peacock via D Remington

C-119L, s/n 53-3186, was photographed while taxying at Wright-Patterson AFB, OH in April 1974. The ANG *Minuteman* insignia was the only unit identification carried on the aircraft. A white cap and overall Aircraft Gray paint were applied to the aircraft. T Brewer

parts, hence a requirement for a hard-timed removal. At the other end of the spectrum is the premature failure due generally to poor workmanship and quality control during overhaul. The 167th ATS had a rash of premature failures on engines being returned from a particular overhaul shop in Miami, FL. At one juncture, they removed the errant engine, crated it, stuffed it into a C-119, and flew to the depot. There the engine was torn down under the supervision of the maintenance personnel from the 167th. During this teardown it was noted that the bearing tolerances were too sloppy for the engine to maintain the requisite design oil pressures. Subsequent overhauled engines from this particular depot were much better.

On 2 June 1963, the 167th received its first C-121G Super Constellation, thus bringing to an end its use of the C-119. The unit was reassigned from TAC to MATS on 13 July 1963.

187th Aeromedical Transport Squadron

In 1961, the 187th FIS from the WY-ANG traded in their F-86Ls, were redesignated the 187th ATS, and obtained their MC-119Js for the aeromedical transport role from Cheyenne

C-119L, s/n 53-8087, from the 130th SOS, 130th SOG, WV ANG, was photographed at Wright-Patterson AFB, OH in April 1974. This overall-black aircraft, with subdued markings, was employed in clandestine operations. T H Brewer

This 187th ATS, WY-ANG crew is cruising at 9,500ft with the aircraft commander hand-flying. The flight engineer sits behind both pilots, observing engine performance and ready to make any power adjustments. The *whiskey* compass is suspended from the top of the windscreen center post. Radio selector controls for both navigation and communications are located on the forward portion of the overhead console. Via Mel Duncan

Municipal Airport, WY. An initial cadre from the WY-ANG went to Meridian, MS for transition training into the MC-119J. The field elevation at Cheyenne is 6,156ft, which resulted in marginal take-off performance with the R-3350 engines. When the ANG unit asked the USAF for advice, a team of experts was dispatched to Cheyenne to show the guard how to operate the airplanes. This team quickly came to the realization that the density altitude at Cheyenne was not conducive to operation of C-119s powered by R-3350s. After almost two months of struggling with the situation, these aircraft were replaced with C-119Cs (actually C-119CFs with hydraulic flaps and landing gear) powered by R-4360 engines.

A USAF ferry crew flew into Cheyenne, parked the unit's first C-119C on the ramp and left town. The savvy ANG crews broke out the flight manuals and began their own transition course for this aircraft powered by R-4360-20-WA water-injected engines. After several days of study followed by ground runs, the initial cadre aircrews began flying the C-119C. The take-off performance was at best marginally better. The engines were equipped with variable speed superchargers with automatic control. Therein lay the problem. The superchargers had a tendency to shift into high blower on take-off, overboosting the engines and momentarily robbing the engines of power at a critical phase during climbout. Working with Pratt & Whitney, the 187th ATS modified the supercharger controls by installing a two-position switch allowing positive control for shifting from low to high stage blower. This modification changed the engine designation to an R-4360-20-WD. In addition, the water-alcohol injection system was reactivated, making 'wet' take-offs a standard procedure.

Operational data was non-existent for the two-stage blower system and Pratt & Whitney enlisted the aid of the 187th to develop the data. Crews took off with huge charts with a multitude of blank spaces for the data that had to be annotated. For several weeks, two dedicated crews recorded the myriad of data. Take-offs were performed in both low- and high-blower and the data duly annotated. Engine readings were taken under a wide variety of flight conditions. Service ceilings were developed to assure reasonable rates of climb.

Operating a C-119 at the high altitudes above Wyoming was not conducive to safety. While loss of engine performance when flying at lower altitudes would have dictated shutting down the ailing engine, crews of the 187th would opt to continue operation under partial power to assure getting to a safe field. This practice usually ruined a faltering engine that otherwise might have been saved had it been shut down.

On occasion, C-119s from the 187th ATS were used to carry personnel to fight forest fires. The clamshell doors were removed, making the back end noisy and drafty. Many of the fire fighters came from local Indian reservations. The passengers had a fantastic view of where they had been, but not where they were going.

After operating the C-119s for about two years, the 187th ATS made a major upgrade into the Lockheed C-121 Super Constellation. These four-engined, pressurized aircraft provided a marked improvement in operating performance and people comfort.

SPECIAL OPERATIONS

Three ANG C-119-equipped squadrons served in the special operations role between 1963 and 1975. Their mission was to work in conjunction with special operations ground units from the Regular Army, ANG, and Army Reserve. Proficiency requirements for the aircrews necessitated 140 flying hours per aircraft per month in each squadron. Each air commando squadron was authorized 43 officers and 57 airmen; while the consolidated aircraft maintenance squadron consisted of six officers and 157 airmen. Each aircrew comprised of two troop carrier pilots, one navigator, an airborne radio operator, a flight mechanic, and a loadmaster.

129th Troop Carrier Squadron/ Special Operations Squadron

Beginning operations as the 129th TCS, the unit was redesignated the 129th SOS. The squadron operated C-119C/G/L aircraft from Hayward Airport between July 1963 and 1975 as part of the CA-ANG. During the late 1960s, the C-119Ls entered the squadron's inventory.

This C-119F-KM, s/n 51-8119, has been converted to an MC-119J with the beavertail door. Dayglo orange trim is applied to the tailbooms, wingtips, and nose. Poor performance of the Wright R-3350 engines at the high altitudes around Cheyenne, WY resulted in this aircraft being replaced after less than a month of operation. Via Mel Duncan

MC-119J-KM, s/n 51-8129, from the 145th Aeromedical Evacuation Squadron (AES), Ohio ANG, was photographed at Baltimore, MD on 26 April 1962. The aircraft was equipped with a beavertail door. The markings consist of the tail number, last three digits of the tail number on the nose gear doors, and the unit name. Dayglo orange paint is applied to the nose, wingtips, and booms. R C Seely via MSgt D W Menard

MC-119J-KM. s/n 51-8123, was operated by the 140th AES, PA ANG. With the 0- in the tail number, the aircraft was at least 10 years old when it was photographed at Olmstead AFB, PA. Dayglo orange trim from the late 1950s-early 1960s is applied to the nose, wingtips, and booms. A red cross is painted on the fins. Only the last two digits of the tail number are applied to the nose of the aircraft. Four F-101Bs appear in the background. R C Seely via MSgt D W Menard

Aircraft and aircrews from the 129th SOS supported Operation *Biglift* between 22 December 1964 and 22 January 1965, when heavy storms inundated California and Oregon. The unit airlifted medical supplies, blankets, food, and four-wheel drive vehicles to many of the cities that were completely surrounded by water.

In 1965, the 129th SOS was scheduled to deploy to Panama for their summer training camp where they worked with an active duty USAF unit, the 605th Air Commando Squadron, Composite, stationed at Howard AB. Unforeseen circumstances precluded this deployment.

Many of the ANG members had World War Two combat experience. The experience level of the ANG aircrew members generally outstripped that of their Regular Air Force counterparts. Consequently during 1966 and 1967, the USAF sent air and ground crews to Hayward for training with the 129th SOS. Many missions were flown to Alaska by the unit for joint maneuvers with the Army Special Forces units.

In 1975, the mission was changed to air rescue and the C-119s were replaced by the Lockheed C-130 Hercules and helicopters.

130th Special Operations Squadron

The 130th SOS from the WV-ANG also performed special operations with C-119Cs, C-119Gs and C-119Ls between 1965 and 1975. The unit was based at Kanawa County Airport, WV. In addition, the squadron operated Helio U-10B Super Couriers and Sikorsky H-19 Chickasaws.

While most members of the 130th Air Commando Squadron (ACS) were away at summer camp during August 1963, a team went to Martinsburg to begin ferrying C-119s from the 167th AES to Kanawa County Airport. Between 1 and 10 October the members of the 130th accepted six of the 167th's C-119s. These aircraft were later all judged to be unfit for future service and were ferried to Davis-Monthan AFB, AZ for salvage. A second lot of C-119s was found to be more airworthy and found their way into the inventory of the 130th ACS.

It was the first such ANG unit to train outside of the CONUS. Between 24 January and 12 February 1965, the squadron deployed to Howard Field, Panama for training. While there, the unit conducted jungle survival, air-sea rescue, and parachute drops. Four C-119s airlifted the U-10Bs and H-19s to Panama. C-121s from the 167th also assisted in the airlift. During this deployment, the 130th ACS was completely self-sustaining.

The 140th AES, PA ANG, flew this MC-119J, s/n 51-8167 from Spaatz Field, PA. The aircraft carries faded dayglo orange conspiscuity markings, a red cross on the tail, and only the last two digits of the tail number on the nose. Frank Lamm

C-119G, s/n 53-7884, was frequently used to drop members of the Army's *Golden Knights* parachute demonstration team.

The 130th ACS operated the only known ANG C-119C in Southeast-Asia camouflage paint, s/n 49-156. In addition, it flew the only known overall black C-119, s/n 53-8086. The paint reduced its radar signature when used in clandestine operations. Little is known about the black bird, except that it had been converted into a C-119L at Kanawa County Airport with the help of personnel dispatched from the Warner Robins Air Material Center, Robins AFB, GA during the winter of 1972-1973. Additional modifications included installation of special engine exhaust shields and mission equipment. Testing was accomplished at Wright-Patterson AFB, OH. One mission for this aircraft was nocturnal crowd surveillance and control. Cameras and listening devices were installed for this mission.

On 8 August 1968, the 130th ACS was redesignated the 130th Special Operations Squadron (SOS).

The Guard Bureau annually recognizes its top unit. During this period, there were 92 units in contention. The 130th SOS was recognized as the best flying unit within the Guard during 1968 and 1970.

The 130th SOS retired its last C-119 in October 1975. While the C-119 had a 5,000-hour design life, the 130th SOS retired one aircraft that had accrued 7,400 flying hours. This is yet another testament to the dedication and skill level of Reserve Component maintenance personnel. During 1963, the 130th SOS briefly operated six C-119Cs received from the 167th AES. These were followed by eight C-119Cs that were flown between 1963 and 1969. The 130th received nine C-119Gs, one of which was salvaged during the first year. The remaining eight C-119Gs were operated between 1969 and 1974. These aircraft were all converted to C-119Ls.

The 130th SOS was the last ANG unit to transition out of the C-119s resulting in the unit being the butt of a number of jokes. For their last hurrah, the 130th deployed their Flying Boxcars to England in 1975 so that they could participate in field exercises in Germany. The other units were equipped with the new Lockheed C-130 Hercules. During this exercise, the 130th SOS flew more tonnage and had a higher in-commission rate than any other unit participating in the exercise.

The 167th AES from the WV ANG operated C-119B, s/n 48-0332. Dayglo paint was carried on the airplane. While the aircraft was retrofitted with dual nosewheels and ventral fins, the horizontal stabilizer tip extensions were retained. In addition, the black paint in the engine exhaust areas indicates that the airplane was powered by the R-4360 engines. The airplane was eventually retired to MASDC. R C Seely via MSgt D W Menard

C-119J-KM, s/n 51-8121, is being parked at NAS Floyd Bennett Field on a cold winter's day. Note the sage green parkas on the ground personnel. These parkas were fitted with wolverine collars that did not freeze with one's breath. The aircraft is in natural metal finish with a white cap and minimal markings. Dayglo orange conspiscuity markings are applied to the nose wingtips and booms. NY ANG

Chapter 16

Gunships

While contemplating the problems associated with a limited war and counterinsurgency operations, Ralph E Flexman, an Assistant Chief Engineer at Bell Aerosystems in Buffalo, NY, became an early proponent of the gunship. On 27 December 1962, Flexman submitted a proposal to Dr Gordon A Extrand with the Behavioral Sciences Laboratory at Wright-Patterson AFB, OH. The idea was to make an aircraft a lateral-firing platform that would fly in a pylon turn to control the effectiveness of an aircraft engaged in anti-aircraft suppression operations. Flexman had worked with the man who should be credited with being the father of the gunship, Gilmour Craig MacDonald. As early as April 1942, as a first lieutenant with the 95th Coast Artillery (AA), MacDonald had proposed using civilian aircraft equipped with a side-firing gun to fly in a banked circle to suppress enemy submarines. In September 1961, MacDonald was a lieutenant colonel in the USAF. He then recommended to TAC that aircraft be equipped with transverse-firing rockets or guns.

In a brainstorming session at Bell, Flexman introduced his theory. The result was the proposal suggesting that an aircraft could spot the enemy, immediately roll into a banked turn to keep the enemy in sight, and then keep the enemy under sustained fire without ever losing sight of them. Three major problem areas required further investigation, these being: the ballistics of the projectiles as they were fired and their subsequent dispersion, the ability of a pilot to aim his lateral weapon and hold the target, and the reaction time required to change from straight-and-level flight to a pylon-turn. Investigation and testing proved the theory to be viable.

Aircraft Conversions

The first aircraft to be converted into operational gunships were Douglas C-47s. Known as Spooky ships, the AC-47s went into combat with the 4th and 14th Air Commando Squadrons in December 1967. These aircraft were equipped with three 7.62mm miniguns.

The Gunship II program consisted of Lockheed C-130 Hercules aircraft with a pair of 20mm Vulcans, a 7.62mm minigun, and a pair of 40mm Bofors cannon. These ships, designated as the AC-130 Spectre, were by far the most effective of the gunships and they continue today in the USAF inventory.

Typical electrical equipment locations on the AC-119.

A number of C-119s also were converted into gunships, with the designation of AC-119 Shadow, under Project *Combat Hornet*. These modifications were accomplished under the Gunship III project. The AC-119s were about 25 per cent more effective than the earlier AC-47s. Two versions of Shadows were developed: the AC-119G had four 7.62mm miniguns installed in a basic C-119G; while the AC-119K had an additional pair of 20mm Vulcans and jet pods for added power. A total of 26 AC-119Gs was produced between 21 May and 22 October 1968. Another 26 aircraft were converted into AC-119Ks between 14 October 1968 and 31 March 1969. These conversions were accomplished by the Fairchild-Hiller Corporation at their St Augustine, FL facility.

The AC-119G Shadow was modified to incorporate the installation of four MXU-470/A module 7.62mm guns, a LAU-74/A flare launcher, fire control computer, lead computing optical gunsight, fire control display, night observation sight (NOS), illuminator, and additional navigational and communications equipment. Armor plating was added in the floor in critical areas only so as to control the weight of the aircraft. The existing Solar APP was replaced by a 60 KvA Garrett Industries auxiliary power unit (APU), the latter being installed in the cargo compartment on the right side. New ducting was provided for the APU air inlet and exhaust outlet. The design gross weight of the airplane was 64,000 lb. The basic crew consisted of a pilot, co-pilot, navigator/safety offi-

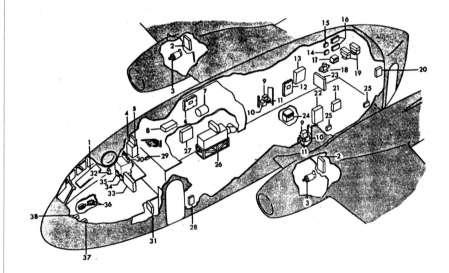

LOCATION OF ELECTRICAL EQUIPMENT (Typical)

1. OVERHEAD PANEL
2. NACELLE JUNCTION BOX
3. ENGINE GENERATOR
4. RADIO JUNCTION BOX NO. 2
5. FCS AUXILIARY JUNCTION BOX
6. AUXILIARY FLOOR JUNCTION BOX
7. TRANSFORMER/RECTIFIER UNIT
8. GYRO PALLET
9. ENGINE GENERATOR VOLTAGE REGULATORS
10. FIELD CONTROL RELAY
11. OVERVOLTAGE RELAY
12. RIGHT MAIN JUNCTION BOX
13. GUN CONTROL PANEL
14. PILOT'S INSTRUMENT INVERTER RELAY
15. FLARE LAUNCHER JUNCTION BOX
16. PILOT'S INSTRUMENT INVERTER
17. AUTOPILOT POWER JUNCTION BOX
18. AUTOPILOT INVERTER
19. SINGLE PHASE INVERTERS
20. APU CONTROL PANEL
21. AUTOPILOT CONTROLLER JUNCTION BOX
22. LEFT MAIN JUNCTION BOX
23. OVERHEAD JUNCTION BOX
24. BATTERY
25. GUN JUNCTION BOX
26. APU-DRIVEN GENERATOR
27. AC POWER DISTRIBUTION BOX
28. NOS JUNCTION BOX
29. EMERGENCY CIRCUIT BREAKER PANEL
30. ARN-21 JUNCTION BOX
31. NOSE JUNCTION BOX
32. NAVIGATOR'S CIRCUIT BREAKER JUNCTION BOX
33. MAIN RADIO JUNCTION BOX
34. UHF-DF JUNCTION BOX
35. MONITOR BUS BOX
36. EXTERNAL POWER RECEPTACLES
37. PILOT'S ATTITUDE AND DIRECTIONAL INDICATOR
38. ADI CONTROLLER

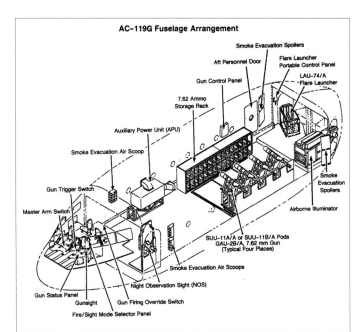
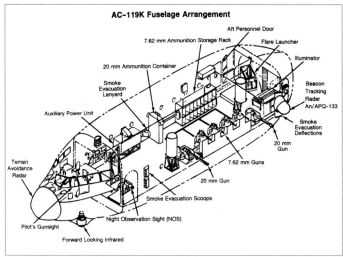

General arrangement of operational equipment installed in the AC-119G (left) and the AC-119K (right).

cer, flight mechanic, illuminator operator, two gunners, and the NOS operator.

Gunship performance differences are shown in this table.

Aircraft	Endurance	Max TOW	Engine-Out Climb
AC-47	4.5 hours		*
AC-119G	6.5 hours	64,000 lb	*
AC-119K	5.0 hours	80,400 lb	500 FPM
AC-130A	6.5 hours	124,200 lb	400 FPM

* Unsatisfactory at combat gross weight.

The AC-119K Stinger was made from the C-119G brought up to the AC-119G standard and then further modified. A pair of 2,850-lbst General Electric J85-GE-17 turbojets were added under the wings. A pair of M61A1 20mm Vulcans were added. The Texas Instruments AN/AAD-4 FLIR was installed along with a Motorola AN/APQ-133 side-looking beacon tracking radar, a Texas Instruments AN/APQ-136 search radar with a moving target indicator mode, and an AN/APN-147 Doppler terrain following radar. With all of these modifications, the AC-119K weighed in at 80,400 lb maximum gross ramp (ground) weight. A major weight reduction program was instituted to get the aircraft at this weight. Three-bladed Hamilton Standard propellers later replaced the four-bladed propellers.

A major concern arose over crew survival due to the lack of cabin smoke evacuation in the event of a magnesium flare igniting. The requirement was for the smoke to be evacuated within 10 seconds. The AC-47 Spooky had such a system; therefore the USAF believed Fairchild-Hiller would have no problems adapting such a system for the AC-119s. On 19 April 1968, USAF officials informed the company that they were dissatisfied with potential deficiencies in the system and the contractor's attitude toward fulfilling the requirement. Testing supported the Air Force's position and reluctantly the contractor made the requisite adjustments. The system consisted of a set of air scoops in the forward cabin and spoilers in the aft fuselage. Installation of this simple fix ended 26 months of strained relations between the USAF and Fairchild-Hiller over this matter.

The first AC-119G, serial number 53-8069, was accepted by the USAF at Robins AFB, Georgia on 19 May 1968. The first AC-119K, serial number 53-7877, was accepted in the same year.

AC-119 Missions

AC-119s were capable of performing the following seven missions:

Armed Reconnaissance: The AC-119Ks would be assigned an area to search and have the authority to strike valid targets discovered within the area.

Close Support: The AC-119s could provide supporting fire and illumination for extended periods to ground units and static positions. These operations required reliable communications with friendly ground forces. Offset distances in excess of 300 meters were not recommended. After making a few firing passes, pilots had to reset their gyro compass to preclude precession in the instrument from affecting both offset firing and wind correction. The AN/APQ-113 radar and offset computer permitted the AC-119s to deliver firepower under adverse weather conditions with low ceilings.

Convoy Escort: These missions were preplanned between both the gunship crew and the convoy commander. The AC-119 would fly irregular patterns over and ahead of the convoy, while staying alert for evidence of enemy activity, movement, or possible ambush. Pilots maintained proper firing altitudes above the ground and the entire crew was prepared for immediate action. If the convoy was large, one rear scanner would have the primary responsibility of rear element safety for the convoy, including watching for stragglers. If the gunship was working with a forward air controller (FAC), both the aircrew and FAC would use the same radio frequency. If possible, the convoy commander would also monitor the same radio frequency. If guerrilla activity was spotted, the convoy was to be immediately halted by radio, smoke flare, or other preplanned briefed signal. The aircrew would maintain close coordination with the convoy commander before and during attacks on detected or suspected unfriendly positions. The same procedures applied in the case of a surprise ambush by the enemy. Clearance to fire came from either the FAC or the convoy commander. The gunship commander would assess the enemy strength and defenses, and consider asking for support from other strike aircraft in the area (that is, F-105 or F-4). When operating at night with a blacked-out convoy or if the convoy was moving under heavy foliage, homing systems could be employed.

Train Escort: While basically the same as convoy escort, special considerations had to be given to train escort. Trains are particularly vulnerable to guerrilla activity. Depending upon the speed and size of the train its stopping distance is time-consuming.

Naval Escort: Flotillas of barges or small native boats made up water convoys that could have required gunship escort. While the procedures are similar to convoy and train escort, special consideration was given to the narrowness of the waterway and density of the foliage along the banks.

Airborne Illuminator: The airborne illuminator could be used for battlefield illumination, and as a light source for sensor operation and visual flying. Other aircraft could also find targets illuminated by the gunship.

Flare Operations: Flare illumination was not considered to be a primary mission for the gunships. Usually only a limited number of flares were carried on each flight. Flares were used to support on-board sensors and pilots in visual

Antenna locations on the AC-119G.

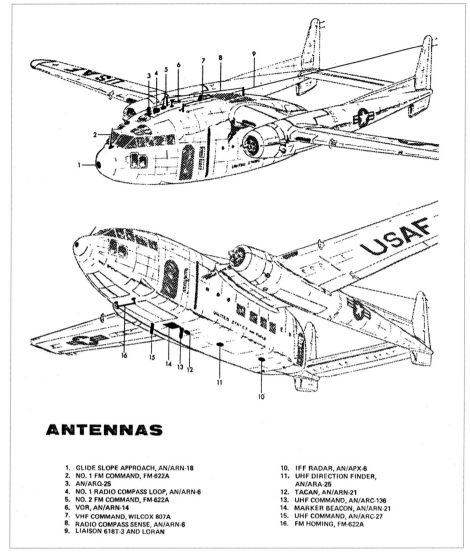

ANTENNAS

1. GLIDE SLOPE APPROACH, AN/ARN-18
2. NO. 1 FM COMMAND, FM-622A
3. AN/ARQ-25
4. NO. 1 RADIO COMPASS LOOP, AN/ARN-6
5. NO. 2 FM COMMAND, FM-622A
6. VOR, AN/ARN-14
7. VHF COMMAND, WILCOX 807A
8. RADIO COMPASS SENSE, AN/ARN-6
9. LIAISON 618T-3 AND LORAN
10. IFF RADAR, AN/APX-6
11. UHF DIRECTION FINDER, AN/ARA-25
12. TACAN, AN/ARN-21
13. UHF COMMAND, AN/ARC-136
14. MARKER BEACON, AN/ARN-21
15. UHF COMMAND, AN/ARC-27
16. FM HOMING, FM-622A

of a 500-gallon auxiliary fuel tank. With 12 years of experience with the C-119s, the Reservists developed their own ferry kits, allowing them to deploy with relative ease. Engine changes were required at Tinker AFB, OK and Wake Island for two of the airplanes. The ferry route was around 9,800 nautical miles long, requiring 10 legs, and 72 flight hours; and made the following stops: England AFB, LA; March AFB, CA; McClellan AFB, CA; McChord AFB, WA; Elmendorf AFB, AK; NAS Adak, AK; Midway Island; Wake Island; Andersen AFB, Guam; Clark AFB, Philippines; and Nha Trang AB, Republic of Vietnam. Deployment data for the 71st SOS:

Departure Date	Arrival Date	Aircraft S/N
2 Dec 1968	12 Jan 1969	53-8155
4 Dec 1968	26 Jan 1969	53-7852
5 Dec 1968	25 Jan 1969	53-3192
5 Dec 1968	27 Jan 1969	53-3189
6 Dec 1968	27 Jan 1967	53-8069
6 Dec 1968	30 Dec 1969	53-3178
10 Dec 1968	30 Dec 1969	53-5905
10 Dec 1968		53-3136
18 Dec 1968	11 Jan 1969	52-5907
18 Dec 1968	8 Jan 1969	52-5927
26 Dec 1968	20 Jan 1969	52-5942
7 Jan 1969	22 Jan 1969	52-5925
13 Jan 1969	13 Jan 1969	52-5938
14 Jan 1969		53-7851
22 Jan 1969	18 Feb 1969	52-3205
24 Jan 1969		53-3170
29 Jan 1969	2 Mar 1969	53-7848
		52-5892

firing. Flares could also be used to illuminate targets for ground forces or other strike aircraft. The LAU-74/A flare dispenser could accommodate up to 24 flares. It was recommended that the launcher be used instead of hand-throwing the flares. The latter procedure could result in personnel injury and/or aircraft damage due to inadvertent actuation, malfunction, or failure to clear the drop exit.

Shadow Evaluation

The 71st Tactical Airlift Squadron, 434th Tactical Airlift Wing, a Reserve unit at Bakalar AFB, IN, was activated on 13 May 1968. By 15 June 1968, the squadron and its 18 C-119Gs moved to Lockbourne AFB, OH, for training in gunship operations by the 4413th Combat Crew Training Squadron (CCTS). Upon this relocation, the 71st Troop Carrier Squadron (TCS) was redesignated as the 71st Air Commando Squadron (ACS). In less than a month, on 8 July 1968, they were again redesignated as the 71st Special Operations Squadron (SOS). By 21 November the unit had 24 fully formed crews. Their deployment was delayed as Headquarters USAF mulled over whether to send the AC-119Gs into combat or wait until the newer AC-119Ks were available. The decision came down advising that the 71st SOS with its AC-119Gs would deploy to Southeast Asia. On 5 December 1968, Lt Col John W Lewis and his crew departed Lockbourne AFB for Nha Trang AB, South Vietnam. Formal orders were received, and on 9 December other elements of the 71st boarded Lockheed C-141 Starlifters headed for Southeast Asia. By 25 December all elements of the unit had departed Lockbourne. An enroute stop in the Philippines allowed aircrews to attend the PACAF Jungle Survival School (affectionately called the *snake school*). The 71st SOS's higher headquarters would become the 14th Special Operations Wing (SOW) at Nha Trang AB.

The initial aircraft were flown from Lockbourne AFB to the Fairchild-Hiller plant in St Augustine, FL to prepare the aircraft for the long ferry flight to South Vietnam. The major modifications consisted of removal of the four 7.6mm miniguns and mounts, and installation

Lt Col Donald Beyl, Commander of the 930th Consolidated Aircraft Maintenance Squadron at Lockbourne AFB, OH, was assigned as the Advanced Echelon (ADVON) commander when the 71st SOS deployed to Southeast Asia.

The 71st SOS operated out of three locations in South Vietnam, listed in the table below.

The AC-119G Shadow would navigate to a patrol box via TACAN with a ground radar backup. Within the patrol box, a Shadow would maintain a 500ft terrain clearance while searching for a target. Upon acquisition, the target would be marked and its coordinates relayed to a controlling agency with a request to fire. Upon gaining clearance, the Shadow would climb to 3,500ft, bank into a left orbit, and commence firing.

Initial operations with the AC-119Gs were flown by the 71st SOS. Advanced elements of

Base	Unit	No of Aircraft	Commander	Operations Officer
Nha Trang AB	71st SOS HQ		Lt Col Donald F Beyl	
	A Flight	5	Lt Col James E Pyle	Lt Col Warren L Johnson
Phan Rang AB	B Flight	6	Lt Col William A Long	Lt Col Earl W Scott
Tan Son Nhut AB	C-Flight	5	Lt Col Donald F Beyl	Lt Col Robert S Mulgrew

This was the business side of the four side-firing 7.62mm miniguns installed in the left side of both the AC-119Gs and AC-119Ks. Each gun could fire 6,000 rounds per minute. USAF

The first AC-119K was delivered to the USAF on 24 September 1968, at St Augustine, FL. A pair of General Electric J85 jet pods were added to the aircraft. The large protuberance on the aft fuselage was the AN/APQ-133 tracking beacon. USAF via Air Force Association

the 71st SOS arrived in country by mid-December 1968. The first aircraft arrived on 27 December.

The first live-fire mission with the AC-119G was flown as a demonstration off the coast of Nha Trang. The crew of nine consisted of five officers, the flight engineer, illuminator operator, and two gunners. In addition, six observers on the aircraft brought the total to 15 souls on board. For this demonstration, a small one-man life raft was dropped into the water. A penetration was made into the firing orbit. Only two of the miniguns were on line as Lt Col Donald Beyl locked onto the target. With the first burst, the raft was shredded.

The 71st SOS began operational sorties and combat evaluation that were accomplished between 5 January and 8 March 1969. Lt Col Donald F Beyl was the aircraft commander of AC-119G, 52-5907, when it made its debut in combat on 5 January as *Shadow 41*. The aircraft lifted off at 2226 hours, flew a 4:28-hour mission, and expended 1,300 rounds of 7.62mm minigun ammunition.

Officer crew aboard *Shadow 41* for both the demonstration flight and the first combat mission on January 1971 were Lt Col Harold E Mitchell, Instructor Pilot; Lt Col Donald F Beyl, Pilot; Maj Herman A Heuss, Co-pilot; Capt William R Joyce Jr, Navigator; Capt Robert Busse, Student Navigator.

Lt Col Mitchell, the 14th SOW Assistant Director of Operations, was not rated in the AC-119G, but had prior C-119 experience that permitted him to serve as an Instructor Pilot. By way of note, he was the aircraft commander on *Pelican 9* that snared the first space capsule (see Chapter 13).

During the night of 9/10 May 1969, Lt Col Earl W Scott, commander of *Shadow 62,* was operating in a sector in support of ARVN troops. The command post ordered *Shadow 62* to depart the area because a B-52 *Arc Light* mission was scheduled for the area. A heated exchange followed over the radio as Lt Col Scott tried convincing the command post that he was protecting friendlies. Finally the command post acquiesced and the *Arc Light* mission was redirected to a secondary target. For their efforts that night, the crew of *Shadow 62* received a Letter of Appreciation signed by Gen George S Brown, Seventh Air Force Commander, Col William K Bush, Commander, and Col William H Ginn, Deputy Commander for Operations of the 14 SOW. The letter read in part: 'When placed in a unique situation, Lt Col Scott and his crew did not respond routinely. They instead, properly analyzed the danger to friendly ground forces and made the fact known. At the risk of censure, they persisted until corrective action was taken. The validity of their judgment has since been established and there can be little doubt that a potentially tragic situation was averted.'

The first 71st SOS ship to sustain damage from enemy fire was 52-5927, which picked up two bullet holes on 7 March 1959. Five other gunships were damaged in May. Four of the aircraft received minor damage while flying missions on 1, 6, 11 and 22 May. The most serious damage occurred when a gunship took six rounds of 12.7mm fire that put 19 holes in the aft fuselage, resulting in minor injury to an active-duty gunner flying with the Reserve aircraft.

Two instances of damage to the AC-119Gs occurred while the aircraft were on the ground. Minor damage was incurred by one aircraft from A Flight when it was struck by six rounds of 75mm recoilless rifle fire on 24 January. Aircraft 52-5907 was struck by ricocheting mortar fragments at Phan Rang AB on 22 February. Ninety minutes later the aircraft took off in defense of its base.

The aft cabin of the gunships was open and drafty resulting in gunners and illuminators experiencing numerous head colds, throat and ear infections, and back ailments. Their illnesses precluded them from flying on many occasions, resulting in an increased workload being imposed on well crewmen. The solution was to add baffles and windscreens in the aft cabin so as to afford the personnel a less drafty environment. As a result of the modifications, the time lost for related ailments decreased by around 80%.

On one mission, a Shadow had a flare misfire resulting in the parachute being wrapped around the boom and stabilizer. The flare severely burned the boom. Some of the active-duty maintenance personnel on the base recommended replacing the boom and ordered a new part. The savvy reservist sheet metal technicians opted to repair the boom. Within a few days the airplane was back on flying status. Several months later a spare boom arrived at the base and may have never been used, only to be left in country after the war.

In one instance, a Shadow was directed towards an outpost near Dak To. The ground unit was under fire. Enemy mortar rounds hit around the command post and probed the perimeter. When the Shadow lit up the area, the enemy withdrew, without even receiving a single round from the gunship.

Near Pleiku AB, a Shadow fired on a suspected enemy troop concentration and storage area. The attack set off 80 secondary explosions.

In another instance, a Shadow aided a US Army unit that was pinned down by enemy fire. After the Shadow attack, the ground unit's radio operator told the story: 'Thanks a lot, Shadow, you made my trip home possible.'

One night an American doctor was operating on a South Vietnamese soldier when the compound came under enemy attack. A generator was hit and all of the lights went out. An AC-119G flew in and lit up the area with its one-million-candlepower illuminator, exposing itself to the potential of enemy gun fire. The operation was successfully completed thanks to the actions of the Shadow.

During six months of operation in Southeast Asia, the 71st SOS left this impressive record of accomplishments.

Fragged Missions	1,209
Sorties	1,516
7.62mm Rounds Expended	14,555,150
Flares Dropped	10,281
Combat Hours Flown	6,251
Confirmed Hostiles Killed	682
Probable Hostiles Killed	1,104
Confirmed Vehicles Destroyed	43

Before leaving Southeast Asia, members of the 71st SOS were awarded 117 Air Medals and one Purple Heart. In addition, nominations were in for 634 Air Medals, 143 Distinguished Flying Crosses, 18 Bronze Stars, 47 Air Force Commendation Medals, and a second Purple Heart. The 71st SOS was also nominated for the Air Force Outstanding Unit Award. On the departure of the 71st SOS, MG Royal N Baker, Seventh AF Commander, stated: 'They've come from civilian life, worked with a new weapon system, brought it into the country, and have done a tremendous job since they've been here.'

On 1 June 1969, the 17th SOS was activated and replaced the 71st SOS which returned to the United States. While the AC-119Gs performed satisfactorily in all mission categories except forward air controlling, it was cited for being rather slow, hard to maneuver, and vulnerable to enemy fire. The latter shortcoming prevented the AC-119G from being a good forward air control aircraft. The gross weight of the aircraft held its mission flying time to about six hours. Because the aircraft lacked an all-weather capability, it would be ineffective in fog or haze. While the target illuminator worked well, its reliability fell when it encountered maintenance problems. As a final note of its evaluation, it was recommended that the aircraft not be deployed into a high-threat environment.

Regular Air Force Gunship Assignments

The Shadows served with two squadrons in Southeast Asia. The 17th SOS, headquartered at Phan Rang, operated the AC-119Gs; while the 18th SOS, also at Phan Rang, flew the AC-119Ks. The 17th and 18th SOSs along with the AC-47-equipped 4th SOS, all reported to the 14th SOW at Nha Trang, which in turn reported to Headquarters 7th Air Force at Tan Son Nhut.

Each squadron had three flights that were distributed as shown herein during November 1969.

Unit	Base	No of Aircraft
17th SOS	Phan Rang	16
A Flight	Tuy Hoe	4 AC-119G
B Flight	Phan Rang	7 AC-119G
C Flight	Tan Son Nhut	5 AC-119G
18th SOS	Phan Rang	12
A Flight	Da Nang	6 AC-119K
B Flight	Phu Cat	3 AC-119K
C Flight	Phan Rang	3 AC-119K

By mid-1970, the AC-119 gunship basing was as shown.

Base	No of Aircraft
Phan Rang AB, RVN	7 AC-119G/ 4 AC-119K
Phu Cat AB, RVN	5 AC-119G
Tan Son Nhut AB, RVN	5 AC-119G
Da Nang AB, RVN	9 AC-119K
Udorn RTAFB, Thailand	3 AC-119K

An AC-119K firing a 7.62mm minigun. Via MSgt D W Menard

An all-black AC-119G, s/n 53-8087, equipped with three-bladed Hamilton Standard propellers. The aircraft was photographed at Wright-Patterson AFB, Ohio, in 1973. Note the paint erosion on the dorsal fin and boom. W Clark via MSgt D W Menard

On 29 December 1970, A Flight, 17th SOS was inactivated at Phu Cat and its personnel and aircraft were reassigned to B Flight at Phan Rang.

At the end of the year in 1970, the gunships were located as shown.

Base	No of Aircraft
Phan Rang AB, RVN	7 AC-119G
Tan Son Nhut AB, RVN	5 AC-119G
Phan Rang AB, RVN	5 AC-119G
Da Nang AB, RVN	9 AC-119K
Nakhon Phanom RTAFB, Thailand	3 AC-119K

Call Sign Commotion

The 18th SOS was given its choice of three call-signs: *Gun Shy*, *Poor Boy*, and *Charlie Brown* They picked the latter as the 'least of the evils.' It was soon learned that the 366th Tactical Fighter Wing had an unused callsign: *Stinger* With the backing of the 14th SOW, the 18th SOS made a claim for the callsign.

Earlier, the 17th SOS had an even greater indignation bestowed upon them. They were issued the callsign *Creep*. A great commotion arose and the callsign was changed to *Shadow*, in keeping with their mission.

Command and Control

Overall American operations in Southeast Asia came under the Commander, United States Military Assistance Command, Vietnam (COMUSMACV); whereas USAF Command and Control stemmed from the Commander of the Seventh Air Force. Command flowed down through the Seventh Air Force Deputy Chief of Staff – Operations, then the Director of Combat Operations. Next Command and Control branched to the combat wings and the Airborne Battlefield Command and Control Center (ABCCC).

Air operations were planned and packaged by the Directory of Combat Operations and resulted in an Air Tasking Order (ATO) that defined: units, aircraft type, ordnance load, target(s), radio frequencies, and package routes An ABCCC that coordinated, directed, and controlled all air strikes. FACs were the on-site eyes for the ABCCC. These were the callsigns for the ABCCCs:

Zone	Daylight Ops	Night Ops
Tiger Hound/Tally Ho	Hillsboro	Moonbeam
Steel Tiger/Barrel Roll	Cricket	Alley Cat

The unsophisticated North Vietnamese and Viet Cong forces were quite capable of intercepting unencrypted radio transmissions. Over time, secure-voice equipment was provided to the units operating in SEA.

One night an AC-119 was receiving a heavy dose of AAA fire. The crew called the second ship in their flight and advised of the conditions. The second ship replied that they had fighter escort. The pilots of the second ship disguised their voices and stated that they were the escort package. They went on to state that they were armed with new 'atomic bullets'. *Alley Cat* chimed in and asked who the fighters were – they were not part of the ATO. The two enterprising airmen mumbled that *Alley Cat* was breaking up. It didn't matter that *Alley Cat* was not hip to the program, the ruse worked. The enemy picked up the transmission and wanted no part of the 'atomic bullets'. The AAA fire ceased!

AC-119G Shadow Casualties

The 17th SOS experienced its first battle damage on 6 August 1969, when four ships took hits. Another aircraft sustained .50 caliber hits in one engine and the fuselage.

The first 17th SOS aircraft to be lost was *Shadow 76* on 11 October 1969. The aircraft crashed on take-off from Tan Son Nhut, with six crew members being killed and the aircraft being destroyed.

Another AC-119G sustained extensive damage when its right landing gear collapsed on landing at Chu Lai AB.

A second 17th SOS AC-119G was lost on 28 April 1970, when the aircraft crashed on take-off from Tan Son Nhut AB, killing six of the eight crew members. As a result of this crash, the Air Force reduced the maximum gross take-off weight by cutting back on both fuel and ammunition, thereby permitting the aircraft to achieve a 150ft per minute rate of climb on a single engine.

Cambodian Operations

The AC-119G Shadows joined in the Duffel Bag Unit Systems Evaluation of new airborne equipment used to monitor signals from ground sensors. Between 3 April and 31 May 1970, the gunships from Tan Son Nhut AB carried a portable UHF receiver that was capable of receiving, decoding, and displaying the sensor signals and audio transmissions. On 18 April, *Shadow 77* detected signals that signified movement in a sensor field. The gunship fired about 6,000 7.62mm rounds into the area. The next night signals were again detected in the same

This top view reveals the camouflage pattern on the upper surfaces of AC-119G, s/n 52-5927. Red fuel filler caps appear on top of the wings. Note how the black paint wrapped up onto the aft portions of the dorsal fins and vertical fins. USAF K41173

This complementary right side view of AC-1119G, s/n 52-5927, shows more of the camouflage pattern. The aircraft ws flying near Nha Trang AB, South Vietnam, on 25 January 1969. USAF

Above: **This was the calling card of the AC-119s.**

Right: **AC-119K, s/n 53-7850, being inspected by military and civilian personnel. To the rear was OV-10A-1A, s/n 66-13557, an FAC aircraft that typically acted as spotters for the gunships in Southeast Asia.** Seattle Museum of Flight

area and another 28,500 rounds were fired. The Shadow also participated in an airstrike in the region that night. A subsequent ground sweep revealed 150 enemy dead. Seventeen more enemy troops were captured, as were nine crew-served weapons and 67 individual weapons. As a result, the new equipment was recommended as a standard installation on the AC-119s.

United States and South Vietnamese forces crossed into Cambodia on 1 May 1970. They had a dual objective. One was to shore up the weak Cambodian army engaged with North Vietnamese units and the other was to destroy the enemy forces and supplies that had been stored for some time in numerous border base camps. The AC-119s were called in to support this operation. In anticipation of the support requirements, especially in the Parrot's Beak area (tip of Cambodia west of Saigon), the gunships were moved to Tan Son Nhut and Phan Rang on 3 May 1970.

The first priority of the redeployed gunships was the support of troops engaged with the enemy in Cambodia, followed in succession by convoy escort and armed reconnaissance. On numerous occasions AC-119G support of friendly forces under night attack resulted in the enemy disengaging.

Previously, the gunships would depart on a night mission and coordinate with Army forces to obtain artillery clearances. Such practices oftentimes necessitated the gunships making course changes in order to avoid guns that had not been shut down. With the new activity in Cambodia, artillery clearances were obtained prior to take-off, thereby allowing the AC-119s greater time over the target.

Petroleum shortages in the Cambodian capitol region of Phnom Penh necessitated extra protection for both road and river convoys. An armed escort package from all three services was orchestrated by the Seventh Air Force in support of Navy convoys plying the Mekong River. An Army light fire team consisting of a command-and-control helicopter, a pair of Huey Cobra helicopter gunships and two light observation helicopters (LOACHes) flew escort at 1,500ft during daylight hours. This escort team cycled between the convoy and their home base at Chi Lang. At night the Navy provided two UH-1Bs and two OV-10As (Black Ponies) for low-altitude coverage. This Navy team cycled from their command-and-control vessel anchored in the Mekong River at Tan Chau in South Vietnam. All the while, the convoy was also escorted by an AC-119G circling the convoy at 3,500ft.

Road convoys were also escorted by the Shadow gunships, either alone or with the assistance of forward air controller (FAC) aircraft. When working together, a FAC aircraft would search for enemy ambush preparations along the route of the convoy, while the gunship flew in a large elliptical orbit. On 30 June 1971, a 51-truck convoy left Phnom Penh along Route 4 towards Kompong Som. Enemy movement was spotted north of Route 4 by a FAC aircraft. The FAC crew anticipated an ambush and requested a strike aircraft. An AC-119G was diverted for the operation. A recheck of the area by the FAC confirmed his suspicions and the gunship was cleared for an attack. The gunship opened up with 7.62mm fire that was countered from the ground. Then the AC-119G saturated the area with fire until the last truck had cleared the area, marking another success for the gunships.

Armed reconnaissance missions by the AC-119Gs in Cambodia concentrated on trucks and river sampans. The 7.62mm miniguns on the AC-119Gs had little effect on the sampan armor. In July 1970, AC-119Ks with their 20mm armor-piercing incendiary cannon were able to sink the sampans; however, they found that 20mm high-explosive incendiary rounds were ineffective. The crews of the AC-119Gs obtained 7.62mm armor-piercing incendiaries from the US Army and were able to improve their effectiveness against the targets and had the added benefit of gauging their accuracy.

The Cambodian area was lightly defended and small-caliber fire resulted in no gunship losses. As a result, the AC-119Gs and some AC-119Ks began daylight interdiction.

Between 5 May and 30 June 1970, the AC-119 gunships flew 178 sorties in support of US ground operations in Cambodia. The gunships continued their support of Cambodian and South Vietnamese forces in the area between July 1970 and March 1971, destroying or damaging 609 enemy vehicles, destroying 237 sampans and damaging another 494, and killing 3,151 enemy troops.

Combat King

The AC-119Ks had suffered serious delays in their conversion due to the technical complexity of their system. One of the most critical was the development of the Texas Instruments Forward-Looking Infra Red (FLIR). By the end of October 1968, it was apparent that the first 18 AC-119Ks would be delivered with only the basic components to accommodate and support the FLIR. The first FLIR was scheduled to reach Fairchild-Hiller in June 1968, but did not arrive until 3 May 1969. Initial testing commenced on 30 May. The last FLIR for the program arrived in April 1970.

Three AC-119Ks, without the FLIR, were deployed to Southeast Asia for combat evaluation. These aircraft were forced to fly the AC-119G mission profile until the FLIR could be installed.

Laotian Operations

In the beginning of 1970, an enemy offensive took a heavy toll on Meo General Vang Pao's forces in northern Laos. Consequently, with PACAF's permission, the Seventh Air Force deployed AC-119Ks to Udorn RTAFB, Thailand, to support Operation *Barrel Roll* during February's high moon phase. Three AC-119Ks with four crews and 30 maintenance personnel left Phu Cat AB, on 15 February 1970, for a trial operation. Their mission would be armed reconnaissance along Routes 7 and 61 in *Barrel Roll* and secondarily to provide support to Lima sites under attack. Their first mission was flown on 17 February. Their test deployment was to be from 17-27 February. The gunship operations soon intensified to counter an enemy offensive into the Plain of Jars. At the end of the gunships' 10-day test period, Seventh Air Force ordered an extension until 2 July. The AC-119Ks significantly strengthened the Allied efforts in northern Laos. By 21 March the Stinger strength increased to four aircraft, seven crews, and 40 maintenance personnel.

Charlie Chasers was AC-119G, s/n 52-5892, operated by the 17th SOS from Phu Cat AB, South Vietnam. This ship was photographed on 20 September 1970. N E Taylor via USAF Museum A1/(A)C-119G/pho7

AC-119K, s/n 53-3187, as she appeared at an open house at McClellan AFB, CA, on 7 October 1972. The tail number is changed from 0-33205 in red to AF/53 187 in white. The aircraft is devoid of any unit markings. Fresh paint obliterates the former unit insignia forward of the 'CUT HERE' marks. To the rear is C-124A-DL, s/n 51-0175 from the AFRES. MSgt D W Menard

In June, Seventh Air Force requested that PACAF allow the gunships to remain at Udorn RTAFB for an additional 120 days.

During Operation *Barrel Roll*, AC-119K Stingers were responsible for 70 per cent of the enemy trucks destroyed in eastern and later northern Laos, thus making the gunship the number one truck-killer in the operation.

During Operation *Steel Tiger*, the Stingers were credited with destroying 2,125 trucks during one month. The AC-119K flew four sorties per night during the operation in southern Laos.

In December 1970 a single AC-119K set an all-time record for destroying 29 trucks and damaging another 6 on one mission. During the last three months of 1970, the Stingers collectively bagged 312 trucks and damaged another 196. During the first quarter of 1971, these figures rose to 1,845 destroyed or damaged. On 28 February 1971, the Stingers were credited with destroying six PT-76 tanks.

This table reveals the relative effectiveness of the three aircraft types as truck hunters.

Aircraft Type	Trucks Destroyed/Damaged	
	Per Sortie	Per Truck Sighted
AC-130	5.37	0.89
AC-119	2.14	0.67
F-4	0.29	0.29

Operation *Lam Son 719*

The Republic of Vietnam Army (ARVN) launched a major ground offensive in the Laotian panhandle between 30 January and 24 March 1971. Dubbed Operation *Lam Son 719*, the operation was designed to cut the enemy's supply lines.

Enemy anti-aircraft fire was unusually quite heavy. One night an AC-119K and an OV-10A FAC were teamed together. The gunship began taking on heavy AAA fire. The FAC called in and said he would bring his 'death ray' into action. The FAC turned on his landing lights and beamed them on the offending anti-aircraft gun. It was a known fact that the enemy monitored our air-to-air radio communications. The gun silenced itself and the gunship spotted the gun crew dusting themselves off after having been hit by the 'death ray'!

Tank Busting

On the night of 28 February, an AC-119K with callsign *Stinger 04* was assigned to fly an armed reconnaissance mission for an ARVN convoy that was advancing towards Tchepone, Laos. It began as a boring night and the gunship crew decided to depart their orbit above the convoy and reconnoiter further down the highway. Then they spotted a pair of hot spots moving in the same direction as the convoy near Hill 13. There was no doubt that they were tanks. The Stinger crew called for FAC verification and got confirmation that there were two tanks on the road. Until now no tanks had been destroyed by gunships.

A nearby AC-130 Spectre begged *Alley Cat* for the target, but they were denied. The Stinger had found the target and they would have first dibs on it. Soon three more tanks rolled out of some trees onto the road, making five. Three more tanks were waiting at an intersection further up the road. Now there were eight tanks. The FAC made a low-level pass and determined that they were Soviet PT-76 light amphibious tanks. He called for the Stinger to take out the tanks.

The Stinger rolled into its firing orbit and marked the target with its miniguns, followed by the 20mm cannon. Next the crew opened up with a withering barrage of a mix of armor-piercing high explosive and miniball tracer rounds. The lead tank was stopped dead and a secondary explosion followed. Then, the trailing tank was taken out, effectively boxing in the tank column. AAA became more intense and the AC-119 began rolling in and out of its orbit to avoid being hit. Soon all eight Soviet PT-76 tanks had been destroyed.

The crew that night consisted of these personnel: Maj Earl R Glass, Pilot/Aircraft Commander; Maj Edward J Kroon, Navigator/Sensor Operator; Maj Boyd E Phillips, Navigator/Sensor Operator; Maj Douglas A Frost, Navigator/Sensor Operator; 1Lt Charles T 'Tony' Robertson Jr, Co-pilot; TSgt Herbert S Simons, Flight Engineer; SSgt Raymond Garcia, Gunner; SSgt William O Petrie, Illuminator Operator/Scanner; Sgt Thomas E Nolan, Gunner; A1C Stephan B McCloskey, Gunner.

Charles T 'Tony' Robertson retired as a general and CINCAMC/CINCUSTRANSCOM. Upon his retirement, he was the last Regular Air Force pilot to have flown the C-119.

During Operation *Lam Son 719*, Spectre and Stingers had these tank kill tallies.

Aircraft	Engagements	Kills
AC-119K	11	10
AC-130	28	14
Total	39	24

Stinger Casualties

The first AC-119K Stinger was lost on the night of 19 February 1970, when the aircraft crashed short of the runway at Da Nang AB, when

AC-119G, s/n 53-8089, with the IH tail code, was flown by the 4413th CCTS, 4410 CCTW, Lockbourne AFB, OH. The aircraft was photographed at Langley AFB, VA, on 23 June 1970. The squadron color, yellow, appears on both the prop hub and main gear hub cap. The APU inlet and exhaust ducts appear on the side of the fuselage under the engine. D Remington

returning from a combat mission. The final approach had gone normally until the landing gear and flaps were lowered about two miles out at an altitude of 500-600ft. Apparently fuel starvation caused a sudden loss of power from both the jet and reciprocating engine on the left side, thereby precluding the pilot from maintaining directional control of the aircraft. While the aircraft was destroyed, all crew members miraculously escaped with only minor injuries.

An AC-119K was lost, severely damaged when a 37mm round shattered the nose section as the aircraft worked an area a few miles north of Ban Bak, Laos. The crew was able to bring the aircraft back to Da Nang.

A second AC-119K from the 18th SOS was lost on the night of 6 June 1970, when its propeller ran away shortly after take-off from Da Nang. The crew safely bailed out when the situation deteriorated and the aircraft crashed in the South China Sea.

Anti-aircraft fire experienced by the AC-130 aircraft led to the use of F-4s as escorts. A similar practice was instituted for the AC-119Ks. The 366th Tactical Fighter Wing (TFW) at Da Nang provided an F-4 Phantom as a constant escort for the Stingers on their armed reconnaissance flights. At the peak of the truck-hunting season, the 366th TFW averaged six sorties per night.

On the night of 8 May 1970, an AC-119K Stinger from Udorn RTAFB was heavily damaged by anti-aircraft fire. The record of its mission follows: 'Capt Alan D Milacek and his nine-man crew had been reconnoitering a heavily defended road section near Ban Ban, Laos, when they discovered, attacked, and destroyed two trucks. Capt James A Russell and Capt Ronald C Jones, the sensor operators, located three more trucks. As the aircraft banked into attack orbit, six enemy positions opened up with a barrage of AA fire. The co-pilot, Capt Brent A O'Brien, cleared the fighter escort for attack and the gunship circled as the F-4s worked to suppress the AA fire. Amid the heavy enemy fire, Captain Milacek resumed the attack and killed another truck. At 0100, just about 2 hours into the mission, "the whole cargo compartment lit up" as enemy rounds tore into the Stinger's right wing. A "sickening right dive of the aircraft" ensued and Milacek called "Mayday, Mayday, we're goin' in." He shouted orders to SSgt Adolfo Lopez Jr, the IO (Illuminator operator), to jettison the flare launcher.

AC-119K, s/n 52-6910, in the markings of the 1st SOW, with the AH tail code. A TAC badge appears on the fin, while the wing insignia is applied to the nose. R T O'Dell via MSgt D W Menard

'Capt Milacek directed the entire crew to get ready for instant bailout. As the gunship dropped about 1,000ft within seconds, Capts Milacek and O'Brien pooled their strength to pull the aircraft out of its dive. By using full-left rudder, full-left aileron, and maximum engine power on the two right engines, they regained stabilized flight. The full-engine power fueled 2-3ft exhaust flames – torchlights for enemy gunners as the crippled Stinger desperately headed for friendly territory. The navigator, Capt Roger E Clancy, gave the correct heading but warned that they were too low to clear a range of mountains towering between them and safety. What's more, the crew discovered that fuel consumption would likely mean dry tanks before reaching base.

'The crew tossed out every possible item to lighten the load and the aircraft slowly climbed to 10,000ft. TSgt Albert A Nash, the flight engineer, reported the fuel-consumption rate had been reduced. Capt Milacek elected to land the damaged plane and when he approached the base area he ran a careful check of the controls. He found that almost full-left rudder and aileron would allow him to keep control. With uncertain flap damage, Milacek chose a no-flap landing approach at 150 knots (normally 117 knots). Utilizing every bit of his pilot skill he landed the plane. Upon leaving the Stinger, the crew saw about one third of the right wing (a 14ft section and aileron) had been torn off.'

During a ceremony held at the Pentagon on 5 August 1971, Gen John D Ryan, USAF Chief of Staff, presented Capt Milacek and his crew the Mackay Trophy for 'the most meritorious flight of the year.'

Mekong River Convoy Escort

During early January 1971, the American Embassy in Phnom Penh, Khmer Republic (Cambodia) expressed considerable concern over the POL shortages resulting from enemy attacks on commercial shipping vessels plying the Mekong River in Cambodia. During this period, land Route 4 from the port city of Kompong Som had been closed, further exacerbating the situation. A request was made for convoy protection between Tan Chau, on the Vietnamese border, to Phnom Penh. The approximately 70-mile long meandering river between the two cities was within easy range of Viet Cong rockets and recoilless rifles. Depending upon the season, the width of the river was between 300 and 2,000 meters. An agreement was achieved between the US, Cambodia, and the Republic of Vietnam to provide convoy support.

Vessels between 4,000 and 6,000 tons normally plied the Mekong River, and the Defense Intelligence Agency believed that the Mekong could easily be blocked by sinking of just one of these boats. Viet Cong attacks averaged three per month; however between 17 and 30 January 1971, there were ten attacks.

To counter the threat, an armed flotilla of eleven vessels was added to the convoy. For a convoy of ten commercial vessels, the flotilla consisted of four mechanized landing craft modified as minesweepers, a pair of river patrol boats, a command and control boat, one mechanized landing craft converted into a heavy weapons platform, and three amphibious assault patrol boats. In addition, a pair of river patrol boats provided protection for each ship.

A third group of support vessels consisted of a command and control boat for the deputy convoy operations commander, a pair of amphibious assault patrol boats, and five armored troop carriers. The latter carried Republic of Vietnam and Cambodian ground troops who could be brought ashore if required. Lastly, ground troops were dispersed along the banks of the river to provide additional surveillance and protection. To escort ten commercial vessels, a total of 46 Republic of Vietnam naval vessels were required. This was an expensive and logistically complex operation.

The original plan called for only USAF and US Army assets to provide additional convoy coverage. Army helicopters and USAF Cessna O-2 Super Skymasters, North American OV-10A Broncos, and AC-119G Shadows were employed. On 17 January 1971, the US Navy was also tasked for supporting the operation with helicopters and OV-10A Black Ponies. To assist in coordination with the air support units, FACs were added to the command vessel.

On 18 August 1971, considerable concern with the overall plan arose within Headquarters Seventh Air Force when it was determined that the AC-119Gs were scheduled to be transferred to the Republic of Vietnam Air Force on 10 September. To ease the transition, five USAF gunship aircrews were provided for the missions until the Vietnamese became proficient with the aircraft.

A total of 33 convoys traveled up the Mekong River between 17 January and 24 September 1971, each with its armed flotilla support and constant air coverage. Of the 640 vessels escorted, only one barge was sunk, two tugs were heavily damaged and one was beached, eight ships were damaged, and several vessels sustained light damage. There were 3 fatalities and 11 injured on the surface vessels or from the air support teams. To ensure the success of the convoy support, 2,240 sorties were flown. However, only 23 air strikes were required. As stated earlier, just the presence of the gunships reduced the enemy's desire to engage targets under their surveillance.

End of An Era

On 1 September 1971, the 819th Combat Squadron was activated in the Vietnamese Air Force and became known as the *Fire Dragons*. Based at Tan Son Nhut, the 819th obtained the C-119Gs from the 17th SOS. Crew experience was a major factor in the speedy transition of the Vietnamese. Many of the pilots had flown the C-47 since 1958, accruing in excess of 6,000 hours with some logging over 12,000 hours. The average American AC-119 pilot had 800 hours in the *Gooney Bird* before transitioning into the C-119. Notwithstanding the Vietnamese pilot experience level, their night and weather capabilities were lacking. Gradually the Vietnamese pilots gained experience in the C-119 and their familiarity with the terrain allowed them to spot targets at night quicker than their American counterparts.

Experience showed that following the initial use of airpower, guerrillas hesitated to attack a convoy escorted by even a light spotter FAC aircraft. On occasion, just the noise and presence of a gunship had such an adverse psychological effect on the enemy that they might opt not to ambush a convoy. The C-119 gunships proved their worth in the war in Southeast Asia. They flew cover for both troops and convoys, and were responsible for destroying numerous enemy trucks and sampans bringing reinforcements into the war. This aircraft had returned to fly in its second war in a mission for which it was never intended and yet still performed the job well.

Known named AC-119 gunships. Names and nose art were only briefly used because the markings were found to be easily illuminated by enemy searchlights at night.

Name	Model/Series	Serial No	Unit	Remarks
Black Killer Duck	AC-119K	53-7830	18th SOS	Transferred to VNAF
Burks Law	AC-119G	53-3136	71st SOS	Transferred to 17th SOS. Transferred to VNAF
Buzzard Eyes	AC-119G	52-5892	71st SOS	Transferred to 17th SOS
Charlie Chasers	AC-119G	52-5892	17th SOS	Transferred to VNAF
City of Columbus	AC-119G	53-8069	71st SOS	1st AC-119 in inventory. Transferred to 18th SOS. Transferred to VNAF
Devil's Advocate	AC-119G	52-5927	71st SOS	
Egg Sucking Dog	AC-119G			
Fly United	AC-119K	53-7830	18th SOS	Transferred to VNAF
Hoosier Hunter	AC-119G	52-5907	71st SOS	
Ghost Rider	AC-119G	53-3192	71st SOS	Transferred to 17th SOS. Transferred to VNAF
Montezuma's Revenge	AC-119K	53-7864	18th SOS	Lost over Thailand during mission on 2 Aug 1972
The Peanut Special	AC-119K	53-3154	18th SOS	Transferred to VNAF
The Polish Cannon	AC-119K		18th SOS	
The Super Sow	AC-119K	52-9982	18th SOS	Transferred to VNAF

AC-119K, 53-7839, operated by the 415th SOTS, 1st SOW, at Hurlburt Field, Florida. The aircraft nose is red. A 1st SOW insignia appears on the nose. The TAC insignia and AH code are applied to the fins. A red turbine warning band appears on the jet pod. The aircraft is equipped with three-bladed Hamilton Standard propellers. This picture dates from 6 February 1972. T H Brewer

The forward fuselage details of an AC-119K operated by B Flight, 18th SOS, 14th SOW, at Da Nang AB, South Vietnam, in August 1970.
SSgt R Faust via D Remington

Chapter 17

United States Marine Corps and Navy Boxcars

The United States Marine Corps (USMC) employed a number of Flying Boxcars in the transport role in both their active duty and reserve units whereas the US Navy operated these airplanes in a limited role with one known unit. A total of 97 R4Q-1 and R4Q-2s were procured through USAF contracts for use by the Navy and Marines. Although the aircraft had noted shortcomings, they provided valuable service for over 20 years.

USMC OPERATIONS

As with the USAF, the United States Marine Corps lacked an adequate heavy-lift transport. Seeing the potential in the USAF C-119B, the Marines opted for this aircraft in their inventory. In keeping with the US Navy Bureau of Aeronautics (BuAer) numbering system, the Flying Boxcars would carry the designation of R4Q-1 – the **R** for transport, the **4** for the fourth model procured from the manufacturer, **Q** which stood for Fairchild, and the **-1** indicating the first series of the aircraft type.

Deliveries of the 39 R4Q-1s began in 1950. These aircraft were essentially C-119Cs, upgraded from the earlier C-119B, powered by P&W R-4360-20W water-injected engines and the airframes incorporating certain structural improvements. In 1953, the Marines took delivery of their first R4Q-2s, these being essentially C-119Fs powered by Wright R-3350-85 turbocompound engines. The Marines acquired 58 R4Q-2s, all of which were delivered with dual nosewheels.

A number of R4Q-2s were subsequently modified to incorporate the AN/APS-42 search radar. These aircraft were readily identifiable by their extended noses. The radar was employed both as a navigational aid and as an anti-collision warning device. It provided a visual indication of the position of cities, landmarks, shore lines, islands, ships, other aircraft, and cloud formations. Target position was visually presented in both range and azimuth on the pilot's range azimuth indicator (an IP-35/APS-42 or IP-217/APS-42), one was located on the left side of the navigator's rack, and the other above the main instrument panel between the pilots.

Initial Inventory

An initial batch of eight R4Q-1s was acquired by the Marines and evaluated at the Naval Air Test Center located at NAS Patuxent River, MD. On 1 September 1950, the aircraft were assigned to their first operational unit, VMR-252, stationed at the Air Fleet Marine Headquarters for the Atlantic Fleet at MCAS Cherry Point, NC, under the command of Col Henry C Lane. The unit's initial allocation of eight R4Q-1s grew to 15 by June 1952. Beginning in April 1953, VMR-252 gained 15 R4Q-2s, and all of their R4Q-1s were sent to other units. VMR-252 was assigned to MAG-11, also stationed at MCAS Cherry Point. The squadron flew throughout the ZI, the Caribbean, Europe, and Africa in support of Marine requirements. A small one- or two-plane detachment from VMR-252 was established at NAS Port Lyautey, Kenitra, Morocco in August 1953 to support Marine operations in the Mediterranean. This detachment provided support to Marine ground forces during the July 1958 crisis in Lebanon.

Three Marine Air Groups were equipped with the R4Qs in the early 1950s: MAG-35 at MCAS

The Marines operated this R4Q-1, BuNo 124324, from NAS Patuxent River, MD for flight testing. This was the first aircraft in this series assigned to the Marines. Note the NATC on the vertical tail and outboard on the right wing. The last three digits of the BuNo appear on the top of the right ring and on the nose. VR0661 via R L Lawson

BuNo 124344 was another USMC test aircraft. The only distinctive markings are the last three digits of the BuNo on the nose and the 'UNITED STATES MARINES' boldly painted on the lower portion of the fuselage. This picture dates from 4 August 1953. Via P Mersky

R4Q-2, BuNo 131666, as she appeared on 10 May 1954. The last three digits of the BuNo appear on the nose and under the left wing inboard of the word 'MARINES'. The AC tail code indicates that the aircraft ws assigned to VMR-153, NAS Itami, Japan. An F-51 Mustang appears in the background. Note that the aircraft is equipped with the large single nosewheel. This was the fifth R4Q-2 built. The aircraft was accepted by the Navy on 27 February 1953, assigned to VMR-153 on 30 March 1953, transferred to VMR-353 on 19 November 1957, transferred to VMR-253 on 19 May 1959, went to storage on 1 December 1961, and was dropped from the inventory on 24 February 1954, after accruing 5405 flying hours. Olson via P M Bowers

R4Q-1, BuNo 124330, lumbered along at NAS Cherry Point on 27 April 1950. The LH on the tail indicated VMR-252. Marine Corps 508720

R4Q-1, BuNo 128735, was assigned to VMR-253 as indicated by the AD unit markings on the boom and tail. 'MARINES' is applied beneath the left wing. H S Gann

Second Round

Two additional units, VMR-153 and VMR-353, began receiving R4Qs in 1952 and 1953.

VMR-153, based at MCAS Cherry Point, began receiving its R4Q-1s in June 1952. The unit gained six of these aircraft that they retained until April 1953 when factory-new R4Q-2s came into the squadron's inventory. The squadron had its full complement of 15 R4Q-2s by the end of April. VMR-153 formed a small detachment, with two aircraft, at NAS Port Lyautey, Morocco where they operated alongside VMR-252. VMR-153s R4Qs flew logistical support missions to England, western Europe, throughout the Mediterranean, and across North Africa. This detachment operated for less than two months and returned to MCAS Cherry Point. VMR-153 operated as many as 20 R4Q-2s by January 1959 however this number was drastically reduced to 12 by 1 July 1959, when the unit was disestablished and its remaining aircraft were distributed amongst remaining R4Q units.

The last unit to receive the R4Qs was VMR-353, based at MCAS Miami (Opa Locka), FL. Its first aircraft, BuNo 131699, arrived on 1 May 1953 and the squadron had its full complement of 15 aircraft by the end of the month. VMR-353 became the designated training squadron for all Marine R4Qs. The squadron made daily flights to Guantanamo Bay, Cuba bringing fresh foods, PX supplies, and mail to the sailors and Marines assigned there. The squadron also participated in a number of humanitarian missions, an example being airlifting supplies from NAS Corpus Christi and Monterey, Mexico, and dropping them for flood victims in Tampico, Mexico.

The last Marine squadron to operate the R4Qs was VMR-352, stationed at MCAS El Toro. The unit has the distinctions of operating the fewest aircraft, five, and using the aircraft for the least amount of time, two years. VMR-352 gained its first R4Q in mid-May 1959 to supplement its

Cherry Point, NC; MAG-25 at MCAS El Toro, CA; and MAG 45 at NAS Miami, FL.

Under the command of Col Ben Z Redfield, MAG-35 had two squadrons equipped with the Flying Boxcar; VMR-153, under Maj William E Baird, and VMR-252, under Maj W H Costello. VMR-252 gained its R4Qs in April 1950, with VMR-153 following in April 1953.

At El Toro, MAG-25 was commanded by Col P K Smith. Two of his squadrons were equipped with Douglas R5D Skymasters, while VMR-253 had R4Qs under the command of Lt Col Carl J Fleps. By February 1952, the unit had its full complement of 16 R4Qs. VMR-253 was the second unit to receive the R4Qs, and was the first west coast unit to gain the aircraft, with BuNo 126582 being accepted on 22 December 1951. The squadron's aircraft flew missions throughout the ZI and across the Pacific. Starting in mid-1953, VMR-253 operated out of MCAF Itami and MCAF Iwakuni, Japan, in support of Marine operations in Korea.

In early 1955, the unit's headquarters was moved to MCAF Iwakuni and VMR-253 was reassigned to MAW-1. VMR-253 replaced its R4Q-1s with R4Q-2s in May 1959. Equipped with 10 of the new aircraft, the squadron made routine logistics flights to bases in Japan, Okinawa, the Philippines, and Southeast Asia. In November 1961, VMR-253 disposed of its last R4Q and gained the new Lockheed GV-1 Hercules.

Col W A Willis headed MAG-45 that had one R4Q-equipped squadron, VMR-353, under Lt Col Lee C Merrell. VMR-353 received its first aircraft in May 1953.

R5D (C-54) Skymasters. The squadron employed the aircraft for routine training exercises, logistical support for west coast Marine bases, and ferrying Marine reservists for training.

R4Q-1s

The first two R4Q-1s, BuNo 124324 and 124326, were delivered to NATC R&D Patuxent River, MD, for a six-month flight test program on 8 February 1950. Subsequently both aircraft found their way into the inventories of several Navy and Marine overhaul and repair facilities before being retired from service with relatively low time. The aircraft had accrued 830 and 565 flying hours, respectively, at retirement.

Most of the 39 R4Q-1s quickly became outdated with the advent of the R4Q-2s. Many of the R4Q-1s were relegated to Marine Headquarters and Maintenance Squadrons, Marine training groups, NATC Patuxent River for flight testing, and MCAS station Operations and Engineering Squadrons. Several R4Q-1s were reassigned to VMR-253 at Itami and Iwakuni, Japan, where they operated between 1953 and 1959. In mid-1959, the remaining 33 R4Q-1s were ferried to NAS Litchfield Park, AZ, for storage. On 13 May 1960, the aircraft were dropped from the inventory and scrapped.

Operational Anecdotes

Between 1 July and 31 December 1952, VMR-252 flew 2,805,264 passenger miles and 625,597 freight ton miles. These missions were flown without an accident. In addition, the unit had an on-going pilot training program.

In January 1951 Marines on maneuvers in the mountains south of Lake Tahoe, CA, became snowbound. On the 17th, the sole R4Q in the inventory of VMR-253 made an emergency airdrop of medical supplies to the troops. Five 300lb paratainer packs of medical supplies were dropped into a valley too narrow for the aircraft to make a 180° turn. The supplies were dropped in a single pass by the R4Q; whereas the Curtiss R5C Commandos would have to have made manual drops in several passes, resulting in widely dispersed supplies.

R4Q-2, BuNo 131690, reveals its original nose. The aircraft was assigned to VMR-353, NAS Miami, FL, displaying its MZ tail code. In the background are FJ4 Furies. H S Gann

**18-9
C-119F (R4Q-2), BuNo 131685 was assigned to VMR 352, as indicated by its QB tail code and unit identifier beneath the 'UNITED STATES MARINES'. A rescue arrow appears near the astrodome. The aircraft was painted with a white cap, black cheat line, and extensive dayglo red paint on the forward fuselage and empennage. The aircraft was photographed at MCAS Quantico, VA on 15 May 1961.** Marine Corps 528037

R4Q-2, BuNo 131679, was operated by MARTAD from NAS Seattle, displaying its 7T tail code. In July 1963, the aircraft shared the ramp at Elmendorf AFB, AK with a MATS C-124. N E Taylor

Within seven seconds the *parapacks* were dropped from the R4Q at an altitude between 300 and 400ft and all landed within a 200ft area. Several days later, the R4Qs flew 37 sorties carrying 588 of the snowbound Marines over a 430 mile trip back to camp.

Much of the flying within the United States was in support of training operations, delivering troops between east and west coast bases.

VMR-352, based at MCAS El Toro from December 1948, transitioned into R4Qs during July 1950. Between that date and January 1953, their primary mission was to airlift personnel and supplies in support of combat troops in the western Pacific. They made daily flights between El Toro and WESTPAC bases. On 23 June 1951, a pair of their R4Qs departed Dallas, TX, with four Bell HTL-4 Sioux helicopters for Korea, marking the first time transports flew helicopters directly from the factory to a combat zone. During the fall of 1958, VMR-352 supported Navy and Marine units staging for action in the Taiwan straits during the artillery duel for control of Matsu and Quemoy Islands. The squadron transitioned into Lockheed GV-1 Hercules tankers in March 1961.

During the ill-fated Bay of Pigs Invasion, both VMR 252 and VMR-353 had their aircraft loaded and airborne in a single day in May 1961 to support the operation. While enroute to their destination, CINCLANT ordered the aircraft to return to home base.

Political Redesignation

In 1962, Secretary of Defense Robert Strange McNamara became confused between the air-

Later in its career, BuNo 131679 was assigned to VMR-234, NAS Glenview, IL as indicated by its QH tail code. This picture dates from 30 July 1972. To the rear is BuNo 131707. Devoid of their brilliant dayglo red colors, these aircraft were repainted in an overall matt Sea Gray. BuNo 131679 last served as QH-679 with VMR-234 before retiring to MASDC on 11 April 1974. The aircraft was spared the scrap heap on 15 September and went to the Pratt Museum at Fort Campbell, KY. N E Taylor

C-119F (R4Q-2), BuNo 131706, was photographed at Waterloo, IA, on 10 May 1965. The aft portion of the booms and stabilizers appears to have been painted with the dayglo red conspiscuity markings. White-outlined red rescue arrows were applied below the entry door and near the astrodome. The bulbous nose housed the AN/APS-42 search radar. USMC

R4Q-2, BuNo 131581, was operated by VMR-253, seen here in natural metal finish with its QD tail code. Note the A-4 Skyhawks in the background. H S Gann

Marine Corps Accidents

The lowest time R4Q to be dropped from the inventory was BuNo 131661 with 253 hours of flying time. The aircraft was accepted from the factory on 27 February 1953, and assigned to VMR-153 at MCAS Cherry Point on 12 March 1953. After an accident, it was stricken from the records on 18 July 1953.

BuNo 126579 was accepted at the factory on 1 December 1951, and assigned to the Overhaul & Repair unit at MCAS Cherry Point on 13 December. VMR-252 gained the aircraft on 18 March 1953. The airplane was reassigned to MTG-10 at MCAS El Toro on 19 June 1953, and then to VMR-253 at MACF Iwakuni, Japan on 22 December 1953. An accident resulted in the aircraft being stricken from the inventory on 4 June 1954, after having accrued only 590 hours.

R4Q-2 BuNo 121703 was accepted from the factory on 28 April 1953, and was assigned to VMR-353, MCAS Miami on 18 May. The aircraft accrued 1,171 hours and suffered an accident, resulting in its being scrapped on 4 February 1956.

BuNo 131716 was accepted on 21 May 1953 and assigned to HAMRON-32 (Headquarters Marine Squadron 32), MCAS Miami on 8 June. The aircraft was transferred to H&MS-32 (Headquarters & Maintenance Squadron 32), MCAS Cherry Point on 10 February 1954, then to VMR-153 at the same base on 6 May. The aircraft returned to MCAS Miami where it was assigned to VMR-353 on 11 September 1956. After accruing 1,607 hours, the aircraft experienced propeller control problems during a local training flight. A heads-up crew feathered the propellers and shut down the engines on the final approach, and brought the aircraft in for a remarkable belly landing. The aircraft slid into a canal resulting in severe structural damage and was dropped from the inventory on 11 October 1956.

BuNo 128744 was accepted from the factory on 31 January 1952, and assigned to the

craft designations used by the USAF and the Navy. To solve his confusion he mandated that the Navy change its designations to conform with that of the USAF. This change took place in October 1962. Consequently, the American taxpayer had to fund the reprinting of all of the BuAer manuals used in support of their aircraft – that is, flight manuals and maintenance manuals. At this time the R4Q lost its identity as a USMC aircraft and became a C-119. The R4Q-1s became C-119Cs and the R4Q-2s became C-119Fs.

Marine Reserve Units

Beginning in 1961, three Marine reserve units gained the newly redesignated C-119Fs to support their operations throughout the country. Approximately 20 of the aircraft were distributed amongst these Marine Reserve units units.

Unit	Base	First Aircraft
VMR-216	MARTD, NAS Seattle, WA	Apr 1962
VMR-222	MARTD, NAS Grosse Isle, MI	Dec 1961
VMR-234	MARTD, NAS Twin Cities, MN	Dec 1961

These units operated the C-119F for about ten years for weekend drills and two weeks of active duty training during the summer.

With the closure of NAS Twin Cities in 1970, VMR-234 moved to NAS Glenview, IL.

Bureau of Aeronautics Research & Development Branch at Baltimore, MD, on 15 February 1952. It was then transferred to the Overhaul & Repair facility at MCAS Cherry Point on 18 June 1952. The aircraft was reassigned to VMR-253 at MCAS El Toro on 20 March 1953, then moved with the unit to MCAF Itami on 25 November 1953. When the squadron relocated to MCAF Iwakuni on 25 May 1955, the aircraft continued its service with the unit. On 11 May 1956, the aircraft was involved in an accident after flying 1,890 hours. The aircraft was dropped from the inventory on 22 May 1956.

BuNo 128726 was accepted from the factory on 28 December 1951, and assigned to VMR-253, MCAS El Toro, on 14 February 1952. The aircraft moved with the unit to MCAF Itami on 30 November 1953. It was reassigned to the Overhaul & Repair facility at NAS San Diego then MCAS Cherry Point on 7 December 1953. H&MS-25 at MCAS El Toro received the aircraft on 31 January 1955. The aircraft was again assigned to VMR-253, now at MACF Iwakuni, on 9 March 1955. After accruing 1,920 hours, the aircraft was involved in an accident and stricken from the records on 16 May 1956.

BuNo 128741 was accepted from the factory on 29 January 1952, and assigned to AirFMLANT (Air Fleet Marine Force Atlantic), MCAS Cherry Point, on 8 April 1952. The aircraft was reassigned to VMR-252 at the same base on 5 June 1952. MTG-10 at MCAS El Toro gained the aircraft on 8 June 1953. The aircraft was reassigned to VMR-253 at MCAF Itami on 28 October 1953, and moved with the unit to MCAF Iwakuni on 1 January 1955. After accruing 3,117 hours, the aircraft was involved in an accident at MCAF Iwakuni on 7 March 1958, and dropped from the inventory on 15 May.

BuNo 128738 was accepted at the factory on 28 January 1952, and assigned to VMR-252, MCAS Cherry Point, on 3 April 1952. MTG-10, MCAS El Toro, gained the aircraft on 8 June 1953. The aircraft was reassigned to VMR-253 at MCAF Itami on 24 November 1953, then moved with the unit to MCAF Iwakuni on 23 February 1956. The Overhaul & Repair facility at NAS Corpus Christi gained the aircraft on 3 March 1955. The aircraft was returned to VMR-253 at MCAF Iwakuni on 24 September 1955. During take-off for a flight from Iwakuni to Itami on 3 May 1958, the landing gear failed to retract. The crew elected to make an emergency landing at Iwakuni with the gear partially retracted. Apparently the aircraft was repaired sufficiently to continue operation until 17 March 1959, when it was sent to NAF Litchfield Park, AZ, where it was dropped from the inventory on 13 May 1960, after having flown 3,462 hours

BuNo 131708 was accepted at the factory on 30 April 1953, and assigned to VMR-353 at MACS Miami on 22 May. Then the aircraft was assigned to MARS/MWSG-37 (Marine Air Repair Squadron/Marine Wing Support Group-37) at MCAS Miami on 1 November 1954. VMR-252, MCAS Cherry Point, gained the aircraft on 9 February 1955. The aircraft was placed in storage at NAF Litchfield Park on 6 March 1956. It was withdrawn from storage on 26 May 1956, and again assigned to VMR-353. The aircraft was sent to MCAS Cherry Point where it was sequentially assigned to VMR-153 and VMR-252 on 19 August 1958, and 15 May 1959,

BuNo 131717, with its 5T tail code, was photographed at NAS Whidbey Island in September 1971. The aircraft is painted overall matt Sea Gray with a white cap. Note the red and white prop tips. P M Bowers

BuNo 131669 is parked on the snowy ramp at NAS Grosse Isle. A tow bar is hooked up to the nose gear. Eric Lundahl via H S Gann

After accruing 4051 hours, C-119F BuNo 131688 left VMR-352 on 3 April 1961 for storage at NAF Litchfield Park, AZ. Subsequently, VMR-234 operated the aircraft out of NAS Glenview, IL, when it was photographed on 16 August 1973. Its squadron code had changed to QH. J D Morris via T H Brewer

BuNo 131670 was photographed at NAS Whidbey Island with tail code MV for VMR-216. The aircraft last served with VMR-234 at NAS Glenview with tail code WH. She was retired to MASDC on 1 June 1972, then on 14 July 1981 she was relegated to Dross Metals for scrapping. D B McCullough

BuNo 131670 carried the 7Y tail code when operating with the MARTAD at NAS Grosse Isle, MI. H S Gann

When VMR-234 operated out of NAS Minneapolis, MN, its tail code was 5E. C-119F, BuNo 131708, was photographed at Forbes AFB, KS, in May 1969. On 28 February 1971, this ship experienced a landing gear malfunction on a flight from NAS Glenview, IL to NAS Twin Cities. The aircraft made a gear-up landing at NAS Glenview. T H Brewer

respectively. On 19 May 1959, the aircraft was reassigned to VMR-253 at MCAF Iwakuni. On 18 December 1961, the aircraft was reassigned to MARTD, NAS Grosse Isle, Michigan. The aircraft then was assigned to MARTD, NAS Seattle on 20 September 1968. It was pulled from the inventory after accruing 7,292 hours on 14 July 1965. MARTD, NAS Twin Cities, MN, operated the aircraft from 1968. While on a flight from NAS Glenview, IL, to NAS Twin Cities, the aircraft experienced a landing gear malfunction and returned to NAS Glenview for a gear up landing. The aircraft was subsequently sold and ended up as N7051U with Hawkins & Powers at Greybull, Wyoming.

US NAVY OPERATIONS

The only known US Navy unit to operate the R4Qs was VR-24 based at Port Lyautey, Kenitra, Morocco, with a detachment at Naples, Italy. This unit operated as many as four Flying Boxcars between 1954 and 1962. Their mission was to provide air logistical support to the US Sixth Fleet and other Naval units and shore establishments throughout the European and Mediterranean areas. Other aircraft operated by VR-24 during this time frame included Douglas R5D Skymasters for long-range missions and Grumman TF-1 Traders for Carrier On-Board Delivery (COD) operations. VR-24 also served as host for Reserve VR squadrons deployed to the theater for training.

On 27 October 1960, while under the command of Capt W A Hood Jr, VR-24 was commended by the Commander-in-Chief, US Naval Forces, Europe, for meritorious achievement in the performance of their duties in air evacuation between 1 and 10 March 1960, after the earthquake at Agadir, Morocco.

A special flight by an R4Q was flown on 1 February 1961, from Port Lyautey to Rota, Spain, and on to Cape Verde Islands, a Portuguese territory in the Atlantic. This mission was in support of fleet units in the area.

An Operational Readiness Inspection was conducted between 26 and 27 March 1961, and an overall grade of excellent was attained.

During their service with VR-24, the R4Qs flew as little as 19 hours and as much as 365 hours per month. Their numbers of flights were as low as 10 per month and as high as 121. Two of the four R4Qs were dropped from the inventory of VR-24 in early 1962. BuNo 131665 departed on 19 January 1962, followed by BuNo 131668 on 12 February. These aircraft were flown to Litchfield Park, AZ, for retirement. By the end of June 1962, the remaining two R4Qs were dropped from the squadron inventory, thus ending the career of the Flying Boxcar in the US Navy. The Lockheed GV-1 Hercules became the replacement aircraft.

In addition to VR-24, the Navy operated a few R4Qs for flight testing at NATC Patuxent River, and as maintenance trainers or base support aircraft at several bases.

BuNo 131708 displayed its dayglo red finish as it faded into orange. Note how 'MARINES' is applied to the bottom of the left wing. N E Filer

This top view of BuNo 131708 reveals the dayglo conspicuity markings pattern, walkway demarcations, and the 708 7T on top of the right wing. N E Filer

BuNo 131692 was flown by VMR-353 from NAS Miami. The DZ tail code indicates that the photograph was taken after 1957 when the unit designation changed from MZ. In the background, an Air Force C-123 Provider shares the ramp with the Navy S2F. H S Gann

EPILOGUE

The Marine Corps Flying Boxcars soldiered on as C-119Fs until the mid-1960s. When the active duty units transitioned into the Lockheed GV-1 Hercules, that would be redesignated as the KC-130F after the McNamara change, a number of Marine Corps air stations used the Flying Boxcars as station support aircraft. In addition, these aircraft found their way into the Marine Corps Reserve inventory. The last of these aircraft, from VMR-234, went into storage at Davis-Monthan AFB, AZ, in July 1975.

While a cantankerous beast, the aircraft served the Marines quite well and filled an essential mission requirement until a better aircraft could be developed. While remembered for propeller failures, engine shutdowns, and landing gear malfunctions, the aircraft afforded the Marines an excellent airdrop platform and offered a rest and recreation escape for many of the men.

Chapter 18

Royal Canadian Air Force

A need for a larger transport was seen by both the Royal Canadian Air Force (RCAF) and the Royal Canadian Army. The Fairchild C-119 appeared to be a viable aircraft for the transport mission. Between 10 and 21 October 1950, the USAF dispatched C-119C 49-181 to Rivers, Manitoba, for trials. Using standard Canadian equipment and procedures, the aircraft demonstrated its air supply, airborne troop drop, air transport, heavy equipment drop and emergency evacuation capabilities. The impression left on the evaluators at Rivers led to the airplane going to Ottawa to perform for the top military officials. Again the Flying Boxcar proved itself. As a result, a total of 35 C-119 Flying Boxcars were procured directly by the RCAF for use as replacements for the venerable Douglas C-47 Dakota. These aircraft were operated by three squadrons between 1952 and 1967 in routine transport operations, air resupply missions, paratroop training drops, and a variety of special duties.

RCAF Squadrons

Chinthe, or 435 Squadron, based at Namao near Edmonton, Alberta, was the first unit to receive the aircraft in September 1952. They performed routine transport duties in western Canada and airlift support for Royal Canadian Army paratroops training near Rivers, Manitoba. Between November 1956 and January 1957, they airlifted more than 1,600 troops (including Canadian Army personnel) and nearly 225,000 lb of freight, 115,000 lb of baggage, and 2,000 lb of mail from Italy to Egypt in more than 900 flying hours while supporting the United Nations (UN) operations there. In 1960, 435 Squadron re-equipped with the Lockheed C-130 Hercules.

Elephant, or 436 Squadron, based at Dorval, Montreal, became the second unit to receive the Flying Boxcars in April 1953. The squadron's motto is *Onus Portamus – We Carry the Load*. On 9 March 1956, a major conflagration erupted after an explosion in 'A' Bay of the Air Transport Command hangar. A strong wind fanned the flames, resulting in the loss of the hangar, a pair of adjacent office buildings, and three aircraft, including a C-119. On 1 July 1956, the unit relocated to Downsview, Ontario, where they continued operations with the C-119s. The Squadron also supported the UN airlift between November 1956 and January 1957. In August 1964, the squadron relocated to Uplands, Ontario. The following year 436 Squadron transitioned into the Lockheed C-130.

The third unit to be equipped with the C-119 was 408 (Goose) Squadron located at Rivers, Manitoba. They acquired the aircraft in April 1964, concurrent with their move to Rivers. At this time they relinquished their reconnaissance role and became a transport and air rescue squadron. They supported the Royal Canadian Army paratroop forces at Rivers. In May 1965 408 Squadron traded their C-119s for C-130s.

On 1 March 1952, 4 (Transport) Operational Training Unit at Dorval, Montreal, Quebec, began training operations with the C-119. They moved to Trenton, Ontario, on 23 January 1954, to begin training operations with the C-130.

The first two RCAF C-119F-FAs, 22101 and 22102, in formation over Edmonton. Note the absence of the ventral fins. Minimal markings appeared on these aircraft when this picture was taken. The pair of radar altimeter antennas are visible beneath the wings. Aircraft 22101 is preserved at the Pratt Museum, Fort Campbell, KY, where it is painted as a USMC R4Q-2 with BuAir No 131679. RCAF PL 54582

The second C-119F procured by the RCAF was serial number 22102. The last three digits were applied to the boom aft of the national insignia when the aircraft was photographed in 1957. Both the tail numbers and boom numbers were stencil cut. This aircraft now resides at the National Warplane Museum, Geneseo, NY.
Via P M Bowers

Aircraft 22110 was employing the paratainer delivery system that permitted the clamshell doors to be installed to retain a modicum of cabin heat. Supplies were being dropped to Royal Canadian Army personnel on a field exercise near Quebec City on 4 February 1955. Red paint is applied to the horizontal stabilizer and wingtips only. The last three digits of the serial number are applied to the booms ahead of the roundel. The aircraft is in overall natural metal finish. RCAF PL101513

Later in its career, aircraft 22110 had the AN/APS-42 search radar retrofitted, as denoted by its bulbous nose. The dayglo orange conspicuity markings had been replaced with the red Arctic trim on the wingtips, dorsal and ventral fins, and vertical fins and horizontal stabilizer. The prop hub appears to have been painted blue. RCAF PCN 79-163

Air Resupply Operations

Flying in the arctic regions is anything but a picnic. Magnetic compasses are all but worthless when flying near the North Pole. Radio navigation can be limited by storms and other electromagnetic disturbances. Weather can take its toll through high winds, icing, and reduced visibility. All of these hazards were taken in stride by the RCAF C-119 crews. Radio altimeters, gyro compasses, and the skills of highly trained navigators helped make flying in the northern latitudes successful.

The C-119s performed resupply operations to bases, weather stations, and the Mid-Canada Line radar sites. The weather stations were co-operated by Canadian and US personnel. In summer, ice breaker-escorted sea supply provided the bulk of logistics requirements. However, during spring and fall, air resupply became a necessity. In 1956 a record 1,200,000 lb of food, fuel oil drums, helium cylinders for weather balloons, heavy equipment, plywood and lumber, and so on were airlifted in by the C-119s. In spring it was daylight 24 hours per day, while in fall it was always dark.

At Resolute Bay there was a 5,800ft long runway with a 600ft high hill at one end. In blowing snow it was not uncommon to have to let down to an altitude of 40ft before the runway could be seen. Once down, the flight crew did their own unloading. Records are there to be made and broken. In early 1956, an aircrew led by F/O A Pickering had unloaded their aircraft at Mould Bay in just seven minutes. Shortly thereafter, another crew led by F/O N D Edwards accomplished their unloading is six minutes. Then F/O W C Badger's crew beat that time by unloading their ship in five minutes. The best time was made by F/O N C Woods' crew when they offloaded 13,000 lb of oil drums in just three minutes, 45 seconds. Of all the types of equipment and supplies carried, oil drums were by far the easiest to unload.

Runways, located on sea ice or land, were marked by red flags and lines of empty oil drums. Once on the ground, the crews worked for a rapid turnaround. The longer the aircraft sat in the cold the more difficult it was to get started.

On occasion a sudden snow storm would prevent a departure, the aircraft had to be dug out and the runway cleared before crew could depart. In 1955, one aircraft landed at a satellite landing strip during a whiteout. The aircraft hit a high snow drift that was unseen by both the flight crew and those on the ground. The aircraft was repaired and was able to participate in the resupply operations during the following year.

During the resupply operations, the ground crews worked 12-hour shifts round the clock. Servicing the aircraft in arctic gear is no small chore. It takes as much as twice as long to perform any task. Refueling of a C-119 necessitated standing on top of the wing and dragging a hose up from a refueling truck. The crews ceased refueling only when in danger of being blown off the wings. Oil in buckets had to be heated in a nearby servicing shed and rushed out to the aircraft. At best, only half of a five-gallon bucket actually got into an engine before the oil congealed to the sides of the bucket. Often the oil was blown out across the snow. Worse yet was when the oil had blown onto the aircraft where it had to be chipped off prior to flight.

At Christmas time, the C-119s made special airdrops to the remote arctic sites, in addition to routinely dropping the mail during the long winter. Dubbed Operation *Santa Claus*, crews would fly on the nights of the last full moon before Christmas in order to ensure their locating the small arctic settlements. Air Transport Command headquarters added Christmas trees to the supplies for each detachment. Both No 435 and No 436 Squadrons allocated one aircraft to Operation *Santa Claus*. Aircraft from 435 Squadron flew out of Frobisher Bay while 436 Squadron staged out of Resolute.

RCAF C-119F, 22115, had ventral fins added to the booms. The last three digits of the construction number, 10859, appears on the nose. Narrow black anti-corrosion panels are applied aft of the upper exhaust stacks.
Via P M Bowers

To the original markings, C-119F, s/n 22130, added the red and white lightning bolt, 'ROYAL CANADIAN AIR FORCE', and 'TROOP CARRIER COMMAND' on the fuselage. Note the corroded skin panels aft of the top exhaust stacks. This aircraft went on to serve as a fire fighter with Hawkins & Powers, Greybull, WY.
Via Eric Dumigan

C-119F, s/n 22131, added the Insignia Red Arctic trim to its full-up markings. The last three digits of the serial number were added to the nose, and deleted from the booms. P M Bowers A.3965

In support of the Mid-Canada Line radar sites, 436 Squadron delivered 8,085,488 lb and airdropped an additional 550,573 lb of cargo. Braving the elements provided essential support to the remote stations and gave vital training in arctic operations to the air and ground crews.

On 16 March 1956, a 436 Squadron C-119 may have set a cold-start record when they fired up in -62°F weather.

UN Operations

Hostilities broke out between Egypt and Israel in early October 1956. Quickly the Israelis took control of the Sinai Peninsula. The British and French intervened and began attacking military targets within Egypt. Within ten days a cease-fire was called and a request was made for a UN peacekeeping force. The UN reacted quickly and formed a United Nations Emergency Force (UNEF) to police the troubled area. Canada had

Aircraft 22123 carries the UN markings. 'CANADIAN AIR FORCE' is replaced by 'UNITED NATIONS' (in red), yet the' TROOP CARRIER COMMAND' lettering is retained. The red paint is applied to the wingtips, horizontal stabilizer, dorsal fins, and the inspar surfaces of the vertical fins and dorsal fin. T Panopalis

Ship 22127 was assigned to No 436 Elephant squadron, as identified by its unit insignia beneath the cockpit window. The last two digits of the serial number appears on either side of the nose landing light. Via T Panopalis

Royal Canadian Army troops prepares to board one of 20 RCAF C-119Fs participating in Exercise *Globetrotter*, on 20 October 1958. Note that three of the four aircraft in this picture had been retrofitted with the AN/APS-42 search radar, as denoted by their elongated noses. In the foreground is C-119F, 22134, replete with an inverted lightning bolt on its fuselage. In the rear, from the left are 22126, 22123, and 22131. RCAF PL-113882

volunteered to contribute a battalion of troops. Both 435 and 436 Squadrons were to fly almost 2,000 Canadian Army troops from Calgary to Halifax where they would board ship for Egypt. This was to be known as Operation *Rapid Step*. The sailing never happened. Instead, it was decided that Canada would provide air transport support and troops for administration and communication for the UNEF. As a result, the RCAF provided one squadron of C-119s. This squadron was made up of 16 aircrews, ground personnel, and aircraft from 435 and 436 Squadrons. Twelve aircraft came from 435 Squadron, while four more C-119s were provided by 436 Squadron.

The RCAF roundels were replaced with blue and white UN insignia. The name 'ROYAL CANADIAN AIR FORCE' was removed from the fuselage sides and replaced by 'UNITED NATIONS'. However, the RCAF lightning bolt on the sides of the aircraft remained.

On 21 November 1956, the first RCAF Flying Boxcars departed from Downsview for Capodichino Airport near Naples, Italy. The aircraft had been fitted with auxiliary fuel tanks mounted on the cabin floor. Ironically, the first ship off would be the last to arrive in Italy.

Around two hours out of Gander AB, Newfoundland, the right engine failed on F/O W W Empringham's aircraft, serial number 22133. The aircraft was carrying a spare engine as its cargo – an item that was not jettisonable. The single-engine performance of the C-119 was not the best. A fuel jettison capability was not featured on the Flying Boxcar. Crew ingenuity was not lacking, however. Cpl R C Hutton, the flight engineer, improvised a fuel jettison system. He took metal tubes from the parachute racks and connected them to the auxiliary fuel tanks. Next he ran the fuel from the cross-flow control valve through his improvised piping. He was able to dump 7,000 lb of fuel out the paratroop doors. Through Cpl Hutton's efforts, F/O Empringham was able to maintain the single-engined aircraft at a 4,000 ft altitude for two and

Paratroops from the Princess Patricia Canadian Light Infantry board C-119F, 22114, at RCAF Station Namao, near Calgary, Alberta, during Operation *Bulldog IV*. A unit code, OU, appears on the boom. RCAF PL-76871

C-119F, 22133, is being loaded at North Luffenham, England, as part of the 1 Fighter Wing move to Marville, France on 13 January 1955. RCAF PL-63644

Note how the RCAF national insignia on the boom and the fin flash have been replaced by the NATO insignia. These aircraft from 435 Squadron were photographed at Abu Sueir, Egypt, on 10 December 1956. RCAF PL-106264

a half hours. The deteriorating weather forced the crew to declare an emergency and a Lancaster was dispatched as an escort. With a 300ft ceiling and three and a half mile visibility, F/O Empringham let down at Torbay. For their efforts in saving the aircraft, crew, and cargo, they received a commendation from the Chief of the Air Staff. A second aircraft, serial number 22130, departed Canada as a replacement, but it too experienced problems. Maintenance delayed its arrival in Italy until 2 December.

On 22 November 1956, air transport units were established at Capodichino, Italy, and Abu Sueir, Egypt, with 114 and 115 Communications Flights based at those two bases, respectively, to direct and control air operations. Group Captain H A Morrison was the first UNEF RCAF component commander. He was succeeded by Group Commander W P Pleasance, in January 1957.

The RCAF C-119s assigned to the UNEF mainly flew a 1,300-mile shuttle between Capodichino and Abu Sueir three times per week carrying troops, equipment, and supplies. On one occasion, a crew from 436 Squadron flew Egyptian prisoners of war on a 1,900 mile trip from Djibouti, French Somaliland, via Wadi Halfa and Khartoum, to Cairo. The POWs were the one-time crew of a ship sunk in the Red Sea during hostilities in the Suez crisis.

Precise flying operations had to be adhered to, lest the peacekeeping aircraft become involved in the fray. Departures from Capodichino were made around 0200 hours in order to ensure an on-time arrival at Souda Bay for refueling. Landfall had to be made at Rosetta, about 30 miles east of Alexandria. When returning, the same point had to be used for departure. The crossings at Rosetta had to be made during daylight hours between 30 minutes past sunrise and 30 minutes before sunset. Later some of the restrictions were lifted and the Egyptian terminal was relocated to El Arish. This change eliminated the fuel stop at Souda.

Christmas 1956 was not without its difficulties. Bad weather had temporarily halted the flying however, the conditions improved and the perishables made it in time for the holidays.

By the end of December 1956, the Flying Boxcars had delivered 614,000 lb of cargo and

One of three electronic warfare C-119s operated by the RCAF, 22112, was taxying at St Hubert, in May 1964. RCAF PL-150200

1,712 passengers. During a three-day airlift between Beirut and Abu Sueir they had flown 570 Indian and Indonesian troops and 144,000 lb of their equipment.

While the bulk of the RCAF detachment had left the Middle East by the end of January 1957, two communications flights remained. Members of 114 Squadron at Capodichino held four C-119s and 115 Squadron at El Arish had three Dakotas and four Otters to continue their support of the UNEF in the Sinai Desert until the spring of 1958. The UNEF continued its presence for about ten years. When the UNEF was withdrawn, 436 Squadron participated in their redeployment.

During the Belgian Congo airlift into Leopoldville, in September 1961, a pair of RCAF C-119s, aircrews and ground support personnel provided airlift assistance.

Exercise Rising Star

Between 15 July and 1 August 1957, RCAF Regular and Auxiliary units participated in Exercise *Rising Star*, a large-scale summer training exercise conducted with the Royal Canadian Army at Camp Gagetown, New Brunswick. The units flew C-119s, North American Mitchells, Avro Lancasters, North American Mustangs, and Douglas Dakotas for the exercise.

Routine Operations

In addition to their arctic supply operations, the C-119s flew routine cargo missions. Between 6-9 March 1957, 436 Squadron flew 86,000 lb of sheet metal to the Mid-Canada Line radar sites. In May of the same year they delivered de Havilland Otters to Abu Sueir. On 20 February 1958, the squadron flew 10,000 lb of cargo from Dartmouth to Guantanamo, Cuba. Tailplanes for the de Havilland Comets were flown to Chester, England, on 1 January 1959. On 9 February 1959, a replica of the *Silver Dart* was flown from Mountainview to Sydney, Australia, as part of a 50th Anniversary of Flight celebration. A Ginie rocket, used on the CF-101 Voodoo, was flown from Utah to Toronto in May 1959. An iron lung was flown from Downsview to Ottawa in September 1959. During that same month, a C-119 delivered fire-fighting equipment to Summerside. The heaviest single item to be transported was a 19,000-lb generator.

During May and June 1959, the royal couple, Queen Elizabeth and Prince Philip, made a tour of Canada. The royal car, a Cadillac Series 75 limousine (18ft 8¾in long and 6ft 8¼in wide, was flown from Windsor to Ottawa for use in a royal tour. An RCAF C-119 would fly the royal car overnight to the next stop for royal couple's use.

The C-119s flew in support of surveys and scientific expeditions, taking them north to the polar regions and south to the jungles of South America.

In January 1955, four aircraft participated in Operation *Rumba Queen* deploying the men and equipment of 1 Fighter Wing, a Sabre unit, from North Luffenham, England, to Marville, France. No 435 Squadron provided aircraft 22125 and 22128; while 22126 and 22133 came from 436 Squadron. All four aircraft left Dorval on 3 January, headed for Gander AB, Newfoundland. One ship diverted to Harmon AFB, while the remaining aircraft went on to Goose Bay and Bluie West 1, Keflavik, and Prestwick. The first three aircraft arrived at North Luffenham on 9 January, followed by the fourth ship on the 10th. The Flying Boxcars could not refuel at Marville, and consequently had to fly the 300-mile leg with reduced loads of 6 to 8 tons (9 tons was normal). During Operation *Rumba Queen*, they airlifted 250 tons of equipment. Though dogged by bad weather, the C-119s completed the move of 1 Fighter Wing by 24 January, and arrived back at Dorval on 1 February.

A Boeing IM-99 BOMARC interceptor missile was flown to Ottawa, by 436 Squadron on 8 November 1958. Missiles of this type would become operational with 446 Squadron at North Bay, Ontario, on 28 December 1961, and 447 Squadron at La Macaza, Quebec, on 15 September 1962. The political uproar surrounding the IM-99 is another story – it did little to cement US/Canadian relationships.

During the first nine months of 1961, the RCAF *Golden Hawks* flight demonstration team performed at 53 airshows in Canada and another five in the United States. During this tour they were supported by C-119s from 436 Squadron.

A C-119 from 435 Squadron was participating in a medical airlift to Thule AB, Greenland, on 11 November 1960. During that flight, the crew assisted in delivering an Eskimo baby boy. When interviewed by the press, one crewman quipped that they were just maintaining their squadron motto – Certi Provehendi – Determined on Delivery.

Airborne Operations

The Flying Boxcars provided routine support to the Canadian Army for their paradrop operations. They flew paratroops for the following operations: *Loup Garou*; *Bulldog I* and *II*; *St. Kits I*, *II*, and *III*; *Breakey*; *Jaques Cartier*; *Falcon*; and *Dash*.

On 18 June 1956, nine Flying Boxcars from 436 Squadron set an RCAF peacetime record for the longest airlift. The ships had taken off from Edmonton and headed east via Winnipeg and Dorval. They arrived over Frederickton and dropped 350 paratroops from the 1st Field Regiment.

Electronic Countermeasures

The C-119 Flying Boxcar was employed in a most unlikely mission by the RCAF between May 1956 and April 1967. This role was that of electronic countermeasures. Three C-119s were modified by Northwest Industries in Edmonton, Alberta, and operated by 104 Composite Squadron at St Hubert, Quebec. The unit designation was in a state of flux between 1 November 1958 and April 1959, when it became 104 Communication and Calibration Flight on 1 January 1959 and then the RCAF Electronic Warfare Unit. In addition to the C-119, the unit operated a number of Douglas C-47 Dakotas. Later, these propeller-driven airplanes were replaced by the Avro CF-100 Canuck.

These aircraft were equipped with a variety of jamming devices and chaff. They routinely were flown against North American Air Defense (NORAD) installations.

The three aircraft converted for this role carried RCAF serial numbers 22112, 22113, and 22122.

EPILOGUE

The C-119 Flying Boxcars served the RCAF faithfully from September 1952 until July 1965, in a variety of roles. During these years the aircraft proved to be most reliable in airdropping troops, supplying remote sites, and assisting in peacekeeping operations.

A number of RCAF C-119s were sold to fire fighting companies such as Hawkins & Powers in Greybull, WY. Others are serving in USAF base museums, ironically with their large radar noses. Disposition of many of these aircraft may be found in Appendix 5.

Chapter 19

Indian Air Force Boxcars

The new commander of the *Bharatiya Vayu Sena* (Indian Air Force), Air Marshal Subroto Mukerjee, had taken over from the last Royal Air Force commander-in-chief in 1954. At this time, the Indian Air Force obtained the first of 26 C-119Gs to relieve the fleet of 70 war-weary C-47s that had remained in country after World War Two. No 12 Squadron was the first to receive the Flying Boxcars, and initially was a composite unit with C-47s. The C-119s were assigned to a Conversion & Training Flight within No 12 Squadron. During 1954, the Indian Air Force received a total of 25 C-119s. Several years later, the C-47s were transferred to the newly formed No 43 Squadron.

Indian Air Force C-119 Operations

The C-119s performed numerous airlift functions, including troop lifts, supply and cargo lifts, and aircraft hauling. A Hindustan Aircraft HT-2 trainer was flown to Indonesia in August 1956 by a C-119G, serial number IK447. Relief supplies were airlifted from India to Egypt and Hungary in 1956 by IAF C-119s. In 1957, C-119G serial number IK451 flew the first Folland Gnat from England to India for evaluation.

During July 1960, the Indian Army had assumed the responsibility for manning the Himalayan front. To perform this mission, airlift was essential. A second batch of 29 C-119Gs was ordered in July 1960. These aircraft were assigned to No 19 Squadron. Under a US emergency military aid program, the Indian Air Force obtained another 24 C-119Gs in May 1963, bringing the total to 79 Flying Boxcars. These aircraft were assigned to No 12 and No 19 Squadrons; while the remaining four transport squadrons were equipped with C-47s and de Havilland U-1 Otters.

By late 1967, the Indian Air Force had expanded its airlift capabilities to include these inventories spread over these 12 transport squadrons.

Aircraft Type	No of Aircraft	No of Sqns	Sqns	Base
An-12B	16	2	No 25	Chandigrah
			No 44	
C-119G	79	3	No 19	Chandigrah
			No 42	Chandigrah
			No 48	Tezpur
C-47		3	No 12	Agra
			No 43	
			No 49	
U-1		2	No 41	Kashmir
IL-14	24	1	No 42	Palam
V-2	18	1	No 33	Tezpur
HS.748	34	1	No 11	Palam

During the UN operation in the Belgian Congo during the early 1960s, No 12 Squadron dispatched aircrew and maintenance personnel to operate the UN C-119s in that country. A second contingent went in June 1961.

Support of the ground forces in Ladakh necessitated that the C-119s operate from four remote airfields located at elevations as much as 14,000ft above sea level. The airplanes routinely operated off 4,000ft-long dirt runways that were 3,500ft above sea level. On hot days, the density altitude took its toll on the operational capability of the C-119s' R-3350 engines. The operational capability of the Flying Boxcars was greatly improved by the installation of a jet engine on top of the fuselage. This *Jet Pack* increased the safety margins by offering an additional 3,400 lb of thrust. The first installation of a Westinghouse J34 turbojet was accomplished at the Overhaul Division of Hindustan Aircraft Limited, in Bangalore, India, with assistance from Steward-Davis, of Long Beach, CA. Eventually, a total of 27 C-119s were retrofitted

The first C-119G, IK450, was delivered by MATS' 1739th Ferrying Squadron. The national insignia, patterned after the British, consist of a green dot in a white circle surrounded in orange. The national insignia were applied to the tops and bottoms of each wing and on each boom. The fin flash is green, white, and orange, front to rear. The serial number is applied to each boom and under the wings – read normal on the left and reversed on the right. W Loyd

IK450 displays its underwing roundels along with its boom markings. W Loyd

Here is a flight line full of Indian Air Force C-119s. Via Steward-Davis

By 1975, aircraft IK450 was retrofitted with the Steward-Davis *Jet Pack*. The aircraft carries its green, white and orange fin flash and roundels. The serial number is applied above the fin flash and repeated beneath the wing. 'INDIAN AIR FORCE' has been added to the fuselage.
Courtesy, *Aviation Week*

Aircraft IK442 carried the letter B on the nose.
E M Sommerich via P M Bowers

with this engine. A world's record was established on 23 July 1962, when one of these modified aircraft successfully transported 32 personnel to and from a forward landing strip at Daulet Beg Oldi, located 16,800ft above sea level in the Karakorams Mountains.

The Chinese were engaged with Indian forces along the Himalayan front in the fall of 1962. During the third week of October, C-119s from No 12 and No 19 Squadrons flew in reinforcements of troops and artillery from Pathankot and Srinagar to the embattled 14th Infantry Brigade at Chushul. On 24 October, they flew in a troop of AMX-13 tanks from the 20th Lancers for the defense of the Chushul airfield that was under attack from the Chinese. Between October and December, the C-119s flew day and night in support of the Indian forces. They made a significant contribution by airlifting the 5th Infantry Division from the plains of the Punjab to the foothills of Tezpur – a distance of 1,200 miles.

In May 1963, under the Military Defense Assistance Program (MDAP) the United States furnished the Indian Air Force with an additional 24 ex-USAF C-119Gs along with 176 overhauled engines. Most of these airplanes were assigned to the newly formed No 48 Squadron. The Paratroop Training School at Agra operated nine C-119Gs as replacements for their C-47s. By the end of 1963, over 70 C-119Gs were in the Indian Air Force inventory, making up the bulk of their airlift capability.

One Indian Air Force C-119G was destroyed on the ground at Pathankot by Pakistani F-86F Sabres during a raid in August 1965. A subsequent Pakistani Sabre mission to the airfield at Baghdogra claimed another C-119.

The Indian Air Force resupplied the airfield at Argatala, some 200 miles northeast of Calcutta, with the Flying Boxcars. These missions were flown only at night because of the possibility of being shot down by Pakistani fighters.

During the battle against the Pakistani forces in December 1971, C-119s were preparing to airdrop paratroops behind Jessore. The Boxcars were loaded with the troops and equipment of the 2nd Battalion Parachute Regiment who were to link up with the 95th Infantry Brigade. The Pakistani surrender negated the requirement for the airdrop.

In October 1960, the Indian government began negotiations with the Soviet Union for replacement transport aircraft. In March 1961, the first Antonov An-12 *Cub* arrived to fill the airlift role in the Indian Air Force. Sixteen of these aircraft were initially obtained by India.

The *Bharatiya Vayu Sena* lost all 46 aboard a C-119 that crashed at Agra on 22 February 1980. Another C-119 was lost at Srinagar on 7 February 1982, killing all 23 aboard.

Between 1953 and 1984, the *Bharatiya Vayu Sena* operated 89 C-119Fs.

OVERVIEW

The advertised performance of the An-12 was much greater than that of the C-119s. Powered by four 4,000 equivalent-horsepower Ivechenko AI-20K turboprops driving four-bladed AV-68 reversible-pitch propellers, the aircraft had a maximum gross weight of 134,480 lb (as compared to 74,400 lb for the C-119). While advanced in some respects, Antonov suffered two major technological defeats with this aircraft. First, the cabin pressurization system that would have given the aircraft a service ceiling of 33,500ft had to be deleted. Second, the flight-operable rear ramp/doors had to be deleted thus eliminating its specification capability to drop 100 paratroops in under one minute. In essence, this later-generation airplane which first flew in 1958 could not perform the heavy cargo drops already being done by the 10-year-old C-119s.

Chapter 20

Republic of Vietnam Air Force

Beginning in 1968, President Richard M Nixon announced his *Vietnamization* program which was designed to reduce American involvement in the unpopular war in Southeast Asia. By the fall of that year, the Republic of Vietnam Air Force (VNAF) transitioned from C-47s to C-119G Flying Boxcars. Selected *Armée de l'Air Vietnamienne* (Republic of Vietnam Air Force) aircrews were either dispatched to the CONUS for training or attended a crew conversion course taught by a USAF detachment stationed at Tan Son Nhut. The payload capacity and loadability of the aircraft greatly enhanced the VNAF's tactical airlift capabilities. While the C-119s could not operate out of the high altitude, short runways at some of its bases located in the mountains, they more than doubled the organization's monthly cargo airlift capacity.

ACQUISITION AND TRAINING

The VNAF gained 16 C-119Gs in 1968 and another six in 1969. They acquired 24 AC-119Gs in 1971 and 22 AC-119Ks in 1972. In addition, an unknown number of RC-119Gs were also delivered to the Republic of Vietnam Air Force in 1972.

The 413th Transport Squadron (TS), 53rd Tactical Wing (TW), VNAF traded in its C-47 *Gooney Birds* for C-119Gs. By March 1968, a total of 16 Flying Boxcars was assigned to the unit. Three more C-119Gs were transferred to the 413th TS in 1970. Both flight and maintenance personnel received transition training at Ellington AFB, TX, that was conducted by reservists from the 446th TCW. Additional training was provided for the maintenance personnel at Tan Son Nhut AB, South Vietnam.

The Chief of Staff of the Air Force, Gen John D Ryan, directed that one squadron of AC-119s would be transferred to the VNAF in FY 72. The 413th TS was activated in September 1971. CONUS training was established as follows:

The eight-week Phase I training was provided to the VNAF crews by the 1st CCTS, Air Force Reserve, at Clinton County AFB, OH. Phase II training was conducted by the 4413th CCTS at Lockbourne AFB, OH. It increased the standard USAF training by 25% (23 flying training days and 10 ground training days).

Eligibility requirements for the 48 pilots entering training were:
- Pilots had to enter training not later than January 1971, and graduate prior to 1 September 1971.
- Pilots – Experienced C-47 (non-gunship) upgraded to the C-119 in Vietnam.
- Co-pilots – T-28 graduates who later attended C-119 Phase I training with the 1st CCTS.

Another 21 VNAF pilots entered training in FY 72. Additional training classes were provided for an initial cadre of: flight mechanics, weapons mechanics, illluminator operators, and navigators.

Initially, seven AC-119Gs were transferred to the VNAF beginning in November 1968. These aircraft came from the 71st SOS. All but two went through extensive corrosion control and an Inspect and Repair As Necessary (IRAN) program. These aircraft were serialled 53-8114, 53-8089, 53-3145, 53-7833, 53-8115, 53-8123, and 53-8131.

AC-119 OPERATIONS

To counter the North Vietnamese advance that began on 30 March 1972, the United States expanded the VNAF's capabilities through Projects *Enhance* and *Enhance Plus*. During the first phase, a large number of squadron-strength aircraft deliveries commenced. During this phase the VNAF gained a squadron of C-119Gs and a squadron of AC-119Ks. The first AC-119K transfer occurred on November 1969. This aircraft had previously served with the 18th SOS. Project *Enhance Plus* provided an additional AC-119K squadron's worth of aircraft. In total, Projects *Enhance* and *Enhance Plus* provided more than 700 aircraft to the VNAF.

The VNAF 5th AD was activated in January 1971, with its headquarters at Tan Son Nhut AB. During September 1971 the 819th Attack Squadron (AS) was activated at the base and equipped with AC-119G Shadows. In December 1972 the 821st AS was activated at the base and equipped with AC-119Ks. Both squadrons reported through the 53rd TW. Another unit, the 720th Combat Squadron was also based at Tan Son Nhut AB and assigned to the 33rd TW. While equipped with RC-119s, the reconnaissance equipment never became operational and the aircraft were employed in the transport role.

The Republic of Vietnam Air Force obtained a number of C-119s. This aircraft, C-119G-36-FA 53-3161, was assigned to the 413th TS. It was taxying at Da Nang AB, on 16 February 1971. The last three digits of the serial number appear on the forward fuselage. The letters NG are on the nose. N E Taylor

C-119G-84-KM, s/n 53-8133, was also assigned to the 413th TS. Compare the camouflage pattern on the left side of this aircraft with that on aircraft 53-3161.

In addition, C-119G-36-FA, 53-3157, was assigned to the 413th Transport Squadron, 33rd Wing, of the Republic of Vietnam Air Force. The aircraft was at Tan Son Nhut AB, on 15 December 1970. The squadron insignia was applied to the nose. N E Taylor

C-119G-36-FA, s/n 53-3180, was photographed next to a C-124 at Paine Field, WA in April 1973. The C-119 was enroute to Southeast Asia to serve with the VNAF with its brand new SEA paint scheme. Note the external rudder lock.
P.B. Lewis via MSgt D.W. Menard

In 1972, the 53rd TW, 1st AD, based at Tan Son Nhut AB, Saigon, had five operational squadrons, two of which were equipped with the Flying Boxcar. The 413th TS had C-119Gs, while the 819th AS had AC-119Gs.

In December 1972, the 821st AS was activated at Tan Son Nhut and was equipped with AC-119K Stinger gunships. This unit was redesignated from the 417th TS. The VNAF aircrews were more adept at night target acquisition than their American counterparts due to their indigenous familiarity with the terrain.

By June 1974, the VNAF was the fourth largest air force in the world, with six air divisions. Attrition due to accidents, combat losses, retirement, and budgetary constraints resulted in the loss of around 300 aircraft from the VNAF by the end of 1974. President Nixon's administration, reeling from the aftermath of *Watergate*, could not provide any more support to South Vietnam. The North Vietnamese repeatedly violated the peace treaty agreements achieved only after the Christmas bombings during December 1972 in Operation *Linebacker II*. A new administration under President Gerald Ford was unable to sway an intractable Congress and no further aid was forthcoming for South Vietnam.

The North Vietnamese seized the opportunity and launched a massive attack during the night of 9 March 1975. By 22 April they had driven the last of the Army of Vietnam defenders from Xuan Loc; thereby making the defense of Bien Hoa AB impossible. Republic of Vietnam ground troops streamed towards Saigon in a massive retreat. During the night of 28 April 1975, infiltrating North Vietnamese pilots (or renegade VNAF pilots under personal threats and threats against their families) took off and attacked Tan Son Nhut AB. Saigon was now surrounded by 13 North Vietnamese Divisions. On 29 April President Ford ordered Operation *Frequent Wind* – the helicopter evacuation of Saigon. VNAF A-1 Skyraiders and an AC-119K provided cover. There were no FACs in the air that night. The AC-119 circled around the south end of Ton Son Nhut AB, firing at enemy troop concentrations and illuminating targets with flares and tracers for the A-1s. VNAF pilots flew out every aircraft they could, with their families, and headed for Thailand. North Vietnamese gunners downed an A-1 flown by a major from the 514th CS. Around 0700 hours on 30 April the AC-119 was struck by an SA-7 Strela missile and began to break apart. While three of the crew managed to bail out, one had his parachute tangled in the falling wreckage and was burned to death during his plunge. That night, 165 Republic of Vietnam Air Force aircraft made it to U-Tapao RTNAB, Thailand, including three AC-119s; thus ended an era for a nation and the airplane.

At least 36 C-119Gs were captured in southern Vietnam in 1975 and operated by the 918th Transport Regiment of the *Khong Quan Nha Dan* (Vietnamese Peoples' Air Force).

Chapter 21

Other Military Packets and Flying Boxcars

After World War Two, the United States and its allies began forming coalitions to assure mutual security. Two of these coalitions were the Organization of American States and the North Atlantic Treaty Organization.

Organization of American States
With its roots in the Monroe Doctrine, a collective security agreement for the Western Hemisphere was established on 30 April 1948, and became known as the Organization of American States (OAS). The first meeting of the OAS was held in Bogota, Colombia with 21 nations in attendance. These nations joined together to preclude intervention from nations outside of the OAS.

North Atlantic Treaty Organization
As an outgrowth of the Marshall Plan, the North Atlantic Treaty Organization (NATO) was formed on 4 April 1949. The Brussels Pact, signed on 17 March 1948, stated that if one of the signatories was attacked in Europe the other members would provide all requisite military and other assistance. These signatories were Britain, Belgium, France, Luxembourg, and the Netherlands.

In the US Senate, the Vandenberg Resolution was agreed to on 11 June 1948. It called for US participation in regional and other collective security arrangements outside the Western Hemisphere under United Nations (UN) auspices and led to talks with European nations for a military defense alliance across the Atlantic Ocean.

Twelve nations met in Washington, DC, to sign such a military alliance agreement. They included the signatories of the Brussels Pact and added Canada, Denmark, Iceland, Italy, Norway, Portugal, and the US In a Senate vote of 82 to 13, the US accepted this collective security agreement on 21 July 1949. Ironically a similar concept had been rejected after World War One. Article V of the North Atlantic Treaty stated that attacking one member of the alliance would be perceived as attacking all of them.

Top: **This C-82 was operated by the Força Aérea Brasileira. National insignia are carried on the top and bottoms of each wing. The s/n, 2200, is applied to the tail while the last three digits are repeated on the forward fuselage. 'C82' appears above the tail number. The upper portions of the rudder are painted green and yellow. An anti-corrosive black paint is on the lower half of the booms and ventral fins.** G S Williams

Left: **C-119s in the Brazilian Air Force had a natural metal fuselage with a white cap separated by a black cheatline. Black anti-corrosive paint was applied to part of the upper portion of the nacelle, cowl flaps, and lower half of the booms and ventral fins. The rudders were painted green and yellow. C-119 and the s/n, 2303, were carried on the vertical fins. In addition, the unit insignia for 2°/1° was applied on each fin. The last three digits of the tail number were painted on the forward fuselage.** G S Williams

144 *Fairchild C-82 & C-119*

Mutual Defense Assistance Act

The Mutual Defense Assistance Act was passed on 21 September 1949. It provided military aid to the NATO allies. Known as the Mutual Defense Assistance Program (MDAP), the main emphasis was placed on training and the furnishing of equipment. The MDAP remained in existence until 1954 when it was renamed the Military Assistance Program (MAP). For the USAF in particular, that was backed by *America's Arsenal of Democracy*, allied nations were supplied with used aircraft and equipment, and the requisite training for its maintenance and operation. This program permitted the American industry to develop newer weapons systems for the United States while providing continuity of compatibility with its allies.

Several smaller air forces also operated the C-82 Packets and C-119 Flying Boxcars for both transport and paratroop missions. These aircraft were provided to the various nations as part of the Military Assistance Program.

Brazilian Air Force

The *Força Aérea Brasileira (FAB)*, or Brazilian Air Force, traces its lineage back to 2 February 1914. Transport operations began in earnest in 1944 with the acquisition of Douglas C-47 Skytrains. These were followed by a pair of Curtiss C-46 Commandos in 1948.

In January 1956, 12 C-82s arrived at *Base Aérea dos Afonsos* for operation with *2° Grupo de Transporte* (2nd Transport Group) which was redesignated *1° Grupo de Tropas* (1st Troop Carrier Group) on 22 January 1958–the latter for operations in conjunction with Brazilian Army's parachute brigade. The 12 C-82s carried serial numbers ranging between 2200 and 2211. The C-82s were replaced by the de Havilland CC-115 Buffalo in April 1958.

These C-82s were transferred to the *Força Aérea Brasileira*: FAB serial 2065 (USAF serial 48-584), 2200, 2201 (48-586), 2202 (48-585), 2203, 2204 (48-580), 2205, 2206 (48-578), 2207, 2208, 2209, 2210.

Eleven C-119Gs were transferred to the Brazilian Air Force under MDAP during the latter half of 1963. A twelfth aircraft was subsequently delivered to Brazil. The aircraft were assigned to *1° Grupo de Tropas* and carried serial numbers between 2300 and 2311 (see Appendix 5). The C-119s were replaced by the Lockheed C-130 Hercules in November 1974.

Under the direction of the UN, the *Força Aérea Brasileira* dispatched four squadrons to the Congo in July 1960, in two contingents, to assist in the evacuation operation. The aircraft operated out of Leopoldville in the west and Kamina in the South Central Congo.

These units and aircraft made up the the second contingent of *Força Aérea Brasileira* the units dispatched to the South Central Congo.

Unit	Quantity	Type
1st Sqn	20	Douglas C-47s
2nd Sqn	6	Fairchild C-119s
3rd Sqn	8	De Havilland Beavers/Otters
4th Sqn	16	Bell H-13s & Sikorsky H-19s

The *Força Aérea Brasileira* lost C-119, serial number 2301, on 26 June 1974. The aircraft crashed at Rio de Janeiro, Brazil killing both crew members.

Belgian Air Force

The Belgian Air Force is officially known as *Force Aérienne Belge*. Belgian air transport operations started during World War Two from the British Isles. Beginning in August 1946, Belgian air transport operations were based at Evère under 169 Wing. On 1 February 1948, the unit was redesignated *15 Vevoers-en Verbindinswing (VVbW)* [15 Wing Air Transport]. The 15 VVbW had No 20 and 21 Squadrons equipped with C-47s.

The first two C-119s arrived at Melsbroek Airport on 24 September 1952, and were assigned to No 20 and No 40 Squadrons for 15 VVbW. They were followed by another 44 Flying Boxcars. The 30,027-lb payload of the C-119 was a great improvement over the 7,496-lb payload capability of the venerable C-47.

Following the British and French withdrawals from their African colonies in 1959, the Belgian government decided to give independence to the Belgian Congo. Independence was declared on 30 June 1960. Joseph Kasavubu was named president and a radical by the name of Patrice Lumumba became prime minister. The Europeans in the Congo began a mass exodus. Beginning in July 1960, airlift was provided by 15 Wing, using C-47s, C-54s, DC-6s, and C-119s operated out of Leopoldville in the west, and Kamina in the south. Security at these bases was provided by the newly formed Congolese Army under the command of Colonel Joseph-Desire Mobutu. Tensions escalated as the Belgians began to intervene in the Congo. A force of 10,000 UN troops was airlifted to the theater, primarily by the USAF's 322nd AD operating C-130s and C-124s. A number of USAF Reserve units also participated in this operation.

C-119G, serial number CP-36, crashed at Rushengo on 19 July 1960, after an engine had

C-119G-30-FA, s/n 52-6051, was OT-CBR, CP-38. She was later scrapped at Koksijde.
MSgt D W Menard

This C-119F was identified as OT-CAK, CP-11. Note the retrofitted white flat blade antenna on top of the fuselage. The aircraft was later scrapped at Koksijde. G Pennick via MSgt D W Menard

C-119F-35-FA, s/n 52-6022, was OT-CBA, CP-21, also served with the Belgian Air Force. She was scrapped at Koksijde. Via J W R Taylor

C-119G, 52-6020, became part of the Italian Air Force inventory with the code 46-34. A silver aluminized finish was applied to the aircraft for corrosion protection. This aircraft supported the Italian Air Force aerobatic team and was photographed at Buchel AB, West Germany in July 1960. Subsequently the aircraft was painted in the camouflage scheme and recoded as 46-84. Today, the aircraft is on display at Rivolto. MSgt D W Menard

46-28 was C-119G, s/n 52-6041. The aircraft was painted in standard camouflage with dayglo orange trim. Note the red spinner and natural metal lower engine cowl. The aircraft was later scrapped at Pisa. MSgt D W Menard

The Italian Air Force operated C-119G-36-FA, s/n 53-3200, originally carrying code 46-48. Subsequently the code was changed to 46-38, as shown here with its faded camouflage finish. The aircraft was eventually scrapped at Pisa.
Via T Panopalis

C-119G, s/n 52-5866, was 46-61 in the Italian Air Force and was one of 47 that were converted to the C-119J configuration with the installation of the beavertail doors. This picture was taken at Koksijde, Belgium, on 9 August 1969. This aircraft was later scrapped at Pisa.
Via J W R Taylor

departed the aircraft. Of the 40 paratroops and crew of 5, 37 were killed in the crash when the aircraft struck 60ft below the ridgeline. The eight survivors began a 50-mile hike through narrow mountain passes and brush. Only half made it to safety.

Realistic training can be hazardous. During an exercise on 23 June 1963, C-119G CP-45, carrying 42 paratroops and a crew of five, was struck by an errant phosphorous mortar shell fired by a British Army unit. The aircraft caught fire and crashed near Augustdorf, West Germany. While nine of the paratroops managed to safely jump from the aircraft, 33 of the paratroops and the five crew members perished in the ensuing crash.

15 Wing operated 18 C-119Fs between September 1953 and October 1956, and 28 C-119Gs between August 1953 and September 1973.

Italian Air Force

After World War Two, the *Aeronautica Militare Italiano (AMI)*, or Italian Air Force, operated a variety of transport aircraft, some of their own design, and others obtained as part of the MDAP. By 1948, the AMI was limited to 350 aircraft, 200 of which could be fighters and reconnaissance, while the remainder had to be trainers and transports. Transports of Italian design used in the immediate post-war period included the Savoia-Marchetti SM.79, SM.82 and SM.102, and Fiat G.12 and G.212.

Italy joined NATO in 1949. Expansion requirements for the AMI in late 1948 resulted in a request for DC-3/C-47s that were being flown by almost every other nation in Europe. The MDAP board turned down the Italian request and directed that such aircraft be purchased on the open market. Hence, 12 C-47s were obtained through civilian sources. However, a more benevolent MDAP board authorized the transfer of 124 Beech C-45 Expeditors to the AMI These aircraft had been derelict in West Germany since the end of World War Two. Italian engineers worked on salvaging the C-45s and by the end of 1949, 27 were operational.

The *Aeronautica Militare Italiano* acquired 70 C-119Gs and C-119Js between May 1953 and January 1979. The first two C-119Gs were delivered to the 46° Stormo Trasporti on 19 May 1953. On 16 April 1954, the AMI transport unit was redesignated 46ª Aerobrigata Trasporti. These transports were operated by three squadrons, one transport and two aeromedical evacuation, assigned to 46ª Aerobrigata Trasporti stationed at Arturo Dell Oro, Pisa, San Giusto.

Adapting to the new aircraft was a major undertaking and required a new mindset in maintenance and operations. The C-119s, with almost twice the horsepower, in essence doubled speed and tripled the payload compared with the G.12 and G.212 aircraft they replaced. Such performance differences brought an instant halt to airlift operations as both air and ground crews went to school to learn new operational procedures, instrument flight rules, and weight and balance techniques. Flight without the rear clamshell doors also posed problems for the crews. To assist the AMI in coping with the new aircraft, USAFE instructors were dispatched to offer training along with a Mobile Training Unit. Other AMI personnel were sent to Canada and the United States to gain additional experience with the C-119s. Some crews were also sent to airlines for training.

Shortly after the C-119 was declared operational in the AMI, crews began making overseas trips. The first occurred on 11 March 1954, when a crew went to a depot at Chateauroux

AB, France to obtain spare parts for their recently gained Republic F-84 Thunderjets and North American F-86 Sabres.

An aerobatic team was formed within the *Aeronautica Militare Italiano* in 1953. It was designated the *Getti Tonati* within the 5ª Aerobrigata. Between 1953 and 1955, a C-119 from 46° Stormo Trasporti/46ª Aerobrigata Trasporti provided logistical support for the team.

The prestige gained by the Italians led to tasking by the UN. A civil war broke out in the Congo in July 1960 and a flight of two C-119s from the 46ª Aerobrigata Trasporti was sent to the area to evacuate Italian citizens. On 26 August 1960, a permanent base was established at N'Djili, near Leopoldville where they operated until December 1962. Between three and fourteen AMI C-119s were stationed there. The aircraft were marked with large letters describing 'UNO' and 'ITALIAN AIR FORCE' as a sign of neutrality. The *Aeronautica Militare Italiano* C-119s delivered food and medical supplies to the Congolese people. Crews were faced with a lack of radio navigational aids and maps riddled with inaccuracies. Many of the so-called airfields were merely dirt strips. A lack of facilities resulted in the aircraft frequently being rotated back to Italy for heavy maintenance. Crews never knew who occupied the airstrips until after they landed. On 11 November 1961, 13 crew members from two C-119s were killed by rebel forces at Kindu airport. During the evacuation of the Congo in 1961, *Distaccamento Congo,* 46° Gruppo lost four C-119s.

Four *Distaccamento Congo,* 46° Gruppo C-119s were lost in the Congo operations, these are listed in the table below.

After being in service for about 10 years, the C-119s were sent to SIAI for refurbishment. The aircraft were returned to service with a camouflaged paint scheme.

The AMI would have liked to have replaced the C-119s with C-130s, but financial constraints made this idea impossible. Instead, 25 C-119Js were obtained from MASDC supplies at Davis-Monthan AFB, Arizona between January and March 1964. The C-119Js were equipped with beavertail doors that the Italians named 'screwdrivers'. Twenty of these aircraft went into the inventory of the newly formed 50° Gruppo, 46ª Aerobrigata Trasporti.

One C-119J crashed on its delivery flight. A second was destroyed in April 1970 when seven C-119 crew members and 10 ground crew personnel from the *Frecce Tricilori* aerobatic team died in a crash that happened during take-off. These four C-119Js were converted into VIP transports.

Serial No	Code	Remarks
MM51-8144	46-55	Converted for VIP use in 1969. Scrapped at Vergiate.
MM51-8158	46-62	Converted for VIP use. Written off July 1971 and scrapped at Vergiate.
MM52-5631	46-30	Converted for VIP use in 1960. Converted for EW in 1975.
MM53-8103	46-68	Converted for VIP use. Written off July 1979 and scrapped at Pisa.

Another five C-119Js were converted for electronic countermeasures operations and assigned to 14° Stormo, 71° Gruppo Guerra Elettronica. These aircraft were originally delivered to the USAF as C-119Gs and subsequently retrofitted with beavertail doors and redesignated as C-119Js. 14° Stormo employed these aircraft as electronic warfare testbeds. The conversions were accomplished by SIAI Marconi. Externally visible were radomes on the nose, fuselage sides, and/or belly.

Five C-119s were converted for electronics warfare testbeds.

Serial No	Remarks
MM51-8130	Converted for EW in 1975. Dropped from inventory in 1989.
MM52-5884	Converted for EW in 1969. Written off in 1974, and scrapped at Vergiate.
MM52-5896	Converted for EW in 1973. Scrapped at Pisa.
MM52-6031	Converted for EW in 1975. Scrapped at Vergiate in April 1977
MM53-8146	Converted for EW in 1976. Dropped from inventory in January 1984.

During 25 years of service with the *Aeronautica Militare Italiano*, it is estimated that the C-119s accrued a total of 301,619 flying hours.

Republic of China Air Force

The *Chung-Kuo Kung Chuan* (Republic of China Air Force [RoCAF]) on Taiwan received a total of 16 C-119Gs under MDAP in 1959. Eventually, a total of 120 surplus C-119s were transferred to the RoCAF. Many of these aircraft were probably used as a source for spares. While some of these aircraft were replaced by 18 C-119Ls, a number of C-119Gs were retrofitted to the C-119L standard on Taiwan. The aircraft were operated by the 101st, 102nd and 103rd Troop Carrier Squadrons, 6th Troop Carrier and Anti-Submarine Combined Wing, based at Pingtung. In addition to logistical support within the island of Taiwan, the C-119s provided urgently needed airlift to the much contended islands of Matsu and Quemoy. The venerable Flying Boxcars were phased out of the RoCAF in 1997 and replaced by Lockheed C-130s, much to the consternation of the Communist Chinese on the mainland.

Royal Norwegian Air Force

No 335 Squadron, Royal Norwegian Air Force operated eight C-119G from Gardermoen, Norway between June 1956 and July 1969.

On 6 December 1968, aircraft BW-E, named *Elmer*, had been on a training mission with the clamshell doors removed. The landing approach was too low and the left main gear contacted the ground 13 meters short of the runway. The aircraft slid down the runway for 800 meters before coming to rest 10 meters to the left side of the runway. While there were no injuries, the C-119 was severely damaged when ground crews moved the aircraft. Equipment was salvaged and the aircraft was scrapped.

Eight C-119Gs were assigned to No 335 Squadron, Royal Norwegian Air Force and carried its Norwegian serial number and squadron code. In addition, a name was applied to the left side of the nose of each aircraft. The USAF serial on the fin was retained.

Date	Serial No	Code	Callsign	Remarks
2 Feb 1961	MM52-6037	46-22	Unknown	Kwamouth, Congo.
15 Feb 1961	MM52-6011	46-15	*Lyra 15*	Lulabourg, Congo. Crashed on take-off, total loss with some survivors.
15 Sep 1961	MM52-6009	46-24	Unknown	Kamina. Sustained heavy damage.
17 Nov 1961	MM52-6014	46-10	*Lyra 10*	Entebbe-Tanganyika, Congo. Crashed on take-off, total loss with some survivors.

Initially, C-119s transferred to the ROKAF were in natural metal finish. This aircraft, C-119G-36-FA, s/n 53-3153, retained its USAF number. National insignia were placed on the top and bottom of each wing, and on the booms. The rudders were painted with alternating blue and white stripes. Via N E Taylor

Right: **C-119L-FA**, s/n 51-7985, was assigned ROKAF s/n 3160. It too was retrofitted with three-bladed propellers. A blue stripe was applied from the nose aft beneath the cockpit windows, and the prop hubs were painted blue, indicating that the aircraft was assigned to 103 Squadron. The squadron insignia was carried above the nose number. Benjamin Yu via Ruud Leeuw

Below left: **C-119L-FA**, s/n 51-8060, appeared in the SEA camouflage scheme, and carried ROKAF s/n 3120. The blue propeller hub indicates that the aircraft was assigned to No 103 Squadron. While the squadron insignia was placed on the nose, the 6th Antisubmarine & Transport Wing insignia was applied to the vertical fins. Benjamin Yu via Ruud Leeuw

Below right: **C-119L-KM**, s/n 51-8150, was given ROKAF s/n 3204, and assigned to No 103 Squadron. Benjamin Yu via Ruud Leeuw

C-119G, s/n 51-2693, was supplied to the Royal Norwegian Air Force and became BW-B, serving with the 335th Transport Squadron. It had dayglo orange paint on the nose, wingtips, and booms. This picture dates from April 1967. The fuselage lettering read 'LUFTFORSVARET'. By 7 May 1969, this aircraft was in storage at MASDC On 23 January 1976, the aircraft was sold to Kolar, Inc, Tucson, AZ, where the airplane was cut up for scrap. S Peltz via P M Bowers

C-119F, s/n 51-2705, as she appeared in the later Norwegian Air Force markings and carrying the code BW-G. This aircraft was at MASDC by 10 July 1969, and sold to Southwestern Alloys, Inc, Tucson, AZ, on 13 July 1976, and scrapped. Via V D Seely

Chapter 22

Civilian Packets and Boxcars

A number of C-82 Packets and C-119 Flying Boxcars found their way into the civilian market after they no longer had any military value for the United States. Their civilian uses ranged from standard transports to fire bombers; however several were put to unique uses. More than a dozen C-82 Packets and 50 C-119 Flying Boxcars carried US civil registrations as of the mid 1980s. Some of these airplanes were employed in air cargo operations while a number of C-119s were used in support of US Forestry Service fire fighting operations in the western United States. A listing of these US-registered airplanes is presented in Appendix 6.

Civilian Type Certificates
As the C-82s and C-119s became excess to US military requirements, they were made available on the civilian market and carried limited type certificates that were issued by the Civil Aeronautics Agency (CAA) (predecessor of the Federal Aviation Administration [FAA]). The CAA, and later FAA, issued a Type Certificate Data Sheets for certain modifications made to these airplanes. These Type Certificates (TCs) were applied for, and granted to specific companies, allowing a variety of special purpose operations including: specialized cargo transport, carriage of fish, forest & wildlife conservation, aerial spray, and aerial surveying

The table opposite summarizes the civilian Type Certificates (TCs) issued by the FAA.

Steward-Davis Jet-Pak Conversion
The Steward-Davis Company, Los Angeles, CA, has always been a nuts-and-bolts engineering firm. They began development with the US Navy surplus Westinghouse 1,600-lbst J30 turbojets. These were the first jet engines to be built solely on US technology. Normally the government provides aircraft components in a piecemeal fashion through their surplus programs. In an unprecedented move, Steward-Davis bid on the entire stock of J30 engines, spare parts, and technical orders when the McDonnell FH-1 Phantoms were declared surplus to Navy requirements. The bid was accepted, and Steward-Davis went to work making the C-82 a real performer.

A number of engineering changes were made to the C-82 to reduce its empty weight from 31,498 lb to something in the order of 27,000 lb. The electric landing gear actuating system was replaced with a hydraulic system. The heavy main gear wheels and brakes were replaced with lighter ones coming from the Douglas DC-4. In a conservative engineering effort, a pair of J30s was installed in a single side-by-side pod above the wing center section. Even with these engines the empty weight was only approximately 29,000 lb.

During certification testing at Edwards AFB, CA, in 1960, a C-82 with a single J30 engine proved a maximum gross weight of 43,000 lb without use of the jet and 62,400 lb with the jet.

As a follow-on to their C-82 Jet-Pak efforts, Steward-Davis began engineering development of a similar installation for the C-119 in January 1961. By March 1962, construction of a prototype was begun and the first flight occurred in September of the same year.

The initial 26 C-119s retrofitted with the Jet-Pak were accomplished as field modifications for the Indian Air Force, which are described elsewhere in this volume. The installation was centered

Formerly an ARS aircraft, C-82A-FA, s/n 44-23029, the aircraft carried the scars on the boom from its prior service. N4829V was converted into a sprayer for use by Skyspray from Redmond, CA, under a restricted license, as denoted aft of the forward entry door. Spray bars were mounted under the wings. The lettering on the nose read 'UNITED Heckathorn'.
E M Sommerich via P M Bowers

C-82A, s/n 48-578, carried US registry N4752C when she was operated by the Shelton Oil Company. Remnants of the Insignia Red Arctic trim remained on the empennage, whereas the national insignia and tail number had been removed. The aircraft was photographed at Anchorage, AK, on 21 September 1963.
Via N E Taylor

150   *Fairchild C-82 & C-119*

TC No	Issue Date	TC Holder	Model	Major Modifications	Limitations	Serial Numbers
AR-15	7 Jul 1955	Steward-Davis Inc 3200 Cherry Ave Long Beach, CA	C-82A	I. None	I. Weight limitations (lb) Over congested areas 43,560 T/O 42,000 ldg Over uncongested areas 43,560 T/O 43,500 ldg Pilot & co-pilot + seats & seatbelts for other personnel necessary to operate special equipment	42-22959 thru 44-22968 All others
	21 May 1961			II. Alternative recip engines. 1 Westinghouse J30 jet engine Restricted Category.	II. Weight limitations (lb) Over all areas 50,000 T/O 42,000 ldg. 50,000 T/O 47,200 ldg. 54,000 T/O 54,000 ldg. 54,000 T/O 54,000 ldg. Pilot & co-pilot + seats & seatbelts for other personnel necessary to operate special equipment	44-22959 thru 44-22968 44-22969 thru 44-22993 & 44-23004 44-22994 thru 44-23058, except 44-23004 45-57733 and subsequent
	23 Jul 1963			III. Recips as II. 1 Westinghouse J34 jet engine Restricted Category.	III. Weight limitations (lb) Over all areas 50,000 T/O 42,000 ldg. 50,000 T/O 47,200 ldg. 54,000 T/O 54,000 ldg. 54,000 T/O 54,000 ldg. Pilot & co-pilot plus seats & seatbelts for other personnel necessary to operate special equipment	44-22959 thru 44-22968 44-22969 thru 44-22993 & 44-23004 44-22994 thru 44-23058, except 44-23004 45-57733 and subsequent
A21WE	11 Mar 1970	Aero Union Corp Municipal Airport Chico, CA	C-119C	I. None, other than floor rollers per Aero Union engineering drawing. Also certified for special purpose of forest & wildlife conservation with cargo door installed. Restricted Category.	I. Limited to flight crew & number of persons essential to perform its intended function. Cargo handlers must wear safety harnesses that are secured to aircraft structure during all drop operations.	48-319 thru 48-355; 49-101 thru 49-199 50-119 thru 50-171 51-2532 thru 51-2584 51-2587 thru 51-2661 51-8233 thru 51-8273
	29 Sep 1971		C-119G	II. None, other than floor rollers per Aero Union engineering drawing. Also certified for special purpose of forest & wildlife conservation with cargo door installed. Restricted Category.	II. Limited to flight crew & number of persons essential to perform its intended function. Cargo handlers must wear safety harnesses that are secured to aircraft structure during all drop operations.	51-2662 thru 51-8168 51-17365 thru 17367 52-6000 thru 52-7884 52-5840 thru 52-5954 53-8069 thru 53-8156
A24WE	20 Mar 1972	Hawkins & Powers Aviation, Inc Greybull, WY	C-119G	I. Recips plus 1 Westinghouse J34 turbojet. Modified per Hawkins & Powers engineering drawings. Restricted Category.	I. Limited to flight crew & number of persons essential to perform special purpose operation. Certified for special purposes of: agricultural operations, forest & wildlife conservation, aerial surveying, carriage of cargo. For carrying fish & fish industry related cargo, aircraft must be additionally modified per Hawkins & Powers engineering drawings.	51-2662 thru 51-8168 51-17365 thru 17367 52-6000 thru 52-7884 52-5840 thru 52-5954 53-8069 thru 53-8156 53-3137 thru 53-3193 53-3201 thru 53-3216 53-7836 thru 53-7884
A5NW	31 May 1979	Starbird, Inc 933 Stitch Road Lake Stevens, WA	C-119L	None Restricted Category.	Certified for special purpose carriage of cargo. Operation over populated areas is prohibited.	51-2662 thru 51-8168; 51-17365 thru 17367 52-6000 thru 52-7884; 52-5840 thru 52-5954 53-8069 thru 53-8156
A6NW	24 Apr 1981	Pacific International Foods, Inc 18306 59th NE Arlington, WA	C-119F/ R4Q-2	None except a loading assist device. Restricted Category.	Limited to flight crew & number of persons essential to perform its intended operation. Certified for the special purpose carriage of cargo. Operation over densely populated areas is prohibited.	BuNo 131696
A32CE	7 May 1981	William Warra 2861 14th Ave Columbus, OH	C-119L	Modified per Warra engineering drawings for the special purpose of agricultural dry chemical spraying. Aft cargo doors must be installed. Restricted Category.	Limited to flight crew & number of persons essential to perform its intended operation.	53-7884
A35CE	12 Nov 1981	Bud's Flying Service, Inc RFD 1 Rising City, NE	C-119L	None Aft cargo doors must be installed. Restricted Category.	Limited to flight crew & number of persons essential to perform its intended function. Operation over densely populated areas is prohibited.	53-3144
A8NM	31 Mar 1982	DMI Aviation 5080 East Nebraska Tucson, AZ	C-119F/ R4Q-2	None Restricted Category.	Limited to flight crew & number of persons essential to perform its intended function. Operation over densely populated areas is prohibited.	BuNo 131669, 131673, 131700 & 131677

The Steward-Davis Jet-Pak installation on top of a C-82 at Long Beach CA. A flapper door closed off the inlet when the engine was inoperative. Steward-Davis

N74127 was formerly C-82A-FA, s/n 45-57807, after service with Latin American operators. She served as the Steward-Davis prototype for the C-82 Jet-Pak. The company logo appeared both on the nose and tail of the aircraft. Steward-Davis

This Steward-Davis-modified C-82 reveals its flight characteristics with the No 1 engine feathered. The boost from the small jet engine permitted straight and level flight with an engine out. Steward-Davis

around a single 3,400-lbst Westinghouse J34 engine mounted above the wing center section.

Later, at the request of the Indian Air Force, Steward-Davis developed a three-jet version that added a detachable J34 under each wing. These units were designed for quick disconnect, thereby permitting field removal should a mission not require all three jet engines. With all three engines, a 77,000-lb maximum take-off weight could be achieved. With the both the piston and jet engines, the maximum cruise speed was 168-175 knots (194-202mph). 203-262 knots (234-302mph). A phenomenal 1,200-3,500ft per minute rate of climb could be achieved at sea level. Airplanes with this modification were known as Steward-Davis/Aircraft International STOLmasters.

The Jet-Pak nacelles incorporated inlet doors that eliminated the drag induced from windmilling engines. With the Steward-Davis modifications to the Westinghouse J34, the power package was designated Jet-Pak 3402. The detachable wing pods were interchangeable, left and right, and between airplanes, through the use of quick-attach fittings at the wing hard points.

In a rebuttal to an *Aviation Week & Space Technology* Letters to the Editor entry in January 1966, Herb Steward, President of Steward-Davis, Inc, stated that a C-119 with R-3350 reciprocating engines and an appropriate Steward-Davis Jet-Pak configuration could operate out of any field which the de Havilland CV-2B Caribou or Lockheed C-130 Hercules could operate from at far lower cost. The Jet-Pak 3402 provided a 10,205-lb lift increase, using FAA performance standards, at a mere six cents per mile increase in operating cost, or $0.000005 per pound. Friendly nations who could not afford the C-130 could easily have afforded a C-119 with a Jet-Pak 3402. The Steward-Davis installation cost $56,000.

In 1961, the US Federal Air Regulations were amended to permit certification of surplus C-82s with the Jet-Pak. Steward-Davis obtained some investors by early 1964 and went into the conversion business in earnest. Their first commercial installation was made on TWA's *Ontos*, using a 3,400-lbst Westinghouse J34. Eventually their business partners went bankrupt and Steward-Davis, unable to find another partner quickly, was forced to scrap around 50 C-82s.

Steward-Davis later developed a twin-jet retrofit package for the C-119. The prototype *STOLMASTER* was installed on N383S, formerly RCAF C-119F-FA, 22133. Steward-Davis

Flying Mail Car

Fairchild had converted a C-82 for use as a Flying Mail Car. The conversion made a *working section* in the middle of the cargo compartment; a mail bag stowage area in the forward area; and a bag rack, locked registered mail file, and a locker in the aft section. The aircraft had about 93% of the capacity of a standard railroad mailcar. Up to six tons of mail could be carried on a 500-mile leg, or in excess of four tons could be carried 1,200 miles.

A new 5 cent airmail service was instituted by the US Postal Service on 1 October 1946. At 0900 hours the United Air Lines Flying Mail Car lifted off from LaGuardia Field, NY, and began its flight along US Air Mail Route No 1, which had been pioneered in 1920 as the first transcontinental plane/train fast three-day mail service. The original service had cost 24 cents.

The Flying Mail Car route was from LaGuardia to Cleveland, Chicago, Omaha, Denver, Cheyenne, Salt Lake City, and San Francisco, thus completing US Air Mail Route No 1. The flight then continued over United Air Lines route AM-11 to Sacramento, CA; Medford and Eugene, OR; and on to Seattle, WA. The entire trip took about 12 hours.

The inaugural flight carried 13 people including: Captain Edgar Hale, UAL's New York flight superintendent; Dan Henry, Fairchild's chief test pilot, Dean Smith, Fairchild's Director of Development; E L Green, UAL's assistant superintendent of maintenance; John J Hart, UAL's postal supervisor; Charles Roggie, Fairchild's Director of Commercial Sales; Ray Connors, UAL's New York publicity manager; and A B Meldrum, a Fairchild mechanic. Postal officials included B E McCaskill, William H Nichols, and E S Ransome.

This operation was of little practical value and had a short duration.

TWA's *Ontos*

In Greek, *Ontos* means 'thing' – appropriate for this C-82 flown by Trans World Airlines as a maintenance support ship. The USAF had recently released 120 of these aircraft for civilian purchase. However, this aircraft was obtained in a rather unusual manner. The TWA pilot, W L Trimble, was introduced to the aircraft through 40 hours of flying with Al Schwimmer, director of Bedek Aviation at Lydda Airport, Israel. Schwimmer had been demonstrating the aircraft for the Israeli Air Force.

The aircraft was originally powered by a pair of 2,100-hp P&W R-2800-85 engines. Trimble found a pair of surplus R-2800-CB16 engines, with a single-stage supercharger, which had come from TWA's Martin 404 inventory. With the consultation of Fairchild, Pratt & Whitney, and Hamilton Standard, it was suggested that a Fairchild J44 turbojet engine with 1,000 lbst be added. The engine had a diagonal-flow compressor followed by a single axial stage and had been used on the Ryan Firebee drone missile. This change would permit increasing the gross take-off weight from 49,000 lb to 50,000 lb, and also enhance the single-engine performance of the aircraft. TWA approved of these changes, procured the aircraft for $50,000, and budgeted another $100,000 for the flying maintenance base that this aircraft would become. TWA purchased the C-82 from Schwimmer in June 1956.

Further modification consisted of replacing all of the wiring with 50,000ft of wiring based on the Lockheed Constellation. In addition, all of the radios would be replaced to the Constellation standard. Some of the equipment was so new that it would not appear until the advent of the Boeing 707. The modified aircraft went into service in April 1957.

Ontos operated out of TWA's maintenance base at Orly Airport, France. On occasion TWA contracted with Air France for the use of their hangar and aircraft weighing facilities. The aircraft served to transport engines and other spare parts throughout TWA's European, North African, Middle Eastern, and Western Pacific areas of operations. *Ontos* would be used to fly a pair of R-3350 engines in support of TWA's Lockheed Constellation operations. Once per month the aircraft would make a 112-hour round trip along the following route: Paris, France - Nice, France - Rome, Italy - Brindisi, Italy - Athens, Greece - Rodhos, Greece - Nicosia, Cyprus - Beirut, Lebanon - Benghazi, Libya - Chandigarh, India - Karachi, India -

Steward-Davis engineers and technicians install a Westinghouse J34 turbojet on the prototype C-119 Jet-Pak airplane. A field-detachable engine strut is mounted on the wing hard points. Steward-Davis

United Air Lines operated this C-82, NC8855, named *The Flying Mail Car*, with its NC (US commercial) registry. The aircraft, photographed in 1955, flew as a mail carrier on US Air Mail Route 1. P M Bowers

The completed Steward-Davis jet pod mounted on the TWA C-82 is shown in this left oblique view of the aircraft. Steward-Davis

Wien Alaska Airlines operated N5102B, Steward-Davis conversion of former USAF C-82A-FA s/n 45-57782. During this stage of its career the aircraft carried this blue and white paint scheme. D D Olson via P M Bowers

Subsequently, Interior Airways of Alaska operated N5102B with a modified livery. Note how the word 'RESTRICTED' was added behind the entry door. Museum of Flight

When Studebaker announced its new automobile, the *Avanti*, they went first class with a Steward-Davis jet pod-equipped Packet. C-82 N5102B appeared brightly polished as she hauled the car around the country. W J Balogh via MSgt D W Menard

Still later in its in its career, N5102B was stripped of her markings and had a name befitting of her age and condition – *Ol' Rattler*. She was photographed on the east side of Boeing Field, WA, in 1961. P M Bowers

N383S was later operated by the Alaskan Bureau of Land Management when photographed at Anchorage International Airport, AK, in April 1972. To the rear is ex-USAF C-119C-14-FA, s/n 48-0152, now carrying registry N13746. MSgt D W Menard

Bombay, India - Calcutta, India - Bangkok, Thailand - and Manila, Philippines. One engine would be dropped off at Bombay, and the other at Manila. A shorter, 57-hour, 10-day trip would be flown as far as Bombay. In one year the C-82 could save $250,000.

Later *Ontos* was retrofitted with the Steward-Davis *Jet Pack* consisting of a single Westinghouse J34 axial flow turbojet mounted on top of the wing center section. The *Jet Pack* modification is described below. Certification was accomplished by the former co-pilot and then pilot Captain Claude Girrard. He later became TWA's Paris-based VP for Flight Operations.

The airplane was ugly as sin, being a refugee from Israel with a Greek name operated under Ethiopian registry by an American airline flying from a French airfield. It was a mixed up creature with four engines – one on each wing, one on its roof, and one in its belly.

Built as a C-82A-FA, serial number 45-57814, the aircraft was registered N2047 when initially operated by TWA. When the Steward-Davis jet pod was added it was re-registered ET-T-12 and then N9701F. The aircraft later returned to the United States and was operated by Briles Wing and Helicopter. Subsequently the aircraft served with Northern Air Cargo, and later Hawkins & Powers. Today the aircraft is main-

The complete Steward-Davis Jet-Pak J3402 installation on a C-119 was nestled under the wing. The bulged fairing accommodated the engine accessories. Steward-Davis

The Steward-Davis Jet Packet J3402, with both engines feathered and the gear down, was able to maintain straight and level flight. Steward-Davis

This immaculate three-tone C-82 was operated by Flying B, Inc of Anchorage, AK. The dual engine inlet is revealed in this view. N E Filer

tained by Hawkins & Powers at the South Big Horn County Airport, Wyoming and on occasion is flown to airshows and other events where it is a welcome addition to the program.

Latin American Operations

A number of Latin American airlines obtained the C-82 Packet during the mid-1950s and 1960s. These aircraft were known as *Vagoes Voladores*.

CMA/Mexicana acquired five of these aircraft in 1956 for use in their cargo operations. In order to improve the yaw characteristics of the aircraft, they installed long dorsal fillets. Mexicana's fleet included these aircraft:

Registry	USAF S/No
XA-LIZ	45-23051
XA-LOJ	45-57740
XA-LOK	45-57756
XA-LOL	45-57766
XB-PEK	45-57807

These aircraft were in the Transportes Aereos Mexicanos, SA fleet:

Registry	USAF S/No
XA-LIZ	45-23051
XA-LIY	44-2348

Transportes Aereos Guatemalecos operated C-82A 45-23050 as TG-DAC-79. The airplane was eventualy scrapped in Miami, FL.

Aerovias Condor flew a pair of C-82As with disastrous results.

Registry	USAF S/No	Remarks
CP-677	45-57747	Crashed at Sasasama on 15 March 1970
CP-678	45-57758	Crashed at Santa Cruz on 26 November 1960.

Aviateca Guatemalteca also operated C-82 Packets.

Registry	USAF S/No
TG-ATA	44-22962
TG-AVA	44-57832
TG-AXA	44-23034
TG-AZA	45-23025

Ex-USAF C-82A-FA, s/n 44-23001, was initially given US registry N6690C. Rivaereo, of Chile, operated this Packet with registry CC-CRB, then CC-CAE. A Steward-Davis jet pod had been installed when this photograph was taken.
W J Balogh via MSgt D W Menard

Aerovias Guest acquired a pair of C-82s in 1955.

Registry	USAF S/No
XA-LIK	45-57758
XA-LIL	45-57747

Cruzeiro, the domestic operator in Brazil, took delivery of a number of C-82s in 1958. These aircraft were primarily used to haul spare engines. One of these aircraft, PP-CFE, had the ignominy of ending its career as a night club in Rio de Janeiro in 1965.

Registry	USAF S/No	Notes
PP-CEH	45-57745	Crashed at Guanabara Bay, Rio de Janeiro on 11 Jan 1958.
PP-CEJ	45-57786	
PP-CEK	45-57777	
PP-CEL	45-57783	
PP-CEM	45-57810	
PP-CFE	45-57830	
PP-CFF	45-57812	
PP-DEI	45-57815	

Honduras obtained a single C-82, FAH 793, through a different route. The aircraft was purchased as surplus in Miami, FL, sometime in 1957, but it was not delivered until April 1958. This aircraft, being a single ship, proved to have serious mechanical difficulties – probably due to a shortage of spare parts. Over a five-year period, the aircraft was used only intermittently before being sold.

Brazil obtained 12 C-82s directly from the USAF as part of the Mutual Defense Assistance Program (MDAP) in 1956. One of these aircraft, 45-57783, subsequently flew with VARIG of Brazil as PP-CEL and now is preserved at the Brazilian Air Force Museum in Rio de Janeiro. VARIG, the Brazilian international carrier, obtained a number of C-82s in 1958. These aircraft were:

Registry	USAF S/No	Name
PP-CEE	45-57774	*Hercules*
PP-CEF	45-57830	*Centauro*
PP-CEG	45-57771	
PP-CEH	45-57745	
PP-CEI	45-57815	
PP-CEJ	45-57786	
PP-CEK	45-57777	
PP-CEL	45-57783	
PP-CEM	45-57810	
PP-CFF	45-57812	

Guest Aerovias Mexico operated XA-LIL on its cargo routes. Later the aircraft operated with Aerovias Condor as CP-677. The aircraft was ex-USAF C-82A-FA, s/n 45-57747. Museum of Flight

Several minor Peruvian airlines operated the C-82. Compania Aereo Mercantil, SA (CAMSA) had one Packet. Rutas Aéreas del Peru, SA (RAPSA) also operated a single C-82. Expreso Aereo Peruano, SA flew three of these aircraft between 1956 and 1962. Transperuana de Aviacion operated a single C-82 between 1964 and 1967.

In Columbia, Lineas Aéreas del Caribe (LIDCE) operated three C-82s for their cargo operations from Barranquilla and Bogota. One of these aircraft, HK-426, with the name *Arauca* under the cockpit, was last known to be resting without engines at Eldorado International Airport.

During the late 1950s Aerovivas Monder operated a C-82 with the registry CX-AQA. The company provided non-scheduled service to Miami, Florida.

The Ohio Oil Company of Guatemala operated at least four C-82s.

Registry	USAF S/No
TG-OOC-2	45-57802
TG-OOC-3	45-57734
TG-OOC-4	45-57795
TG-OOC-5	45-57793

Tale of a Caribbean Packet

C-82, 45-5773, had been purchased by David Losley. He leased the Packet to an affiliate of Pan American World Airways, Servicio Aero de Honduras (SAHSA), that operated a number of DC-3s and a Consolidated PBY Catalina. While with SAHSA, the C-82 carried registry HR-SAM. The company had won a contract from Esso Oil to fly gas cooking stoves for the oil company.

The Packet was subsequently sold to 'Doc' George Byron Adler Alder, an entrepreneur who was a Cessna dealer in the Caribbean. Alder had been in medical school, dropped out and joined the Navy: hence the moniker 'Doc'. The aircraft was re-registered as N4834V. On the afternoon of 29 July 1965, the C-82 was flying between Lake Front Airport, New Orleans and Guatemala City while under the command of Captain Wendell W Levister, aka *Black Eagle*. While approaching their destination, they encountered a number of tropical thunderstorms, which resulted in one airport after another going below minimums. The ADF was all but worthless because of the static created by the storm's electrical activity. As the storms enveloped the entire Yucatan Peninsula, it was getting dark and the fuel state was becoming precarious.

Using dead reckoning, the crew of three broke out of the clouds, headed for what they thought was Merida, and spotted some lights on what appeared to be a coastline. As they circled the lights, the No 2 engine sputtered and died due to fuel exhaustion. The decision was made to put the airplane down immediately.

The No 1 engine died of fuel starvation and the pilots set the aircraft up for a stall. Shortly thereafter the crew felt the aircraft strike the water. An order was given to open the top hatch and egress before the airplane sank – it did not. They had come to rest on a sand bar with the waterline at the level of the escape hatch.

Local rescue personnel launched a boat and met the forlorn aircraft. The rescuers asked if there were any injuries. With the entire crew intact, the rescue officer yelled, 'Then welcome to Campeche, Mexico.' A cool head on the part of Captain Levister averted injuries and fatalities under most daunting conditions.

The aircraft was not salvageable and salt water immediately began corroding its aluminum structure.

Latin American Losses

At least 11 C-82s were lost during Latin American civilian operations. Known losses are listed in the table below.

Hollywood Packet

In 1965, Twentieth Century Fox Studios released a film entitled *Flight of the Phoenix*, that was directed by Robert Aldrich. Buttercup Valley, Arizona served as the backdrop for the film. The movie featured Jimmy Stewart, Richard Attenborough, Peter Finch, Hardy Kruger, and Ernest Borgnine. A C-82 belonging to Steward-Davis was used in the movie. In the film, a C-82 became lost over the African desert and crashed. One of the passengers, a model airplane designer, suggested building a single engined aircraft from the wreckage. After much haggling, an air-

Date	Operator	Registry	USAF S/No	Location	Remarks
30 Oct 1957	TAMSA	XA-LIW		Campoeche, Mexico	During climb out from Campeche International Airport with a load of freight. 3 on board/3 fatalities.
11 Jan 1958	Cruzeiro	PP-CEH	45-57745	Rio de Janeiro, Brazil	During initial climb out from Rio de Janeiro-Santos Dumont Airport on a training flight. Instrument flying screens were in place. The aircraft lost altitude and struck a barrier before crashing into Guanabara Bay. 2 on board/0 fatalities.
16 Jan 1958	Cruzeiro	PP-CEF	45-57812	Belem, Brazil	The No 1 engine caught fire after take-off while on a freight flight. 3 on board/3 fatalities.
26 Jan 1960	Cruzeiro	PP-CEM	45-57810	Rio de Janeiro, Brazil	Damaged beyond repair.
24 Aug 1960	DAC	CP-665		El Palmar, Bolivia	The aircraft crashed.
26 Nov 1960	Aerovias Condor	CP-678	45-57758	Santa Cruz, Bolivia	The aircraft crashed.
29 Jul 1965	'Doc' George Byron Alder	N4834V	45-5773	Campoeche, Mexico	Ditched on a sand bar. 3 on board//0 fatalities.
15 Mar 1970	TABSA	CP-677	45-57747	Sasasama, Bolivia	
Oct 1970	Amazonia Comercio e Industria	PT-DLP	48-584	Unknown	
28 Oct 1970	Amazonia Comercio e Industria	PT-DNZ	48-578	Serra do Norte, Brazil	
27 Jan 1977	T A Itenez	CP-983	45-57777	San Ramon Airport, Bolivia	Crashed on take-off. 6 fatalities

Initially this aircraft was given civil registry XB-PEK. C-82 XA-MAW was flown by Mexicana Airlines along its cargo routes. It is interesting to note that dorsal fillets were added on top of the booms to increase longitudinal stability. The aircraft was ex-USAF C-82A-FA, s/n 45-57807. Subsequently, the aircraft was re-registered as CP-697 with Aerovias Condor, and then returned to the US where she operated with New Frontier Airlift as N74127. The aircraft also served as the prototype for the Steward-Davis Jet-Pak installation. D D Olson via P M Bowers

plane is built utilizing one nacelle and tailboom, a pair of outboard wing panels, and an intriguing pair of skis supported by some of the fuselage frame structure. For the passengers to hang on to, handholds were attached to the wing top surfaces. The result was a cobbled-up machine utilizing parts from a North American T-6 Texan and a Beech C-45 Expeditor. The flying scenes were performed by Paul Mantz. He was killed flying the mongrel machine and the movie was dedicated to him. To complete the film, a North American O-47 was employed for the flying scenes of the strange airplane The filming was so well done that only a skilled observer can discern the switch.

For some of the flying shots in the film, Steward-Davis provided C-82 N6887C.

Hollywood Déja Vu

After protracted negotiations for a suitable aircraft, Hollywood was able to remake the *Flight of the Phoenix* using C-119s instead of C-82s. The Comutair R4Q-2, BuAir 131700, was resting in Nairobi, Kenya, and would have been ideal for the new film – relatively easy to restore to operational condition, and closer to the filming locale. It is believed that this aircraft was one employed in the movie as a prop.

Hawkins & Powers had C-119F, RCAF s/n 121131, in storage at Greybull, WY, with registry N15501. This aircraft was restored to airworthiness standards. The 50-year-old aircraft was flown to Namibia for use in the flying scenes in the film and returned to Greybull, after an epic flight via Brazil in June 2004.

In addition, the filmmaker found a pair or derelict R4Qs in an aircraft boneyard in Tucson. They paid $50,000 each, had them dismantled and trucked to Galveston, TX, and then shipped the parts to Namibia.

The remake of *Flight of the Phoenix* was done by Fox Studios, under the direction of John Moore, and stars Dennis Quaid.

FOREST FIRE FIGHTING

Several operators employed C-119s in support of fire fighting operations in the west; including Hawkins & Powers in WY, and Aero Union and Hemet Valley Flying Service in CA.

Hawkins & Powers

Hawkins & Powers Aviation, Incorporated has been in business since 1969, operating a variety of aircraft for fire fighting and seismic exploration from their base in Greybull, WY. The company evolved from Chrysler-Avery Aviation, a company specializing in agricultural spraying and fire fighting since 1958. Hawkins & Powers was founded by co-owners Dan Hawkins and Gene Powers. Duane Powers is currently the principal in the company. Included in their inventory was the Fairchild Flying Boxcar. At least 21 ex-RCAF and two ex-USAF C-119s were operated by Hawkins & Powers.

The aerial tanker fleet numbers were carried on the Steward-Davis Jet-Pak cowling. As may be seen, the fleet numbers were duplicated over time. All but two of these aircraft were former RCAF C-119Fs. Information is given in the table below.

During the summer of 1981 Hawkins & Powers ship No 138, registry N8682, was employed under contract for the Bureau of Land Management to drop fuel bladders to fire fighting helicopter pads in northern Alaska. One 4,500-lb fuel bladder had been dropped at a site some 30 miles south of Bettles Field near the village of Allakaket close to the Koyukuk River. Each fuel bladder was mounted on a pallet that rolled on roller trays mounted to the main cabin floor. A pair of 64ft diameter parachutes eased the load to the ground when dropped from an altitude of about 400ft above ground level. The first drop was successful and the plane headed towards the second drop zone. The No 2 engine began smoking then exploded. Fire spread along the right tailboom. (Remember that the control surfaces on a C-119 are fabric covered.) The pilot, Ed Dugan, a former USAF F-100 pilot in Southeast Asia with over 1,500 skydiving jumps to his credit, and Jim Slocum the co-pilot, with more than 150 jumps, flew the

Tanker Fleet No	Registry	Military Serial	Jet Pods	Remarks
	N15501	22130		
	N15502	22114		
	N15505	22101		
	N15506	22105		
	N15508	22134		
	N3003	22106		
137	N3559	22118	Single Steward Davis	To Dover AFB Museum. Jet pod removed.
140	N3560	22132		Crashed 10 Jun 1978
133	N383S	22133		
29	N3935	22113	Single Steward Davis	
	N37636	53-8150		
135	N48076	52-5846		Crashed 16 Sep 1987
	N5215R	22108		
136	N5216R	22131	Single Steward Davis	
	N5217R	22116		
140	N807Z			
	N8091	22122		
138	N8092	22103	Single Steward Davis	Crashed near Bettles Field, AK 1981
140	N8093	22111	Single Steward Davis	
136	N8094	22135		
28/138	N8682	22115	Single Steward Davis	Crashed 127 Jun 1981
134	N8832	22123		
	N961S	22120		
	N966S	22107		

aircraft. Four smoke jumpers served as kickers in the main cabin. They were Chris Fairinetti from Fairbanks, AK; Jack Firestone from McCall, ID; and Jim Olson and Tony Pastro from Fairbanks. Dugan contacted Bettles Field and declared an emergency. Although he had both feet on the left rudder pedal, the aircraft continued to yaw to the right. Dugan ordered the others to bail out and he remained with the ship. The co-pilot and kickers had new quick-opening parachutes that had been issued that year for the first time. The second fuel bladder was jettisoned and the crew bailed out. Dugan cleared a ridge and saw the south fork of the Koyukuk River and a sandbar. He had no flaps or landing gear. C-119s were not good in belly landings. Dugan kept the nose slightly high and brought the aircraft down onto the sandbar. A helicopter in the area rescued the co-pilot and kickers, then went after Dugan. The crew was taken to Fairbanks. Three days later Dugan and Slocum had a new Hawkins & Powers C-119 waiting for them.

Aero Union

Aero Union, of Chico, CA, was founded by Dale Newton in July 1961. The company specalizes in aerial firefighting and providing modifications for firefighting aircraft. Aero Union modified C-119s for firefighting operations through FAA Type Certificate A21WE.

The C-119s were known to have been in Aero Union's inventory are detailed in the table to the left.

Hemet Valley Flying Service

Hemet Valley Flying Service had as many as 23 aircraft employed in the fire fighting mission, at least four of which were C-119s. The Flying

Aero Union C-119s

Tanker Fleet No	Registry	Military Serial	Jet Pods	Remarks
	N13742		Single Steward Davis	Cargo operations only
				Sold to Hemet Valley Flying Service
12	N13743	49-0132	Single Steward Davis	Sold to Hemet Valley Flying Service
13	N13744	49-0199		Sold to Hemet Valley Flying Service
14	N13745	49-0122	Single Steward Davis	Cargo operations only
				Sold to Hemet Valley Flying Service
	N13746	49-0152		
	N8682	22115	Single Steward Davis	Retained RCAF markings
				Sold to Hawkins & Powers
	N383S	22133	2 Under-Wing Steward Davis	Sold to Hemet Valley Flying Service

Top: **After service with Mexicana, this C-82, CP-693, went to Bolivia. It too had the dorsal fillet additions.** D D Olson via P M Bowers

Below: **This ex-RCAF bird, 22114, became N15502. The first five characters of the registry were stencil-applied, while the last digit was hand-written. The photograph was taken in August 1975. This aircraft was eventually moved to the museum at McClellan AFB, CA.** Douglas E Slowiak via MSgt D W Menard

160 Fairchild C-82 & C-119

Carrying US Forestry Service fleet number 81, N13743 was ex-USAF C-119C-13-FA, s/n 49-0132. The aircraft was operated by Hemet Valley Flying Service and carried these distinctive red and black markings. G S Williams

Boxcars were equipped with the Steward-Davis J34 *Jet Pack*. These aircraft could carry 2,400 gallons of water or fire retardant versus the 1,000 gallons carried by the Convair PBY Catalinas. Hemet Valley's C-119s had a maximum gross weight of 70,000 lb, and could be operated from hard surfaced runways that were a mere 4,000ft in length. The aircraft had a 5-hour endurance and could carry up to 20 fully equipped fire fighters. A typical crew consisted of two pilots and a flight engineer/mechanic. In addition to working with the US Forest Service and the California Division of Forestry, the company worked with the Chilean government for several years.

The C-119s listed in the table below were known to have been in Hemet Valley Flying Service's inventory. The aerial tanker fleet numbers were carried on the vertical fin.

NANTUCKET LUMBER COMPANY

The Nantucket Lumber Company operated R4Q-2, registry N175ML (ex-USMC BuNo 131677), to haul lumber to Block Island, RI, in support of the relocation of the Southeast Lighthouse. The aircraft had originally served in VMR-252 based at MCAS Cherry Point, North Carolina and was deployed to Port Lyautey, Morocco, to support Marine ground forces during the Lebanon crisis in 1958. Subsequently it served with USMC Reserve units in Miami, Seattle, and Minneapolis, with VMR-352, VMR-216 and VMR-234, respectively. The aircraft sat derelict in one of the boneyards at Tucson International Airport after serving with the Nantucket Lumber Company. Currently the aircraft is being cared for by the Mid Atlantic Air Museum in Reading, PA and may well be the last Flying Boxcar in flying condition.

CIVILIAN ACCIDENTS

While there are numerous examples of accidents with C-82s and C-119s in civilian operation, only a few will be described. Alaska is known for short fields, high density altitude airfields, snow and ice conditions, rugged terrain, adverse winds, and tight operation conditions. Each of these factors makes flying in Alaska challenging.

A C-82 was obtained by the John W Mecom Oil Company of Houston, TX, from Humble Oil & Refining in July 1963. The aircraft was then used to fly regular 900-mile flights between Jordan and Benghazi. On 20 December 1964, Hoyt Williams, a US pilot, and Kejel Grup, a Swede, had filed a flight plan from Amman to Cairo at 0435 hours. As was the practice, no Egyptian acknowledgment was required, and none was received. Egyptian authorities claimed that around 1000 hours the C-82 was detected by radar and a pair of MiGs were dispatched for an intercept. The fighters broke off when the Packet appeared to be heeding their directions to land at Cairo. The Egyptians claimed that, when the aircraft turned away, the fighters returned and shot it down near Alexandria.

On 7 July 1983, Northern Air Cargo C-82A, registry N9701F, experienced an incident at Anchorage, AK. The main gear collapsed after landing. While the nose gear was down and locked with a green gear indicator light in the cockpit, there was no down and locked gear indicator light for the main gear. Examination revealed signatures that are consistent with extreme overload resulting from an event such as attempting to extend the gear with the aircraft on the ground. The crew claimed to have searched for a checklist in the cockpit. The probable cause was listed as the pilot in command not following the checklist. There was a crew of two aboard the aircraft. Both escaped without injuries. This aircraft, that had previously served with TWA as *Ontos*, was repaired and returned to service.

On 26 June 1984, a Northern Air Cargo

Hemet Valley C-119s

Tanker Fleet No	Registry	Military Serial	Jet Pods	Remarks
	N13742		Single Steward Davis	Obtained from Aero Union
81	N13743	49-0132	Single Steward Davis	Obtained from Aero Union
	N13744	49-0199		Obtained from Aero Union
82	N13745	49-0122	Single Steward Davis	Obtained from Aero Union
	N13746	49-0152		
	N383S	22133	2 Under-Wing Steward Davis	Obtained from Aero Union

Hemet Valley Flying Service also operated N13744, ex-USAF C-119C-17-FA, s/n 49-199. The hoses and hydrants in the foreground were for loading fire retardant on the aircraft. T Panopalis

C-82A, N4753C, was on approach to their destination in Alaska when the crew was unable to extend the landing gear using either the normal or emergency extension systems. The crew opted to return to Anchorage where emergency equipment was available. Fuel was reduced on the return leg. A wheels-up landing was made on a foamed runway. Both crew members escaped injuries in the accident. A subsequent examination revealed that the right gimbal ring/travel nut had traveled beyond its normal distance and jammed against the collar on the electric gear actuator.

On 24 April 1984, the crew of Hawkins & Powers C-119, registry N15509, was attempting a take-off on an airstrip at Venetie, AK. Braking action at the 3,000ft elevation airstrip was considered good during the normal summer season. The runway was covered with snow during most of the year, as on the day of the accident. Grading and construction permitted take-offs to the south only; resulting in many take-offs being made with a tailwind. On the day of the accident, there was a 5-knot wind from the north, gusting to 10 knots. The pilot in command stated that nosewheel steering was not effective and the rudder did not respond due to the tailwind. Most pilots used a 25° right turn dogleg of the runway at the north end to start their take-off, especially when a tailwind was present. The airplane went off the runway to the left and collided with a snowbank, where it nosed over. All four crewmen escaped without injuries. The probable causes were identified as improper planning and decision on the part of the pilot-in-command, and selection of unsuitable terrain for taxi and take-off. The numerous contributing factors were:

- Over-confidence in the aircraft's ability by the pilot-in-command
- Self-induced pressure by the pilot-in-command
- Weather conditions – high density altitude
- Weather condition – tailwind
- Airport facilities – inadequate, snow covered, icy, rough and uneven
- Terrain condition – snowbank

Known Civilian C-119 Losses
The known civilian C-119 losses are shown in the table at the foot of this page.

Airworthiness Directive
A C-119 from the Hemet Valley Flying Service crashed north of Los Angeles in the Frazier Park area while enroute to a firedrop. The entire crew was lost. During the ensuing National Transportation Safety Board investigation, evidence of a failure in an aileron bellcrank due to a casting flaw induced during manufacture was found. This resulted in a loose aileron. The aileron departed the aircraft along with the outboard wing panel. All of the reinforcing tape strips over the aileron ribs were found missing.

As a result, the FAA issued an Airworthiness Directive (AD) calling for an inspection to prevent possible wing failure due to loads induced by a free aileron. AD 81-18-06 became effective on 10 September 1981, and was applicable to Model C-119 series airplanes certificated in all categories under various type certificates including, but not limited to, Pacific International Foods (TC A6NW), William Warra (TC A32CE), Starbird (TC A5NW), Aero Union (TC A21WE), and Hawkins & Powers (TC A24WE).

The AD called for inspections of the inboard and outboard aileron, aileron control system, and all aileron attach fittings of the outboard wing panel using close visual (10x magnification), dye penetrant and X-ray procedures. The components were to be inspected for evidence of cracks, corrosion, pitting; loose, distorted or corroded fasteners; excessive wear and elongated holes. These inspections were to be conducted within 100 hours time in service or within 60 days of the effective date of the AD. Any discrepancies found had to be repaired or parts replaced prior to further flight. Repeat inspections were to be conducted at intervals not to exceed 3,000 hours time in service or one year from the last inspection, whichever occurred earlier.

EPILOGUE
After ably serving the United States military for more than two decades, the C-82s and C-119s not only soldiered on in Allied air forces but served in a variety of challenging roles in the civilian world. For the civilians, the price of the airplanes was right, they had a proven track record, and had the capacity and performance to serve in a niche market. Today some of these airplanes may be seen in museums or on the airshow circuit.

Date	Operator	Registry	Location	Remarks
10 Jun 1978	Hawkins & Powers	N3560	Greybull, WY	While on a test hop out of Greybull, WY, the No 2 engine propeller ran away shortly after take-off. The aircraft made a belly landing 5 miles NE of the airport. 3 on board/3 fatalities.
5 Jul 1980	J D Gifford & Associates	N90268	King Salmon, AK	While on approach into King Salmon Airport, AK, during a freight flight, the crew received a No 1 engine fire warning. The left wingtip exploded. 2 on board/0 fatalities.
27 Jun 1981	Hawkins & Powers	N8682	Nr. Bettles, AK	While climbing out from a cargo airdrop at a forest fire, the No 2 engine suffered a massive internal failure, resulting in a fire and explosion. The cargo was jettisoned and the 4 kickers and co-pilot bailed out. The pilot made an emergency landing on a sand bar. 6 onboard/0 fatalities.
8 May 1983	Supra International	N13626	River Kagiak, AK	While taxying, the aircraft sank through the ice.
21 Apr 1984	Hawkins & Powers	N15509	Venetie Airport, AK	The aircraft departed Venetie Airport for Fairbanks International Airport while on a freight mission. The aircraft departed a snow-covered runway. Crew of 2 and 2 passengers/0 fatalities.
13 May 1987	J D Gifford & Associates	N8504X	Shagekluk, AK	5 on board/0 fatalities.
16 Sep 1987	Hawkins & Powers		Castle Crags State Park, CA	3 on board/3 fatalities.

C-82 Packet & C-119 Flying Boxcar Summary Unit Histories & Markings

After World War Two, the C-82 Packets, followed by the C-119 Flying Boxcars, quickly became the mainstay of the USAF troop carrier units. With wholesale replacement in the Regular Air Force inventory of these aircraft with the Lockheed C-130 Hercules, the C-119s then became the main airlift aircraft for the USAF Reserve. In addition, some C-82s and over 300 C-119s found their way into the air forces of at least nine foreign nations through the Mutual Defense Assistance Program (MDAP).

United States Air Force

REGULAR AIR FORCE

60th Troop Carrier Wing, Medium

During World War Two, the 60th Troop Carrier Wing, Medium (TCG) flew C-47s in support of Twelfth Air Force operations in the Mediterranean Theater. The group moved to Waller Field, Trinidad on 4 June 1945, and operated as part of the Air Transport Command until 31 July 1945, when they were inactivated. The 60th TCG (Medium) was reactivated at Munich AB, West Germany on 30 September 1946, and assigned to United States Air Forces Europe (USAFE). On 14 May 1948, the group moved to Kaufbeuren AB, West Germany. Initially operating with C-47s, the unit was augmented with C-54s during the latter part of 1948. The 60th TCG moved to Wiesbaden AB, West Germany, on 15 December 1948, were redesignated the 60th TCG (Heavy), and began to re-equip with C-54s. While there they had no specific mission, they did provide airlift support to USAFE and other units in the theater. They participated in Operation *Vittles*, the Berlin Airlift, between June 1948 and September 1949. On 26 September 1949, the unit moved to Rhein-Main AB, West Germany, where they replaced the 61st TCG. The unit was redesignated the 60th TCG (Medium) in November 1949, and resumed the tactical airlift role.

Commanders of the 60th TCG during the C-82 and C-119 eras were:

Col Jay D Bogue	5 Dec 1950
Col Donald J French	29 Feb 1952
Lt Col John W Osborne	14 Jun 1952
Col Lorris W Moomaw	25 May 1953
Lt Col Robert L Olinger	13 Jun 1954
Col Howard J Withycombe	1 Jul 1954
Col Randolph E Churchill	c5 Jul 1955

Commanders of the 60th TCW during the C-82 and C-119 eras were:

Col Aubry C Strickland	2 Jun 1951
Col Lawrence B Kelly	13 Jul 1952
Col Harry S Bishop	1 Nov 1953
Col Clyde Box	1 Aug 1955
Unknown	14 Feb 1956
Col Randolph E Churchill	c22 May 1956

C-82s came into the inventory in 1951, and the 60th TCG began to transition into C-119s during 1953. Between August 1951 and July 1952, the 60th TCG provided training for the recently reactivated 433rd TCW from the USAF Reserve. Between July 1952 and March 1953, the 60th TCW provided training for the 317th TCW. On 22 September 1955, the 60th TCW moved to Dreux AB, France, where they continued operations with the C-119s until their inactivation on 25 September 1958. The 60th TCW operated C-119s out of both Rhein-Main AB, West Germany, and Dreux AB, France, with the following squadrons (colors were applied to the nose and fin tips): 10th TCS/Red, 11th TCS/Green, and 12th TCS/Blue.

With the inactivation of the 60th TCW, the component squadrons were assigned to the 322nd Air Division in September 1958.

The wing was reactivated as the 60th Military Airlift Wing on 17 December 1965, and organized on 8 January 1966. Redesignated the 60th Air Mobility Wing, the unit currently operates Lockheed C-5 Galaxies and McDonnell Douglas/Boeing KC-10 Extenders from Travis AFB, California.

61st Troop Carrier Wing, Medium

The 61st TCW (Medium), based at Rhein-Main AB, West Germany, was equipped with C-47s and C-54s. Its component squadrons were the 14th, 15th, and 53rd TCSs. The 61st TCW was to re-equip with C-119s and on paper such action took place in August 1950. However, the outbreak of the Korean War dictated that the wing's primary operating unit, the 61st TCG, be redeployed to McChord AFB, Washington in July. By December, the wing and its component squadrons were all relocated to Ashiya AB, Japan. The C-119 transition never took place.

62nd Troop Carrier Wing, Medium

The 62nd TCW flew C-47 and C-53 Skytrains during World War Two. Initially based at Keevil, England, where they received additional training, the unit was assigned to the Twelfth Air Force and moved to North Africa in time to participate in the Battle for Tunisia. Between April and June 1944, the 4th TCS operated out of

The 129th SOG insignia was applied to many of the unit's C-119s. In addition, the Air Force Outstanding Unit Award (AFOUA) was added above the insignia. Bergagnini via D Remington

bases in India in support of the assault on Myitkyina, Burma. After the secession of hostilities in the European Theater, elements of the 62nd TCG assisted in the redeployment of personnel until 14 November 1945, when the unit returned to the ZI. The group was inactivated in Naples, Italy on 14 November 1945. It was reactivated at Bergstrom Field, Texas, between 7 September 1946 and August 1947 when it was reassigned to McChord Field, WA and transitioned into C-82 Packets.

Commanders of the 62nd TCG during the C-82 era were:

Col Donald J French	7 Sep 1946
Col Adriel N Williams	1 Mar 1948

Colonel Julius A Kolb commanded the 62nd TCW during the C-82 era.

The component squadrons and colors (applied to the nose) were: 4th TCS/Red, 7th TCS/Yellow, and 8th TCS/Blue.

The 62nd Airlift Wing is currently stationed at McChord AFB, Washington where it has transitioned out of the Lockheed C-141 Starlifter into the McDonnell Douglas/Boeing C-17 Globemaster III.

64th Troop Carrier Wing, Medium

The 64th TCG flew C-47s during World War Two in support of Twelfth Air Force operations in the Mediterranean Theater. During June 1944, the bulk of the group was on temporary duty in the China-Burma-India Theater. The group was assigned to Air Transport Command and relocated to Waller Field, Trinidad on 4 June 1945, where it remained until their inactivation on 31 July 1945. Though activated in the ZI at Langley AB, Virginia, on 10 May 1947, the unit remained unmanned until its inactivation on 10 September 1948.

The 64th TCG was reactivated at Donaldson AFB, South Carolina, assigned to Tactical Air Command, and began training in C-82s on 14 July 1952. By July 1953, the 64th TCG began transition into C-119s. The group was inactivated on 21 July 1954. Colonel Kenneth L Johnson commanded the 63rd TCG during this era. Wing commanders for the 64th TCW were:

Brig Gen Glynne M Jones	cMar 1953
Brig Gen Edgar W Hampton	Feb 1955

The 64th TCG operated C-119s with the following squadrons: 17th TCS, 18th TCS, and 35th TCS.

The wing was discontinued and inactivated on 1 January 1963. It was redesignated the 64th TCW on 1 July 1966, and organized on 1 July 1966. The unit was redesignated the 64th Tactical Airlift Wing on 1 May 1967, and inactivated on 31 May 1971. Redesignated the 64th Flying Training Wing on 14 April 1972, the unit was reactivated on 1 October 1972.

313th Troop Carrier Wing, Medium

After service during World War Two with the Twelfth Air Force, operating C-47 and C-54 aircraft, the unit returned to the ZI and was inactivated at Baer Field, Indiana. Reactivated at Tulln AB, Austria, on 30 September 1946, the 313th TCG (Heavy) was assigned to USAFE and resumed operations with C-47 and C-54 aircraft.

It returned to the ZI on 25 June 1947, was assigned to TAC and resumed training in gliders and C-82s. It moved to Germany on 9 November 1948 and participated in the Berlin Airlift. In February 1949 it was redesignated the 313th TCG (Special). The unit was inactivated at Fassberg, West Germany, on 18 September 1949.

Again redesignated, the unit became the 313th TCG (Medium) and was activated at Mitchel AFB, New York, on 1 February 1953, assigned to TAC, and equipped with C-119s. On 2 October 1953 the group moved to Sewart AFB, Tennessee, where they served until their inactivation on 8 June 1955.

Commanders of the 313th TCG during this era were:

Col Clinton W Davies	30 Sep 1946
Lt Col Walter W Washburn Jr	15 Aug 1947
Col Frank P Bostrom	3 Dec 1947
Lt Col Conway S Hall	unk to Sep 1949
Col Benton R Baldwin	Feb 1953
Col Steward H Nichols	1 Oct 1953-55

Commanders of the 313th TCW during this era were:

Col Thomas K Hampton	18 Aug 1948
Col William A Ross	c15 Aug 1949 to c14 Sep 1949
Col Donald J French	14 Jul 1952
Col Harry M Pike	23 Jul 1954
Col Clarence B Hammerle Jr	29 Jul 1954
Col Joseph A Cunningham	9 Sep 1954

Markings for the C-119s assigned to the 313th TCG consisted of a solid colored nose with a scalloped edge along the aircraft centerline beneath the cockpit. The squadrons and their colors were: 29th TCS/Red, 47th TCS/Green, and 48th TCS/Blue.

The 313th TCW was inactivated on 25 August 1953. Reactivated on 15 June 1964, the 313th TCW operated Lockheed C-130s from Forbes AFB, Kansas until its inactivation on 30 September 1973.

314th Troop Carrier Wing, Medium

After World War Two, the 314th TCG flew C-47s out of Bolling Field, District of Columbia, until late September 1946, when they moved to Albrook Field, Canal Zone, on 1 October 1946. Between 10 March and early October 1948, the group operated out of Curundu Heights, Canal Zone.

When the 314th TCG returned to the ZI, it was assigned to Tactical Air Command, redesignated the 314th TCG (M), and based at Smyrna (later Sewart) AFB, Tennessee, on 21 October 1948. The unit was equipped with C-82s. The 20th TCS saw detached service at Rhein/Main AB, West Germany and Bergstrom AFB, Texas.

Commanders of the 314th TCG during this era were:

Col Richard W Henderson	8 Oct 1948
Col William H DeLacey	27 Aug 1951

Colonel Hoyt L Prindle commanded of the 314th TCW during this era.

Component squadrons of the 314th TCG and their colours were: 20th TCS/Yellow, 50th TCS/Red, 61st TCS/Green, 62nd TCS/Blue, 334th TCS.

The 314th TCG began operation with C-119s at Sewart AFB, Tennessee in 1949, with the 50th TCS, 61st TCS, and 62nd TCS. The 314th TCG relocated to Ashiya AB, Japan, in September 1950, where they remained until 15 November 1954. The group was assigned to the Far East Air Forces, 315th Air Division (Combat Cargo). In addition to the 314th TCG's three assigned squadrons, it was augmented by the 37th TCG (from the 316th TCG) which was attached between 21 August 1950 and 8 May 1952. During the Korean War, the 314th transported troops and supplies from Japan to Korea, and evacuated wounded personnel. The group participated in two major airborne operations: the paratroop and equipment drop over Sunchon in October 1950 in support of the UN assault on Pyongyang and the paradrop over Munsan-ni during the airborne attack across the 38th Parallel in March 1951. After the armistice, the 314th TCG remained in Japan to transport supplies to Korea and to evacuate prisoners of war. For action between 28 November and 10 December 1950, the group was awarded the Distinguished Unit Citation. The Republic of Korea Presidential Unit Citation was awarded for service between 1 July 1951 and 27 July 1953. The 314th TCG was also awarded campaign ribbons for the following: UN Defensive, UN Offensive, CCF Intervention, 1st UN Counteroffensive, CCF Spring Offensive, UN Summer-Fall Offensive, Second Korean Winter, Korea Summer-Fall 1952, Third Korean Winter, and Korea Summer-Fall 1953.

Commanders of the 314th TCG during this era were:

Col William H DeLacey	27 Aug 1948
Col David E Daniel	28 Sep 1951
Lt Col Harold V Sommers	1 May 1952
Col William H DeLacey	Nov 1954

Commanders of the 314th TCW during this era were:

Col Hoyt L Prindle	1 Nov 1948
Col Norton H Van Sicklen	31 Aug 1950
Col Hoyt L Prindle	28 Dec 1950
Col Norton H Van Sicklen	1 Jun 1952
Col William H DeLacey	2 Jul 1952
Col Hoyt L Prindle	23 Aug 1952
Col Marvin L McNickle	6 Jul 1954
Col William Lewis Jr	1 Jul 1956

On 15 November 1954, the 314th TCG returned to Sewart AFB, Tennessee, where it continued

troop carrier operations with the C-119 until 1957. The component squadrons of the 314th TCG were: 50th TCS, 61st TCS, 62nd TCS, and 321st TCS. Between 11 January and 14 February 1955, the group participated in TACAIR exercise 55-3 and Exercise *Snowbird*, designed to test their combat capability under extremely cold weather conditions. As a result of these operations the 314th TCG received the Air Force Outstanding Unit award.

In October 1955, the 62nd TCS, under the command of Lieutenant Colonel W H Kellerher, departed with 12 aircraft for Dreux AB, France, to perform airlifts as part of NATO's Air Logistic Force operated by the 322nd Air Division USAFE. The unit remained TDY for a period of six months.

During the winter of 1955, the 314th TCG participated in a large USAF/US Army maneuver called Operation *Sagebrush* in Louisiana. For this operation the 321st TCS was deployed to England AFB, Louisiana, between 5 November and 8 December to furnish the bulk of the airlift. The remaining squadrons fulfilled airborne commitments assigned to the 314th TCG from higher headquarters.

The markings for the C-119s operated by the 314th TCG changed over time. Initially they carried a pair of insignia blue diagonal stripes on the vertical tails, reminiscent of their C-82 Packets. Then their markings were as follows: Medium Blue nose with a series of six parallel stripes in graduated lengths – small at the bottom and long at the top. A series of four similar parallel stripes extended aft from the cockpit windows. The upper third of the vertical fins were Insignia Blue with a series of six parallel stripes extending over the rudders. The squadron colors were applied to the cowl rings as follows: 50th TCS/Red, 61st TCS/Green, 62nd TCS/Blue, 37th TCS/Yellow (Attached 21 August 1950 to 8 May 1952).

The markings were subsequently changed to delete the parallel stripes. The entire upper third of the vertical tail surfaces were painted in the squadron color. The center of the nose on some aircraft carried the earlier group insignia depicting a pair of cowboy boots. A quartered nose with scalloped trailing edges was employed. The colors of the nose markings were white and the squadron colors and names were as follows: 50th TCS/Red/*Red Barons*, 61st TCS/Green/*Green Hornets*, 62nd TCS/Blue/*Blue Barons*.

Some aircraft, in particular from the 61st TCS, carried the squadron name on the dorsal fins.

Still later, the nose markings were modified to include a lightning bolt extending aft from the former scallop in the squadron color.

The 314th TCW transitioned into Lockheed C-130s. It was redesignated the 314th Tactical Airlift Wing on 1 August 1967. During the war in Southeast Asia, the wing operated from bases in Taiwan. The 314th TAW returned to the CONUS and has been stationed at Little Rock AFB, Tennessee since 31 May 1971.

316th Troop Carrier Wing, Medium

During World War Two, the 316th TCG was assigned to the Twelfth Air Force and operated C-47 and C-53 aircraft primarily in the Mediterranean. They were reassigned to the Ninth Air Force and moved to England to participate in Normandy Invasion.

By 25 May 1945, the 316th TCG had returned to the ZI and established their headquarters at Pope Field, North Carolina, where they operated C-82s. On 25 August 1947, the group moved to Greenville AAB, South Carolina. Commanders of the 316th TCG during this era were:

Col Harvey A Berger	13 May 1944 to 2 Sep 1945
Lt Col Walter R Washburn	2-Sep 1945 to 17 Sep 1945
Lt Col Leonard C Fletcher	17 Sep 1945
Col Jerome B McCauley	5 Oct 1945
Col Clarence J Galligan	2 Feb 1946
Lt Col Leroy M Stanton	31 Sep 1946
Col Clarence J Galligan	1 Nov 1946
Col John H Lackey Jr	cApr 1947
Col Edgar W Hampton	20 Sep 1947
Col Norton H Van Sicklen	1 Aug 1950
Maj Dwight E Maul	31 Aug 1950
Maj Gordon F Blood	6 Sep 1950
Col Norton H Van Sicklen	28 Dec 1950
Col William H DeLacey	1 Jun 1952
Col Richard P Carr	cNov 1954
Col William C Lindley	19 Mar 1955

Commanders of the 316th TCW during this era were:

Col Paul H Prentiss	15 Aug 1947
Col Newton Longfellow	11 Dec 1948
Col Lewis M Merrick	26 Jun 1949

On 4 November 1949, the group moved to Smyrna AFB (later Sewart AFB), Tennessee, where they trained in C-119s. The 16th TCS (Assault, Light) operated C-119s with the group between 5 October 1950 and some time in 1951, and then, transitioned into YC-122s until their transfer to the 463rd TCW at Ardmore AFB, Oklahoma, on 14 November 1954. The 75th TCS was reactivated on 20 December 1952, and assigned to the 316th TCG. On 15 November 1954, the 316th TCG (Medium) transferred without personnel and equipment, to Ashiya AB, Japan, and assignment to FEAF. While assigned to the 316th TCG, the 37th TCS had been attached to the 314th TCG at Ashiya AB, Japan, between 21 August 1950 and 8 May 1952. The 316th TCG remained at Ashiya until some time in 1957. The squadrons involved in this transfer were: 36th TCS, 37th TCS, and 75th TCS.

Markings for the 316th TCG consisted of a horizontally and vertically quartered nose in white and in the squadron color. The color was applied in the upper left and lower right quadrant as were the darkened portion of the wings that were adjacent to the circle. It appears as if the 316th TCG acquired their aircraft from the 314th TCG when it made a paper move back to Sewart AFB, Tennessee, and the wings were added to differentiate the two units. The squadron colors were: 36th TCS Red/White, 37th TCS Blue/White, 75th TCS Green/White.

These markings were changed some time in 1956 when the clocking of the quartered nose was rotated to have the squadron color in the upper and lower quadrants, divided by white in the left and right quadrants.

The 316th TCW was inactivated at Greenville AFB, South Carolina on 20 October 1949. The unit was redesignated the 316th Troop Carrier Wing, Assault and activated at Langley AFB, Virginia on 15 November 1965. The unit was redesignated the 316th TCW on 1 March 1966, and the 316th Tactical Airlift Wing on 1 May 1967. The wing, by then operating C-130Es, was inactivated on 1 October 1975.

317th Troop Carrier Wing, Medium

Assigned to the Fifth Air Force in the Southwest Pacific, the 317th TCG operated a variety of aircraft during World War Two. After the war the group remained at Tachikawa AB, Japan, where it operated C-54s. The 317th TCG (Heavy) relocated, via the ZI, to Wiesbaden AB, West Germany, around 20 September 1948, where it became part of USAFE and participated in the Berlin Airlift. The group was inactivated at RAF Celle, West Germany, on 14 September 1949.

Reactivated at Rhein-Main AB, West Germany, on 14 July 1952, the 317th TCG (Medium) was equipped with C-119s and assigned to USAFE, gaining the assets of the 433rd TCW. The 317th TCW relocated to Neubiberg AB, West Germany, on 21 March 1953, and then moved on to Evreux-Fauville AB, France, 17 April 1957, where it replaced the 465th TCW. The 317th TCG provided troop carrier support and airlift service in support of USAFE, NATO, and UN operations. They participated in numerous exercises and humanitarian missions.

Commanders of the 317th TCG during this era were:

Col Lucion N Powell	14 Jul 1952
Lt Col James E Bauley	1 Mar 1954
Col Harry M Pike	May 1954

Commanders of the 317th TCW during this era were:

Col Thomas K Hampton	18 Aug 1948
Col William A Ross	c15 Aug 1949 to c14 Sep 1949
Col Donald J French	14 Jul 1952
Col Harry M Pike	23 Jul 1954
Col Clarence B Hammerle Jr	29 Jul 1954
Col Joseph A Cunningham	9 Sep 1954

Initially, the 317th retained the markings carried on the C-119s assigned to the 433rd TCG. Subsequently, the squadrons comprising the 317th TCG were identified by the following colors applied to the cowl rings: 39th TCS/Green, 40th TCS/Red, 41st TCS/Blue

The 317th TCW (M) was inactivated on 25 September 1958, activated on 13 March 1963, and organized on 15 April 1963. The wing moved to Lockbourne AFB, Ohio on 20 June 1964 where it operated C-123s, C-124s and C-130s. The unit was redesignated the 317th Tactical Airlift Wing (TAW) on 1 May 1967. The 317th TAW moved to Pope AFB, North Carolina on 31 August 1971.

443rd Troop Carrier Wing, Medium
The 443rd TCG was activated at Sedalia AAF, Missouri, on 1 October 1943, and was equipped with L-3, C-47 and C-53 aircraft. The unit service in the China-India-Burma Theater during World War Two, returned to the ZI, and was inactivated on 26 December 1945.

Allocated to the Reserve and activated on 27 June 1949, at Henley Field, Texas, the 443rd TCG was equipped with C-46s and assigned to Tactical Air Command. The unit relocated to Donaldson AFB, South Carolina, on 9 August 1951, ordered to active service on 1 May of the same year, and was redesignated as a wing.

The 443rd TCW transitioned into C-119s in February 1952, and participated in tactical exercises and operations while assigned to the Eighteenth Air Force from 1 June 1951. The 443rd worked closely with other troop carrier wings in the testing and evaluation of new troop carrier doctrine and procedures. The wing operated C-119s until 8 January 1953, when it was inactivated.

Commanders of the 443rd TCG during this era were:

Lt Col Cornelius P Chima	15 Oct 1950
Col Lucion N Powell	24 Mar to 14 Jul 1952

Colonel William E Shuttles commanded the 443rd TCW during this era.

Component squadrons of the 443rd TCG were: 309th TCS, 310th TCS, 343rd TCS.

Redesignated the 443rd Military Airlift Wing, Training, and activated on 27 December 1965. The wing was organized at Tinker AFB, Oklahoma on 8 January 1966. During this period it operated both the C-124 and Lockheed C-141 Starlifter. On 5 May 1969, the wing moved to Altus AFB, Oklahoma and added the Lockheed C-5 Galaxy to their C-141 inventory.

463rd Troop Carrier Wing, Medium
The 463rd was a B-17 heavy bombardment group assigned to the 15th Air Force during World War Two, and served in the Mediterranean Theater of Operations. Olympic diving gold medalist Colonel Frank A Kurtz took the unit overseas, leading them in his B-17 named *The Swoose*, in honor of his Flying Fortress from the Pacific Theater. The 463rd BG was inactivated in Italy on 25 September 1945.

Redesignated as the 463rd TCG (M), the unit was activated at Memphis Municipal Airport, Tennessee, on 16 January 1953. The unit was equipped with both C-46s and C-119s and assigned to the Eighteenth Air Force. The 463rd TCW moved to Ardmore AFB, Oklahoma, on 1 September 1953, where it continued to operate C-119s until 1957, when it transitioned into C-130s. Along with the C-119s, the wing also operated YC-122s, C-122s, and C-123s. The 463rd TCW airlifted, airdropped, airlanded troops and cargo in support of a variety of tactical operations and special missions as part of US Army and joint airborne exercises at worldwide locations.

Commanders of the 463rd TCG during this era were:

Col John R Roche	16 Jan 1953
Col Woodrow T Merrill	10 Aug 1953
Col Benjamin M Tarver Jr	12 Aug 1954

Commanders of the 463rd TCW during this era were:

Col George L Holcomb	16 Jan 1953
Brig Gen Cecil H Childre	20 Aug 1954
Col James L Daniel Jr	4 Jun 1957

The wartime bombardment squadrons were redesignated as troop carrier squadrons when they continued on with the 463rd TCW. These component squadrons were: 772nd TCS/Red, 773rd TCS/Yellow, 774th TCS/Green, 775th TCS/Blue.

The 463rd TCW operated a variety of twin- and four-engined transports after relinquishing the C-119s. Most notable of the aircraft was the C-130 that entered the inventory in 1956 and remains the primary aircraft of the wing. The unit was redesignated the 463rd Tactical Airlift Wing (TAW) on 1 August 1967. During the war in Southeast Asia, the wing operated from bases in the Philippines and was inactivated there on 31 December 1971. The 463rd TAW was reactivated at Dyess AFB, Texas on 1 June 1972 moving to Little Rock, Arkansas where it continues to operate C-130s.

464th Troop Carrier Wing, Medium
The 464th was a heavy bombardment group equipped with B-24s and assigned to the Fifteenth Air Force in the Mediterranean Theater of Operations during World War Two. The unit was assigned to Air Transport Command and relocated to Waller Field, Trinidad in June 1945. The 464th BG was inactivated there on 31 July 1945.

The 464th TCW (M) was established on 15 December 1952, and activated at Lawson AFB, Georgia, on 1 February 1953. This unit transitioned from Curtiss C-46 Commandos to C-119s during 1953 and 1954. On 21 September 1954, the wing relocated to Pope AFB, South Carolina. Sikorsky H-19 Chickasaw helicopters and Fairchild C-123 Providers came into the wing's inventory in 1955. They provided tactical airlift of troops and cargo, took part in joint airborne training with Army forces, and participated in tactical exercises within the ZI and overseas. The 464th TCW was assigned to the Eighteenth Air Force, TAC, from its activation until 1 September 1957, when it came under the control of the Ninth Air Force.

Commanders of the 464th TCG during this era were:

Col James A Evans	c1 Feb 1954
Col Charles F Franklin	1954
Col Adam A Reaves	1955

Commanders of the 464 TCW during this era were:

Col Troy W Crawford	1 Feb 1953
Col Charles D Birdsall	20 Apr 1953
Col Troy W Crawford	18 May 1953
Brig Gen Theodore G Kershaw	15 Aug 1955

Markings for the C-119s operated by the 464th TCW included a colored nose that scalloped back into a lightning bolt in the squadron color. The wing insignia was applied to both sides of the nose forward of the drop windows. The squadron colors were: 776th TCS/Red, 777th TCS/Blue, 778th TCS/Green, 779th TCS/Yellow.

The 464th TCW operated Sikorsky H-19 Chickasaws and C-123s from 1955. The unit was redesignated the 464th Troop Carrier Wing, Assault on 1 December 1958. The wing gained C-130s in 1963. Redesignated the 464th Tactical Airlift Wing on 1 May 1967, the wing continued operations until its inactivation on 31 August 1971.

465th Troop Carrier Wing, Medium
The 465th was a heavy bombardment group equipped with B-24s and assigned to the 15th Air Force in the Mediterranean Theater of Operations during World War Two. The group was transferred to Air Transport Command and relocated to Waller Field, Trinidad in June 1945, and inactivated there on 31 July of the same year.

The 465th TCW was established on 21 August 1953, and activated at Mitchel Field, New York, on 25 August 1953. Assigned to the Eighteenth Air Force, the wing was equipped with C-119s, and replaced the 313th TCW that was on the base. Between August and 30 November 1953, the 465th TCW operated under the control of other wings until it commenced its overseas movement. No tactical operations were performed between 1 October 1953 and early April 1954. The wing relocated to Toul-Rosières AB, France, on 2 April 1954, where it operated under the control of the 322nd Air Division. The wing then moved to Evreux (later Evreux-Fauville) AB, France, on 23 May 1955, where they remained until 8 July 1957. The 465th TCW participated in many airlift and troop carrier exercises, tests, and operations in the European area in support of NATO and USAFE commitments. The 465th TCW was inactivated on 8 July 1957, and their assets were gained by the 317th TCW.

Commanders of the 465th TCG during this era were:

Maj Clifford F Harris	Feb 1953
Col Earl W Worley	cMar 1953
Lt Col James D Barlow	10 May 1954
Col James A Evans Jr	19 Sep 1954

Col James D Barlow	7 Apr 1955

Commanders of the 465 TCW during this era were:

Brig Gen Franklin Rose	25 Aug 1953
Col Earl W Worley	12 May 1954
Col James A Evans Jr	31 Jul 1956
Col Robert D Forman	13 Aug 1956 to 8 Jul 1957

The wartime bombardment squadrons were redesignated troop carrier squadrons and became part of the 465th TCW. The component squadrons and their colors were as follows: 780th TCS/Red, 781st TCS/Blue, 782nd TCS/Green.

The unit was redesignated the 465th Bombardment Wing, Heavy on 15 November 1962, organized at Robins AFB, Georgia on 1 February 1963, and assigned to SAC. The wing operated B-52s and KC-135s until its discontinuance and inactivation on 25 July 1968.

483rd Troop Carrier Wing, Medium

The 483rd was a heavy bombardment group equipped with B-17s and assigned to the Fifteenth Air Force in the MTO during World War Two. The unit was inactivated in Italy on 25 September 1945. Redesignated the 483rd TCG (M), the unit was reactivated at Ashiya AB, Japan on 1 January 1953. While assigned to TAC, the unit was attached to FEAF for duty in the Korean War. Commanders of the 483rd TCG were:

Lt Col Ernest W Burton	1 Jan 1953
Col George M Foster	1 Mar 1953
Lt Col Kenneth C Jacobs	c Jul 1955
Col Horace W Patch	cAug 1955

The 483rd TCW was established on 15 November 1952, and activated at Ashiya AB, Japan on 1 January 1953. While assigned to TAC, the unit was attached to FEAF for duty in the Korean War, replacing the 403rd TCW that was returned to Reserve status. The 483rd TCW controlled both the 483rd TCG and the 314th TCG, and the 6461st TCS.

Commanders of the 483rd TCW during the C-119 era were:

Col Maurice F Casey	1 Jan 1953
Col Jamie Gough	13 May 1954
Col William C Lindley	6 Aug 1953
Col Leyrom M Stanton	13 Aug 1955

On 23 June 1953, the 483rd TCW launched all available C-119s, using every available pilot in both the 3124th and 483rd TCGs to airlift 3,252 paratroops from the 187th RCT and 1,110.6 tons of their equipment from southern Japan to Seoul and Chunch'on, Korea. Then between 28 June and 2 July 1953 they airlifted 4,397 troops and 1,227,47 tons of cargo from Misawa and Tachikawa. This movement was to preclude enemy breakthroughs as the armistice neared. It was the largest mass movement of personnel in the history of airlift to date.

The 483rd TCW controlled more C-119 units that any other wing. Between 1951 and 1959, the wing had the following units assigned or attached:

Direct Reporting Unit	Colors	Name
483rd TCG		
815th TCS	Red/White	
816th TCS	Green/White	
817th TCS	Blue/White	Sky Runners
21st TCS (attached)		
21st TCS		
36th TCS (attached)	Red/White	
37th TCS (attached)	Blue/White	
75th TCS (attached)	Green/White	
Détachement C-119 de l'Armée de l'Air (attached)		
Det 772 TCS (attached)	Red	
Det 815th TCS (attached)	Red/White	
Det 816th TCS (attached)	Green/White	
Det 817th TCS (attached)	Blue/White	Sky Runners
6461st TCS (attached)		

After serving in the war in Southeast Asia, the 483rd TCW was inactivated at Cam Ranh Bay AB, Republic of Vietnam on 31 May 1972.

SPECIAL OPERATIONS GUNSHIPS

AC-119G and AC-119K Shadow and Stinger gunships were operated by the 17th and 18th SOS in the active USAF and the 71st SOS from the Reserve. The 71st SOS was assigned to Bakalar AFB, Indiana, while the 17th and 18th SOSs, part of the 1st Special Operations Wing (SOW), were based at Hurlburt Field, Florida, for training within the Continental United States (CONUS); a term which began replacing Zone of Interior (ZI) during the 1960s.

The 1st Air Commando was activated and organized at Eglin Air Force Auxiliary Field No 9 (Hurlburt Field), Florida on 27 April 1968, and redesignated the 1st SOW on 8 July 1968. The 1st SOW replaced the 4400th Combat Crew Training Group and assumed air commando operations and training responsibility. On 15 January 1966, the wing moved to England AFB, Louisiana, and returned to Hurlburt Field on 15 July 1969. C/AC-119 aircraft served within the unit between 1968-1969 and 1971-1972. Commanders of the 1st SOW during this era were:

Col Albert S Pouloit	9 Sep 1967
Col Leonard Volet	14 Feb 1969
Col Robert W Gates	15 Jul 1969
Col Michael C Horgan	31 Oct 1970

Gloss Black was applied to the lower surfaces of the airplanes up to a line parallel with the bottom of the cockpit windows. The upper surfaces were painted in a pattern of Olive Drab (FS 34102), Dark Green (FS 34079), and Tan (FS 30219). USAF serial numbers were applied to the fins in Insignia Red. National insignia were applied to the booms and the upper surface of the right wing. The last three digits of the serial number appeared on the nose gear doors in Insignia Red. Unit codes were applied to the fins in Insignia White while the aircraft operated within the CONUS. The 1st SOW insignia was applied to the nose, while a TAC badge was carried on the fins of some aircraft operating within the CONUS. Some aircraft were photographed in an overall Flat Black (FS 37038). Nose art was not common in combat because it could be illuminated by enemy searchlights.

The 1st SOW was redesignated the 834th Tactical Composite Wing on 1 July 1974, and the 1st SOW on 1 July 1975. The wing continues to operate from Hurlburt Field with AC-130s and a variety of other aircraft.

USAF RESERVE

C-119s in the USAF Reserve varied in markings over time. The most colorful units were described above. Initially, other Reserve units had rather bland aircraft in an assortment of natural metal finish and aluminized paint. Some had white tops with blue cheat lines and others did not. Some carried Insignia Red Arctic markings and others did not. Dayglo orange markings were applied to the nose, wingtips, and booms during the late 1950s and early 1960s. With the advent of the Cuban Missile Crisis in 1962, the dayglo trim was either removed or hurriedly painted over with aluminized paint.

Some aircraft carried the Fourteenth Air Force Bengal Tiger insignia on the fins, circa 1958. The 514th TAW carried diagonal fin striping consisting of a broad white band edged in black, with squadron colors applied to the white band in a series of stripes.

White tops and blue cheat lines came into vogue during the mid-1960s. Unit designators were spelled out above the cheat line aft of the cockpit. Unit insignia were also carried aft of the cockpit.

For a period, 'CONAC', for Continental Air Command, was carried on the booms. Later this was replaced by 'AFRES', for Air Force Reserve. White lettering was applied to a blue field surrounded with a yellow edge. With the advent of the AFRES markings, came the application of the Air Force Reserve insignia on the fins.

94th Troop Carrier Wing, Medium

Established as the 94th Bombardment Wing, Light on 10 May 1949, the unit was activated in the Reserve on 26 June 1949. Based at Marietta (later Dobbins AFB), Georgia, the wing was equipped with Douglas B-26 Invaders, and a variety of trainers, namely: the Beech T-7 Expeditor/T-11 Kansan. The wing was ordered to active service on 10 March 1951, and inactivated on 1 April 1951. Redesignated the 94th Tactical Reconnaissance Wing on 26 May 1952, and activated in the Reserve on 14 June 1952. The unit was again redesignated the 94th Bombardment Wing, Tactical on 18 May 1955.

The wing was redesignated the 94th TCW (M) on 1 July 1957, while stationed at Scott AFB, Illinois. On 16 November 1957, the wing moved to Laurence G Hanscom AFB, Massachusetts and transitioned into C-119s. Colonel Arthur C Carroll was commander at this time. The 94th TCG Headquarters was inactivated on 14 April 1959, and replaced by the 901st TCG Headquarters on 11 February 1963. The 731st TCS was the tactical unit assigned to the group and wing.

In addition to flying routine training missions within the CONUS, the wing began flying overseas, including supporting contingency operations in the Dominican Republic in 1965. The wing was briefly activated for the Cuban Missile Crisis in the fall of 1962.

302nd Troop Carrier Wing, Medium

Established as the 302nd TCW (M) on 16 May 1949, the unit was activated in the Reserve on 27 June 1949. While the wing was based at McChord AFB, Washington between 27 June 1949 and 8 June 1951, it operated C-82s and C-54s as the Reserve corollary of the 62nd TCW (M) and the 325th Fighter-All Weather Wing (later Fighter-Interceptor), Regular Air Force units. When the 302nd was ordered to active service on 1 June 1951, its personnel were absorbed by the 325th Fighter Interceptor Wing, and the 302nd was inactivated.

The 302nd TCW was reactivated at Clinton County AFB, Ohio on 14 June 1952, where it gained C-46s that were operated until 1957. The wing began transitioning into the C-119 in 1956. Until the mid 1950s the 302nd trained exclusively as a Reserve unit. Then, it began flying airlift operations within the ZI and overseas. In October 1958, the wing converted to the Air Reserve Technician (ART) program in which a number of personnel were in the full-time employ of the wing; thereby being able to perform missions around the clock like a Regular Air Force unit. Regular Reservists augmented the organization for drill weekends and summer camp.

During the C-119 era, the 302nd TCW was commanded by the following:

Brig Gen Donald J Campbell	14 Jun 1952
Brig Gen Ben J Mangina	15 Jun 1970

In the fall of 1962, the 302nd was called to active duty in support of the Cuban Missile Crisis. Between April 1968 and March 1973, the wing provided C-119 gunship training for pilots, navigators, flight engineers, and mechanics for USAF active duty personnel, and those from Ethiopia, Jordan, Morocco, and South Vietnam.

The wing also operated some Cessna U-3A Blue Canoes between 1970 and 1972. The Lockheed C-130s were also operated in 1970 and 1971. In addition, the 302nd operated Cessna A-37s in 1970, and C-123s from 1971. The C-119s were phased out of the wing's inventory in 1973.

The 302nd TCW was awarded the Air Force Outstanding Unit Award (AFOUA) for the period of 1 January through 31 December 1970, and the Republic of Vietnam Gallantry Cross with Palm for the period between 14 February 1968 and 28 January 1973.

349th Troop Carrier Wing, Medium

The 349th TCW was established on 10 May 1949, and activated in the Reserve at Hamilton AFB, California on 27 June 1949. The unit was equipped with T-6s, T-7s, T-11s, and C-46s. The 349th TCW was activated for the Korean War on 1 April 1951, and inactivated on 2 April 1951. Its personnel were used to fill manpower vacancies in other wings.

The unit was redesignated the 349th Fighter-Bomber Wing on 26 May 1952, and activated at Hamilton AFB on 13 June 1952. The wing was equipped with T-6s, C-46s, T-28s, F-51s, F-80s. C-45s, C-47s, and F-84s.

The wing was again redesignated the 349th TCW on 1 September 1957, and gained C 119s in 1958. Brigadier General Harold P Little was commander at this time, and was succeeded by Brigadier General Rollin B Moore Jr, on 10 January 1959. On 1 April 1958, the 349th TCW came under the Air Reserve Technician program. On 28 October 1962, the wing was activated for one month during the Cuban Missile crisis. The wing was awarded the Air Force Outstanding Unit Award for the period of 23 December 1964 through 22 January 1965.

The tactical squadrons of the 349th TCW reported through the 349th TCG, also stationed at Hamilton AFB until 14 April 1959. Between 14 April 1959 and 11 February 1963, the two tactical squadrons, the 313th and 314th TCSs, reported directly to the 349th TCW. The 313th TCS was stationed at Hill AFB, Utah with C-46s until 16 November 1957 when it was relocated to Portland International Airport, Oregon. The 314th TCS was based at McClellan AFB, California from 14 October 1955. With the advent of the 900-series groups, a new reporting line came into being.

The 939th TCG, and its tactical component, the 313th TCS, were stationed at Portland International Airport from 11 February 1963 until 26 January 1968.

The 940th TCG, and its tactical component, the 314th TCS, were stationed at McClellan AFB from 11 February 1963 until 26 January 1968.

The 941st TCG, and its tactical component, the 97th TCS, were stationed at Paine AFB, Washington, 11 February 1963 until 9 November 1965, when the units moved to McChord AFB, Washington. The units continued operating C-119s until 31 July 1968 when they transitioned into the C-124 Globemaster II.

375th Troop Carrier Group/Wing, Medium

The 375th TCG operated C-47s in the Southwest Pacific during World War Two. The unit was inactivated on Okinawa on 25 March 1946. Allotted to the Reserve, the 375th TCG was activated at the Greater Pittsburgh Airport, Pennsylvania and equipped with C-46s on 3 August 1947. The unit moved to Greenville AFB, South Carolina on 15 October 1950, where it gained C-82s. The 375th TCG was commanded by:

Unknown	
Capt Charles J Newell	15 Oct 1950
Lt Col Charles R Gianque	7 Nov 1950
Col Kenneth L Johnson	13 Nov 1951
Lt Col Arthur J Stavley	1 Feb 1952
Col Stewart H Nichols	17 Apr 1952

The 375th TCW was established on 10 May 1949, and activated in the Reserve on 27 June 1947. The wing was equipped with C-82s and stationed at Greenville AFB, South Carolina. The 375th TCW was commanded by:

Brig Gen Emil H Molthan	27 Jun 1949
Col William S Johnston	14 Sep 1949
Lt Col Stanley V Fowler	cAug 1950
Col Lance Call	cSep 1950
Col Glynne M Jones	3 Mar 1952
Brig Gen Franklin Rose	22 May 1952
Col Arthur R Anderson	14 Jul 1952
Col Jack R Adams	cMar 1953
Col Albert B Starr	1 Sep 1955

During this period, the component squadrons of the 375th TCW were: 55th TCS, 56th TCS, 57th TCS, 58th TCS.

The 375th TCG was called to active duty and assigned to Tactical Air Command on 15 October 1950, and inactivated on 14 July 1952.

The 375th TCG was a component of the wing between 27 January 1949 and 16 November 1957. The 375th TCW was called to active duty on 15 October 1950 and was reallocated to the Reserve on 16 November 1957.

The C-82s were supplemented by C-45s in 1951 and replaced by C-46s during 1952 and 1953. C-119s came into the inventory in 1954 and continued into 1957. During C-119 era, the component squadrons were: 55th TCS, 56th TCS, 57th TCS.

Between June 1949 and October 1950, the wing performed Reserve flying training. While on active duty, the 375th TCW participated in troop carrier/airlift operations and paratroop drops, and other exercises.

Between 14 July 1952 and 16 November 1957, the 375th TCW was stationed at the Greater Pittsburgh Airport, Pennsylvania.

403rd Troop Carrier Wing, Medium

After World War Two, the 403rd TCG was allocated to the Reserve. The unit was activated at Portland Municipal Airport, Oregon, on 27 June 1949, where they operated C-46 and C-47 aircraft until 29 March 1952.

The 403rd TCG transitioned into C-119s and was activated for service during the Korean War. The group operated out of Ashiya AB, Japan, between 14 April 1952 and 1 January 1953, aiding UN forces by dropping paratroops and supplies, transporting personnel and equipment, and evacuating casualties. For service in Korea between 14 April 1952 and 3 December 1952, the group was awarded the Republic of Korea Presidential Citation. In addition, the following campaign ribbons were awarded: Korea Summer-Fall 1952 and the Third Korean Winter. Colonel Maurice F Casey commanded the 403rd TCW during this period; while the 403rd TCG commanders were:

Maj Wallace C Forsythe	22 Apr 1952
Lt Col Ernest W Burton	Aug 1952

When the 403rd TCG arrived in Japan, the markings applied to the aircraft consisted of a series of alternating stripes on the vertical tail (three colored and two white) and four each white and colored diagonal stripes on the nose gear doors. In addition, the nose was painted in the squadron color with a small separating circle in white. The squadron colors were: 63rd TCS/Red/*Flying Jennies,* 64th TCS/Blue/*Blue Tail Flies,* 65th TCS/Green/*Packet Rats.*

When aircraft began arriving with dorsal fins, the squadron names were applied to these fins.

The 403rd TCG was relieved from active duty and inactivated in Japan on 1 January 1953, allotted to the Reserve, and activated at Portland International Airport, Oregon. The wing remained at Portland until November 1957 where they operated C-46s.

On 16 November 1957, the 403rd TCW moved to Selfridge AFB, Michigan under the command of Colonel James H McPartlin. There the wing regained C-119s. The 403rd TCG Headquarters supervised the operations of the 63rd, 64th and 65th TCSs until 11 February 1963.

The 927th TCG Headquarters, also at Selfridge AFB, was assigned to the wing between 11 February 1963 and 31 December 1969, with the 63rd TCS reporting to it.

The 928th TCG Headquarters, based at O'Hare International Airport, Illinois, was assigned to the wing between 11 February 1963 and 1 December 1969, having the 64th TCS assigned.

The 929th TCG Headquarters, based at Davis Field, Oklahoma, was assigned to the wing between 11 February 1963 and 1 January 1964, having the 65th TCS assigned.

When the 403rd TCW moved to Selfridge AFB in November 1957, it absorbed the resources of another Reserve wing. There it continued to train as a Reserve unit until becoming part of the ART program in April 1958. The wing participated in numerous tactical exercises and humanitarian missions, and was activated for a month during the fall of 1962 for the Cuban Missile Crisis.

433rd Troop Carrier Wing, Medium
After World War Two, the 433rd TCG was inactivated at Tachikawa AB, Japan. The unit was allotted to the Reserves and activated at Akron, Ohio, on 6 July 1946. They trained in C-46 and C-47 aircraft. On 27 June 1949, they relocated to Cleveland Municipal Airport, Ohio. The unit was nicknamed 'The Royal Ohio'.

With the advent of the Korean War, the 433rd was activated and relocated at Greenville AFB, South Carolina, on 16 October 1950. They remained there undergoing transition training in C-119s until 20 July 1951. The 433rd TCW was under the command of Colonel Harry W Hopp, a World War Two troop carrier pilot who flew for the airlines after the hostilities. Assigned to USAFE, the 433rd took up residence at Rhein-Main AB, West Germany, on 5 August 1951. While in Europe, they participated in tactical exercises and special missions. The 433rd was inactivated in Europe on 14 July 1952, and their assets were gained by the 317th TCW that was activated at that time.

Commanders of the 433rd TCG during this era were:

Col James B Henson	1 May 1951
Maj Clifford F Harris	c15 Dec 1952

Commanders of the 433rd TCW during this era were:

Col Lewis M Merrick	15 Jan 1951
Col Harry W Hopp	20 Jul 1951
Col Donald J French	14 Jan 1952

When the 433rd TCG was activated and acquired C-119s, they embellished them in attractive colors. A diamond was applied to the nose within a circle and a set of wings extended aft along the fuselage sides. The entire dorsal fin and vertical fins were marked in a solid color divided by three diagonal stripes, the lowest of which covered the top of the dorsal fin. In addition, the squadron colors were applied to the wingtips and the cowl rings. These colors were: 67th TCS Black/Yellow, 68th TCS Red/White, 69th TCS Blue/Yellow.

The assets of the 433rd TCG were acquired by the 317th TCW in 1952, and the markings of the former unit were retained for a brief period.

Allocated to the Reserve, the 433rd was subsequently reactivated at Brooks AFB, Texas on 18 May 1955, reverting to C-46s. The wing operated C-46s between 1955 and 1958. Subsequently the 433rd operated C-119s between 1957 and 1971. The unit moved to Kelly AFB, Texas on 1 November 1960, and operated some C-124s in 1963. The wing began transition into the C-124s in 1966, while continuing to operate the C-119s.

Brigadier General John H Foster assumed command of the wing when it returned to the ZI in 1955. Between 18 May 1955 and 14 April 1959, the 433rd TCG Headquarters directed the operations of the 67th, and 68th TCSs stationed at Brooks AFB, Texas. Both the 67th and 68th TCSs moved to Kelly AFB, Texas along with the 433rd TCW on 1 November 1960.

The 908th TCG Headquarters, stationed at Bates Field, Alabama, between 11 February 1963 and 25 April 1969, had the 357th TCS assigned.

The 916th TCG, based at Carswell AFB, Texas, oversaw operations of the 77th TCS between 18 March and 1 July 1963.

The 921st TCG Headquarters, with its tactical unit the 67th TCS, were assigned to Kelly AFB, Texas, between 17 January 1963 and 26 January 1968, and again between 2 June 1969 and 1971 when they transitioned into C-124s.

The 922nd TCG Headquarters and its subordinate 68th TCS were also assigned to Kelly AFB between 17 January 1963 and 1971 when they transitioned into C-124s.

The 923rd TCG Headquarters was assigned to the 433rd TCW from 17 January 1963 until 25 November 1965. On 1 April 1963 both the group and its tactical component, the 69th TCS, were assigned to Carswell AFB, Texas.

When reactivated in the Reserves, the 433rd TCW replaced the 8707th Pilot Training Wing at Brooks AFB. Until 1958, the wing relied upon an active Reserve Flying Center for assistance. It then became a self-supporting unit under the ART program. Between 28 October and 18 November 1962, the 433rd TCW was activated for the Cuban Missile Crisis. In 1971, the wing transitioned from the C-119 to the C-130.

434th Troop Carrier Wing, Medium
The 434th TCW (M) was established and activated in the Reserve on 1 July 1949, and was stationed at Atterbury AFB, Indiana. Initially the wing was equipped with the Beech T-7 Expeditor/T-11 Kansan and C-45, C-46, C-47, and North American T-6 Texan. C-119s came into the inventory in 1957. The wing had three troop carrier groups assigned. The 434th TCW was commanded by:

Brig Gen John O Bradshaw	22 Apr 1953
Brig Gen John W Hoff	13 Oct 1962
Brig Gen Alfred Verhulst	16 Jul 1967

The 930th TCG Headquarters had the 71st TCS assigned. Both units were at Bakalar AFB, Indiana from 11 February 1963 until 13 May 1968. On that date, the units at Bakalar AFB were redesignated the 434th Tactical Airlift Wing (TAW) and 71st Tactical Airlift Squadron (TAS), respectively. By 15 June 1968 the 71st TAS and its 18 C-119Gs moved to Lockbourne AFB, OH for training in gunship operations by the 4413th Combat Crew Training Squadron. Personnel from the group's command section, 930th Consolidated Maintenance Squadron, and 930th Aerial Port Squadron augmented the 71st TAS that trained in the AC-119G gunship at Lockbourne AFB, Ohio, and then served in Vietnam between January and 4 June 1969. The unit returned to Bakalar AFB on 30 May 1969, where they continued to operate the C-119. The units moved to Grissom AFB, Indiana, on 15 January 1970 and transitioned into the Cessna A-37.

The 931st TCG Headquarters was assigned to the wing on 11 February 1963, with the 72nd TCS as its tactical component. Both units were stationed at Bakalar AFB, Indiana until 15 January 1970. During 1968, the 72nd TCS flew airlift missions into combat areas in Southeast Asia. The C-119s were phased out in late 1969, and replaced by Cessna U-3A Blue Canoes.

The 932nd TCG Headquarters, with its 73rd TCS, was stationed at Scott AFB, Illinois between 11 February 1963 and January 1967. The 73rd TCS was capable of performing the trapeze recovery mission with its beavertailed C-119s. The unit transitioned into the C-124 for the aeromedical evacuation role.

The 434th TCW trained as a Reserve troop carrier until coming under the ART program in October 1958. The wing flew routine training exercises and overseas missions. During the fall of 1962, the wing was activated for one month in support of the Cuban Missile Crisis. Redesignated the 434th TAW on 1 July 1967 and inactivated on 31 December 1971. Redesignated the 434th Special Operations Wing on 12 January 1971, the unit was activated in the Reserve on 15 January 1971. The wing was again redesignated the 434th Tactical Fighter Wing on 1 October 1973 and transitioned into Cessna A-37s. Between 1980 and 1987, the wing operated Fairchild A-10 Thunderbolt IIs or Warthogs. On 1 July 1987, the unit was redesignated the 434th Air Refueling Wing (ARW) and gained Boeing KC-135 Stratotankers and McDonnell Douglas KC-10 Extenders. Currently the 434th ARW operates KC-135Rs from Grissom AFRB, Indiana. The 72nd and 74th ARSs are each equipped with 11 tankers.

435th Troop Carrier Wing, Medium

Established as the 435th TCW (M) on 10 May 1949, the unit was activated at Miami International Airport, Florida on 26 June 1949. The wing was equipped with Beech T-7 Expeditor/T-11 Kansan, C-46, C-47, and North American T-6 Texan until 1951 when the wing transitioned into the C-119. Until 1958, the wing was under the supervision of the 2585th Air Force Reserve Training Center. After operating the C-119s for two years, the wing reverted to C-46s that they operated between 1952 and 1957. The C-119s were transferred to the 456th TCW (M), assigned to SAC.

The wing entered the ART program in April 1958, and was able to operate independently by December that year. The 435th TCW relocated to Homestead AFB, Florida on 25 July 1960, where it remained until 1 December 1965. Two of the squadrons transitioned into C-124s in 1961. The wing was redesignated the 435th TCW (H) for the period between 18 September 1961 and 1 July 1963. The 435th TCW (H) was called to active duty between 1 October 1961 and 27 August 1962. Again redesignated the 435th TCW (M) on 1 July 1963, the wing was discontinued and inactivated on 25 November 1968. During this period, the wing was under the command of Colonel Robert C Hutton.

Between 26 June 1949 and 1 December 1952, the 435th TCG Headquarters oversaw the operations of the 772nd and 773rd TCS. The 435th TCW was replaced at the Miami International Airport, Florida by the 482nd TCW.

The 908th TCG Headquarters, and its 357th TCS, were stationed at Bates Field, Alabama from 11 February 1963, and Brookley AFB, Alabama between 1 October 1964 and 1 December 1965, when both units were transferred to the 446th TCW.

The 915th TCG Headquarters and the 76th TCS were stationed at Miami International Airport, Florida between 17 January 1963 and 1 December 1965.

The 916th TCG Headquarters and the 77th TCS were stationed at Donaldson AFB, South Carolina between 17 January and 18 March 1963.

The 917th TCG Headquarters and the 78th TCS were stationed at Barksdale AFB, Texas between 17 January and 1 July 1963.

436th Troop Carrier Wing, Medium

Established as the 436th TCW (M) on 10 May 1949, the wing was activated in the Reserve at Goodman AFB, Kentucky, on 27 June 1949. The wing was ordered to active service on 1 April 1951, and returned to Reserve status on 16 April 1951, when the unit was inactivated. Reactivated again in the Reserve on 18 May 1955, and assigned to the First Air Force, the unit was stationed at NAS New York. During this period the wing was equipped with C-46s. Then, in 1957 the unit added the C-119. The 79th and 81st TCSs were assigned during this period. Apparently the C-119s were only operated between 1 February and 14 November 1957, while the wing was under the command of Colonel Michael P Yannell. The wing was inactivated on 15 May 1958.

437th Troop Carrier Wing, Medium

Established as the 437th TCW (M) on 10 May 1949, at Chicago-Orchard Airport (later O'Hare Field-Chicago International Airport), Illinois, the wing was activated in the Reserve on 27 June 1949. The wing was ordered to active service on 10 June 1950 and inactivated on 10 June 1952. Apparently the wing only operated the C-119s between 2 May and 16 November 1957, while the wing was under the command of Lieutenant Colonel Joseph E Whitwell. The 437th TCG oversaw operations of the 83rd, 84th, and 85th TCSs.

439th Troop Carrier Wing, Medium

Established as the 439th TCW (M) on 19 May 1949, the wing was activated in the Reserve at Selfridge AFB, Michigan, on 27 June 1949. The wing was ordered to active service between 1 and 3 April 1951, when it was inactivated. Redesignated the 439th Fighter-Bomber Wing on 26 May 1952, the wing was activated in the Reserve on 15 June 1952. Apparently the wing operated C-119s between 25 December 1956 and 16 November 1957, when the 439th was again inactivated. The wing was under the command of Colonel James M McPartlin. Reporting to the wing was the 439th TCG with the 93rd, 471st, and 472nd TCSs.

440th Troop Carrier Wing, Medium

Established as the 440th TCW (M) on 10 May 1949, the wing was activated in the Reserve at Wold-Chamberlain Municipal (later Minneapolis-St Paul International) Airport, Minnesota, on 27 June 1949. The wing was ordered to active service on 1 May 1951, and inactivated on 4 May 1951. During this period the unit operated the C-46 and a variety of training aircraft. Redesignated the 440th Fighter-Bomber Wing on 26 May 1952, the wing was activated in the Reserve on 15 May 1952, at Fort Snelling, Minnesota. The 440th FBW moved to Minneapolis-St Paul International Airport on 15 May 1952, where they flew F-51 Mustangs, F-80 Shooting Stars, and T-33s. Redesignated the 440th TCW (M) on 8 September 1957, and relocated to General Billy Mitchell Field, Wisconsin. The wing transitioned into C-119s at this time, and was under the command of Brigadier General Joseph J Lingle.

The 440th TCW trained as a Reserve troop carrier wing under the supervision of the 2465th Air Force Reserve Training (later Air Reserve Flying) Center between June 1957 and December 1958. It then became part of the ART program. During the Cuban Missile Crisis, the unit was activated for one month during the fall of 1962. Until 14 April 1959, the 440th TCG Headquarters oversaw operations of the 95th and 96th TCSs.

The 914th TCG Headquarters and its flying component, the 328th TCS, operated from Niagara Falls Municipal Airport, New York, between 1 September 1969 and 21 April 1971. Both units were reassigned to the 302nd TCW (M) and transitioned into C-130s.

The 933rd TCG Headquarters and its tactical unit, the 95th TCS, were stationed at General Billy Mitchell Field, Wisconsin, from 11 February 1963. In 1970, the unit transitioned into C-130s.

The 934th TCG Headquarters and the 96th TCS were stationed at Minneapolis-St Paul International Airport, Minnesota, from 11 February 1963. In 1970, the unit transitioned into C-130s.

The 440th TCW garnered the Air Force Association's trophy for the outstanding Air Force Reserve flying unit for 1963, 1964, 1966, and 1968. In addition, the wing was awarded the Republic of Vietnam Gallantry Cross with Palm for operations between 14 February and 11 March 1968.

442nd Troop Carrier Wing, Medium

The 442nd TCW (M) was established on 10 May 1949, and activated in the Reserve at Fairfax Field, Kansas, on 27 June 1949. The wing operated C-46s, C-47s, and a variety of training aircraft. On 15 June 1952, the wing moved to NAS Olathe, Kansas. The 442nd TCW was under the supervision of the 2472nd Air Reserve Training (later Air Reserve Flying) Center between June 1949 and February 1951, and again between June 1952 and March 1959. Next, the 442nd moved to Grandview (later Richards-Gebaur) AFB, Missouri, on 3 April 1955. The wing was under the command of Colonel James H McPartlin during this period.

The 442nd TCW operated C-119s between 1957 and 1961, and again between 1966 and 1967. C-124s were added to the inventory in

1961. The 442nd TCG Headquarters oversaw the operations of its two tactical components, the 904th and 905th TCSs.

The 916th TCG Headquarters and 77th TCS operated from Donaldson AFB, South Carolina between 1 July 1963 and 8 January 1965. The 917th TCG Headquarters and 78th TCS operated out of Barksdale AFB, Louisiana between 1 July 1963 and 5 February 1965.

The 932nd TCG Headquarters and 73rd TCS were stationed at Scott AFB, Illinois between 1 October 1966 and 1 April 1969.

The 935th TCG Headquarters and 303rd TCS were based at Richards-Gebaur AFB, Kansas between 17 January 1963 and 5 February 1965.

443rd Troop Carrier Wing, Medium

The 443rd TCW (M) was established on 10 May 1949, and activated in the Reserve at Hensley Field, Texas, on 27 June 1949. The wing operated C-46s and a variety of training aircraft. On 9 August 1951, the wing moved to Tinker AFB, SC. The 443rd TCW was under the supervision of the 2596th Air Force Reserve Training Center between June 1949 and April 1951.

The 443rd TCG Headquarters over saw operations of the 309th and 310th TCSs while they operated C-119s between 1952 and 8 January 1953, when the wing was inactivated. The wing operated closely with other troop carrier wings to test and evaluate new troop carrier doctrine and procedures. During this period, the 443rd TCW was under the command of Colonel William E Shuttles.

445th Troop Carrier Wing, Medium

The 445th Fighter-Bomber Wing was established on 24 June 1952, and activated in the Reserve at Buffalo, New York, on 8 July 1952. The wing subsequently moved to Niagara Falls Municipal Airport, New York. The wing again moved to Dobbins AFB, Georgia, on 16 November 1957. Redesignated the 445th TCW (M) on 6 September 1957, and the 445th Troop Carrier Wing, Assault on 25 September 1958. While operating C-119s between 16 November 1957 and some time in 1966. The wing was under the command of Brigadier General George H Wilson during this period.

The 915th TCG Headquarters oversaw the operation of the 96th TCS while both were stationed at Miami International Airport, Florida, from 1 December 1965.

The 918th TCG Headquarters and its tactical component, 700th TCS, were stationed at Dobbins AFB, Georgia, from 11 February 1963.

446th Troop Carrier Wing, Medium

The 446th TCW (M) was established on 11 April 1955, and activated in the Reserve at Ellington AFB, Texas, on 2 May 1955, replacing the 8706th Pilot Training Wing. The unit operated C-45s and C-46s between 1955 and 1958. C-119s were in the inventory between 1957 and 1970. Initially Colonel Forrest R Harsh, then Brigadier General Russell F Gustke commanded the 446th TCW during this era. In 1958, the wing came under the ART program.

The 446th TCG Headquarters oversaw operations of the 704th, 705th, and 706th TCSs between 25 May 1955 and 14 April 1959.

The 908th TCG Headquarters and its tactical component, the 357th TCS, operated from Bates Field, Alabama from 1 December 1965 until 1 May 1968. The unit operated C-119s during 1962.

The 924th TCG Headquarters and the 704th and 706th TCSs operated from Ellington AFB, Texas between 17 January 1963 and 1 July 1972. The C-119s were in the inventory between 1963 and 1970.

The 925th TCG Headquarters and the 705th TCS, based at Ellington AFB, Texas, were assigned to the wing between 17 January 1963 and 28 March 1968.

The 926th TCG Headquarters was assigned to the wing between 17 January 1963 and 1 May 1968, and again between 1 October 1969 and 1 July 1972.

The 446th TCW was awarded the AFOUA for the period 1 December 1967 to 10 January 1972. In addition, the wing was awarded the Republic of Vietnam Gallantry Cross with Palm for operations between 1 April 1966 and 29 June 1971.

452nd Troop Carrier Wing, Medium

The 452nd Bombardment Wing, Light was established on 10 May 1949, and activated in the Reserve at Long Beach Municipal Airport, California, on 27 June 1949. The wing was ordered to active service on 10 August 1950, operated Douglas B-26 Invaders in Korea, and was inactivated on 10 May 1952. Redesignated the 452nd Tactical Reconnaissance Wing on 6 June 1952, the unit was activated in the Reserve on 13 June 1952. The wing was redesignated the 452nd Bombardment Wing, Tactical on 25 May 1955. The unit was then redesignated the 452nd TCW (M) on 1 July 1957, and operated C-46s from Long Beach Municipal Airport through 1958. Between 1958 and 1969, the wing operated C-119s. When the Flying Boxcars entered the wing inventory, Major General John R Alison was commander. He was followed by Lieutenant Colonel George F Schlagel on 1 October 1959, and Brigadier General Earl O Anderson on 16 May 1960.

The 452nd TCG Headquarters supervised operations of the tactical units, the 728th, 729th, and 730th TCSs, between 1958 and 14 April 1959.

The 943rd TCG Headquarters and the 729th TCS were assigned to the 452nd TCW and stationed at March AFB, CA between 17 January 1963 and 25 April 1969.

The 944th TCG Headquarters and the 730th TCS were stationed at March AFB, California from 17 January 1963, until 25 March 1968.

The 945th TCG Headquarters and the 733rd TCS were stationed at Hill AFB, Utah between 17 January 1963 and 1969.

The 452nd TCW was awarded the Republic of Vietnam Gallantry Cross with Palm for operations between 1 January 1967 and 31 December 1971.

459th Troop Carrier Wing, Medium

The 459th TCW was established on 30 December 1954, and activated in the Reserve at Andrews AFB, Maryland on 26 January 1955. Between 1955 and 1958 the unit operated both the Beech C-45 Expeditor and Curtiss C-46 Commando. The 459th TCG was component of the wing between 26 January 1955 and 14 April 1959. The 756th TCS was assigned to the 459th TCG during this period. Three 900-series groups replaced the 459th TCG on 17 January 1963, as the wing gained greater geographical responsibilities. During the period the wing operated C-119s, it was commanded by Brigadier General Ramsey D Potts Jr, followed by Brigadier General Charles D Briggs Jr, on 19 June 1960.

The 909th TCG Headquarters and the 756th TCS were assigned to the 459th TCW and stationed at Andrews AFB, Maryland between 17 January 1963 and 1 September 1975. The unit operated C-119s between 1963 and 1967.

The 910th TCG Headquarters and the 757th TCS were assigned to the 459th TCW and stationed at the Greater Pittsburgh Airport, Pennsylvania between 17 January 1963 and 1 July 1966. Both the group and squadron were reassigned to the 302nd TCW on 1 July 1966, at which time the squadron transitioned from C-119Cs to C-119Gs. The last C-119Gs departed the unit in December 1969.

The 911th TCG Headquarters and the 758th TCS were assigned to the 459th TCW and stationed at the Greater Pittsburgh Airport, Pennsylvania from 17 January 1963. The squadron operated C-119s between 1963 and 1967.

482nd Troop Carrier Wing, Medium

Established as the 482nd TCW on 26 May 1952, the unit was activated in the Reserve at Miami International Airport on 14 June 1952. The wing was equipped with C-46 Commandos. On 1 December 1952, the wing was inactivated. Redesignated the 482nd Fighter-Bomber Wing on 12 April 1955, the wing was activated in the Reserve at Dobbins AFB, Georgia on 18 May 1955. C-119s came into the wing's inventory however the unit was inactivated on 16 November 1957. Colonel George H Wilson commanded the wing during this period. Then the wing was replaced the 445th TCW on 16 November 1957.

512th Troop Carrier Wing, Medium

The 512th TCW was established on 4 August 1949, and activated in the Reserve at Reading Municipal Airport, Pennsylvania, on 2 September 1949. The unit was equipped with Beech AT-7s and AT-11s, and Curtiss C-46s. The wing moved to New Castle County Airport, Delaware on 12 April 1951. On 15 March 1951, the wing was ordered to active service and supported

USAF worldwide airlift requirements. The wing reverted to Reserve status on 14 June 1952, and remained at New Castle County Airport, until moving to NAS Willow Grove, Pennsylvania on 20 July 1958. The 512th TCW operated C-119s between 1957 and 1963. During this period the wing was commanded by Brigadier General John S Bagby.

The 512th TCG and its tactical units, the 326th, 327th, and 328th TCSs were assigned to the 512th TCW between 14 June 1952 and 14 April 1959.

The 912th TCG and the 326th TCS, stationed at NAS Willow Grove, Pennsylvania, were assigned to the 512th TCW between 11 February 1963 and 8 January 1965. Both units were reassigned to the 302nd TCW on 8 January 1965, while remaining at NAS Willow Grove.

The 913th TCG and the 327th TCS, stationed at NAS Willow Grove, Pennsylvania, were assigned to the 512th TCW between 11 January 1963 and 8 January 1965.

The 914th TCG and the 328th TCS, stationed at Niagara Falls International Airport, New York, were assigned to the 512th TCW between 11 January 1963 and 1 January 1964.

The 916th TCG and the 77th TCS, stationed at Donaldson AFB, South Carolina, were assigned to the 512th TCW from 8 January 1965.

The 917th TCG and the 78th TCS, stationed at Barksdale AFB, Louisiana, were assigned to the 512th TCW from 5 February 1965.

514th Troop Carrier Wing, Medium

Established as the 514th TCW on 10 May 1949, the wing was activated in the Reserve at Birmingham Municipal Airport, Alabama on 26 June 1949;, the unit was equipped with C/TC-46s, T-6s, T-7s, and T-11s. The wing was reassigned to Mitchel AFB, New York on 10 October 1949, ordered to active service on 1 May 1951, inactivated on 1 February 1953, and reactivated at Mitchel AFB in the Reserve on 1 April 1953. Its 514th TCG and component squadrons began transitioning into C-119s on 31 December 1952 and replaced the 313th TCW at Mitchel AFB on 1 February 1953. For the next two years, the wing reverted to C-46s and trained under the supervision of the 2233rd Air Reserve Combat Training Center (later 2233rd Air Reserve Flying Center). The wing was then again to operate C-119s from July 1954 until 1970. On 1 April 1958, the 514th TCW began participating the Air Reserve Technician Program. Subsequently the wing participated in airlift missions, tactical exercises, humanitarian missions, and mercy flights. Brigadier General Arthur L McCullough commanded the wing while it operated C-119s during 1952 and 1953. When C-119s returned to the wing and operated between 1954 and 1970, the 514th TCW was commanded by: Major General Clayton Stiles, followed by Brigadier General Campbell Y Jackson on 1 October 1959.

The 514th TCW trained both aircrews and maintenance technicians for the VNAF, and Royal Hellenic Air Force. Between 10 August and 18 December 1967, the wing ferried a number of C-119s to South Vietnam.

The 903rd TCG and 335th TCS, stationed at McGuire AFB, New Jersey, were assigned to the 514th TCW from 17 January 1963.

The 904th TCG and 326th TCS were stationed at Stewart AFB, New York, and assigned to the 514th TCW from 17 January 1963 until 1 July 1966.

The 905th TCG and 337th TCS, stationed at Westover AFB, Massachusetts, were assigned to the 514th TCW from 17 January 1963.

The 912th TCG and 326th TCS, stationed at NAS Willow Grove, Pennsylvania, were assigned to the 514th TCW from 1 July 1966.

The 913th TCG and 327th TCS, stationed at NAS Willow Grove, Pennsylvania, were assigned to the 514th TCW from 1 July 1966.

516th Troop Carrier Wing, Medium

The 516th TCW was established on 10 May 1949, and activated in the Reserve at the Memphis Municipal Airport, Tennessee on 26 June 1949. The wing operated T-7s, T-11s, and C-46s. During 1952, the wing transitioned into C-119s, which they operated until 16 January 1953, when the 516th TCW was replaced by the 463rd TCW. The wing was commanded by Colonel Willis W Mitchell.

AIR NATIONAL GUARD

As with the Reserve airplanes, the ANG C-119s evolved from anonymous airplanes to those with unit identifiers. State abbreviations first appeared on the fuselage; that is, 'PA. AIR GUARD', 'N.J. AIR GUARD', and 'N.Y. AIR GUARD'. Subsequently, standard USAF markings were applied and the ANG insignia was added to the fins. As with the Reserve airplanes, some unit identifiers were spelled out on the forward fuselage above the cheat line. Unit insignia were also applied to the forward fuselage. A number of aeromedical evacuation aircraft were equipped with beavertail doors and carried a red cross on the fins. Some carried Insignia Red Arctic trim and others did not. Dayglo orange markings were applied to the nose, wingtips, and booms during the late 1950s and early 1960s. Some had white tops with blue cheat lines and others did not. Some carried red Arctic trim and others did not. Dayglo orange markings were applied to the nose, wingtips, and booms during the late 1950s and early 1960s. With the advent of the Cuban Missile Crisis in 1962, the dayglo trim was either removed or hurriedly painted over with aluminized paint.

Some special operations airplanes were painted in an overall Gloss Black (FS 17038).

'U.S. AIR FORCE' appeared beneath the two aft-most cockpit windows and extended aft to the prop warning line. The white tops and blue cheat lines varied – some came straight back from the top of the cockpit window line and ran aft to the prop warning line; others started at the middle of the aft vertical frame of the cockpit window and ran aft to the prop warning line; still others had the full white top with the cheat line running aft from the bottom frame of the cockpit windows to the prop warning line, then dropping diagonally to just above the main cabin windows and ran aft parallel to the airplane waterlines and wrapped around the clamshell doors. Some aircraft carried the squadron insignia on the forward fuselage in lieu of the last three digits of the tail number. An ANG *Minuteman* insignia was applied to the outboard surfaces of the vertical fins on some of the aircraft, while other aircraft carried the squadron insignia within the white cap above the word 'AIR' in 'U.S. AIR FORCE'. In the latter case, the last three digits of the tail number were applied in reduced size, beginning below the aft drop window and running aft.

There were 12 ANG units in 10 states operating C-119s.

California ANG

The 129th TCS, from the California ANG, was equipped with C-46Ds that were supplemented with Grumman SA-16A Albatrosses in the summer of 1958. Helio U-10A Couriers were added to the inventory in early 1963. The 129th TCS was a TAC-gained unit. On 1 July 1963, the unit was redesignated the 129th Air Commando Squadron (ACS) and C-119Cs were added to the squadron inventory. Between 1966-1967, the unit replaced its U-10As with de Havilland Canada U-6A Beavers. On 1 August 1968, the unit was again redesignated as the 129th Special Operations Squadron (SOS). During FY68, the C-119Cs were replaced with C-119Gs. Then during FY73, the C-119Gs were replaced with C-119Ls. The 129th SOS operated C-119C/G/L aircraft from Fresno Airport between 1963 and 1975.

Mississippi ANG

Pilots began transition training for the anticipated Republic RF-84Fs the 183rd Tactical Reconnaissance Squadron (TRS), Mississippi ANG were to use as replacements for their RB-26s, but a lack of suitable facilities precluded consummation of the transition. On 15 November 1957, the unit was redesignated the 183rd Aeromedical Transport Squadron (ATS) and became a MATS-gained organization. The 183rd ATS operated C-119Fs in the aeromedical transport role from Hawkins Field between November 1957 and July 1962, when they transitioned into C-121Cs.

New Jersey ANG

The 150th ATS from the New Jersey ANG operated C-46Ds from Newark Airport. During October 1958, the squadron transitioned into the C-119G/MC-119J for the aeromedical transport role and became a MATS-gained organization. During October 1962, the unit transitioned into C-121Cs.

The 150th ATS C-119s where painted in an overall aluminum finish and had a white cap and blue cheat line extending aft from the upper cockpit window frames. The noses were dayglo orange. 'N.J. AIR GUARD' appeared on the forward fuselage from beneath the next to the last cockpit window to the prop warning line. A red cross was applied to the outboard surfaces of the vertical fins above the tail numbers. Apparently nose numbers were not applied.

New York ANG

The 102nd Fighter Interceptor Squadron (FIS), New York ANG operated Lockheed F-94B Starfires from Floyd Bennett Field (NAS New York). During September 1958, the unit converted into C/MC-119Js and was redesignated the 102nd ATS. MATS was the gaining command. During the winter of 1962, the unit transitioned into C-97As.

North Carolina ANG

The 156th FIS, North Carolina ANG, flew F-86Ls. On 1 February 1961, the unit was redesignated the 156th ATS and became a MATS-gained organization. Beginning in May 1961, the squadron operated C-119Cs from Douglas Municipal Airport until June 1962, when they transitioned into C-121C/Gs.

Ohio ANG

The 145th ATS from the Ohio ANG operated C-46Ds from the Akron-Canton Municipal Airport. The squadron converted to C-119Js for the aeromedical transport role on 1 February 1968 and became a MATS-gained organization on 1 July 1960. During the winter of 1961, the unit transitioned into KC-97Fs.

Pennsylvania ANG

The 140th ATS from the Pennsylvania ANG operated C-46Ds from Spaatz Field, Reading. Redesignated the 140th Aeromedical Evacuation Squadron (AES) on 1 February 1957, the unit converted to C-119Js and at least two MC-119Js in April 1958. MATS would gain the squadron upon activation. On 1 February 1961, the squadron moved to Olmstead AFB where the runways were longer.

The 140th AES aircraft were in natural metal fnish, marked with dayglo orange trim. 'P.A. AIR GUARD' appeared below the aft-most two cockpit windows and extended back to the prop warning line. The last two digits of the tail number were centered below the guard designation.

The 147th FIS from the Pennsylvania ANG operated F-86Ls from the Greater Pittsburgh Airport. On 1 May 1961, the unit was redesignated the 147th ATS, and gained C-119Js for the aeromedical transport role. On 18 February 1964, the unit began transitioning into C-121Gs.

The 147th ATS aircraft were marked with dayglo orange trim and had white tops with blue cheat lines. 'P.A. AIR GUARD' appeared below the aft-most two cockpit windows and extended back to the prop warning line. The last two digits of the tail number were centered below the guard designation. Some aircraft carried the last three digits of the tail number on the nose gear doors.

Rhode Island ANG

The 143rd ACS from the Rhode Island ANG operated UH-16B Albatrosses, then added U-6As and U-10Ds to their inventory for the special operations role from T F Green Airport, Rhode Island. On 19 August 1968, the unit was redesignated the 143rd SOS. During the fall of 1961, the squadron began replacing their UH-16Bs with C-119Gs that were subsequently converted into C-119Ls. During the summer of 1975, the 143rd SOS phased-out its C-119Ls and U-10Ds, and gained C-130As.

West Virginia ANG

The 130th Air Resupply Squadron from the West Virginia ANG operated both C-46Ds and SA-16s from Kanawha County Airport. Redesignated the 130th TCS on 10 October 1958, the unit became a TAC gained organization on 1 July 1960. The squadron transitioned into C-119Cs and Helio U-10Bs in January 1962. Subsequently C-119Gs and C-119Ls came into the unit's inventory. The squadron was redesignated the 130th ACS on 1 July 1963. During August 1965, the U-10Bs were replaced by U-6As. Then in June 1967, the U-6As were replaced by U-10Ds. Redesignated the 130th SOS on 8 August 1968, the C-119s continued in the squadron's inventory until the last C-119L departed in September 1975. Then the primary mission aircraft became the C-130E.

After trading in their F-86Hs, the 167th FS operated C-119Cs from Kanawha County Airport between the spring of 1961 and July 1963 when the unit began transitioning into C-121Cs. By January 1964, the transition was complete. While operating the C-119s, the unit was designated the 167th ATS.

Wyoming ANG

The 187th TFS from the Wyoming ANG operated F-86Ls, from Cheyenne Municipal Airport. In February 1961, the unit began conversion into C/MC-119Js in the aeromedical transport role. On 1 May 1961, the unit was redesignated the 187th ATS and became a MATS-gained organization. Poor performance of these aircraft at higher field elevations led to conversion into the C-119CFs. In April 1963, the unit began transitioning into C-121Gs. 'USAF' was deleted from wings and 'WYO AIR GUARD' was applied to the forward fuselage in lieu of 'U.S. AIR FORCE'.

47th BOMB GROUP

The 47th BG was activated on 12 March 1951, at Langley AFB, Virginia, and assigned to Tactical Air Command. The group was equipped with North American B-45 Tornados and departed for RAF Sculthorpe, England, where they operated between 1 June 1952 and 8 February 1955. Their mission was to provide all-weather/night back-up to the nuclear-capable F-84Fs flown by the 81st Fighter Bomber Wing stationed at RAF Bentwaters. In addition to C-47s, the 47th Operations Squadron operated at least two C-119s as base support aircraft. These were C-119C-70-FA, serial number 51-8247, and s/n 51-8258.

On one occasion a B-45 had blown a main gear tire at a remote base resulting in the runway being shut down for several hours. A C-119 was dispatched from Sculthorpe with a spare wheel assembly. In the mean time the B-45 crew jacked their airplane. The C-119 landed and taxied up to the disabled Tornado and the wheel replacement was accomplished. The B-45 was then towed off the runway.

The C-119 markings were: nose – white with a black stripe; vertical fin – white truncated wedge edged in black; forward fuselage – large 47th BG insignia below cockpit with the black disk trailing a pair of long white wedges edged in black.

STRATEGIC AIR COMMAND

A number of SAC units operated C-119s as base support aircraft. They were not known to have carried any unit markings. However, a SAC 'Milky Way' band was applied to the forward fuselage and the SAC insignia was placed on the left side over the band.

In addition, there was one highly unusual wing in SAC that operanded the C-119 for one year.

456th Troop Carrier Wing, Medium

The 456th TCW was established on 15 October 1952, and activated at Miami International Airport, Florida, on 1 December of the same year, when it gained the assets of the 435th TCW, a Reserve unit. The 456th TCW was assigned to the Eighteenth Air Force between 1 December 1952 and 9 July 1956. The wing was attached to the 1st Air Division (Meteorological Survey), Strategic Air Command, between 22 April 1955 and 26 March 1956, and as such were the only troop carrier unit in SAC. Colonel James L Daniel commanded the 456th TCW. The 456th TCW moved to Charleston AFB, SC, on 25 July 1953, and to Shiroi AB, Japan, for service between 10 November 1955 and 10 May 1956. Between 1952 and 1955, the 456th TCW participated in numerous tactical exercises both within the ZI and overseas, mostly in conjunction with Army airborne forces. On 1 May 1955, the wing was reorganized and the tactical group and all support components were inactivated. The wing then gained control over three squadrons and three squadron-sized detachments. The 456th TCW then participated in Project *Drag Net*, part of Project *Grand Union*. Each squadron was equipped with eight C-119s. Their mission was the recovery of balloon-borne instrument packages. The 456th TCW returned to Ardmore AFB, Oklahoma, were it was inactivated between 25 May and 9 July

1956. The wing's aircraft were dispersed to other units.

Colored bands around the nose identified the squadrons; while checks applied to the nose and ventral fins identified the detachments. Components of the 456th TCW were: 744th TCS Red, 745th TCS Green, 746th TCS Blue, Det 1 744th TCS Red/White, Det 1 745th TCS Green/White, Det 1 746th TCS Blue/White.

AIR DEFENSE COMMAND

As with SAC, a number of ADC units operated C-119s as base support aircraft. Their only distinguishing markings were ADC insignia applied to the outer surfaces of the vertical fins.

MILITARY AIR TRANSPORT SERVICE

Air Rescue Service

A number of squadrons and detachments of the Air Rescue Service operated C-82s. The aircraft were in natural metal finish. The national insignia was applied to the top left and lower right outboard wing panels, and on the outboard surface of the booms. The 'CQ' buzz numbers were carried on both sides of the nose and on the lower left outboard wing panel. The upper surfaces of the inboard wing, to just outboard of the nacelles and extending over the top of the fuselage, was painted orange-yellow and a six-inch-wide black stripe was added along the outboard edges of the markings. The word 'RESCUE' was applied in black, extending from inboard of the nacelles over the top of the fuselage. Either the last three digits of the tail number or the buzz number was applied under the word 'RESCUE' on top of the fuselage. The orange-yellow band was extended down along the fuselage sides and wrapped under the belly. This band too was edged with a six-inch-wide black band. 'AIR RESCUE SERVICE', in black, was applied across the orange-yellow fuselage band centered between the windows and the lower waterline of the fuselage. orange-yellow bands, 36-inches wide with six-inch-wide black stripes, was applied to the booms approximately three feet forward of the leading edge of the horizontal stabilizer. Some aircraft carried the MATS globe emblem on the booms forward of the orange-yellow bands. A small portion of the nose was also painted orange-yellow with a narrow black band along the aft edge.

Airways & Communications Service

Several C-82s and C-119s were operated by the Airways & Communications Service. These aircraft were in natural metal finish and usually carried the Insignia Red Arctic trim on the empennage and outboard wing panels. The MATS globe emblem was located on the booms half way between the national insignia and the leading edge of the horizontal tail. Some aircraft from the 1st AACS Installation and Maintenance Squadron had the unit insignia applied to the forward fuselage.

1739th Ferrying Squadron

Based at Amarillo AFB, Texas, the 1739th Ferrying Squadron was part of the MATS Continental Division. This unit was equipped with a variety of its own aircraft including a pair of C-119s.

Their markings were somewhat unique in that the entire upper half of the fuselage was painted white. An insignia blue cheat line was also applied. These colors extended diagonally from the forward windscreen, across the tops of the two drop windows, down to the aircraft waterline that bisected the round portholes. 'U.S. AIR FORCE' was applied in the white area ahead of the red prop warning stripe. Along the lower fuselage beneath the wings were the words 'MILITARY AIR TRANSPORT SERVICE'. A MATS insignia was applied along the booms aft of the national insignia. A typical MATS yellow-edged blue band was applied to the outer surfaces of the vertical fins and rudders and the word 'CONTINENTAL' was inscribed in white within the band.

Air Resupply and Communications Service

Because of their clandestine mission, it is not believed that the C-119s assigned to the Air Resupply and Communications Service carried any unique markings.

United States Marines & Navy

The R4Q-1s operated by the Marines were in natural metal finish. The national insignia was placed on the top left and lower right outboard wing panels and on the outboard surfaces of the booms. 'UNITED STATES MARINES' was applied in black to the fuselage sides between the window belt and bottom waterline of the airplane. The unit designator, that is, 'VMR-253' was applied in black aft of the national insignia on the booms. R4Q-1 with the BuNo beneath were applied in black aft of the unit designator on the booms. The last three digits of the BuNo were generally applied in black on each side of the nose. A pair of distinguishing letters was applied to the vertical tails in black. The last three digits of the BuNo, followed by the two-letter unit designator, were applied to the top of the right wing upper surface in what was known as the MODEX identifier. These letters may be found in Appendix 4.

Anti-corrosive silver paint was subsequently applied to the aircraft and a white cap was added to the top of the fuselage with a black stripe at the bottom.

Some time after the arrival of the R4Q-2s, VMR-252 added an Insignia Yellow wing design that was bordered in black to the nose of the aircraft. In addition, a black-edged Insignia Yellow band was applied above the tail code on the outboard surfaces of the vertical tails.

By 1958, VMR-153 had added an Insignia Red wing design bordered in black to the nose of the aircraft. In addition, a black-edged Insignia Red band was applied above the tail code on the outboard surfaces of the vertical tails.

By the early 1960s, the Marine R4Qs had added dayglo red conspicuity markings to the forward fuselage, outboard wing panels, and empennage.

The first R4Q-1, BuNo 124324, was delivered to the Naval Air Test Center at NAS Patuxent River, Maryland in June 1950. This aircraft was in natural metal finish and carried the national insignia on the top left and lower right outboard wing panels and on the outboard surfaces of the tailbooms. The last three digits of the BuNo, '324', were applied to the aft fuselage forward of the troop doors. 'NATC' in black was applied mid-height on the outboard surfaces of the vertical tail. 'NATC' in black was also applied to the upper outboard wing panel.

Station aircraft assigned to operation and engineering units, repair squadrons, headquarters and maintenance squadrons, and the like, had the station name applied in black to the outboard surfaces of the vertical tails (see Appendix 4).

Belgian Air Force

15 Wing

Lineage of the 15 Wing goes back to 169 Wing that was formed at Evère, Belgium, on 1 April 1947. 366 and 367 Squadrons were assigned and equipped with Douglas C-47s, Avro Ansons, Hawker Siddeley Dominies, and Airspeed Oxfords. The Belgian Air Force underwent a general reorganization on 1 February 1948, and 169 Wing was redesignated 15 Wing. Its squadrons became 20 and 21 Smaldeel. 15 Wing was relocated to Melsbroek in 1950.

15 Wing of the Belgian Air Force, stationed at Melsbroek (Brussels) received their complement of 22 C-119Fs between 10 August 1953 and 20 March 1954. The two squadrons equipped with the C-119s were 20 and 40 Smaldeel.

The airplanes were finished in an aluminized paint. Black, yellow, and red flashes were applied to the outboard surfaces of the vertical fins. National insignia replaced the USAF star and bar markings on the booms and wings. Squadron colors were applied in two horizontal stripes on the dorsal fins. Their colors and markings were: 20 Smaldeel, blue horizontal stripes, OT-CAA thru OT-CAR; 40 Smaldeel, green horizontal stripes, OT-CBA thru OT-CBT. The insignia for 20 Smaldeel was a Sioux Indian head within a blue disk.

40 Smaldeel was established on 1 April 1954, but was disbanded two months later when it was deemed not to be economical to operate two squadrons. All of the C-119s were then operated by 20 Smaldeel.

The USAF's 322nd Air Division transferred an additional six C-119Gs to the Belgian Air Force during February 1958, to replace 18 C-119Fs that were returned to the United States for modification. Ten of these aircraft were returned to the Belgian Air Force, while the remaining eight were transferred to the Norwegian Air Force. By July 1973, all C-119s were withdrawn from the inventory and replaced by the Lockheed Hercules. In over 20 years of service with the Belgian Air Force, the C-119s had accrued 154,157 hours.

Brazilian Air Force

Twelve C-82 Packets were acquired by the *Força Aérea Brasileira* in 1956. These were followed by 11 C-119s in the latter half of 1963.

Markings applied to the Brazilian Air Force C-82s and C-119s consisted of their yellow, green, white, and blue star on the wings and booms, and yellow and green rudder trim.

Ethiopian Air Force

At least two C-119s, serial numbers 52-6047 and 52-6055, from the Norwegian Air Force went to the *Ye Ityopya Ayer Hayl* (Imperial Ethiopian Air Force) in 1973. Both flight and ground crews from the Ethiopian Air Force received training from the 302nd TAW stationed at Bakalar AFB, Indiana. Details on the aircraft markings are unknown.

France

L'*Armée de l'Air* – Détachement C-119
France's *Armée de l'Air* operated a number of C-119s between May 1953 and August 1954, during their war in Indochina. These airplanes were loaned by the USAF and operated both by French Air Force crews and Claire Chennault's Civil Air Transport. The Flying Boxcars were assigned to the Détachement C-119, and operated out of Hanoi-Gai Lam, Bach Mai, Haiphong-Cat Bi, and Tourane.

The C-119s left Korea and transited Clark AB, Philippines, where the USAF insignia were painted out and French roundels were applied. Existing USAF serial numbers, unit markings, and nose art were retained.

Indian Air Force

C-119s entered the *Bharatiya Vayu Sena* (Indian Air Force) inventory during 1954, and entered service with No 12 Squadron. Additional aircraft were assigned to No 19 Squadron in July 1960, followed by still more in May 1963. These aircraft carried red, white, and green roundels and red, white, and green fin flashes. Indian Air Force serial numbers in black were carried aft of the roundels on the booms. A large black aircraft identification letter was usually applied to the forward fuselage. Some aircraft were painted with dayglo orange conspiscuity markings. The squadron insignia was carried on the forward fuselage of some aircraft.

Italian Air Force

The *Aeronautica Militare Italiano* (Italian Air Force) operated a total of 65 C-119s between 1965 and 1979.

46° Stormo
Beginning as a bomber unit, the 46° Stormo was established at Pisa, on 15 February 1940. After the Armistice of September 1943, the 46° Stormo became a transport unit operating in southern Italy. The unit was reconstituted at Centocelle (Rome) on 1 November 1948, and equipped with Savoia-Marchetti SM.70s and SM.82s, and Fiat G.12s. The unit relocated to Pisa in stages between July 1949 and July 1950.

C-119s were introduced into the Italian Air Force beginning on 19 May 1953. The first two airplanes were turned over to the Italians at Ciampino (Rome) and they were ferried to their new base at San Guisto (Pisa). The 2° Gruppo became the first squadron to be equipped with the C-119s. A USAF training unit was in place there to assist with the transition of the 46° Stormo.

The airplanes were finished in aluminized paint. USAF national insignia were removed and replaced by the Italian roundel. Codes for the 46° Stormo were applied to either side of the roundel; for example, 46 ● 2 on airplane serial number 51-17366. The USAF serial numbers were retained on the vertical fins. Squadron colors were applied to the nose: 2° Gruppo/Red, 50° Gruppo/Yellow, 98° Gruppo/Green.

On 16 April 1954, the 46° Stormo was redesignated the 46ª Aerobrigata Transporti Medi (Medium Transport Brigade). At this time, the *Lira* (constellation) insignia for 2° Gruppo and the *Lupo* (wolf) insignia for 98° Gruppo were combined to form a new unit insignia that was applied to the vertical fins.

50° Gruppo was formed in late 1960 when the first C-119Js came into the inventory. This unit was the first to transition into the Lockheed Hercules on 27 March 1972.

Initially, the Italian C-119s were in the natural metal fnish. In 1963, the C-119Gs received a camouflaged scheme. The C-119Js followed in 1965. A green-gray paint was applied. An irregular pattern of dark gray and dark green were applied to the upper surfaces, while the bottom was a metallic gray. dayglo orange (later yellow) bands were applied to the nose, wingtips, and booms. Smaller USAF-style serial numbers were applied to the fins with an 'MM' prefix, standing for *Matricola Militaire* or military serial. While the nose colors remained for each squadron, the codes were changed to provide squadron identity as follows: 2° Gruppo 46-20 thru 46-39, 50° Gruppo 46-50 thru 46-69, 98° Gruppo 46-80 thru 46-99.

Two C-119s entered the VIP role pending delivery of the DC-9. These airplanes were coded 46-62 and 46-68.

14° Stormo
Three C-119s were also converted for use by the 71° Gruppo, 14° Stormo, in the ECM role. The first airplane, 46-63, had antennas added to the fuselage sides and belly. Airplanes 46-30 and 46-35 had antennas added beneath the nose and below the forward fuselage.

Republic of China Air Force

A total of 16 C-119s were delivered to the *Chung-Kou Kung Chaun* (Republic of China Air Force [RoCAF]) on Taiwan, in 1956 and replaced by 18 C-119Ls in 1959. During the 1960s and 1970s, 120 C-119s were diverted to the RoCAF.

Originally, these airplanes were finished in natural metal and carried the blue and white 12-pointed Chinese star on the wings and booms, and 12 blue and white rudder stripes. These stripes represent two-hour intervals throughout the day. USAF serial numbers were retained.

Subsequently, standard USAF camouflage, consisting of Olive Drab (FS 34102), Dark Green (FS 34079), and Tan (FS 30219) over Camouflage Gray (FS 36622) was applied. White 24in-high numerals were applied to the nose. Unit insignia were carried on both the nose and fins – the squadron insignia was applied aft of the drop windows on the nose, while the group insignia was carried on the outboard surfaces of the vertical fins. The controlling unit for the RoCAF C-119s was the 6th Troop Carrier & Antisubmarine Combined Wing (TC&ASCW) based at Pingtung. The transports were assigned to the 10th Transport Group. In addition to the individual squadron insignia on the nose, each squadron carried a colored stripe painted beneath the cockpit windows: 101 Sqn/Yellow, 102 Sqn/Red, 103 Sqn/Blue

The first to transition into C-130s during 1986 was 101 Squadron. Next, to phase out the C-119s, was 102 Squadron, and lastly No 103 Squadron.

Royal Canadian Air Force

The Royal Canadian Air Force purchased 35 C-119Fs directly from Fairchild in 1964. They were operated by 408, 435, and 436 Squadrons, and the 104 Composite Unit.

RCAF markings consisted of the Maple leaf roundel applied to the booms and wings; red

Royal Canadian Air Force C-119F 22133 is loaded with equipment at North Luffenham, England, as part of the 1 Fighter Wing move to Marville, France on 13 January 1955. RCAF PL-124070

and white lightning bolt applied to the fuselage, and black serial numbers on the fins. For a period, unit codes were carried on the booms. During activation for UN peacekeeping operations, the roundels were replaced by the UN wreath, and 'ROYAL CANADIAN AIR FORCE' on the fuselage was replaced by 'UNITED NATIONS'.

Royal Hellenic Air Force

While the 514th TCW, stationed at McGuire AFB, New Jersey, provided C-119 training for both aircrews and maintenance technicians of the Royal Hellenic Air Force between 10 August and 18 December 1967, there is no indication that an MDAP aircraft transfer actually was consummated.

Royal Jordanian Air Force

Members of the *Al Quwwat al-Jawwiya al-Malakiya al-Urduniya* (Royal Jordanian Air Force) are known to have been given instruction in the C-119 by the 302nd TAW at Bakalar AFB, Indiana, in 1973. Apparently four C-119Ks were operated by Jordan between 1972 and 1977. Details on any aircraft transferred to that nation are unknown.

Royal Moroccan Air Force

The *Al Quwwat al-Jawwiya al-Malakiya Marakishiya* (Royal Moroccan Air Force) was founded on 19 November 1956. First three, followed by an additional ten C-119F/Gs were delivered to Morocco during the 1962-1963 and 1966 time frames and operated by the 1st Air Transport Squadron.

These aircraft were painted in a desert scheme of irregular patterns of desert tan and black over camouflage gray. It is suspected that some of these aircraft were RC-119s that were equipped with a camera pallet mounted in the aft fuselage. For this reconnaissance mission, the aircraft would have been operated with the clamshell doors removed.

Royal Norwegian Air Force

The *Kongelige Norske Flyvapen* (Royal Norwegian Air Force) operated eight C-119Gs between 1956 and 1969.

No 335 Squadron

The primary transport unit within the Royal Norwegian Air Force was No 335 Squadron. It had its origins with the No 20 Training Flight in May 1945, when it operated Douglas C-47s. In November 1945, No 335 Squadron was established.

C-119s for the Royal Norwegian Air Force came by way of the Belgian Air Force. All eight of their C-119s were operated by No 335 Squadron. These airplanes were silver with dayglo orange applied to the nose, wingtips, and booms. The codes straddled the boom roundels; that is, **BW ● A** on the right and **A ● BW** on the left. USAF serial numbers were retained on the fins.

The Lockheed Hercules replaced the C-119 as Norway's primary transport during May and June 1969. During 13 years of service in Norway, the C-119s had flown 37,584 hours.

Republic of Vietnam Air Force

Four squadrons of the *Armée de l'Air Vietnamienne* (Republic of Vietnam Air Force) [VNAF] operated the C-119s between 1968 and 1975. Because of the operational limitations of these airplanes (that is, poor short field and rough strip capabilities) the airplanes were based at Tan Son Nhut where they enjoyed the luxury of flying off well-prepared runways. The aircraft were painted in standard USAF Southeast Asia colors. The following units were assigned to the VNAF.

53rd Tactical Wing

The 53rd Tactical Wing was in place at Tan Son Nhut when the first C-119s were assigned.

413th Tactical Squadron

The letter 'N' was carried on the tails of their C-119Gs. The unit was activated in January 1963 and equipped with C-47s. The unit was re-equipped with C-119Gs in January 1968. They were named the *Red Dragons*.

720th Reconnaissance Squadron

The unit was activated in December 1972 and equipped with RC-119s for use in maritime patrol. Because of the lack of mission equipment, these airplanes were operated in the transport role. No known distinctive markings were applied to these airplanes.

819th Combat Squadron

The letters 'HR' were carried on the tails of their AC-119Gs. The unit was activated in September 1971. They were named the *Black Dragons*.

821st Combat Squadron

The letter 'F' was carried on the tails of their AC-119Ks. The unit was activated in December 1972. A detachment also operated out of Da Nang. They were named the *White Dragons*.

Vietnamese People's Army Air Force

The *Khong Quan Nhan Dan* (Vietnamese People's Army Air Force) operated at least 36 captured C-119s between 1975 and 1988. The aircraft retained the Southeast Asia camouflage and the US tail numbers. A red flag with a yellow star was applied to the outboard vertical fin surfaces above the tail numbers.

The aircraft were flown by the 918th Air Transport Regiment.

Appendix 1

Production and Mishap Data

Production Summaries

Aircraft	No Built	Air Force Letter Contract	Contract Date
XC-82	1	W33-038-AC30435	6 Aug 1942
C-82A-FA	90	W33-038-AC124	28 Sep 1943
C-82A-FA	100	W33-038-AC124	28 May 1945
C-82A-FA	20	W33-038-AC124	30 Mar 1948
C-82N-NT	3	W33-038-AC7179	19 Dec 1944
XC-82B-FA	1*		
XC-119A	1*	W33-038-AC124	28 May 1945
C-119B-FA	36	W33-038-AC19200	4 Mar 1948
C-119B Static Test Article	1	W33-038-AC19200	4 Mar 1948
C-119B-FA	99	W33-038-AC19200	4 Mar 1948
C-119C-FA	53	W33-038-AC19200	22 Nov 1949
C-119C-FA	128	W33-038-AC19200	23 Dec 1949
C-119C-FA	41	AF(33)-18499	2 Oct 1951
C-119D	0	CANCELLED	
C-119E	0	CANCELLED	
YC-119F-FA	1	W33-038-AC19200	23 Dec 1949
C-119F-FA	53	W33-038-AC19200	23 Dec 1949
C-119-FA	80	W33-038-AC19200	30 Jun 1951
C-119F-FA	85	AF(33)-18499	2 Oct 1951
C-119G-FA	45	AF(33)-18499	2 Oct 1951
C-119F-WR	71	AF(33)-18481	16 May 1952
C-119G-FA	177	AF(33)-18499	13 Oct 1952
C-119G-FA	87	AF(33)-22285	22 Aug 1952
C-119G-FA	2	AF(33)-18499	29 Dec 1952
C-119G-KM	88	AF(33)-16021	23 Aug 1954
C-119G-FA	87	AF(33)-22285	22 Aug 1953
AC-119G	26†	Sustaining Funds	
YC-119H	1	W33-038-AC19200	23 Jul 1951
C-119I	Not Used		
C-119J	68‡	AF36(600)-2199	
YC-119K	1†		
C-119K	5†		
AC-119K	26†	Sustaining Funds	
C-119L	22†		
XC-120-FA	1	W33-038-AC19200	4 Mar 1948
R4Q-1 (C-119C)	39	AF(33)-18499	26 Feb 1951
R4Q-2 (C-119F)	58	AF(33)-18499	26 Feb 1951

* C-82A Conversion; † C-119G Conversion; ‡ C-119F/G Conversion

C-82 Mishap Statistics 1950-1955*

Year	Hours	Mishap Major Rate†	Fatal Mishap Rate	Destroyed Aircraft Rate	All Type Mishap Rate	Cost ($)
1950	52,210	14/26.8	4/7.7	7/13.4	17/32.5	3,640,660
1951	45,808	15/32.7	3/6.5	4/8.7	19/41.5	2,053,687
1952	34.280	11/32.0	3/8.7	2/5.8	26/75.8	1,541,546
1953	9,384	4/42.6	0/0	1/10.6	4/42.6	491,829
1954	5,653	2/35.4	1/17.7	2/35.4	2/35.4	652,300
1955	1,003	0/0	0/0	0/0	0/0	0

C-119 Mishap Statistics 1950-1975*

Year	Hours	Mishap Major Rate†	Minor Mishap Rate	Fatal Mishap Rate	Destroyed Aircraft Rate	All Type Mishap Rate	Cost ($)
1950	45,734	23/50.2		4/8.7	9/19.7	26/56.8	5,598,950
1951	83.250	28/33.6		6/7.2	8/9.6	38/45.6	5,883,447
1952	106,060	34/32.0		7/6.6	10/9.4	53/50.0	5,242,981
1953	198,327	30/15.1		6/3.0	12/6.1	64/32.3	10,163,414
1954	260,911	27/10.3		9/3.4	12/4.6	54/20.7	11,202,672
1955	331,713	25/7.5		7/2.1	17/5.1	40/12.1	
1956	344,296	19/5.5		4/1.2	10/2.9	24/7.0	
1957	301,570	13/4.3		2/0.6	8/2.7	15/5.0	
1958	261,271	11/4.2		3/1.2	5/1.9	3/1.2	3,586,736
1959	208,374	1/14.1		2/0.5	3/1.0	5/1.9	1,841,845
1960	174.588	4/2.3		0/0	2/1.1	4/2.3	1,229,320
1961	164,553	6/3.6	1/0.6	2/1.2	3/1.8	7/4.3	1,671,185
1962	169,787	5/2.9	4/2.4	2/1.2	3/1.8	9/5.3	1,745.548
1963	158,719	5/3.2	1/0.6	0/0	5/3.2	6/3.8	
1964	158,270	3/1.9	1/0.6	2/1.3	5/3.2	4/2.5	
1965	164,882	2/1.2	2/1.2	1/0.6	2/1.2	4/2.4	
1966	111,853	7/6.3	0/0	3/2.7	6/5.4	7/6.3	
1967	87,068	0/0	1/1.2	0/0	0/0	1/1.2	
1968	78,605	2/2.5	0/0	2/2.5	2/2.5	2/2.5	
1969	84,801	2/2.4	0/0	1/1.2	1/1.2	2/2.4	
1970	67,525	3/4.4	0/0	2/3.0	3/4.4	3/3.4	
1971	44,512	0/0	0/0	0/0	0/0	0/0	
1972	26,019	1/3.8	0/0	1/3.8	1/3.8	1/3.8	
1973	6,983	0/0	0/0	0/0	0/0	0/0	
1974	6,076	0/0	0/0	0/0	0/0	0/0	
1975	3,355	0/0	0/0	0/0	0/0	0/0	

* Last year flown.
† Mishap rates are based on 100,000 flying hours, that is, $\frac{14 \times 100,000}{52,210} = 26.8$ rate

Appendix 2

C-82 & C-119 Block Numbers and Serial Numbers

Model/Series	Serial Numbers	No Built
XC-82-FA	43-13202	1
C-82A-1-FA	44-22959/44-22968	10
C-82A-5-FA	44-22969/44-22988	20
C-82A-10-FA	44-22989/44-23003	15
C-82A-15-FA	44-23004/44-23018	15
C-82A-20-FA	44-23019/44-23033	15
C-82A-25-FA	44-23034/44-23048	15
C-82A-30-FA	44-23049/44-23058	10
C-82A-FA	45-57733/45-57832	100
C-82A-FA	48-0568/48-0587	20
XC-82B-FA	45-57769	1*
C-82N-NT	45-25436/45-25438	3
C-82N-NT	45-25439/45-26435	Cancelled
XC-119A-FA	45-57769	1*
C-119B-FA	48-319/48-329	11
XC-120-FA	48-330	1
C-119B-FA	48-331/48-355	25
C-119B-10-FA	49-101/49-109	9
C-119B-12-FA	49-110/49-118	9
C-119C-12-FA	49-119/49-124	6
C-119C-13-FA	49-125/49-139	15
C-119C-14-FA	49-140/49-154	15
C-119C-15-FA	49-155/49-169	15
C-119C-16-FA	49-170/49-184	15
C-119C-17-FA	49-185/49-199	15
C-119C-18-FA	50-119/50-131	13
C-119C-19-FA	50-132/50-146	15
C-119C-20-FA	50-147/50-161	15
C-119C-21-FA	50-162/50-171	10
C-119C-22-FA	51-2532/51-2556	25

Model/Series	Serial Numbers	No Built
C-119C-23-FA	51-2557/51-2584	28
YC-119H-FA	51-2585	1*
C-119C-25-FA†	51-2587/51-2617	31
C-119C-26-FA†	51-2618/51-2661	44
	51-2662-51-2667	6
C-119F-FA†	51-2668/51-2686	19
	51-2687-51-2689	Cancelled
	51-2690-51-2707	18‡
	51-2707/51-2717	10
	51-7968/51/51-8052	85
	51-17365/51-17367	3‡
C-119F-WR¶	51-8098/51-8168	71
C-119F-KM	22101/22135§	35
C-119C-70-FA†	51-8233/51-8273	41
C-119G-FA†	51-8053/51-8097	45
	52-5840-52-5954	115
	52-5955-52-5954	Cancelled
C-119G-35-FA	52-6000-52-6058	59‡
	52-9981/52-9982	2
C-119G-36-FA	53-3136-53-3222	87
	53-4637/53-4662 ‖	26‡
	53-7826/53-7884	59
C-119G-84-KM	53-8069/53-8156	88

* Conversion from an earlier series; † C-119CF-FAs essentially C-119Cs with hydraulically actuated landing gear; ‡ Purchased directly by the Canadian government; § MDAP production; ¶ WR plant changed to KM; ‖ Purchased directly by the Indian government and given IAF serials IK441 through IK466.

Manufacturer codes:
FA=Fairchild, **KM**=Kaiser, and **NT**=North American.
WR=Willys, Willow Run became **KM** for Kaiser.

Major Conversions

Model/Series	Serial Numbers	No Built
AC-119G-FA	52-8089, 52-5892, 52-5898, 52-5905, 52-5907, 52-5925, 52-5927, 52-5938, 52-5942, 53-3136, 53-3145, 53-3170, 53-3178, 53-3189, 53-3192, 53-3205, 53-7833, 53-7848, 53-7849, 53-7851, 53-7852, 53-8114, 53-8115, 53-8123, 53-8131, 53-8155	26
AC-119K	52-5864, 52-5889, 52-5910, 52-5911, 52-5926, 52-5935, 52-5940, 52-5945, 52-9982, 53-3154, 53-3156, 53-3187, 53-3197, 53-3211, 53-7826, 53-7830, 53-7831, 53-7839, 53-7850, 53-7854, 53-7877, 53-7879, 53-7883, 53-8121, 53-8145, 53-8148	26
C-119K	52-5932, 53-3142, 53-3160, 53-8180, 53-3188	5
YC-119K	53-3142	1
C-119J	51-7968, 51-8030, 51-81035/51-8143, 51-8145/51-8046, 51-8049/51-8052, 51-8113/51-8116, 51-8119, 51-8121/51-8132, 51-8134, 51-8137/51-8138, 51-8140/51-8141, 51-8144, 51-8152/51-8154, 51-8159, 51-8164/51-8165, 51-8167, 52-5845, 52-5849, 52-5851, 52-5866, 52-5875, 52-5877, 52-5895/52-5897, 52-5903, 52-5906; 52-5942, 53-3213, 53-7855, 53-8089, 53-8101, 53-8103	67

Model/Series	Serial Numbers	No Built
EC-119J	52-5884, 52-5896	2
C-119L	53-3184, 53-3186, 53-3193, 53-3206, 53-3216, 53-7849, 53-7853, 53-7858, 53-7865, 53-8073, 53-8074, 53-8076, 53-8083, 53-8084, 53-8087, 53-8126, 53-8127, 53-8142, 53-8149, 53-8150, 53-81553, 53-8154	22
RC-119L	53-3160, 53-3181	2

USMC R4Q-1 (C-119C) & R4Q-2 (C-119F)

Model/Series	Serial Numbers	No Built
R4Q-1	BuNo 124324/124331	8
R4Q-1	BuNo 126574/126582	9
R4Q-1	BuNo 128723/128744	22
R4Q-2	BuNo 131662/131719	58

Appendix 3

C-82 Packet Units

United States Air Forces Europe (USAFE)

Group/Sqn	Color	Base	Dates
60th TCG		Wiesbaden AB, West Germany	1949-1949
- 10th TCC	Red	Rhein-Main AB, West Germany	1949-1949
- 11th TCS	Green	Wiesbaden AB, West Germany	1949-1950
- 12th TCS	Blue	Rhein-Main AB, West Germany	1950-1953
61st TCG		Rhein-Main AB, West Germany	1949-1951
- 60th TCG (Attached)			

Tactical Air Command (TAC)

Group/Sqn	Color	Base	Dates
62nd TCG		Bergstrom AFB, TX	1947-1948
- 4th TCS	Red	McChord AFB, WA	1948-1950
- 7th TCS	Yellow		
- 8th TCS	Blue		
64th TCG		Donaldson AFB, SC	1952-1953
- 17th TCS			
- 18th TCS			
- 35th TCS			
302nd TCG		McChord AFB, WA	1949-1951
- 335th TCS			
- 356th TCS			
313th TCG		Bergstrom AFB, TX	1947-1948
- 29th TCS	Red		
- 47th TCS	Green		
314th TCG		Smyrna AFB, TN	1947-1949
- 20th TCS (Det)		(Rhein-Main AB, West Germany)	-1948
- 50th TCS			
- 61st TCS	Red		
- 62nd TCS	Green		
- 334th TCS	Blue		
316th TCG		Pope Field, NC	1946-1947
		Greenville AAB, SC	1947-1949
		Smyrna AFB, TN	1949-1950
- 36th TCS			
- 37th TCS			
- 75th TCS			
- 77th TCS			
375th TCG		Greenville AFB, SC	1950-1952
- 55th TCS			
- 56th TCS			
- 57th TCS			

Air Rescue Service (MATS)

Unit	Base	Dates
1st ARS	Albrook AFB, Canal Zone	1949-1952
4th ARS	Hamilton AFB, CA	1949-1952
- B Flight, 4th ARS	March AFB, CA	
5th ARS	MacDill AFB, FL	1947-1949
- D Flight, 5th ARS	Westover AFB, MA	1951-1952
6th ARS	Westover AFB, MA	1949-1951
	Pepperell AFB, Newfoundland	1951-1952
7th ARS	Wheelus AB, Libya	1951-1952
9th ARS	Bushy Park, England	1951-1952
9th ARS, Flight D	Wheelus AB, Libya	-1951
41st ARS	Hamilton AFB, CA	1952-1953
48th ARS	Eglin AFB, FL	1952-1953
58th ARS	Wheelus AB, Libya	1952-
59th ARS		
66th ARS	RAF Manston, England	1952-1953
2151st Rescue Unit	Lowry AFB, CO	1948-1949
2156th ARS	MacDill AFB, FL	1950-1952
	Palm Beach Airport, FL	1951-1952

Miscellaneous USAF Units

Unit/Sqn	Color	Base	Dates
1st ACCS I&M Sqn		Tinker AFB, OK	1953-1954
57th Fighter Wing		Elmendorf AFB, AK	1948-1950
- 4th TCS (Attached)	Red		1948-1949
- 7th TCS (Attached)	Yellow		1949-1949
- 7th TCS (Attached)	Blue		1948-1949
- 37th TCS (Attached)	Yellow		1948-1950
55th SRW (SAC)		Ramey AFB, PR	
- 7th Geodetic Sqn	Green		1949
91st SRW (SAC)		Barksdale AFB, LA	1949-1951
- Base Flight		Lockbourne AFB, OH	1951-1952
92nd BW (SAC)		Fairchild AFB, WA	
- Base Flight			
1455th Air Force Base Unit (ATC)		Great Falls AFB, MT	1947-1948

For unit abbreviations see foot of page 183.

Appendix 4

United States C-119 Units

Regular Air Force Troop Carrier Units

Unit	Sqn Color	Base	Dates
60th TCG		Rhein-Main AB, West Germany	1953-1955
		Dreux AB, France	1955-1958
- 10th TCS	Red		
- 11th TCS	Green		
- 12th TCS	Blue		
61st TCW *		Rhein-Main AB, West Germany	1950-1950
63rd TCW		Donaldson AFB, SC	1953-1954
- 64th TCS (Attached)			
64th TCG		Donaldson AFB, SC	1953-1954
- 17th TCS			
- 18th TCS			
- 35th TCS			
313th TCG		Mitchel AFB, NY	1953-1953
		Sewart AFB, TN	1953-1955
- 29th TCS	Red		
- 47th TCS	Green		
- 48th TCS	Blue		
314th TCG†		Sewart AFB, TN	1949-1950
		Ashiya AB, Japan	1950-1954
- 50th TCS	Red/White		
- 61st TCS	Green/White		
- 62nd TCS	Blue/White		
- 37th TCS (Attached)	Yellow	Komaki AB, Japan	1950-1950
		Ashiya AB, Japan	1950-1952
		Sewart AFB, TN	1952-1954
316th TCW		Sewart AFB, TN	1952-1954
- 316th TCG		Sewart AFB, TN	1952-1954
- 316th TCG		Ashiya AB, Japan	1954-1955
- 36th TCS	Red/White		
- 37th TCS	Blue/White	Detached 1950-1952	
- 75th TCS	Green/White		
317th TCG		Rhein-Main AB, West Germany	1952-1953
		Neubiberg AB, West Germany	1953-1957
		Evreux-Fauville AB, France	1957-1958
- 39th TCS	Yellow/Black		
- 40th TCS	Red/White		
- 41st TCS	Blue/White		
374th TCW		Tachikawa AB, Japan	1956-1957
- 21st TCS (Attached)		Kisarazu AB, Japan	1956-1957
		Naha AB, Okinawa	1958-1959
433rd TCW		Rhein-Main AB, West Germany	1951-1952
- 433rd TCG			AFRES
- 67th TCS			activated
- 68th TCS			during
- 69th TCS			Korean War
443rd TCG (M)		Donaldson AFB, SC	1952-1953
- 309th TCS			
- 310th TCS			
- 343rd TCS			
463rd TCW		Memphis, TN	1953-1953
		Ardmore AFB, OK	1953-1957
- 772nd TCS	Red		
- 773rd TCS	Yellow		
- 774th TCS	Green		
- 775th TCS	Blue		
464th TCW		Lawson AFB, GA	1953-1954
		Pope AFB, NC	1954-1958
- 776th TCS	Red		
- 777th TCS	Blue		
- 778th TCS	Green		
- 779th TCS	Yellow		
465th TCW		Mitchel AFB, NY	1953-1954
		Toul-Rosières AB, France	1954-1955
		Evreux-Fauville AB, France	1955-1957
- 780th TCS	Red		
- 781st TCS	Blue		
- 782nd TCS	Green		
483rd TCW		Ashiya AB, Japan	1951-1959
		Tachikawa AB, Japan	1956-1957
- 21st TCS (Attached)		Naha AB, Japan	1957-1958
- 21st TCS		Kisarazu AB, Japan	1958-1959
- 36th TCS (Attached)	Red/White		1956-1957
- 37th TCS (Attached)	Blue/White	Ashiya AB, Japan	1956-1957
- 75th TCS (Attached)	Green/White	Ashiya AB, Japan	1956-1957
- Détachement C-119		Ashiya AB, Japan	1953-1954
l'Armée de l'Air (Attached)†			
- Det 772nd TCS (Attached)	Red	Ashiya AB, Japan	1958
- 815th TCS (Attached)	Red/White†	Ashiya AB, Japan	1956-1958
- 816th TCS (Attached)	Green/White†	Ashiya AB, Japan	1956-1958
- 817th TCS	Blue/White†	Ashiya AB, Japan	1956-1958
- 6461st TCS/ATS (Attached)		Ashiya AB, Japan	1953-1955
- 316th TCG (Attached)		Ashiya AB, Japan	1954-1955

Other Regular Air Force Troop Carrier Units

Unit	Base	Dates
9th ABW (SAC)	Mountain Home AFB, ID	circa 1956
28th ABW (SAC)	Ellsworth AFB, SD	circa 1956
42nd TCS (Special)	Molesworth, England	1956-1957
	RAF Alconbury, England	1957-1957
47th BW (L)	RAF Sculthorpe, England	1952-1956
- 47th ABG		
53rd FG (ADC	Sioux City AFB, IA	circa 1956
67th TRW	Yokota AB, Japan	1957-1958

180 Fairchild C-82 & C-119

Unit	Base	Dates
89th FBW	Hanscom Field, MA	1957-1957
92nd ABW (SAC)	Fairchild AFB, WA	circa 1956
93rd ABW (SAC)	Castle AFB, CA	circa 1956
97th ABW (SAC)	Dyess AFB, TX	circa 1956
322nd AD	Evreux-Fauville AB, France	1954-1958
	Dreux AB, France	1958-1960
- 10th TCS		1958-1960
- 11th TCS		1958-1960
- 12th TCS		1958-1960
- 60th TCW (Attached)	Dreux AB, France	1954-1955
- 60th TCW	Dreux AB, France	1955-1958
- 317th TCW (Attached)	Evreux-Fauville AB, France	1954-1955
- 317th TCW	Toul-Rosières AB, France	1955-1958
		1954-1955
- 465th TCW (Attached)	Evreux-Fauville AB, France	1954-1955
- 465th TCW		1955-1957
322nd TCS (Special)	Kadena AB, Okinawa	1956-1957
328th FG (ADC)	Grandview AFB, MO	circa 1957
	(Renamed Richards-Gebaur AFB)	
405th FBW	Langley AFB, VA	1954-1956
421st ARS	Yokota AB, Japan	circa 1960
521st ADFG	Sioux City AFB, IA	circa 1956
566th ADFG	Hamilton AFB, CA	circa 1956
580th AR&CS	Mountain Home AFB, ID	1951-1952
	Wheelus Field, Libya	1953-1956
581st AR&CS	Mountain Home AFB, ID	1951-1952
	Clark AB, Philippines	1952-1953
	Anderson AFB, Guam	1953-1956
582nd AR&CS	Mountain Home AFB, ID	1951-1953
	Great Falls AFB, MT	1953-1953
	RAF Molesworth, England	1953-1956
1739th FrySqn (MATS)	Amarillo AFB, TX	1952-1955
2578th ABS	Ellington AFB, TX	circa 1966
3345th TTW	Chanute AFB, IL	circa 1957
3415th TTW	Lowry AFB, CO	circa 1956
3499th TTW (Mobile)		
3560th PTW	Webb AFB, TX	circa 1956
3750th TTW	Sheppard AFB, TX	circa 1955
3919th ABG	RAF Fairford, England	circa 1955
4440th ADG (ADC)	Langley AFB, VA	circa 1960
4600th ABW (ADC)	Peterson AFB, CO	circa 1959
4750th ADFW	Yuma AFB, AZ	circa 1957
4756th ADFW	Tyndall AFB, FL	circa 1958
4900th ABG (AFCS)	Kirtland AFB, NM	circa 1956
5039th ATS	Elmendorf AFB, AK	1955-1957
6102nd ABG	Yokota AB, Japan	circa 1958
6594th TG (AFSC)	Hickam AFB, HI	1958-1962

* Plans changed swiftly with the outbreak of the Korean War. The 61st TCW (Medium) headquarters was located at Rhein-Main AB, West Germany, and its component squadrons (14th, 15th, and 53rd TCSs) were equipped with C-47s and C-54s. The 61st TCW was to re-equip with C-119s and such action began in August 1950. However, with the exigencies of the emerging conflict in Korea, the wing's primary operating unit, the 61st TCG, with its C-54s, was redeployed to McChord AFB, Washington, in July, and by December 1950, while the wing and its component squadrons were based at Ashiya AB, Japan.

† The three squadrons from the 314th TCG; 50th, 61st, and 62nd, were transferred back to the ZI to rejoin their parent wing in 1954; however, the assets were retained at Ashiya AB, Japan, and gained by the 483rd TCW. The new squadrons assigned to the 483rd TCW were the 815th, 816th, and 817th TCSs. The names of the 50th/815th TCS, 61st/816th TCS, and 62nd/817th TCS were *Red Barons, Green Hornets*, and *Blue Barons*, respectively. Their colors matched their names. The 314th TCG squadrons retained their names and colors upon returning to the ZI. When the aircraft were gained by the 483rd TCW, the colors and markings remained, however the squadron names changed. The 817th changed their name from *Red Barons* to *Sky Runners* on their dorsal fillets.

It should be noted that the USAF underwent a major reorganization in the early 1950s and the basic operating unit went from being a group to a wing. For some period the groups were still assigned to the new wing and the units continued to identify themselves as groups even after the wing designation had been established. A number of miscellaneous units also operated the C-119 as a combat support airplane, usually as part of the base flight unit providing training and utility transport for an operational wing. SAC operated as many as 50 C-119s, sprinkled by ones and twos, at various bases and assigned to the air base group that supported the wing. A number of C-119s also served as combat support aircraft for various air defense, tactical bombardment, and tactical fighter units.

Air Force Reserve Units

Unit	Group/Sqn	Base	Dates
94th TCW (M)		Hanscom AFB, MA	1957-1966
	94th TCG	Hanscom AFB, MA	1957-1959
	901st TCG	Hanscom AFB, MA	1963-1966
	- 731st TCS	Hanscom AFB, MA	1953-1966
302nd TCW (M)	906th TCG	Clinton Co AFB, OH	1956-1963
	- 335th TCS	Lockbourne AFB, OH	1963-1973
	907th TCG	Lockbourne AFB, OH	1963-1973
	- 356th TCS	Lockbourne AFB, OH	1963-1973
	908th TCG	Bates Field, AL	1963-1964
		Brookley AFB, AL	1964-1969
	- 357th TCS	Brookley AFB, AL	1964-1969
	910th TCG	Youngstown Apt, OH	1966-1969
	- 757th TCS	Youngstown Apt, OH	1966-1969
	912th TCG	NAS Willow Grove, PA	1965-1966
	- 326th TCS	NAS Willow Grove, PA	1965-1966
349th TCW (M)		Hamilton AFB, CA	1963-1968
	939th TCG	Portland Apt, OR	1963-1968
	- 313th TCS	Portland Apt, OR	1963-1965
	940th TCG	McClellan AFB, CA	1963-1968
	- 314th TCS	McClellan AFB, CA	1963-1968
	941st TCG	Paine AFB, WA	1963-1965
	- 97th TCS	Paine AFB, WA	1963-1965
	941st TCG	McChord AFB, WA	1965-1968
	- 97th TCS	McChord AFB, WA	1965-1968
375th TCW	375th TCG	Greater Pittsburgh Apt, PA	1952-1957
	- 55th TCS		
	- 56th TCS		
	- 57th TCS		
403rd TCW (M)	403rd TCG	Portland Apt, OR	1952
		Ashiya AB, Japan	1952-1953
		(Activated for Korea)	
		Portland Apt, OR	1957-1963
	927th TCG	Selfridge AFB, MI	1963-1970
	- 63rd TCS	Selfridge AFB, MI	1963-1970
433rd TCW (M)		Greenville AFB, SC	1950-1952
		Rhein-Main AB, W Germany	1952-1957
		(Activated for Korea)	
		Brooks AFB, TX	1957-1960
		Kelly AFB, TX	1960-1971

Wing	Group	Base	Dates
	433rd TCG	Brooks AFB, TX	1955-1959
	- 67th TCS	Brooks AFB, TX	1957-1960
	- 68th TCS	Brooks AFB, TX	1957-1962
	916th TCG	Carswell AFB, TX	1963-1971
	- 77th TCS	Carswell AFB, TX	1963-1971
	921st TCG	Kelly AFB, TX	1962-1971
	- 67th TCS	Kelly AFB, TX	1960-1971
	922nd TCG	Kelly AFB, TX	1962-1971
	- 68th TCS	Kelly AFB, TX	1962-1971
	923rd TCG	Carswell AFB, TX	1963-1965
	- 69th TCS	Carswell AFB, TX	1963-1969
434th TCW (M)	930th TCG	Atterbury/Bakalar AFB, IN	1957-1969
		Bakalar AFB, IN	
	930th TCG	Lockbourne AFB, OH	1963-1968
		Bakalar AFB, IN	1969-1969
	- 71st TCS	Lockbourne AFB, OH	1963-1968
		Bakalar AFB, IN	1969-1969
	931st TCG	Bakalar AFB, IN	1963-1969
	- 72nd TCS	Bakalar AFB, IN	1963-1969
	932nd TCG	Scott AFB, IL	1957-1969
	- 73rd TCS	Scott AFB, IL	1963-1969
435th TCW (M)	435th TCG	Miami Apt, FL	1951-1952
		Homestead AFB, FL	1952-1957
	917th TCG	Barksdale AFB, LA	1962-1965
	- 78th TCS	Barksdale AFB, LA	1961-1965
436th TCW	436th TCG	NAS New York, NY	1957-1957
	- 79th TCS	NAS New York, NY	1957-1957
437th TCW (M)	437th TCG	O'Hare Apt, IL	1957-1957
	- 83rd TCS	O'Hare Apt, IL	1957-1957
439th TCG (M)	439th TCG	Selfridge AFB, MI	1956-1957
	- 93rd TCS		
	- 94th TCS		
	- 472nd TCS		
440th TCW (M)	440th TCG	Gen Mitchell Field, WI	1963-1970
	914th TCG	Niagara Falls Mun Apt, NY	1969-1969
	- 328th TCS	Gen Mitchell Field, WI	1969-1969
	933rd TCG	Gen Mitchell Field, WI	
	- 95th TCS		1963-1970
	934th TCG	Minneapolis-St Paul Apt, MN	1963-1970
	- 96th TCS		1963-1970
442nd TCW (M)		Richards-Gebaur AFB, MO	1957-1967
	442nd TCG	Richards-Gebaur AFB, MO	1957-1959
	935th TCG	Richards-Gebaur AFB, MO	1963-1967
	- 303rd TCS	Richards-Gebaur AFB, MO	1959-1967
	936th TCG	Tinker AFB, OK	1963-1967
	- 304th TCS	Tinker AFB, OK	1959-1967
	937th TCG	Tinker AFB, OK	1957-1967
	- 305th TCS	Tinker AFB, OK	1957-1967
443rd TCW (M)	443rd TCG	Donaldson AFB, SC	1952-1953
	- 309th TCS	Donaldson AFB, SC	1952-1953
	- 310th TCS	Donaldson AFB, SC	1952-1953
445th TCW (M)	445th TCG	Dobbins AFB, GA	1957-1959
	915th TCG	Miami Int'l Apt, FL	1965-1966
	- 96th TCS	Miami Int'l Apt, FL	1965-1966
	- 918th TCG	Dobbins AFB, GA	1963-1966
	- 700th TCS	Dobbins AFB, GA	1963-1966
446th TCW (M)	446th TCG	Ellington AFB, TX	1957-1970
	908th TCG	Bates Field, AL	1961-1970
	- 357th TCS	Bates Field, AL	1961-1970
	924th TCG	Ellington AFB, TX	1963-1970
	- 704th TCS	Ellington AFB, TX	1963-1970
	- 705th TCS	Ellington AFB, TX	1963-1970
452nd TCW (M)	452nd TCG	Long Beach Apt, CA	1958-1960
		March AFB, CA	1960-1969
	- 728th TCS	March AFB, CA	1958-1962
	- 729th TCS	March AFB, CA	1958-1962
	- 730th TCS	March AFB, CA	1962-1962
	943rd TCG	March AFB, CA	1963-1969
	- 729th TCS	March AFB, CA	1963-1969
	944th TCG	March AFB, CA	1963-1969
	- 928th TCS	March AFB, CA	1962-1969
	- 929th TCS	March AFB, CA	1962-1969
	- 930th TCS	March AFB, CA	1962-1969
	945th TCG	Hill AFB, UT	1962-1969
	- 733rd TCS	Hill AFB, UT	1962-1969
459th TCW (M)		Andrews AFB, MD	1957-1967
	459th TCG	Andrews AFB, MD	1957-1959
	909th TCG	Andrews AFB, MD	1962-1967
	- 756th TCS	Andrews AFB, MD	1957-1967
	910th TCG	Youngstown Apt OH	1963-1966
	- 757th TCS	Youngstown Apt OH	1963-1966
	911th TCG	Greater Pittsburgh Apt, PA	1963-1967
	- 758th TCS	Greater Pittsburgh Apt, PA	1963-1967
482nd TCW (M)	482nd TCG	Dobbins AFB, GA	1957-1957
512th TCW (M)	912th TCG	NAS Willow Grove, PA	1963-1968
	- 326th TCS	NAS Willow Grove, PA	1957-1968
514th TCW (M)	514th TCG	Mitchel AFB, NY	1954-1961
	903rd TCG	McGuire AFB, NJ	1961-1970
	- 335th TCS	McGuire AFB, NJ	1961-1970
	904th TCG	Stewart AFB, NY	1963-1966
	- 336th TCS	Stewart AFB, NY	1963-1966
	905th TCG	Westover AFB, MA	1966-1970
	- 337th TCS	Westover AFB, MA	1966-1970
	914th TCG	Niagara Falls Apt, NY	1963-1964
	- 328th TCS	Niagara Falls Apt, NY	1963-1964
516th TCW (M)	516th TCG	Memphis Mun Apt, TN	1952-1953

Regular Air Force AC-119 Gunship Units

Unit	Code	Base	Dates
1st ACW		England AFB, LA	1968-1969
1st SOW		Hurlburt Field, FL	1969
- 71st SOS*	IC		
- 317th ACS/SOS*	AH		
- 415th SOS†			
4408th CCTS*	IH	Lockbourne AFB, OH	1961-1971
- OL #1¶		Clinton County AFB, OH	1969
14th SOW		Phan Rang AB, RVN	1968-1971
- 17th SOS*	EF‡		1969-1971
- 18th SOS*	EH‡		1969-1971
- 71st SOS*			1968-1969
24th SOW		Howard Field, Panama	1971-1973
- (Various rotational sqns)			
56th SOW		Nakhon Phanom RTAFB, Thailand	1971-1972
- 18th SOS†			
4410th CCTW		Eglin AFB, FL	1969-1969
		England AFB, LA	1969-1973
- 71st SOS*	IC	Lockbourne AFB, OH	1969-1969
- 18th SOS†	II	Lockbourne AFB, OH	1969-1970
		England AFB, LA	1972-1973
- 4413th CCTS*§	IH	Lockbourne AFB, OH	1969-1970

Air Force Reserve AC-119 Gunship Units

Unit	Code	Base	Dates
302nd SOW		Lockbourne AFB, OH	1968-1973
- 1st CCTS*			1968-1970
- 1st TATS*			1970-1973

* AC-119G; † AC-119K; ‡ Not carried because they would be seen when painted with a searchlight. § While the 4413th CCTS (Auxiliary) was assigned to the 1st ACW, it was attached to the 317th TAW, Lockbourne AFB, OH (equipped with C-130s) for administrative and logistics support. ¶ Operating Location #1, 4408th CCTS. Was in use between 10 March and 15 July 1969.

Air National Guard Units

Unit	Base	Type	Dates
102nd ATS	Mitchel AFB, NY	MC-119J	1958-1962
129th TCS*	Hayward Airport, CA	C-119C/G/L	1963-1975
130th SOS	Kanawha Co Airport, WV	C-119C/G/L	1965-1975
140th ATS	Spaatz Field, PA	C-119J	1958-1961
	Olmstead AFB, PA		1961-1962
143rd SOS	T F Green Airport, RI	C-119G/L	1971-1975
145th ATS	Akron-Canton Municipal Airport, OH	C-119J	1957-1961
	Clinton Co AFB, OH		1961-1962
147th ATS	Greater Pittsburgh Airport, PA	C-119J	1961-1973
150th ATS	McGuire AFB, NJ	MC-119J	1958-1961
156th AAS	Douglas Municipal Airport, NC	C-119C	1961-1962
167th ATS	Kanawha Co Airport, WV	C-119C	1961-1963
183rd ATS	Hawkins Field, MS	C-119F	1957-1961
187th ATS	Cheyenne Municipal Airport, WY	MC-119J	1961-1963

* Changed to Air Commando Squadron then Special Operations Squadron

US Marine Corps and Navy Units

Squadron	Code	Base	Dates
US Marine Corps			
VMR-153	AC	NAS Itami, Japan	1952-1953
VMR-216	5T	NAS Seattle, WA	1961-1967
	7T	NAS Seattle, WA	1967-1972
	MV	NAS Whidbey Island, WA	1972-1972
VMR-234	5E	NAS Minneapolis, MN	1972-1972
	QH	NAS Glenview, IL	1972-1975
VMR-252	LH	MCAS Cherry Point, NC	1950-1957
	BH	MCAS Cherry Point, NC	1957-1971
VMR-253	AD	NAS Itami, Japan	1953-1955
	AD	NAS Iwakuni, Japan	1955-1957
	QD	NAS Iwakuni, Japan	1957-1959
VMR-352	LB	MCAS El Toro, CA	1950-1957
	QB	MCAS El Toro, CA	1957-1961
VMR-353	MZ	NAS Miami, FL	1953-1957
	DZ	NAS Miami, FL	1957-1960
MARTAD	7Y	NAS Grosse Isle, MI	circa 1960
	5T	NAS Seattle, WA	1961-1966
	5V	NAS Glenview, IL	1966-1967
Other Units			
AirFMLANT		MCAS Cherry Point, NC	1952
AES-12		MCAS Quantico, VA	1953
H&MS MAW-1		Pohang, Korea	1954-1955
H&MS-13		MCAS Kaneohe, HI	1954
H&MS-14		MCAS Edenton, NC	1953-1954.
H&MS-25		MCAS El Toro, CA	1954-1955
HAMRON-15		MCAS El Toro, CA	1953
HAMRON-26		MCAS Cherry Point, NC	1953
HEDRON-2		MCAS Cherry Point, NC	1953
HEDRON-25		MCAS El Toro, CA	1954-1955
HAMRON-32		MCAS Miami, FL	1953-1954
MARS-27		MCAS Cherry Point, NC	1953
MARS-37		MCAS El Toro, CA	1955-1956
MTG-10		MCAS El Toro, CA	1953
NATC R&D		NATC Patuxent River, MD	1950, 1957
SO&ES		MCAS Cherry Point, NC	1958-1959
US Navy			
VR-24	JM	NAS Port Lyautey, Morocco	1954-1962
FASRON-117		NAS Barber's Point, HI	1954
NABTC		NAS Pensacola, FL	1955, 1957-1959
5th ND		NAS Norfolk, VA	1956-1958
6th ND		NAS Jacksonville, FL	1958-1959
11th ND		NAS North Island, CA	1958-1959
12th ND		NAS Alameda, CA	1958-1959

The tail codes beginning with a numeral were for Marine Reserve units assigned to the 4th Marine Air Wing which were not assigned to a Marine Reserve transport squadron, and based at a reserve naval air station. These aircraft carried the tail code assigned to the facility where they were based.

Unit Abbreviations

AAB	Army Air Base	FW	Fighter Wing
AAS	Aeromedical Airlift Squadron	H&MS	Headquarters & Maintenance Sqn
AB	Air Base	HAMRON	– Headquarters & Maintenance Sqn
ABG	Air Base Group	I&M Sqn	Installation & Maintenance Squadron
ABS	Air Base Squadron	MARS	Marine Air Repair Squadron
ABW	Air Base Wing	MARTAD	Marine Air Reserve Training
ACCS	Airways & Air Communications Service		Detachment
ACS	Air Commando Squadron	MATS	Military Air Transport Service
ACW	Air Command Wing	MATS	Military Air Transport Service
AD	Air Division	NABTC	Naval Air Basic Training Center
ADC	Air Defense Command	NATC	Naval Air Test Center
ADFG	Air Defense Fighter Group	ND	Naval District
ADFW	Air Defense Fighter Wing	RTAFB	Royal Thai Air Force Base
ADG	Air Defense Group	RU	Rescue Unit
AES	Aviation Engineering Squadron	RVN	Republic of Vietnam
AF	Air Force	SAC	Strategic Air Command
AFCS	Air Force Communications Service	SAC	Strategic Air Command
AFSC	Air Force Systems Command	SO&ES	Station Operation & Engineering Sqn
AirFLMLANT	– Fleet Marine Force Atlantic (Air)	SOS	Special Operations Squadron
AR&CS	Air Resupply & Communications Sqn	SOW	Special Operations Wing
ARS	Air Refueling Squadron	SRW	Strategic Reconnaissance Wing
ARS	Air Rescue Squadron	TATS	Tactical Airlift Training Squadron
ATC	Air Transport Command	TAW	Tactical Airlift Wing
ATS	Air Transport Squadron	TCG	Troop Carrier Group
ATS	Aeromedical Transport Squadron	TCG	Troop Carrier Group
BU	Base Unit	TCS	Troop Carrier Squadron
BW (L)	Bombardment Wing (Light)	TCS	Troop Carrier Squadron
CCTS	Combat Crew Training Squadron	TCW	Troop Carrier Wing
CCTW	Combat Crew Training Wing	TG	Test Group
CONUS	CONtinental United States	TRW	Tactical Reconnaissance Wing
FASRON	Fleet Air Service Squadron	TTW	Technical Training Wing
FBW	Fighter-Bomber Wing	VMR	Heavier-than-air Marine Transport
Flt	Flight		Squadron
FrySqn	Ferrying Squadron	VR	Heavier-than-air Navy Transport Sqn

C-82s and C-119s in Foreign Service

A number of Allied nations received C-119s from the US. The Brazilian Air Force also received C-82s. While most were provided under the Mutual Defense Assistance Plan (MDAP), Canada and India made direct purchases of the aircraft from Fairchild. Where known, foreign serials are cross-referenced to US serials. Disposition of many of the aircraft is also provided.

Belgium – All assigned to 20th TS/15th TW, Brussels, Oct 1953-Jul 1973

USAF S/n	Model/Series	Codes		Remarks
51-2692	C-119F-FA	CP-1	OT-CAA	To Norwegian AF
51-2693	C-119F-FA	CP-2	OT-CAB	To Norwegian AF
51-2694	C-119F-FA	CP-3	OT-CAC	
Unknown	C-119F-FA	CP-14	OT-CAN	Scrapped at Koksijde
51-2695	C-119F-FA	CP-4	OT-CAD	To Norwegian AF
51-2696	C-119F-FA	CP-5	OT-CAE	
Unknown	C-119F-FA	CP-11	OT-CAK	Scrapped at Koksijde
51-2697	C-119F-FA	CP-6	OT-CAF	To Norwegian AF
51-2698	C-119F-FA	CP-7	OT-CAG	To Norwegian AF
51-2699	C-119F-FA	CP-8	OT-CAH	To Norwegian AF
51-2700	C-119F-FA	CP-9	OT-CAI	Scrapped at Koksijde
51-2701	C-119F-FA	CP-10	OT-CAJ	Preserved Musée Royal de' l'Armée, Zaventem
51-2702	C-119F-FA	CP-11	OT-CAK	To Norwegian AF
51-2703	C-119F-FA	CP-12	OT-CAL	Scrapped at Koksijde
51-2704	C-119F-FA	CP-13	OT-CAM	Scrapped at Koksijde
51-2705	C-119F-FA	CP-14	OT-CAN	To Norwegian AF
51-2706	C-119F-FA	CP-15	OT-CAO	Scrapped at Koksijde
51-2707	C-119F-FA	CP-16	OT-CAP	Scrapped at Koksijde
51-2690	C-119F-FA	CP-17	OT-CAQ	Scrapped at Koksijde
51-2691	C-119F-FA	CP-18	OT-CAR	Scrapped at Koksijde
52-6021	C-119F-35-FA	CP-23	OT-CBC	Crashed at Chièvres 12 Dec 1961
52-6022	C-119F-35-FA	CP-21	OT-CBA	Scrapped at Koksijde
52-6023	C-119F-35-FA	CP-22	OT-CBB	Scrapped at Koksijde
52-6026	C-119F-35-FA	CP-27	OT-CBG	Scrapped at Koksijde
52-6027	C-119F-35-FA	CP-30	OT-CBJ	Scrapped at Koksijde
52-6028	C-119F-35-FA	CP-26	OT-CBF	Scrapped at Koksijde
52-6032	C-119F-35-FA	CP-33	OT-CBM	Scrapped at Koksijde
52-6033	C-119F-35-FA	CP-20	OT-CAT	Scrapped at Koksijde
52-6034	C-119F-35-FA	CP-19	OT-CAS	Crashed at Hofgeishar 22 Oct 1965
52-6035	C-119F-35-FA	CP-31	OT-CBO	Scrapped at Koksijde
52-6038	C-119F-35-FA	CP-24	OT-CBD	Scrapped at Koksijde
52-6039	C-119F-35-FA	CP-28	OT-CBH	Scrapped at Koksijde
52-6043	C-119F-35-FA	CP-25	OT-CBE	Crashed at Chièvres 12 Dec 1961
52-6044	C-119F-35-FA	CP-36	OT-CBP	Crashed at Rushengo 19 Jul 1960
52-6045	C-119F-35-FA	CP-32	OT-CBL	Scrapped at Koksijde
52-6046	C-119F-35-FA	CP-39	OT-CBS	Scrapped at Koksijde
52-6047	C-119F-35-FA	CP-29	OT-CBI	To Ethiopian AF
52-6050	C-119F-35-FA	CP-34	OT-CBN	Scrapped at Koksijde
52-6051	C-119F-35-FA	CP-38	OT-CBR	Scrapped at Koksijde
52-6052	C-119F-35-FA	CP-35	OT-CBO	Scrapped at Koksijde
52-6055	C-119F-35-FA	CP-37	OT-CBQ	To Ethiopian AF
52-6058	C-119F-35-FA	CP-40	OT-CBT	Scrapped at Koksijde
53-7829	C-119G-36-FA	CP-41	OT-CEA	Scrapped at Koksijde
53-7843	C-119G-36-FA	CP-42	OT-CEB	Scrapped at Koksijde
53-8130	C-119G-36-FA	CP-43	OT-CEC	Scrapped at Koksijde
53-8141	C-119G-36-FA	CP-44	OT-CED	Scrapped at Koksijde
53-8143	C-119G-36-FA	CP-45	OT-CEE	Crashed nr Augustdorf, W Germany 26 Jun 63
53-8151	C-119G-36-FA	CP-46	OT-CEH	At Musée Royale de l'Armée, Brussels

Brazil – Assigned to 1° GTT, Area dos Afonsos, C-82s 1956-1967; C-119s 1963-1975

USAF S/n	Model/Series	FAB S/n	Remarks
48-586	C-82-FA	2201	1° Grupo de Transporte de Tropas
48-585	C-82-FA	2202	1° Grupo de Transporte de Tropas
		2203	1° Grupo de Transporte de Tropas
48-580	C-82-FA	2204	1° Grupo de Transporte de Tropas
		2205	1° Grupo de Transporte de Tropas
		2206	1° Grupo de Transporte de Tropas
48-578	C-82-FA	2207	1° Grupo de Transporte de Tropas
		2208	1° Grupo de Transporte de Tropas
		2209	1° Grupo de Transporte de Tropas
		2210	1° Grupo de Transporte de Tropas
51-8064	C-119G-FA		1° Grupo de Transporte de Tropas
51-8065	C-119G-FA		1° Grupo de Transporte de Tropas
51-8066	C-119G-FA	2310	1° Grupo de Transporte de Tropas
51-8067	C-119G-FA		1° Grupo de Transporte de Tropas
51-8074	C-119G-FA	2304	1° Grupo de Transporte de Tropas
51-8075	C-119G-FA		1° Grupo de Transporte de Tropas
51-8076	C-119G-FA	2305	1° Grupo de Transporte de Tropas
51-8077	C-119G-FA	2312	1° Grupo de Transporte de Tropas
51-8080	C-119G-FA		1° Grupo de Transporte de Tropas
51-8084	C-119G-FA		1° Grupo de Transporte de Tropas
51-8086	C-119G-FA		1° Grupo de Transporte de Tropas
51-8092	C-119G-FA		1° Grupo de Transporte de Tropas

Canada – For unit assignments see footnote

USAF S/n	Model/Series	RCAF S/n	Remarks
–	C-119F-KM	22101	To Hawkins & Powers. Museum
–	C-119F-KM	22102	
–	C-119F-KM	22103	To Hawkins & Powers. Museum
–	C-119F-KM	22104	
–	C-119F-KM	22105	To Hawkins & Powers. Museum
–	C-119F-KM	22106	To Hawkins & Powers. Museum
–	C-119F-KM	22107	To Hawkins & Powers. Museum
–	C-119F-KM	22108	To Hawkins & Powers.
–	C-119F-KM	22109	Museum
–	C-119F-KM	22110	Museum
–	C-119F-KM	22111	To Hawkins & Powers. Museum
–	C-119F-KM	22112	To ECM.
–	C-119F-KM	22113	To ECM.
–	C-119F-KM	22114	To Hawkins & Powers. Museum
–	C-119F-KM	22115	To Hawkins & Powers.
–	C-119F-KM	22116	To Hawkins & Powers. Museum
–	C-119F-KM	22117	
–	C-119F-KM	22118	To Hawkins & Powers. Museum
–	C-119F-KM	22119	
–	C-119F-KM	22120	To Hawkins & Powers.
–	C-119F-KM	22121	
–	C-119F-KM	22122	To ECM. To Hawkins & Powers. Museum
–	C-119F-KM	22123	
–	C-119F-KM	22124	
–	C-119F-KM	22125	
–	C-119F-KM	22126	
–	C-119F-KM	22127	

–	C-119F-KM	22128		
–	C-119F-KM	22129		
–	C-119F-KM	22130		
–	C-119F-KM	22131	To Hawkins & Powers. Museum	
–	C-119F-KM	22132	To Hawkins & Powers.	
–	C-119F-KM	22133	To Hawkins & Powers.	
–	C-119F-KM	22134	To Hawkins & Powers. Museum	
–	C-119F-KM	22135	To Hawkins & Powers. Museum	

Units were 408 Sqn, Rivers, Manitoba Apr 1964-May 1965; 435 Sqn, Edmonton, Alberta Sep 1952-Jul 1965; 436 Sqn, Dorval, Quebec Apr 1953-Jul 1956 then Downsview, Ontario Jul 1956-Jul 1965; 104 Composite Unit, St Hubert, Quebec May 1956-Oct 1958 (redesignated 104 Communication & Calibration Flight 1 Nov 1958 and RCAF Electronic Warfare Unit 1 Apr 1959.

Ethiopia – All assigned to 1 Squadron at Bishoftu c1972-1986

USAF S/n	Model/Series	Codes	Remarks
52-5899	C-119G-FA	912	1 Sqn
52-5932	C-119G-FA		1 Sqn
53-3160	C-119G-36-FA	917	1 Sqn
53-3188	C-119G-36-FA	915	1 Sqn
53-7856	C-119G-36-FA	911	1 Sqn
53-8108	C-119G-84-KM	916	1 Sqn

India – Assigned to 12, 19, 48 Sqns and Paratroop Training School at Agra

USAF S/n	Model/Series	IAF S/n	Remarks
53-4637	C-119G-36-FA	IK441	
53-4638	C-119G-36-FA	IK442	
53-4639	C-119G-36-FA	IK443	
53-4640	C-119G-36-FA	IK444	
53-4641	C-119G-36-FA	IK445	
53-4642	C-119G-36-FA	IK446	
53-4643	C-119G-36-FA	IK447	
53-4644	C-119G-36-FA	IK448	
53-4645	C-119G-36-FA	IK449	
53-4646	C-119G-36-FA	IK450	Museum
53-4647	C-119G-36-FA	IK451	
53-4648	C-119G-36-FA	IK452	
53-4649	C-119G-36-FA	IK453	
53-4650	C-119G-36-FA	IK454	
53-4651	C-119G-36-FA	IK455	Stored
53-4652	C-119G-36-FA	IK456	
53-4653	C-119G-36-FA	IK457	Stored
53-4654	C-119G-36-FA	IK458	
53-4655	C-119G-36-FA	IK459	
53-4656	C-119G-36-FA	IK460	
53-4657	C-119G-36-FA	IK461	
53-4658	C-119G-36-FA	IK462	
53-4659	C-119G-36-FA	IK463	
53-4660	C-119G-36-FA	IK464	
53-4661	C-119G-36-FA	IK465	
53-4662	C-119G-36-FA	IK466	

The IAF received further C-119Gs under MDAP; and an additional 176 overhauled engines.

Italy – For unit assignments see footnote. Codes listed in two columns: pre- and post-1965

USAF S/n	Model/Series	Codes		Remarks
51-8046	C-119J-KM	None	None	Ground accident 14 Dec 1964; to instructional aircraft Jan 1965. Used for spares until 1988.
51-8113	C-119J-KM	46-49	46-69	Scrapped at Pisa
51-8121	C-119J-KM	46-50	46-50	At Turin Museum
51-8125	C-119J-KM	46-51	46-51	Scrapped at Pisa
51-8128	C-119J-KM	46-52	46-52	Scrapped at Pisa
51-8130	EC-119J-KM	46-53	46-53	Converted to EC-119J in 1975. Transferred to 71° Gruppo. Scrapped at Pisa
51-8140	C-119J-KM	46-54	46-54	Converted to VC-119J in 1969. Transferred to 50° Gruppo. Scrapped at Pisa
52-6030	C-119G-35-FA	46-27	46-95	Crashed at Pisa 24 Jan 1979
51-8144	VC-119J-KM	46-55	46-55	Scrapped at Vergiate
51-8152	C-119J-KM	46-56	46-56	Scrapped at Pisa
51-8154	C-119J-KM	46-57	46-57	Crashed at Cisterna 23 Jun 1969
51-8156	C-119J-KM	46-58	46-58	Scrapped at Pisa
51-8158	VC-119J-KM	46-62	46-62	Scrapped at Vergiate
51-17365	C-119G-FA	46-9	46-??	Scrapped at Pisa
51-17366	C-119G-FA	46-2	46-80	Scrapped at Pisa
51-17367	C-119G-FA	46-4	46-27	Scrapped at Pisa
52-5849	C-119J-FA	46-59	46-59	Scrapped at Vergiate
52-5851	C-119J-FA	46-60	46-50	Scrapped at Vergiate
52-5866	C-119J-FA	46-61	46-61	Scrapped at Pisa
52-5884	EC-119J-FA	46-63	46-63	Converted to EC-119J in 1969. Transferred to 71° Gruppo. Scrapped at Vergiate
52-5896	EC-119J-FA	46-64	46-64	Converted to EC-119J in 1973. Transferred to 71° Gruppo. Scrapped at Pisa
52-5897	C-119J-FA	46-65	46-65	Scrapped at Pisa
52-5947	C-119J-FA	46-66	46-66	Scrapped at Pisa
52-6000	C-119G-35-FA	46-6	46-98	Scrapped at Pisa
52-6001	C-119G-35-FA	46-13	46-33	Scrapped at Pisa
52-6003	C-119G-35-FA	46-5	46-31	Scrapped at Pisa
52-6004	C-119G-35-FA	46-8	46-34	Scrapped at Pisa
52-6005	C-119G-35-FA	46-3	None	Crashed at Pisa 1963
53-6006	C-119G-35-FA	46-7	46-82	Scrapped at Pisa
52-6007	C-119G-35-FA	46-37	46-87	Scrapped at Pisa
52-6008	C-119G-35-FA	46-20	46-20	Scrapped at Pisa
52-6009	C-119G-35-FA	46-24	46-24	Scrapped at Pisa
52-6010	C-119G-35-FA	46-23	46-23	Scrapped at Pisa
52-6011	C-119G-35-FA	46-15	None	Crashed at Luluaburg 15 Feb 1961
52-6012	C-119G-35-FA	46-29	46-29	Scrapped at Pisa
52-6013	C-119G-35-FA	46-16	46-37	Scrapped at Pisa
52-6014	C-119G-35-FA	46-10	None	Crashed in Lake Tanganyika 17 Nov 1961
52-6015	C-119G-35-FA	46-19	46-19	Scrapped at Pisa
52-6016	C-119G-35-FA	46-31	46-81	Scrapped at Pisa
52-6017	C-119G-35-FA	46-18	46-39	Scrapped at Pisa
52-6018	C-119G-35-FA	46-24	46-86	Crashed at Rivolto 25 Apr 1970
52-6019	C-119G-35-FA	46-21	46-21	Scrapped at Pisa
52-6020	C-119G-35-FA	46-34	46-84	On display at Rivolto
52-6024	C-119G-35-FA	46-41	46-91	Scrapped at Pisa
52-6025	C-119G-35-FA	46-36	46-36	Scrapped at Vergiate
52-6029	C-119G-35-FA	46-43	46-93	On display at Campoformidio
52-6030	C-119G-35-FA	46-27	46-95	Crashed at Pisa 24 Jan 1979
52-6031	C-119G-35-FA	46-30	46-30	VC-119G with 2° Gruppo from 1960. To EC-119G. To 71° Gruppo 1975. Scrapped at Vergiate
52-6036	C-119G-35-FA	46-11	None	Crashed off of Pisa 20 Apr 1964
52-6037	C-119G-35-FA	46-22	None	Crashed at Kwamouth 2 Feb 1961
52-6040	C-119G-35-FA	46-25	46-25	Scrapped at Pisa
52-6041	C-119G-35-FA	46-28	46-28	Scrapped at Pisa
52-6042	C-119G-35-FA	46-32	46-32	Scrapped at Pisa
52-6048	C-119G-35-FA	46-42	46-92	Scrapped at Pisa
52-6049	C-119G-35-FA	46-33	46-83	Scrapped at Pisa
52-6053	C-119G-35-FA	46-35	46-85	Scrapped at Pisa
52-6054	C-119G-35-FA	46-38	46-88	Scrapped at Pisa
52-6056	C-119G-35-FA	46-39	46-89	Scrapped at Pisa
52-6057	C-119G-35-FA	46-40	46-90	Scrapped at Pisa
53-3200	C-119G-36-FA	46-48	46-38	Scrapped at Pisa
53-3219	C-119G-36-FA	46-46	46-96	Scrapped at Pisa
53-7828	C-119G-36-FA	46-47	46-97	Scrapped at Pisa
53-7845	C-119G-36-FA	46-44	46-94	Formerly with Indian AF. Scrapped at Pisa
53-8098	C-119J-KM	46-67	46-67	Scrapped at Pisa
53-8103	VC-119J-KM	46-68	46-68	Scrapped at Pisa
53-8146	C-119G-KM	46-45	46-355	Formerly with Indian AF. Converted to EC-119G in 1976. Transferred to 71° Gruppo

Units were 2° Gruppo, 46° Stormo, Pisa May 1953-Jan 1979; 50° Gruppo, 46° Stormo, Pisa Jun 1964-Mar 1972; 98° Gruppo, 46° Stormo, Pisa Feb 1954-Jan 1979; 14° Stormo, 71° Gruppo, Pratica di Mare 1972-89. 2°, 50°, and 98° Gruppi were assigned to 46ª Aerobrigata, Transport Wing 1.

Jordan – Unit assignment unknown, operated c1972-1977

USAF S/n	Model/Series	Remarks
52-5863	C-119G-FA	
52-5880	C-119G-FA	
52-5918	C-119G-FA	

Morocco – Assigned to 1st Air Transport Squadron c1963-1980

USAF S/n	Model/Series	Codes	Remarks
49-139	C-119C-13-FA		1st ATS
49-171	C-119C-16-FA		1st ATS
49-180	C-119C-16-FA		1st ATS
49-183	C-119C-16-FA		1st ATS
49-187	C-119C-17-FA		1st ATS
49-190	C-119C-17-FA	CAN-MN	1st ATS. Preserved at Marrakech.
53-3160	RC-119L		
53-7862	C-119G-36-FA	CAN-MH	1st ATS. Preserved at Kenitra.
53-8095	C-119G-84-KM		1st ATS

Norway – Assigned to 335 Sqn, Gardermoen Jun 1956-Jun 1969

USAF S/n	Model/Series	Codes	Names	Remarks
51-2692	C-119F-FA	BW-C	*Cappy*	Returned to USAF
51-2693	C-119F-FA	BW-B	*Bamse*	Returned to USAF
51-2695	C-119F-FA	BW-E	*Elmer*	Crashed 16 Dec 1968
51-2697	C-119F-FA	BW-A	*Anton*	Returned to USAF
51-2698	C-119F-FA	BW-F	*Fiimbeck*	Returned to USAF
51-2699	C-119F-FA	BW-D	*Donald*	Returned to USAF
51-2702	C-119F-FA	BW-H	*Hiawatha*	Returned to USAF
51-2705	C-119F-FA	BW-G	*Goofey*	Returned to USAF

Republic of China (Taiwan) – For unit assignments see footnote

USAF S/n	Model/Series	Codes	Remarks
51-2709	C-119F-FA	3125	
51-2710	C-119F-FA	3174	
51-2711	C-119F-FA	3162	
51-2716	C-119F-FA	3112	
51-5924	C-119F-FA		
51-7973	C-119F-FA	3210	
51-7978	C-119F-FA	3123	
51-7979	C-119F-FA		
51-7981	C-119F-FA	3195	
51-7984	C-119F-FA	3220	
51-7985	C-119F-FA	3160	Storage
51-7989	C-119F-FA	3119	
51-7990	C-119F-FA	3206	
51-7996	C-119F-FA	3199	
51-8003	C-119F-FA	3181	
51-8004	C-119F-FA	3186	
51-8016	C-119F-FA	3202	
51-8017	C-119F-FA	3147	
51-8018	C-119F-FA		Storage
51-8031	C-119F-FA	3212	
51-8048	C-119F-FA	3208	
51-8057	C-119F-FA	3157	
51-8058	C-l19F-FA	3151	
51-8060	C-119F-FA	3120	Storage
51-8068	C-119F-FA		
51-8070	C-119F-FA		
51-8071	C-119F-FA	3183	
51-8079	C-119F-FA	3144	
51-8091	C-119F-FA	3126	
51-8094	C-119F-FA		
51-8099	C-119F-FA	3142	
51-8106	C-119FKM	3190	Preserved Gang Shan. AF Academy Museum
51-8120	C-119F-KM	3192	Storage
51-8136	C-119F-KM	3152	Storage
51-8147	C-119F-KM	3198	
51-8150	C-119F-KM	3204	Storage
52-5844	C-119G-36-FA		
52-5848	C-119G-36-FA	3191	
52-5869	C-119G-36-FA	3142	
52-5870	C-119G-36-FA	3187	
52-3140	C-119G-36-FA		
52-3165	C-119G-36-FA	3165	
52-5923	C-119G-36-FA		
52-5924	C-119G-36-FA	3217	
52-5937	C-119G-36-FA	3137	
53-3143	C-119G-36-FA		
53-3144	C-119G-36-FA		
53-3153	C-119G-36-FA		
53-3158	C-119G-36-FA		
53-3164	C-119G-36-FA	3164	
53-3171	C-119G-36-FA	3171	
53-3172	C-119G-36-FA	3172	
53-3176	C-119G-36-FA	3176	
53-3177	C-119G-36-FA	3177	
53-3181	RC-119L-KM	3181	Destroyed in a ground fire at Pingtung AB on 1 June 1996
53-3207	C-119G-36-FA	3129	
53-7870	C-119G-36-FA	3158	
53-7875	C-119G-36-FA	3175	
53-8132	C-119G-84-KM	3139	

Assigned to 101st TCS, Pingtung 1959-1986; 102nd TCS; 103rd TCS 1959-1997.
These squadrons reported to the 6th Troop Carrier and Anti-Submarine Combined Wing.

Republic of Vietnam (South Vietnam) – For unit assignments see footnote

USAF S/n	Model/Series	Codes	Remarks
51-7983	C-119F-FA		413th TS, 53rd TW, 5th AD
52-5892	C-119G-FA		413th TS, 53rd TW, 5th AD
52-5925	C-119G-FA		413th TS, 53rd TW, 5th AD
52-5927	C-119G-FA		413th TS, 53rd TW, 5th AD
53-3145	C-119G-36-FA		413th TS, 53rd TW, 5th AD
53-3147	C-119G-36-FA		413th TS, 53rd TW, 5th AD
53-3148	C-119G-36-FA		413th TS, 53rd TW, 5th AD
53-3157	C-119G-36-FA		413th TS, 53rd TW, 5th AD
53-3161	C-119G-36-FA	NG	413th TS, 53rd TW, 5th AD
53-3167	C-119G-36-FA		413th TS, 53rd TW, 5th AD
53-3173	C-119G-36-FA		413th TS, 53rd TW, 5th AD
53-3175	C-119G-36-FA		413th TS, 53rd TW, 5th AD
53-3185	C-119G-36-FA		413th TS, 53rd TW, 5th AD
53-3189	C-119G-36-FA		413th TS, 53rd TW, 5th AD
53-3194	C-119G-36-FA		413th TS, 53rd TW, 5th AD
53-3196	C-119G-36-FA		413th TS, 53rd TW, 5th AD
53-3202	C-119G-36-FA		413th TS, 53rd TW, 5th AD
53-3203	C-119G-36-FA		413th TS, 53rd TW, 5th AD
53-3218	C-119G-36-FA	NB	413th TS, 53rd TW, 5th AD
53-3218	C-119G36-FA		413th TS, 53rd TW, 5th AD
53-3220	C-119G-36-FA		413th TS, 53rd TW, 5th AD
53-7873	C-119G-36-FA		413th TS, 53rd TW, 5th AD
53-8073	C-119G-84-KM		413th TS, 53rd TW, 5th AD
53-8077	C-119G-84-KM		413th TS, 53rd TW, 5th AD

Serial	Type	Unit
53-8080	C-119G-84-KM	413th TS, 53rd TW, 5th AD
		To Vietnamese People's Air Force
53-8088	C-119G-84-KM	413th TS, 53rd TW, 5th AD
53-8089	C-119G-84-KM	413th TS, 53rd TW, 5th AD
53-8106	C-119G-84-KM	413th TS, 53rd TW, 5th AD
53-8109	C-119G-84-KM	413th TS, 53rd TW, 5th AD
53-8112	C-119G-84-KM	413th TS, 53rd TW, 5th AD
53-8114	C-119G-84-KM	413th TS, 53rd TW, 5th AD
53-8115	C-119G-84-KM	413th TS, 53rd TW, 5th AD
53-8117	C-119G-84-KM	413th TS, 53rd TW, 5th AD
53-8123	C-119G-84-KM	413th TS, 53rd TW, 5th AD
53-8124	C-119G-84-KM	413th TS, 53rd TW, 5th AD
53-8130	C-119G-84-KM	413th TS, 53rd TW, 5th AD
53-8131	C-119G-84-KM	413th TS, 53rd TW, 5th AD
53-8133	C-119G-84-KM	413th TS, 53rd TW, 5th AD
52-5905	AC-119G	819th AS, 53rd TW, 5th AD
52-5938	AC-119G	819th AS, 53rd TW, 5th AD
52-5942	AC-119G	819th AS, 53rd TW, 5th AD
53-3136	AC-119G	819th AS, 53rd TW, 5th AD
53-3145	AC-119G	819th AS, 53rd TW, 5th AD
53-3170	AC-119G	819th AS, 53rd TW, 5th AD
53-3178	AC-119G	819th AS, 53rd TW, 5th AD
53-3192	AC-119G	819th AS, 53rd TW, 5th AD
53-3205	AC-119G	819th AS, 53rd TW, 5th AD
53-7833	AC-119G	819th AS, 53rd TW, 5th AD
53-8069	AC-119G	819th AS, 53rd TW, 5th AD
53-8089	AC-119G	819th AS, 53rd TW, 5th AD
53-8114	AC-119G	819th AS, 53rd TW, 5th AD
53-8115	AC-119G	819th AS, 53rd TW, 5th AD
53-8123	AC-119G	819th AS, 53rd TW, 5th AD
53-8131	AC-119G	819th AS, 53rd TW, 5th AD
52-5864	AC-119K	821st AS, 53rd TW, 5th AD
52-5889	AC-119K	821st AS, 53rd TW, 5th AD
52-5910	AC-119K	821st AS, 53rd TW, 5th AD
52-5911	AC-119K	821st AS, 53rd TW, 5th AD
52-5926	AC-119K	821st AS, 53rd TW, 5th AD
52-5940	AC-119K	821st AS, 53rd TW, 5th AD
52-5945	AC-119K	821st AS, 53rd TW, 5th AD
52-9982	AC-119K	821st AS, 53rd TW, 5th AD
53-3154	AC-119K	821st AS, 53rd TW, 5th AD
53-3187	AC-119K	821st AS, 53rd TW, 5th AD
53-3197	AC-119K	821st AS, 53rd TW, 5th AD
53-3211	AC-119K	821st AS, 53rd TW, 5th AD
53-7830	AC-119K	821st AS, 53rd TW, 5th AD
53-7831	AC-119K	821st AS, 53rd TW, 5th AD
53-7839	AC-119K	821st AS, 53rd TW, 5th AD
53-7850	AC-119K	821st AS, 53rd TW, 5th AD
53-7877	AC-119K	821st AS, 53rd TW, 5th AD
53-7879	AC-119K	821st AS, 53rd TW, 5th AD
53-7883	AC-119K	821st AS, 53rd TW, 5th AD
53-8121	AC-119K	821st AS, 53rd TW, 5th AD
53-8145	AC-119K	821st AS, 53rd TW, 5th AD
53-8148	AC-119K	821st AS, 53rd TW, 5th AD

413th TS, Tan Son Nhut Jan 1968-1975; 720th RS Dec 1972-1975; 819th CS Sep 1971-1975; 821st CS Dec 1972-1975. All units reported to the 53rd Tactical Wing.

The People's Republic of Vietnam's 918th ATR operated C-119s between 1975 and 1988.

Mutual Defense Assistance Program (MDAP) Summary

Type	Dates*	Quantity	Total
Brazil			
C-82A	Jan 1956	12	12
Belgium			
C-119F	Sep 1953	4	
C-119F	Oct 1953	12	
C-119F	Dec 1953	2	18
C-119G	Jul 1953	2	
C-119G	Aug 1953	1	
C-119G	Dec 1953	2	
C-119G	Feb 1954	8	
C-119G	Mar 1954	8	
C-119G	Apr 1954	1	
C-119G	1st quarter 1955	6	22
Brazil			
C-119G	3rd quarter 1963	10	
C-119G	4th quarter 1963	1	11
French Indo-China			
C-119C	1st quarter FY 1953	3	3
C-119B/C	1st quarter FY 1953	15	15
India			
C-119F	1954	26	26
C-119G	2nd quarter 1963	15	15
Italy			
C-119G	May 1953	3	
C-119G	Jun 1953	3	
C-119G	Jul 1953	9	
C-119G	Aug 1953	5	
C-119G	Sep 1953	2	
C-119G	Dec 1953	3	
C-119G	Jan 1954	8	
C-119G	Feb 1954	2	
C-119G	Mar 1954	3	
C-119G	Apr 1954	1	
C-119G	1st quarter FY 1954	1	40
Jordan			
C-119K	1972	3	3
Morocco			
C-119F/G	1st quarter FY 1962	3	
C-119F/G	2nd quarter FY 1963	3	
C-119F/G	1966	10	16
Norway			
C-119F	1st quarter FY 1957	8	8
Spain			
C-119F	3rd quarter FY 1956	10	10†
Republic of China			
C-119B/C	1st quarter 1953	3	3
	1959	16	16
Republic of Vietnam			
C-119G	1968	16	
C-119G		6	22
AC-119G	1971	7	
AC-119G	1972	17	24
AC-119K	1972	22	22
RC-119G‡	1972		

*MDAP accounting system changed from monthly to quarterly in 1955; hence the difference in format; † These airplanes were apparently returned by the 1st quarter of FY 1957, or were never actually delivered; ‡ An unknown number of RC-119Gs were delivered to South Vietnam; however, due to a lack of mission equipment they were operated strictly in the transport role.

Appendix 6

Civil Registered and Museum C-82s and C-119s in the United States

C-82 Packet

Reg No	USAF S/No	Owner	Location
N107	44-23056	NACA/NASM	NAS Moffett, CA
N127E	45-57780	Unknown	Derelict – Athens, Greece
N128E	45-57794	Unknown	
N136E	44-22981	Unknown	
N208M	45-57793	Interior Airways, Inc	Anchorage, AK
N209M	45-57795	Interior Airways, Inc	Anchorage, AK
			Derelict – Fairbanks, AK
N2047	45-57814	TWA	Paris, France
N2054A	45-57832	Donald B Sittman	Miami, FL
N2055A	44-23023	Unknown	
N2059A	44-23058	L B Smith Aircraft Corp	
N2060A	45-57734	Royal International Corp	Miami, FL
N2065A	45-57802	Royal International Corp	Miami, FL
N4752C	48-581	Northern Air Cargo, Inc	Anchorage, AK
N4753C	48-574	Northern Air Cargo, Inc	Anchorage, AK
N4828V	44-23041	New Frontier Airlift Corp	Miami, FL
N4829V	44-23029	M&F, Inc	
N4830V	45-57763	Big Piney Aviation, Inc	
N4832B	44-23026	Booth Leasing Corp	
N4833V	44-23031	New Frontier Airlift Corp	Miami, FL
N4834V	45-57733	Unknown	
N4962V	45-57767	Unknown	
N5095B	44-23027	Unknown	
N5101B	45-57788	Unknown	
N5102B	45-57782	Tanana Investment Corp	
		Northern Air Cargo, Inc	Anchorage, AK
		Hawkins & Powers	Greybull, WY
N5103B	44-57778	Bankers Life and Casualty Co	
N5104B	45-57776	Bankers Life and Casualty Co	
N5105B	45-57775	Bankers Life and Casualty Co	
N5106B	45-57773	Bankers Life and Casualty Co	
N5107B	45-57770	Bankers Life and Casualty Co	
N5108B	45-57765	Bankers Life and Casualty Co	
N5110B	45-57741	Bankers Life and Casualty Co	
N5111B	44-23053	Bankers Life and Casualty Co	
N5112B	44-23051	Unknown	
N5113B	44-23050	Unknown	Scrapped at Miami, FL
N5115B	44-23048	Unknown	
N5116B	44-23045	Unknown	
N5117B	44-23039	L B Smith Aircraft Corp	
N5118B	44-23034	Aviation Facilities	Miami, FL
N5119B	44-23025	Aviation Facilities	Miami, FL
N5120B	45-57793	Unknown	
N5121B	45-57794	Bankers Life and Casualty Co	
N5122B	45-57795	Bankers Life and Casualty Co	
N5123B	45-57808	Bankers Life and Casualty Co	
N5124B	45-57817	Bankers Life and Casualty Co	
N5125B	45-57825	Bankers Life and Casualty Co	
N5126B	45-57800	Bankers Life and Casualty Co	
N5127B	45-57803	Bankers Life and Casualty Co	
N5128B	45-57804	Bankers Life and Casualty Co	
N5203B	45-57778	Unknown	
N53228	44-23036	New Frontier Airlift Corp	
N57886	45-57766	Unknown	
N6233C	45-57827	LEBCA International, Inc	Miami, FL
N6235C	45-57829	LEBCA International, Inc	Miami, FL
N6236C	45-57780	Unknown	
N6240C	45-57734	Unknown	
N6241C	45-57802	Unknown	
N6243C	44-24030	Unknown	
N6245C	44-23011	Unknown	
N6246C	44-23018	Unknown	
N6247C	45-57830	Leeward Aeronautical Sales, Inc	Miami, FL
N6769A	44-23043	Fairchild Hiller Corp	Hagerstown, MD
N6781A	45-57764	Fairchild Hiller Corp	Hagerstown, MD
N6782A	44-23008	Fairchild Hiller Corp	Hagerstown, MD
N6845A	45-57792	Fairchild Hiller Corp	Hagerstown, MD
N6850A	44-23031	Fairchild Hiller Corp	Hagerstown, MD
N6856A	44-23012	Fairchild Hiller Corp	Hagerstown, MD
N6857A	44-23032	Fairchild Hiller Corp	Hagerstown, MD
N6862A	44-23017	Fairchild Hiller Corp	Hagerstown, MD
N6981A	45-57764	Fairchild Hiller Corp	Hagerstown, MD
N6985C	44-23046	New Frontier Airlift Corp	Phoenix, AZ
N6986C	44-23015	Unknown	
N6987C	44-23006	New Frontier Airlift Corp	Berkley, CA
		Steward-Davis, Corp	Los Angeles, CA
N6990C	44-23001	Walter Soplata Collection	
N6996C	44-23005	New Frontier Airlift Corp	Phoenix, AZ
N6997C	44-23006	New Frontier Airlift Corp	Phoenix, AZ
		Pima County Air Museum	Tucson, AZ
N6998C	44-23009	New Frontier Airlift Corp	Phoenix, AZ
N6999C	44-23033	New Frontier Airlift Corp	Phoenix, AZ
N74038	44-23017	New Frontier Airlift Corp	Berkley, CA
N74039	45-57764	New Frontier Airlift Corp	Berkley, CA
N74041	44-23032	New Frontier Airlift Corp	Berkley, CA
N74042	44-23037	New Frontier Airlift Corp	Berkley, CA
N74043	44-23043	New Frontier Airlift Corp	Berkley, CA
N74044	45-57792	New Frontier Airlift Corp	Berkley, CA
N74046	44-23008	New Frontier Airlift Corp	Phoenix, AZ
N74047	44-23012	New Frontier Airlift Corp	Phoenix, AZ
N74048	44-23052	New Frontier Airlift Corp	Phoenix, AZ
N74127	45-57807	New Frontier Airlift Corp	
N7452C	48-581	Unknown	
		USAF Museum as 45-57735	Wright-Patterson AFB, OH
N7453C	45-574	Unknown	
		McChord AFB Museum	McChord AFB, WA
N74810	45-57780	Unknown	
N75398	44-22962	Unknown	
N75399	44-23004	Unknown	
N75585	45-57756	Unknown	
N75888	45-57807	Unknown	
N78408	44-23052	New Frontier Airlift Corp	
N7849B	44-23040	M&F, Inc	Anchorage, AK
		Derelict	Fairbanks, AK
N7850B	44-23054	Unknown	
N7851B	44-23038	Unknown	
N7853B	45-57771	Unknown	
N7854B	45-57815	Leeward Aeronautical Sales, Inc	Miami, FL

188 Fairchild C-82 & C-119

Reg No	USAF S/No	Owner	Location
N7855B	45-57783	Leeward Aeronautical Sales, Inc	Miami, FL
N7856B	45-57777	Leeward Aeronautical Sales, Inc	Miami, FL
N7857B	45-57812	Leeward Aeronautical Sales, Inc	Miami, FL
N7884C	44-23013	New Frontier Airlift Corp	Phoenix, AZ
N8009E	44-23027	Flying B, Inc	Anchorage, AK
		Hawkins & Powers Aviation	Greybull, WY
N9701F	45-57814	Briles Wing and Helicopter, Inc	Los Angeles, CA
		Northern Pacific Transport	Anchorage, AK
		D&G Inc	Greybull, WY
		Hawkins & Powers, Inc	Greybull, WY
NX45210	45-57780	Unknown	
NX54211*	45-57832	Unknown	

* NX denotes an aircraft registered under Experimental conditions.

C-82 Flying Boxcar

Reg No	USAF S/No	Owner	Location
N1040E	53-7849	Dross Metals, Inc	Tucson, AZ
N131DM	131664*	Dross Metals, Inc	Tucson, AZ
N1394N	1311673	John S Reffett	Eagle River, AK
N13626	131669	Unknown	
N13743	49-0132	Hemet Valley Flying Service	Hemet, CA
N13744	49-0199	Hemet Valley Flying Service	Hemet, CA
N13745	48-0322	Hemet Valley Flying Service	Hemet, CA
N13746	48-0152	Hemet Valley Flying Service	Hemet, CA
N1394N	131673*	Delta Associates, Inc	Anchorage, AK
		John S Reffett	Eagle River, AK
N15501	22130†	Hawkins & Powers Aviation	Greybull, WY
		(Used in remake of Flight of the Phoenix)	
N15502	22114†	Hawkins & Powers Aviation	Greybull, WY
N15505	22101†	Hawkins & Powers Aviation	Greybull, WY
N15506	22105†	Hawkins & Powers Aviation	Greybull, WY
N15508	22134†	Hawkins & Powers Aviation	Greybull, WY
N175ML	131677*	Marine Lumber, Inc	Nantucket, MA
		Mid-Atlantic Air Muserm	Reading, PA
N2700	51-2700	John P Downey	East Middlebury, VT
N3003	22106†	D&G Inc	Greybull, WY
		Hawkins & Powers Aviation	Greybull, WY
N3267U	131700*	DMI Aviation, Inc	Tucson, AZ
		Comutair	Gering, NE
		In storage	Nairobi, Kenya
		(Used in remake of Flight of the Phoenix)	
N3559	22118†	Hawkins & Powers Aviation	Greybull, WY
N3560	22132†	Hawkins & Powers Aviation	Greybull, WY
N37483	53-7884	Bud's Flying Service	Rising City, NE
		Unknown	Oklahoma City, OK
N37484	53-3144	American Freight Co	Laredo, TX
N37636	53-8150	D&G Inc	Greybull, WY
		Mike Ivers	Yakutat, AK
N383S	22133†	Aero Union, Corp	Chico, CA
N3935	22113†	Hawkins & Powers Aviation	Greybull, WY
N4234S	131690*	Tobacco Road Farms, Inc	Ronda, NC
N48543	131677	Unknown	
N48706	52-5846	Hawkins & Powers Aviation	Greybull, WY
N5215R	22108†	Hawkins & Powers Aviation	Greybull, WY
N5216R	22131†	Hawkins & Powers Aviation	Greybull, WY
N5217R	22116†	Hawkins & Powers Aviation	Greybull, WY
N55795	52-6050	Unknown	
N7051U	22116†	J B Hubbard Aviation Museum	
N7051U	131708	Marine Air Ground Museum	MCAS El Toro, CA
N8091	22122†	Hawkins & Powers Aviation	Greybull, WY
N8092	22103†	Hawkins & Powers Aviation	Greybull, WY
N8093	22111†	D&G Inc	Greybull, WY
		Hawkins & Powers Aviation	Greybull, WY
N8094	22135†	D&G Inc	Greybull, WY
		Hawkins & Powers Aviation	Greybull, WY
N8501W	131695*	Delta Associates, Inc	Anchorage, AK
		John S Reffett	Eagle River, AK
N8504W	53-8153	J D Gifford & Associates	Anchorage. AK
N8504X	53-8142	Alaska Aircraft Leasing	Anchorage, AK
		Northern Pacific Transport	Anchorage, AK
N8504Y	51-8129	Stebbins Community Assoc.	Stebbins, AK
N8504Z	53-7836	Northern Pacific Transport	Anchorage, AK
		Everts Air Fuel	Fairbanks, AK
N8505A	53-8076	Northern Pacific Transport	Anchorage, AK
		Hawkins & Powers Aviation	Greybull, WY
N8682	22115†	Hawkins & Powers Aviation	Greybull, WY
N8832	22123†	Hawkins & Powers Aviation	Greybull, WY
N9027K	53-8073	Northern Pacific Transport	Anchorage, AK
		Brooks Fuel	Fairbanks, AK
		Classic Air Transport	Anchorage, AK
N90267	53-8154	Stebbins/Ambler Air Transport	Anchorage, AK
N90268	53-3206	Starbird, Inc	Reno, NV
N90269	53-8127	Starbird, Inc	Reno, NV
N961S	22120†	Hawkins & Powers Aviation	Greybull, WY
N966S	22107†	Hawkins & Powers Aviation	Greybull, WY
N9955F	49-0133	Unknown	
N9956F	51-8263	Unknown	
N99574	131688*	Unknown	
N9959F	51-2608	Unknown	
N9961F	51-2610	Unknown	
N9966F	51-2605	Unknown	
N99574	131688	Fred E Weisbrod Museum	Pueblo, CO

* USN /USMC BuAer No; † RCAF Serial No.

Museum (and Stored) Aircraft

Type	Serial No	Location
Argentina		
C-82A	LV-FHZ	National Air Museum, Buenos Aires
Belgium		
C-119F	CP-10/CP-18	Melsbroek, Brussels
C-119G	CP-46	Musée Royale de l'Armée, Brussels
Brazil		
C-82A	PP-CEL (45-57783)	Air Force Museum, Brasilia
C-119G	FAB 2304	Campos Dos Afonsos (stored)
C-119G	FAB 2305	Museu Aerospacial, Campos Dos Afonsos
Canada		
C-82A	CF-XCL (44-23107)	National Aero. Collection. Uplands, Ottawa
Columbia		
C-82A	HK-426	Eldorado Airport, Bogota
Greece		
C-82A	N127E	Athens Airport, Athens
India		
C-119F	IK450	Indian Air Force Museum, Delhi
C-119F	IK455	Paratrooper Training School, Agra AB (stored)
C-119F	IK463	Paratrooper Training School, Agra AB (stored)
Italy		
C-119J	51-8113/46.50	Turin International Airport, Turin
C-119F		Military Air Museum, Vigna di Valle
C-119J	51-8128/56-52	Treviso
C-119G	526020/46-84	Rivolto
C-119G	52-6029/46-93	Udine-Campoformido
C-119G	53-3200/46-38	Pisa-San Giusto

Kenya

C-119F	N3267U/BuAir 131700	Stored in Nairobi.

Morocco

C-119C	49-190/CNA-MH	Marrakech
C-119G	53-7862/CNA-MN	Kenitra

Republic of China (Taiwan)

C-119F	51-8106/3190	Air Force Academy, Gang Shan

South Korea

C-119F	53-3199	Korean War Memorial, Seoul

United Kingdom

C-119F	N2700/G-BLSW	Aces High Flying Museum, North Weald, Essex
	51-2700	(nose preserved)

United States

C-82A	N209M	Fairbanks Airport, AK
C-82A	N4745C	USAF Museum, Wright-Patterson AFB, OH
C-82A	N5102B	Greybull, WY (fuselage dumped)
C-82A	N7849B	Fairbanks Airport, AK
C-82A	N8009E	Greybull, WY (fuselage dumped)
C-82A	N9701F	The Museum of Flight and Aerial Firefighting, Greybull, WY
C-82A	44-23033	Tucson Aviation Center, Tucson, AZ (Storage)
C-82A	44-23056	Pima County Air Museum, Tucson, AZ
	(N6997C)	Restored to 7th Geodetic Sqn, 55th SRW markings.
R4Q-2	131677	Mid Atlantic Air Museum, Reading, PA
R4Q-2	131679 (N15505)	Pratt Museum, Fort Campbell, KY
	(ex-RCAF 22101)	
R4Q-2	131688	Fred Weisbrod Museum, Pueblo, CO
R4Q-2	131700 (N3267U)	Stored in Nairobi, Kenya
R4Q-2	131708	J Hubbard Aviation, El Toro, CA
C-119B	48-0352	AFTC Museum, Edwards AFB, CA
C-119C	49-0157 (N13743)	Pima County Air Museum, Tucson, AZ
C-119C	49-199 (N12744)	Castle AFB Museum, Castle AFB, CA
C-119C	50-0128	Pope Museum, Pope AFB, NC
C-119C	51-2566	Museum of Aviation, Warner Robins AFB, GA
C-119C	51-2567	USAF History and Traditions Museum, Lackland AFB, TX
C-119C	51-2616	Bradley Air Museum, Bridgeport, CT
C-119C	51-2566	Robins AFB Museum of Aviation, GA
C-119F	51-2675	Pate Museum of Transport, Crenow, TX
C-119F	N8093 (RCAF 22103)	National Warplane Museum, Geneseo, NY
C-119F	N15505 (RCAF 22101)	Pratt Museum, Fort Campbell, KY
C-119F	RCAF 22105	Milwaukee, WI
C-119F	N3003 (RCAF 22106)	Greybull, WY
C-119F	RCAF 22110	Hill Aerospace Museum, Hill AFB, UT
C-119F	N5215R (RCAF 22108)	Greybull, WY
C-119F	N8093 (RCAF 22111)	The Museum of Flight and Aerial Firefighting, Greybull, WY
C-119F	RCAF 22114	McClellan AFB, CA
C-119F	RCAF 22116	Battle Mountain Air Museum, NV
C-119F	N3559 (RCAF 22118)	Dover AFB Museum, Dover AFB, DL
C-119F	N8091 (RCAF 22122)	March Field Museum, March AFRB, CA
C-119F	RCAF 22131	National Infantry Museum, Fort Benning, GA
C-119F	RCAF 22134	Travis AFB Museum, Travis AFB, CA
C-119F	N8094 (RCAF 22135)	Greybull, WY
C-119G	52-5850	Museum, Grissom AFB, OH
C-119G	51-8024	SAC Museum, Ashland, NE
C-119G	RCAF 22109	Hill Aerospace Museum, Hill AF, UT
C-119G	53-3144 (N37484)	Hurlburt Field, FL
C-119G	53-8084	Little Rock AFB, AR
C-119G	53-8087	82nd Airborne Division Memorial Museum, Fort Bragg, NC
C-119G	N37636 (53-7837)	Greybull, WY
C-119G	N8504Z (53-7836)	Everts Air Fuel, Anchorage, AK
C-119G	N9027K (53-8073)	Classic Air Transport, Anchorage, AK
C-119J	51-8037	USAF Museum, Wright-Patterson AFB, OH
C-119L	53-8084	Museum, Little Rock AFB, AR

C-82 USAF Serial / US Civil Registry Cross-Reference

USAF S/No	Reg No	USAF S/No	Reg No	USAF S/No	Reg No
44-22962	N75398	44-23043	N6769A	45-57780	N6236C
44-22981	N136E	44-23043	N74043	45-57780	N74810
44-23001	N6990C	44-23045	N5116B	45-57780	NX45210
44-23004	N75399	44-23046	N6985C	45-57782	N5102B
44-23005	N6996C	44-23048	N5115B	45-57783	N7855B
44-23006	N6987C	44-23050	N5113B	45-57788	N5101B
44-23006	N6997C	44-23051	N5112B	45-57792	N6845A
44-23008	N6782A	44-23052	N74048	45-57792	N74044
44-23008	N74046	44-23052	N78408	45-57793	N208M
44-23009	N6998C	44-23053	N5111B	45-57793	N5120B
44-23011	N6245C	44-23054	N7850B	45-57794	N128E
44-23012	N6856A	44-23056	N107	45-57794	N5121B
44-23012	N74047	44-23058	N2059A	45-57795	N209M
44-23013	N7884C	44-24030	N6243C	45-57795	N5122B
44-23015	N6986C	44-57764	N6981A	45-57800	N5126B
44-23017	N6862A	44-57778	N5103B	45-57802	N2065A
44-23017	N74038	45-57766	N57886	45-57802	N6241C
44-23018	N6246C	45-574	N7453C	45-57803	N5127B
44-23023	N2055A	45-57733	N4834V	45-57804	N5128B
44-23025	N5119B	45-57734	N2060A	45-57807	N74127
44-23026	N4832B	45-57734	N6240C	45-57807	N75888
44-23027	N5095B	45-57741	N5110B	45-57808	N5123B
44-23027	N8009E	45-57756	N75585	45-57812	N7857B
44-23029	N4829V	45-57763	N4830V	45-57814	N2047
44-23031	N4833V	45-57764	N6781A	45-57814	N9701F
44-23031	N6850A	45-57764	N74039	45-57815	N7854B
44-23032	N6857A	45-57765	N5108B	45-57817	N5124B
44-23032	N74041	45-57767	N4962V	45-57825	N5125B
44-23033	N6999C	45-57770	N5107B	45-57827	N6233C
44-23034	N5118B	45-57771	N7853B	45-57829	N6235C
44-23036	N53228	45-57773	N5106B	45-57830	N6247C
44-23037	N74042	45-57775	N5105B	45-57832	N2054A
44-23038	N7851B	45-57776	N5104B	45-57832	NX54211*
44-23039	N5117B	45-57777	N7856B	48-574	N4753C
44-23040	N7849B	45-57778	N5203B	48-581	N4752C
44-23041	N4828V	45-57780	N127E	48-581	N7452C

* NX denotes an aircraft registered under Experimental conditions.

C-119 Military Serial / US Civil Registry Cross-Reference

USAF S/No	Reg No	USAF S/No	Reg No	USAF S/No	Reg No
1311673	N1394N	22115†	N8682	51-2610	N9961F
131664*	N131DM	22116†	N5217R	51-2700	N2700
131669	N13626		N7051U	51-8129	N8504Y
131673*	N1394N	22118†	N3559	51-8263	N9956F
131677	N48543	22120†	N961S	52-5846	N48706
	N175ML	22122†	N8091	52-6050	N55795
131688*	N99574	22123†	N8832	53-3144	N37484
131690*	N4234S	22130†	N15501	53-3206	N90268
131695*	N8501W	22131†	N5216R	53-7836	N8504Z
131700*	N3267U	22132†	N3560	53-7849	N1040E
131708	N7051U	22133†	N383S	53-7884	N37483
22101†	N15505	22134†	N15508	53-8073	N9027K
22103†	N8092	22135†	N8094	53-8076	N8505A
22105†	N15506	48-0152	N13746	53-8127	N90269
22106†	N3003	48-0322	N13745	53-8142	N8504X
22107†	N966S	49-0132	N13743	53-8150	N37636
22108†	N5215R	49-0133	N9955F	53-8153	N8504W
22111†	N8093	49-0199	N13744	53-8154	N90267
22113†	N3935	51-2605	N9966F		
22114†	N15502	51-2608	N9959F		

* USN /USMC BuAer No; † RCAF Serial No.

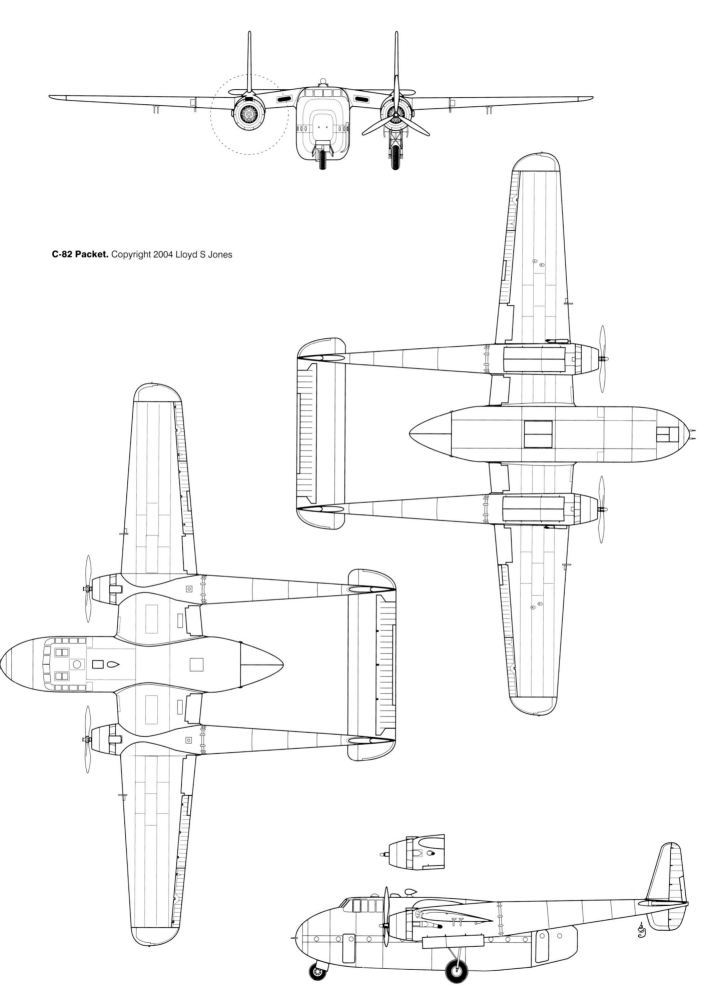

C-82 Packet. Copyright 2004 Lloyd S Jones

Fairchild C-82 & C-119

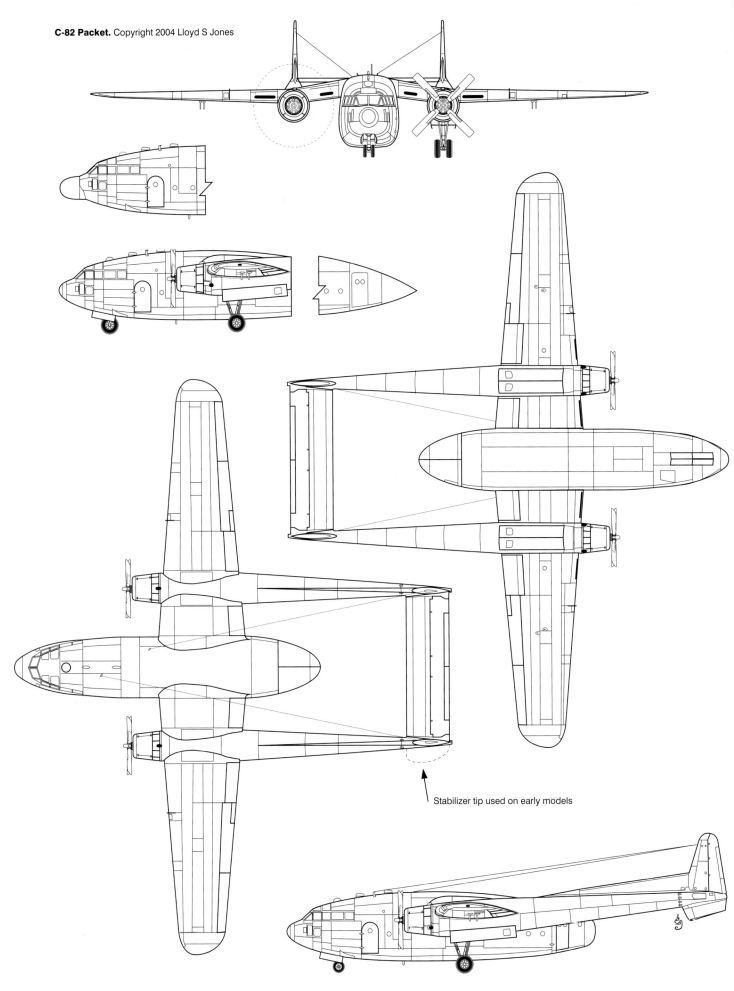

C-82 Packet. Copyright 2004 Lloyd S Jones

Stabilizer tip used on early models